EAT WELL
AND STAY SLIM

THE ESSENTIAL CUISINE MINCEUR

EAT WELL
AND STAY SLIM

THE ESSENTIAL CUISINE MINCEUR

MICHEL GUÉRARD

PHOTOGRAPHS BY CHARLOTTE LASCÈVE
TRANSLATED BY ALEXANDRA CARLIER

Frances Lincoln Limited
74–77 White Lion Street
London N1 9PF
www.franceslincoln.com

Eat Well and Stay Slim - The Essential Cuisine Minceur
Copyright © Frances Lincoln Limited 2014

First edition copyright © Albin Michel 2012

Text by Michel Guérard
Photographs by Charlotte Lascève
Drawings by Michel Guérard

First Frances Lincoln edition 2014

Translated by Alexandra Carlier

A catalogue record for this book is available from the British Library.

978-0-7112-3536-6

Printed in China

1 3 5 7 9 8 6 4 2

EAT WELL AND STAY SLIM: THE ESSENTIAL CUISINE MINCEUR

Why does the idea of combining gastronomy with a healthy, calorie-conscious eating plan still cause surprise, doubt and even derision?

Taste and enjoyment lie at the heart of all French cooking, so I am drawn to conclude that any plan to reform eating habits must not lose sight of the fact that people want to enjoy their food. Any sort of cooking or diet is doomed to failure if it fails to give people pleasure.

This inescapable premise is enshrined in *Eat Well and Stay Slim: The Essential Cuisine Minceur* and should be at the forefront of the minds of nutritionists, dieticians, hospital managers, carers and, of course, caterers in general, many of whom supply food to schools, retirement homes and workplace canteens.

For the French, eating is one of the most instant and accessible routes to pleasure. It is a pleasure to which we feel entitled as human beings. You might even go so far as to say that we regard it as an inalienable social right. But the French do not want to choose between health and pleasure; they want both at the same time. So how can we reconcile the traditions of French cuisine with a healthy regime? How can we avoid the repeated failures of the past and escape the negative idea that diets are about restriction and punishment? How do we counteract the easy 'junk food' option, which can lead to serious health problems, with all the costs that these bring in their wake? How can we invent new ways of healthy eating that are affordable for those on lower incomes? How can we lead the food industry towards new, healthy trends?

The three key players at the heart of these questions are:
- Scientists and nutritionists
- Cooks at all levels and the food industry, whose job it is to prepare and conserve food so it reaches people's plates in the best possible condition
- The consumer, client or patient, who is not necessarily an expert and who may be emotionally attached to certain types of food. (In fact, it is now thought that we have a DNA 'food memory' that accounts for such attachments.)

So it came about that, at the end of 2008, I suggested to Madame Roselyne Bachelot, then Minister for Health in France,

the setting up of an *École de Cuisine de Santé* – a School for Healthy Cooking. She was enthusiastic about the idea and a Steering Committee then prepared a White Paper to which many prestigious scientists contributed. This White Paper covered priority health areas: obesity, diabetes, cardiovascular disease and eating disorders linked to cancer and advancing age. The White Paper became the foundation for the teaching at the École de Cuisine de Santé and was also passed on to faculties of medicine in French universities. It brings together current knowledge on key medical problems and proposes diets for each one. In order to succeed, any healthy eating regime must be rooted in social custom, which means that its meals must include an element of ritual and should be special moments of enjoyment, whether or not they are shared with other people.

Creating recipes for this new, healthy culinary discipline is surely the way forward. We have just measured the results of this dietary approach in a pilot study carried out at Eugénie-les-Bains. The results showed a clear improvement in clients' metabolism after one year, taking into account other factors such as the spa treatments they have received and their level of physical activity.

Eat Well and Stay Slim: The Essential Cuisine Minceur has the edge over the quirky diet books that currently occupy the shelves of our bookshops. Given today's state of knowledge concerning health and diet, I believe that this book makes a very positive contribution to the prevention of many forms of chronic illness, such as obesity, heart disease and diabetes. It does so by giving both the amateur and the professional cook practical instruction as well as intellectual autonomy.

This is an approach that goes beyond short-term dieting: it is more about lifestyle changes that can be implemented continuously and over the long term. The Essential Cuisine Minceur can be adopted by anyone who chooses to eat well and stay slim. To paraphrase the twentieth-century French novelist André Malraux, tomorrow's cooking will either be for health and wellbeing or it will not.

Michel Guérard

HOW TO USE THIS BOOK

Eat Well and Stay Slim: The Essential Cuisine Minceur can be read in several different ways. If you are keen to establish and maintain a calorie-controlled regime, you will, I am sure, find it interesting to learn about the Essential Cuisine Minceur diet plan as used in the Essential Slimming Treatment (Minceur Essentielle) offered at my spa hotel, Les Prés d'Eugénie, in Eugénie-les-Bains. The thinking behind the diet plan is explained and details of the menus are given on the following two pages.

If you want to find out more about the way that cookery methods and key ingredients impact upon health and diet you will find the section Key Principles and Techniques on pages 14–37 of interest. Here I outline the minceur approach to buying, preparing and cooking food. There is information about important everyday basics, such as salt, fats, sugars and sweeteners, as well as advice on the healthiest and leanest ways to cook. As part of this, I discuss the use of gelatine and egg whites – and that magic invention, the multi-purpose gourmet whipper.

I hope that all readers, whether home cooks or professionals, will use the information to free themselves of some popular misconceptions. I hope, too, that you will discover a wealth of ideas and advice to help you incorporate a new, healthy dimension into your cooking and to adapt your own signature dishes.

Moving on beyond the fundamental principles, you will find an exciting and innovative section that I have called The Essential Cuisine Minceur Toolkit (see pages 38–95). This unlocks the secrets of the tools of the trade for my 'minceur', low-calorie approach to gastronomy. It is one of the crucial keys to eating well and staying slim.

The Toolkit includes stocks, flavoured oils, vinaigrettes, classic sauces and condiments and special vegetable and fruit purées, which can be used both as sauces and as low-calorie liaisons, or thickening agents. You can put these 'tools' together in almost endless combinations, thus allowing your imagination to run riot in the kitchen. With practice, you will become ever more confident about adapting the 'tools' to your own style of cooking.

Finally, you can dip into the pool of recipes that I and my team at Eugénie-les-Bains have developed. These fall naturally within the scope of contemporary grande cuisine. I believe that the recipes we have selected will suit a range of budgets and will be accessible to all cooks, whether beginners, experienced or even professional.

I hope that you will find something here for every mood and occasion, whether you are eating alone, cooking for family and friends, or entertaining in grand style.

THE SPIRIT OF ESSENTIAL CUISINE MINCEUR

'Taste and enjoyment lie at the heart of all French cooking'

The need for enjoyment must be recognised in any eating plan, even one that is concerned with weight loss.

Any diet or change in eating habits requires an incentive if it is to work. You cannot expect a normal human being to deprive her or himself indefinitely of certain foods and live in a state of permanent culinary frustration, day after day.

Failure to acknowledge this explains why people who follow an over-restrictive diet, where the daily rations are reminiscent of the processed meals an astronaut is obliged to eat, always fall by the wayside. Such diets simply neglect people's need to experience a sense of pleasure, satisfaction and wellbeing from their food.

Les Prés d'Eugénie at Eugénie-les-Bains is a medically approved thermal spa, registered with the French health authorities for the treatment of weight problems linked to metabolism. Here we offer our Essential Slimming Treatment (Minceur Essentielle) precisely to satisfy the pleasure principle and to give to the usually gruelling – even depressing – period of dietary adjustment a whole new meaning. The spirit of hedonistic refinement at Les Prés d'Eugénie proves that it is possible to eat well while staying slim and healthy. The dietary regime we use there, developed with the assistance of a nutritionist–doctor, consists of three phases, each three or four days long.

It begins with the Attack Phase. During this phase, participants must rid themselves of any preconceived, food-related ideas. Pride of place is given to protein-rich fish and meat, with a view to achieving an optimal balance between calorie count and a feeling of satisfaction. Vegetables are included, too; thanks to their fibrous composition, they play an important role in digestion and, more particularly, in efficient intestinal transit.

The regime continues with the Metabolic Adjustment Phase. During this phase, the inclusion of starches, such as potatoes and semolina, helps to bring the body closer to its ideal energy balance and to a well-regulated metabolism.

The third and final stage is the Stabilisation Phase. This is all about preparing participants for their return home and the adoption of an everyday eating plan based on the recipes in this book.

The menus for each of these phases comprise a starter, followed by a main course and a dessert. All are delicious enough to satisfy the most demanding of tastebuds. No one need feel deprived.

This slimming programme merits five stars, but it is not sufficient on its own. Readers should remember that weight gain is not only caused by bad eating habits. A sedentary lifestyle is another cause, so it is essential to combine a healthy diet with sufficient physical activity. Physical activity leads to the development of muscle mass and, the more muscle mass you possess, the more efficiently your body burns calories. Following my dietary regime and combining it with physical activity will set in train the virtuous circle of health and slimness.

Above all, the success of a diet lies in keeping up your newly acquired improved eating habits. That is why no serious diet should be undertaken without the support offered by long-term nutritional and medical supervision.

The spirit of *Eat Well and Stay Slim: The Essential Cuisine Minceur* embraces all these aspects of diet and is the foundation for the Essential Slimming Treatment offered at Eugénie-les-Bains.

Sample one-day menus

This book gives you all the recipes and techniques you need to follow the Essential Slimming Treatment. Below are some suggested one-day menus for each of the three phases.

Phase I – Attack Phase
LUNCH
Herb-scented prawn skewers (page 182)
Fillet of beef poached in herby beef stock
   (recipe for the stock, page 54)
Garden-fresh lemon sorbet (page 292)
DINNER
Carpaccio of salmon with olives and tapioca (page 139)
Strips of cod in Thai stock (recipe for the stock, page 52)
Tropical meringue floating islands (page 309)

Phase II – Metabolic Adjustment Phase
LUNCH
Crunchy vegetables with coriander seeds (page 200)
Filet of duck with pearl barley in mushroom stock
   (recipe for the stock, page 51)
Verbena-infused semolina mousse (page 283)
DINNER
Courgette quenelles with black olive coulis (page 142)
Cold Beef Salad with a Mustard Sauce (page 192)
Upside-down strawberry and mint tarts (page 310)

N.B. For the methods of cooking meat and fish for Phases I and II, see Key Principles and Techniques, Cooking methods, pages 29–35).

Phase III – Stabilisation Phase
LUNCH
Morsels of rabbit in a vegetable jelly (page 150)
Braised loin of pork with lemongrass and
   tropical fruit (page 250)
Rolled Apple Crêpes with Vanilla Mousse (page 314)
DINNER
Autumnal cep and mushroom soup (page 125)
Tandoori-spiced white fish (page 240)
Herb-scented panna cotta with raspberries (page 316)

Notes on nutrition

Fibre: Fibre consists of the partially digested or undigested remains of foods of vegetable origin. There are two types of fibre: insoluble (for example the outer envelope of vegetables, such as wheat or peas), which help intestinal transit, and soluble (for example, apple pectin), which help the body to absorb food.

Fats: Also known as lipids, these are basic nutrients, which, together with proteins and carbohydrates, contribute part of the energy needed by the body to function (1g of lipids equals 9 calories). Nutritionists estimate that fats should make up 30% to 35% of our daily food intake. There are many types of fat: for example polyunsaturated fatty acids (including the essential fatty acids omega 3 and 6), which are necessary for body function; monounsaturated fatty acids, which are considered neutral from a health perspective; saturated fatty acids, which should be limited; and trans fats (hydrogenated fats), which are found in manufactured food products and are not recommended. In general, you should also be careful about hidden fat in manufactured food products. Such foods often contain large amounts of hidden fat; they are added for their organoleptic role – in other words, they help to make food more tasty.

Proteins: These basic nutrients, together with carbohydrates and fats (lipids), contribute to the energy needed by the body to function (1g of protein equals 4 calories). Nutritionists estimate that proteins should make up 15% to 20% of what you eat each day. Proteins are essential for building bones, skin and muscles. They can come from animal sources (meat, fish, egg) or vegetable sources (leguminous plants).

Carbohydrates: Along with protein and fibre, carbohydrates contribute to the energy that the body needs in order to function (1g of carbohydrate equals 4 calories). Nutritionists estimate that carbohydrates should make up 5% of what we eat daily. Carbohydrates consist of 'simple' sugars, which are very quickly assimilated (for example, comfort foods, which you should avoid eating in large amounts); and 'complex' sugars, which are assimilated much more slowly and help you wait longer between meals. These are recommended for diabetics, as they avoid surges in blood-sugar levels.

Glycaemic Index (GI): A measure of the speed with which food is absorbed into the bloodstream and of its glycaemic impact (its impact on blood-sugar levels). This measurement is useful to diabetics who have to be careful about peaks of sugar in their blood. For example, most vegetables have a low GI, while sliced white bread and sweets have a very high GI.

Minerals (mineral salts and trace elements): These are mineral elements present in food; your body needs them because it cannot make them itself. They should be taken in varying amounts, for example, 1g per day for calcium, as opposed to just a few microgrammes or milligrammes for iron or copper. Minerals are calorie-free and do not alter during digestion.

Nutrients: This is a general term for the components of food that we obtain from the process of digestions. They are indispensable to our physiological and energy requirements. They feed our cells – ensuring growth and regeneration of our body and certain of its components – and they produce energy, enabling us to move, for example.

Nutrients are classified into two groups: macronutrients (fats, carbohydrates, proteins) and micronutrients (mineral salts, trace elements and vitamins).

Vitamins: These are organic elements that are present in food; the body needs them but cannot make them itself. Like dietary minerals, they should be taken in various quantities. There are 13 vitamins, classified into two groups: water-soluble vitamins, found in foods containing water, and fat-soluble vitamins, present in foods containing fats. Vitamins are calorie-free and do not alter during digestion.

PART ONE:
THE BASICS OF
ESSENTIAL
CUISINE
MINCEUR

KEY PRINCIPLES AND TECHNIQUES

Salt

Salt (sodium chloride) has been known since prehistoric times and, until the eighteenth century, was the only way we had to preserve food. Today, salt is used as a condiment to heighten flavour and, incidentally, it is for reasons of flavour that the food-processing industry often uses too much salt, particularly as the products being prepared are sometimes of inferior quality.

Salt originates in two ways: either as sea salt, which is obtained from the evaporation of sea water, or as traditionally mined rock salt.

Natural salt, such as fleur de sel, is unrefined so its minerals remain intact. Such salt is generally rich in magnesium and iron and has a unique flavour linked to its local climate and environment. By contrast, table salt – which is the most commonly consumed type of salt – has been refined in a way that largely rids it of its natural nutritional qualities.

Note
The medical world agrees unanimously that the excessive intake of salt induces high blood pressure and is one of the risk factors of cardiovascular disease. Cutting down your salt intake lowers blood pressure and limits water retention. While salt is indispensible to keeping the human body in good working order (a minimum of 2g per day is recommended), daily intake should not exceed 5g–7g (although it can be more than 12g in certain individuals).

Charcuterie, cheese, bread, snacks (including, for example, crisps) and ready-made dishes all contain a great deal of salt. To find out the salt content in ready-prepared foods, multiply the sodium content indicated on the packaging by 2.54. For example: 0.6g of sodium x 2.54 = 1.5g of salt (sodium chloride).

Correct salting should show the natural qualities of the food to best advantage. Adding more salt than necessary will do nothing to improve a food's quintessential flavour. This means not being too heavy-handed with salt, particularly at the table. It also means limiting the use of various seasonings containing salt, by which I mean a whole range of condiments and sauces that should only be used with caution.

How salt measures up
½ level teaspoon = 2.5g salt
1 level teaspoon = 5g salt
1 heaped teaspoon = 6.5g salt
1 level tablespoon = 10g salt

Note
Always taste what is on your plate before adding salt.

Alternatives to salt

Fortunately, nature has blessed us with almost unlimited resources that cooks can use to impart flavour to food: there is a multitude of wonderful herbs and plant-based aromatics, which have not yet been fully exploited, not to mention simple or compound spices that can be used to create endlessly complex flavours. Marinades and stocks can make the most of these.

Marinades

Marinating, which employs a marinade of herbs and aromatics, is an extremely useful alternative to salt for seasoning fish, poultry and meat. As well as lending aroma and flavour, marinades that contain an acidic element will also tenderize. A marinade can be dry or wet, and the length of time for marinating can vary widely, from one to 24 hours.

The short, one- to two-hour marinade is very useful. You simply coat the food evenly in its marinade, cover it and put it in a refrigerator or a cool place to rest, turning the food from time to time to ensure the flavours are well distributed. Before cooking, wipe off any surplus marinade using a piece of kitchen paper.

- Dry marinades: Poultry, fish and meat can be covered in a dry marinade of herbs (basil, thyme rosemary, etc.) or spices (curry, cumin, turmeric, saffron, allspice, etc.) without the addition of any liquid. This type of marinade flavours the food and often colours its surface.

- Wet marinades: Poultry, fish and meat or fish are also good candidates for a wet marinade. This might employ, for example, a little olive oil, some thyme, a bay leaf and the juice of a lemon. The marinade will impart flavour while the acidity of the lemon will also act as a tenderizer. Similar tenderizing effects can be achieved with yoghurt, wine and good-quality vinegar. The oil used in a wet marinade renders the food ready for cooking but to keep the amount of oil used to a minimum (see Oils, page 55), the food must be turned regularly in the marinade.

For an Asian marinade, use a mixture of sesame oil, soy sauce, rice vinegar, sugar and finely chopped fresh ginger. This marinade gives an agreeable tangy edge to red meats and duck.

Stocks

Stock is another good alternative to seasoning food with salt: it contains all the elements needed to add taste. Some might say it gives a rather salty taste but it also adds the essence of the ingredients that went into it, whether poultry, beef or vegetables, or herbs and spices. A further advantage of adding stock is that it reduces the need for salt.

When immersed in a gently simmering stock and poached (page 32), an item of food, such as a fillet of fish or a piece of chicken, benefits enormously from the exchange of flavours that takes place. Similarly, if a little stock is added to a parcel of food before being cooked en papillotte (page 33), it will create the steamy conditions that are needed for the cooking process as well as imparting flavour and fragrance. The stock will also contribute to the juices that accompany the final dish, and these will not require any extra seasoning.

Stock can be used in many ways and is essential to poaching, steaming, braising, sautéing, and vacuum-sealed cooking techniques. In this book, however, you will also find other ideas for exploiting the virtues of stock. For example, I have made stock an essential ingredient in my modern take on vinaigrette, as well as using it in a new range of purée-type liaisons and sauces – all of which are far lower in fats and calories than their traditional counterparts.

Sugar and sweetening

Nature and science together provide plenty of alternatives to satisfy those of us who like the taste of sugar but who have to limit its intake, whether for health reasons, such as diabetes, or perhaps because we want to control our weight.

Although many studies have tried to prove the dangers of sweeteners other than sugar and honey, none has succeeded to date. This is particularly the case with aspartame (see below). In any event, the tests carried out on these sweeteners have used amounts that are far higher than the Acceptable Daily Intake (ADI). Nevertheless, it seems sensible to advise moderate consumption – as with any type of sugar. It is certain that the excessive intake of sugar, in whatever form, can lead to addiction and to an increase in one's tolerance of sweetness, and this is clearly harmful in the long term.

Ordinary sugar

Ordinary sugar, or sucrose, is a natural product that comes from sugar cane or sugar beet plants. Once the juice is extracted from the plant, it is refined to give it the appearance we know. The juice is crystallized, then cleaned to eliminate any unwanted deposits. The more it is refined, the paler and more neutral in taste it becomes. Although refined beet sugar is always pure white and light in taste, refined cane sugar varies in colour from very dark brown to blonde and has a distinctive flavour.

After it has been refined, the sugar is processed so it acquires its particular form – lump sugar, granulated sugar, soft brown sugar, caster (superfine) sugar or icing sugar (confectioner's sugar). A liquid form of sugar – found, for example, in fizzy drinks – can also be obtained from cane sugar, but diabetics should take care with liquid sugar because it is absorbed into the blood much faster than its solid-form counterparts.

Ordinary sugar is what distinguishes dessert cookery from savoury cookery. This distinction took root as soon as the extraction and transformation of sugar into all kinds of syrups and caramels was mastered.

Ordinary sugar is the benchmark of sweetness, with its sweetening capacity classed as 1. The calorie count of ordinary sugar is around 4 calories per gram. This is its major drawback, which is why alternatives to sugar may be used, as appropriate.

A historical titbit

Dutch traders transported sugar to Europe from around 1640. When Britain captured Jamaica and other parts of the West Indies from Spain in 1655, it made a heavy investment in the sugar industry and immediately integrated sugar into its culinary tradition. France, on the other hand, used sugar initially to sweeten medicines. Americans brought sugar to Jamestown around 1619 and developed an immediate liking for it, a habit that has endured. Today, France is the leading European producer of sugar but it only comes seventh in terms of consumption – 33kg (73lb) per person/per year, compared to the USA where consumptions stands at 59kg (130lb) per person/per year, and Great Britain where consumption is 40kg (88lb) per person/per year.

Honey

Honey is 100% natural, produced by bees from the pollen they collect from flowers. The pollen is then transformed into nectar, which the bees store in their hives. Honey has been used far longer than ordinary sugar and is prized not only for its sweet taste but also for its nutritional benefits, therapeutic qualities and beauty uses. There is a multitude of different types of honey, depending on the nectar of the plant of origin, for example acacia, heather, lavender, rosemary, thyme, pine, chestnut, sunflower, and so on.

Honey's calorie count of 3.2 calories per gram is lower than that of ordinary sugar, but its sweetening capacity is comparable.

Uses in cooking

Due to its pronounced flavour and viscous consistency, honey is only used occasionally in dessert cookery. It is a shame that its characteristic taste becomes accentuated during cooking and its sticky texture prevents it from becoming well incorporated with other ingredients. This becomes an issue particularly when honey is used in any frothy, airy preparation: the work of blending the honey with the other ingredients takes so long that the air bubbles burst.

Despite these inconveniences, honey has many applications. It caramelizes very easily and so is used to make French Montélimar nougat and Spanish turrón. You will also find it in cakes and ice creams. As with sugar, honey remains stable when it undergoes a change in temperature; neither its sweetening power nor its structure alters. Maple syrup (2.7 calories per gram) and agave syrup (3.2 calories per gram) behave in a similar way to honey, so can be used as a replacement for honey in some dessert recipes.

Fructose

Discovered in 1847 by Augustin-Pierre Dubrunfaut, fructose is a natural sugar found in fruit or plants. It has the advantage of having a neutral taste and can be bought as a powder or a syrup. We use only powder in our dessert recipes.

Fructose has an exceptional capacity for sweetening, exceeding 1.2 to 2 times that of ordinary sugar, but with the same calorie count – 4 calories per gram. And that is precisely why fructose is so interesting; you use almost half the quantity of fructose as you would sugar to achieve the equivalent taste, and the fructose has half the number of calories.

Uses in cooking

In cooking, powdered fructose is an attractive substitute for sugar by virtue of the fact that when it is heated and cooked, it guarantees a good balance between stability, sweetening capacity and calorie count. It also has other advantages: it is highly soluble in cold fluids, so it blends well with cold ingredients; and when it is heated, it allows the Maillard Reaction (page 29) to take place. True, its sweetening capacity diminishes very slightly with cooking but fructose can, more or less, be used in the same ways as ordinary sugar.

Its only real disadvantage in dessert cookery concerns texture. Although fructose can produce the same soft, melting texture as sugar, the effect is reduced since you need to use proportionately less fructose.

Note

Fructose has often been criticised, most notably across the Atlantic, where the over-consumption of commercial food products containing glucose-fructose syrup (used in sodas, cakes, snacks, and sweets, for example) contributes to the phenomenon of the USA's escalating obesity. Studies based on a high intake of products made with glucose-fructose syrup have shown that its powerful sweetening capacity could lead to the over-consumption of sweet foods, which is not compensated for by an increased expenditure of energy through physical activity. Fructose syrup may also affect the metabolism, upsetting the signals of satiation and appetite sent by the brain, which then results in unhelpful eating habits. It is best to follow the golden rule of all types of food intake: consume in moderation.

Xylitol

Discovered at the end of the nineteenth century by French and German scientists, Xylitol is a natural sweetener found in vegetable fibres in general, and more particularly in the bark of silver birch. It is produced commercially in powder form.

Xylitol has a sweetening capacity more or less equivalent to that of ordinary sugar and it has a neutral taste. Its calorie count is 2.5 calories per gram – almost half that of ordinary sugar.

Uses in cooking

Xylitol is another interesting substitute for sugar since, when cooked, it guarantees a good balance between stability, sweetening capacity and calorie count. It handles in the same way as ordinary sugar, both in terms of its solubility and its ability to preserve its essential properties when cooked. Thanks to the sensation of freshness that Xylitol leaves on the palate, it lends itself well to ice-cream making.

Note

Xylitol leaves a feeling of freshness in the mouth, it does not ferment in the mouth and, therefore, does not cause dental cavities. For these reasons it is often found in dental hygiene products and in chewing gum. Studies have also shown that Xylitol is associated with beneficial effects in cases of respiratory infections and osteoporosis. It is also used by diabetics as it does not cause hyperglycaemia. Rather, it spreads through the bloodstream more slowly than ordinary sugar. Xylitol has no known harmful effects, other than as a laxative when consumed to excess.

Aspartame-based sweeteners

Discovered by chance in 1965, during laboratory experimentation, aspartame is a synthetic composite sweetener. It has been used in soft drinks and low-calorie or sugar-free foods throughout the world for more than 26 years. During this time, it has also been the subject of controversy concerning its possible adverse effects on health. However, aspartame's safety has been rigorously assessed both by the FSA (Food Standards Agency) in the UK and by the FDA (Food and Drug Administration) in the United States, and it has been found to be safe within the limits set by the ADI.

Aspartame was first approved by the FSA in 1982. In the European Union, its safety was reaffirmed in 1988 by the Scientific Committee on Food (SCF) under the European Code E951. Its recommended ADI was reviewed again by the FSA in 2002 and no evidence was found for the need to revise it. In the UK, the ADI therefore remains set at 40 milligrams per kilogram of body weight per day (40mg/kg bw/day), an intake that is far higher than normal average consumption. For example, an adult of average weight would have to consume 14 cans of sugar-free drink every day before reaching the recommended ADI, assuming the maximum permitted level of sweetener was used in the drink.

In the USA, the FDA initially approved of aspartame as a safe, general-purpose, sweetener in food in 1981. The FDA re-evaluated aspartame in 2006 and found no reason to alter its earlier conclusions. In the USA, the ADI is set at 50 milligrams per kilogram of body weight per day (50mg/kg bw/day). As a rule of thumb, this means that an adult of average weight would have to consume 20 cans of sugar-free drink every day before reaching the recommended ADI. As is the case with all sweeteners, it is important that aspartame's ADI is strictly observed when it is consumed by children.

In its pure compound form, aspartame is not available directly to consumers, though it is available indirectly through the consumption of commercially produced low-calorie foodstuffs and carbonated low-calorie drinks. When bought by consumers as a sweetening powder, it comes mixed with the carrier, maltodextrine. Sweeteners based on aspartame that are available to consumers include: in the UK, Canderel (granular Canderel is used for cooking) and Stevia (see below); in the USA, NutraSweet and Equal. These products generally contain only 3% pure aspartame because the aspartame is usually mixed with other components, notably Acesulfame K. This is an intense synthetic sweetener that is used to preserve the overall sweetening capacity in case aspartame's sweetening power diminishes when heated to a high temperature. The use of Acesulfame K is also controlled.

The advantage of aspartame-based sweeteners lies in their intense sweetening power. Indeed, weight for weight, aspartame has a sweetening power about ten times that of ordinary sugar – in other words, 1g of aspartame-based sweetener is the equivalent of 10g of ordinary sugar. One might therefore say that it is ten times less calorific than sugar, because one uses ten times less.

For a long time it was thought that aspartame was a-calorific, but we now know that we have to differentiate between pure aspartame, as used in the food-industry's low-calorie foods and fizzy drinks, and the aspartame-based sweetening powder that is destined for the general public. In the case of the former, pure aspartame is, indeed, a-calorific, but in the case of the latter, as we have already seen, the aspartame is blended with maltodextrine, which does contain calories. Aspartame-based sweetening powder therefore has a calorie count of 3.5–4 calories per gram.

Uses in cooking

Aspartame-based sweeteners are easy to use cold when mixed into other cold ingredients when preparing desserts. Under these conditions it blends well – better even than ordinary sugar. Unfortunately though, aspartame is unstable when exposed to prolonged heating, which means that there is a loss of sweetness in preparations requiring cooking, such as custards or cakes.

To help offset this, you can sometimes add an aspartame sweetener at the end of the cooking process, once the food has cooled down a little.

Other problems are less easy to overcome: when aspartame sweetener is used, the Maillard Reaction (page 29) cannot take place so it is impossible to give your dessert the golden crunchiness that may be desired. There is also the issue of texture: whereas melted sugar lends a moist, soft, texture to preparations such as ice cream and cakes, aspartame-based sweeteners do not possess this quality and in fact, they become very hard. Once an aspartame sweetener has been frozen – is in the case of ice cream – it becomes as hard as wood and impossible to work without using a Pacojet – a professional ice-cream making machine (page 286). Unfortunately, it is also impossible to make meringues using aspartame sweetener.

Note

Having the same qualities as aspartame, Stevia is a natural sweetener that comes directly from the plant of the same name. As with aspartame in its pure form, Stevia is a-calorific and, like aspartame, it also has a far greater sweetening power than ordinary sugar. At present, it leaves a strong after-taste in the mouth, which makes it tricky to use in cooking. This after-taste is even more pronounced when Stevia is refined. To mask this after-taste, Stevia is usually blended with ordinary sugar, which makes it less appealing from a calorific point of view.

Egg whites

Weighing sugar and sweeteners

In the recipes in this book, the weight of sugar or sweetener is always given in spoonfuls, making it easier to measure. You can find the corresponding equivalent in grams in the chart below. Note that these are average weights, not precise ones.

	½ tsp	1 level tsp	1 heaped tsp	½ tbs	1 level tbsp	1 heaped tbsp
Sugar	2.3g	4g	7.3g	8.5g	12g	20g
Fructose	2.8g	4.6g	8g	7g	12.5g	22g
Aspartame	0.3g	0.5g	0.9g	0.8g	1.3g	2.3g
Xylitol	2.1g	7.5g	8.7g	10.7g	13g	27g

* Xylitol crystals tend to stick together, while those of ordinary sugar slide like a liquid. The weights given for Xylitol therefore correspond to 'tapped' spoonfuls, in other words, after a gentle tap of the finger on the handle of the spoon to make the crystals fall apart.

Incorporating whisked egg white into a mixture is a useful technique. It is easy to do and lends itself to a variety of dishes. Egg white also has many merits. From a nutritional point of view, the white of a 30g egg only contains 13 calories and it does not contain any fats (lipids) or sugars. It also works well in protein-oriented diets since it consists of 10% protein and 90% water.

As well as its inherently low calorie count, whisked egg white traps air and so adds volume, which means that the calorie count of each portion is reduced. For example, a whisked egg white has the same volume as 100g of whipped cream, which creates a very effective culinary illusion!

And last but not least, it would be wrong to be deprived of the airy, frothy dream desserts we love, so I have used whisked egg whites to create two fundamental preparations that can be used in many dessert recipes: a light version of Chantilly Cream (page 280) and the base for bavarois desserts (page 282).

Whisking egg whites

Always whisk egg whites in an ultra-clean, dry bowl using a grease-free whisk, either a balloon whisk or an electric beater. In theory, there is no reason not to use a food processor, but the bowl of a processor is big, calling for the use of at least three egg whites at a time to prevent splattering. As the recipes in this book generally only need one or two egg whites for four servings, a food processor is not the best tool for the job.

The golden rule is to whisk your egg white at the last moment, never in advance. Freshly whisked egg whites are soft but if you wait before using them, they quickly harden and when you try to incorporate them into a mixture, they begin to collapse.

Whisked egg whites are used in soufflés and mousses to lighten the mixture and incorporate air. For this you need soft to fairly firm peaks. If you whisk the whites until the peaks are so firm that they are dry, it will be hard to incorporate them successfully: the air bubbles will burst and you will lose the desired volume.

Meringues are a different matter; for these you should beat the whites to a firmer peak, but you should still make sure they do not become dry.

Note

Tradition has it that, before whisking egg whites, you should always add a pinch of salt. This is supposed to prevent the whites from collapsing if they are kept too long before use. This does not apply to dessert cookery since the addition of sugar at the end of whisking softens and binds the mixture and makes it easier to incorporate the whisked whites in the other ingredients. However, you should still not wait too long before using the whisked whites.

Incorporating whisked egg whites

The way that the whisked egg white is incorporated into the other ingredients is the key to a recipe's success. Firstly, you should add all the freshly whipped egg white in one go because if you do not, the first spoonfuls will be over-worked and will lose some volume.

Secondly, as you work, use the so-called 'planetary movement'. A right-handed person should hold the bowl in their left hand, tilt it slightly and turn it anti-clockwise. Using the right hand, plunge a spatula into the centre of the mixture until it touches the base of the bowl, then lift the mixture, dragging the spatula across the base of the bowl towards the outer edge, from bottom to top, using a clockwise movement.

Cooking whisked egg whites

The traditional method of making a 'floating island' (a poached meringue of whisked egg white) involved poaching the meringue in warm milk, which was then used to make an accompanying crème anglaise, or custard. This method is now used less and less.

Instead, two other methods are used. The first involves using a steamer. Pre-heat the steamer and place the uncooked meringues on a sheet of greaseproof or parchment paper.

This prevents the meringues from sticking to the steamer. Transfer the paper to the steamer and steam them for exactly one minute. If you cook them longer, they will become rubbery.

The second method involves using a microwave oven but you may need several trials before finding the precise cooking time, to the nearest second. For this method, place the meringues on a flat, slightly moistened, plate and microwave for approximately 10 seconds at full power.

Gelatine

Gelatine is a setting agent that lends body to liquid ingredients and, at the same time, binds them into a stiffened form.

With the addition of quite large amounts of gelatine, even thin liquids, such as fruit juices and stocks, will stiffen to a jelly that is firm enough to support its own weight when turned out of a mould. Such gelatine-based preparations remind me of gently swaying palm trees. In our minceur approach to cookery, we use gelatine in a rather more measured and masterly way.

Most gelatine is an animal derivative. It consists of protein extracted from the tendons, ligaments, cartilage and bones of animals, usually cows or pigs. Vegetarians will no doubt prefer to use agar-agar, which is a non-animal derivative, now widely available. Since it does not set quite as firmly as regular gelatine, it is important to follow the instructions for its use.

In our kitchens in France we use sheets of leaf gelatine, choosing from a variety of grades such as platinum, gold, silver and bronze. In the UK, some home cooks use leaf gelatine, usually the gold grade, while others prefer to use powder. In the USA, most home cooks find powdered gelatine easier to obtain than leaf gelatine.

The size of sheets of leaf gelatine varies from country to country and powdered brands differ in their setting strength, which is why you should always be guided by the instructions on the packet. Our recipes give an approximate conversion from leaf to powder. The conversion varies slightly. Where a mixture is supported by eggs, yogurt or cream, and just enough gelatine is needed to hold the preparation together, a sheet of leaf gelatine is equivalent to about ¾ teaspoon, or even less. If the preparation is to be turned out of a mould, you will need more powder; we err on the side of caution.

Using leaf gelatine

To soak leaf gelatine, put it in a shallow dish of cold water ensuring the sheet(s) can lie flat and that several can do so without sticking together. Leave to soak for 5–30 minutes.

The gelatine will usually be sufficiently soft and swollen after 5 minutes but you can leave it longer if convenient. Squeeze it to remove excess water before use.

To dissolve and combine leaf gelatine with warm liquid, add the soaked, squeezed gelatine directly to warm liquid and whisk or stir it thoroughly until smoothly blended. The warmth and the whisking will usually be enough to dissolve the gelatine completely.If necessary, warm the mixture gently but never let it boil.

To dissolve and combine leaf gelatine with cold liquid, place the soaked, squeezed gelatine in a saucepan with just enough cold water to cover. Stir it over a gentle heat and, when it has dissolved completely, combine it with the cold preparation you are setting, mixing the two together thoroughly.

Using powdered gelatine

To dissolve and combine powdered gelatine with hot and cold liquids, for each teaspoon of powdered gelatine, put one tablespoon of very hot – but not boiling – water into a small bowl and sprinkle the powder onto it. (Always add powdered gelatine to the liquid and not the other way around.) The gelatine will swell and start to dissolve. Stand the bowl in a pan of hot water, set over a low heat, for about 3 minutes or until you can see the bottom of the bowl clearly. The dissolved gelatine is now ready to be combined with either hot or cold preparations.

Fats

Fats, also known as lipids, are high-calorie foods: they contain 9 calories per gram, compared with 4 calories per gram for carbohydrates and 4 calories per gram for proteins. If we take an everyday example of one tablespoon of oil, we are talking about 10g of oil and, since oil is 100% fat, that makes 90 calories!

Not all fats are the same, however: some are indispensable to life, while others have no effect on our health. Still others – notably saturated fatty acids – can be harmful if taken in large quantities. Unfortunately, our western eating habits favour foods that fall into this latter category.

Fats are found in animal fats (the most obvious being meat, charcuterie and dairy products) and in fats derived from vegetables. Unfortunately, there are also trans fats, which are the result of the hydrogenation processes often used in the food-processing industry for ensuring, for example, that biscuits, snacks, crisps, margarine and so on, acquire their long shelf-life. (Hydrogenation involves adding hydrogen to unsaturated fatty acids, causing the altered fatty acids – now trans-fatty acids – to become solid at room temperature.)

Today, the uncontested results of numerous scientific studies show a link between cholesterol in foods, saturated fatty acids and trans fats, leading to the risk of developing a cardiovascular problem and a heart attack or stroke.

Note
Omega 3 and 6 are called 'essential' fatty acids with good reason: they play a crucial role in the healthy functioning of the heart and nervous system. They cannot be synthesized. Colza oil and walnut oil are an important source of Omega 3 and 6, as are the fish oils found in salmon, mackerel, herring and sardine.

Milk
There are three kinds of milk, all of which contain fat to a greater or lesser extent:
· Skimmed milk contains less than 0.3% fat
· Semi-skimmed milk contains 1.5%–1.8% fat
· Full-cream milk contains about 3.5% fat

Since fat gives flavour, semi-skimmed milk provides a balance between taste and calorie count. In our minceur approach to cooking, we do not use skimmed milk, even though its taste has been significantly improved recently. Sometimes, though, we use milk in its condensed (or concentrated), unsweetened, form. This is essentially semi-skimmed milk, but with a water content of only 50%–55%. It is useful not only in dessert cookery but also in some savoury preparations, such as emulsified sauces (see the Essential Cuisine Minceur Toolkit, pages 38–95), where it is an ideal substitute for fats such as oil or butter. In the creation of a low-calorie Sauce Béarnaise, for example, you can use unsweetened evaporated milk to create a glistening fluff.

Cream

Cream generally contains around 30%–35% fat. It can be runny, thick and heavy, clotted or something in between. Some cooks think its calorie count too high and prefer to buy reduced-fat cream. In recent years, the choice of reduced-fat cream has increased considerably and you can now easily find creams with a fat content of anything between 5% and 40%. Use these as you see fit, but bear in mind that, if you want whipped cream, you should always choose cream with a fat content above 30%. Lower than this, and you will not be able to get the cream to whip and mount successfully. That is because the structure of its lipids is unsuitable for allowing air bubbles to be trapped, which is what makes the cream hold together in a firm shape.

As a result, you cannot make anything even approaching a successful low-calorie Chantilly Cream (page 280) without adding a certain amount of 30% cream. The trick is to use just a little of this and to mix it with egg whites (see page 20) whipped to snowy peaks.

When using crème fraiche, however, it is possible to cut down the calories by replacing full-cream liquid crème fraiche with reduced-fat thick crème fraiche. This works well as an accompaniment as it is thick enough to be spooned, but it cannot be whipped to a fluff and if it is incorporated into a dessert, the texture will be far less silky.

Fromage blanc

Fromage blanc is one of the French food industry's cherished products. Made from cow's milk, it is prepared in a similar way to crème fraîche, except that crème fraîche is made with cream. Fromage blanc has a slightly bland taste that verges on tartness, as well as a soft texture that blends well with other ingredients, which is useful when it comes to making sauces. In parts of the world where fromage blanc is not available, drained or Greek-style yogurt is a reasonable substitute.

The low-calorie, or 0% fat versions of fromage blanc have become almost indispensible now that people are ever more alert to the dangers of being overweight. However, the food industry has still some way to go in order to market a palatable fromage blanc with a fat content of 0%. The lighter the fromage blanc, the more acidic it becomes, and its plaster-like taste lingers in the mouth. It is for this reason that we use it sparingly in our desserts.

Butter

With its high fat content of 82% and its high calorie count, we use butter only in very limited amounts in *Eat Well and Stay Slim: The Essential Cuisine Minceur*.

Companies in the food industry compete to create substitutes that have butter's consistency and taste without the calories (typically they are 11%–60% fat). Today there are many alternatives to butter of both animal and vegetable origin and some even carry the seductive promise of lowering the cholesterol in the blood. However, even when such substitutes claim to be suitable for cooking, their structure breaks down easily and they do not perform well. Nor do they add a nice traditional buttery taste, so you might just as well forgo the use of such substitutes and instead limit your use of butter as best you can.

When butter is heated, it colours firstly to a light brown and then, very quickly, to a dark, chestnut-brown. At this stage it is known as beurre noisette, or brown butter. It has a highly seductive, tempting aroma and is found in dishes with the word 'meunière' in their name.

However, at this brown stage, the butter's structure starts to break down, which means it is better to limit your intake. If you carry on cooking it, the brown butter will turn black and decompose completely. This black butter was, until very recently, the secret of 'skate in black butter'. Today, we see this dish in a different light because we now know that black butter contains fatty acid peroxides. Some experts think that these fatty acid peroxides are extremely bad for the health, while others claim they are not dangerous if consumed only occasionally. That said, skate in black butter has now been banned from restaurants in France.

When you cook with butter, you should stop it from cooking once it reaches a pale chestnut-brown stage. To do this, simply stand the saucepan or frying pan (skillet) in iced water. To serve, simply reheat the butter gently. You can also slow down the browning stages of butter by adding a little olive, or other oil to the butter before you start heating it.

Chef's tip

If you heat butter and oil together and add a clove of crushed, unpeeled garlic, you end up with a simple basting mixture that can make a world of difference to the food you coat with it. Use it for basting any food that you think will benefit from an intriguing hint of garlic and a heady aroma.

Note

Margarine was created in 1869 in response to a competition launched by Napoleon III, who expressed the wish that his fellow-citizens might benefit from a 'fatty substance, similar to butter, but costing less, able to be kept for a long time without structural alteration and loss of its nutritional value.' The winning substitute, margarine, quickly became a culinary favourite. Margarine's popularity has endured even if, today, thanks to the invention of the hydrogenation of oils – which itself is the subject of many criticisms linking it with weight gain and obesity – it is manufactured very differently.

Oils

The use of oil is even less advisable, from a calorific perspective, than the use of butter: oil contains more fat than butter – 100% compared with butter's 82%. Remember that one gram of lipids contains nine calories, therefore one tablespoonful of oil is the equivalent of 90 calories – and that takes nearly half an hour's walk at a moderate pace to be burned off.

The richer an oil is in either polyunsaturated fatty acids or monounsaturated fatty acids, the less stable it is and the less capable of tolerating high temperatures. What is more, it is believed that high temperatures could provoke the appearance of carcinogens (page 29).

At high temperatures, oil colours and smokes; this is rightly called the 'smoking point' and signals danger. The smoking point of virgin olive oil is 160°C (320°F). For grapeseed oil, the smoking point rises to 216°C (420°F), while for groundnut oil, it is as high as 227°C (440°F), which is why groundnut oil is called the 'queen of frying', especially deep-frying.

Although olive oil has a wonderful flavour, its low smoking point makes it better suited to sautéing and shallow-frying at reasonable temperatures, than to deep-frying, which calls for a high temperature.

Special oils for deep-frying

In discussing cooking oils, it seems natural to talk of deep-frying, which is highly appreciated for its organoleptic qualities – that is to say, the taste and crunch it brings to the food. Today there are special deep-frying oils with a high smoking point. As a result, the dangers of deep-frying are no longer focused exclusively on the high temperatures reached during the cooking process (see The Maillard Reaction, page 29) but also take into account the excessive fat content of many of these frying oils, and the risks of cardiovascular disease that they bring with them.

Fat found in poultry and meat

The first thing a cook should do when preparing poultry, meat and game is to trim off any excess fat – not only external fat but also any internal connective tissue and interlarding. Economy cuts of meat – spare ribs of pork and braising steak, for example – require a considerable amount of trimming, whereas prime cuts, such as fillet steak, do not need much.

Sometimes fat is partially concealed, as is the case with breast of duck. The best way to deal with it is to start by trimming away the visible fatty pieces around the breast, then removing the thickish layer of fat found under the skin. Finally, use a small knife to score a pattern of small slits through the skin so that remaining fat can escape during cooking.

When selecting poultry and meat, be guided by its fat content per 100g (4oz), as shown below.

Beef	
Prime rib	26g
Rib steak or entrecote with fat	17g
Steak with 15% fat	15g
Rib steak or entrecote without fat	8.7g
Rib eye	6.7g
Chuck	6.5g
Flank steak	6g
Cheek	5g
Mince with 5% fat	5g
Shoulder of beef	3.4g

Poultry	
Whole chicken for roasting	11g
Whole guinea fowl for roasting	8g
Duck breast without skin	6g
Chicken breast	2g

Veal	
Rib with fat	12.7g
Sweetbreads	7.5g
Rib without fat	5g
Shoulder	5g
Roast of topside or blade	5g
Liver	3.4g
Shank or leg	2.6g
Round fillet	2.6g
Escalope	2.5g

Lamb	
Cutlets or rack with fat	17g– 23g
Saddle with fat	18.4g
Cutlets or rack without fat	4.5g–17g
Saddle without fat	4.2g
Leg	4.2g

Pork	
Loin cutlets	10g
Spare rib	10g
Roasts of leg, loin and shoulder	8g
Leg fillet	5g

Egg	6g

Chef's tip

If you buy meat ready-coated with, say, herbs or breadcrumbs, you will not be able to trim off the fat prior to cooking. Instead, remove it after cooking. Simply leave the cooked dish to rest in a cool place. The fat will rise to the surface and solidify, at which point you can easily scrape it off with a spoon. This same cooling and degreasing method can be applied to meat stock.

Note

The fat content in meat has been significantly reduced over the past 20 years. Livestock farmers have progressively taken account of public health recommendations, as well as consumer tastes, with the result that new rearing techniques have evolved.

Fat found in fish

Most types of fish are lean and need little or no fat removal. That is why health experts recommend that we give fish pride of place in our diets, eating it at least two or three times a week instead of meat, and thereby reducing our intake of saturated fatty acids. However, some fish have a high lipid content. Eels are a case in point. Indeed, connoisseurs used to hang eels in their chimneys above the flames; this encouraged the fat to ooze out naturally, after which the eels were grilled.

Fish is thought by some to be challenging to cook: the flesh is fragile and dries out quickly during cooking. And, in the eyes of many, fish is bland and uninteresting. However, this should not be the case. This book offers many recipes that showcase the wonderful qualities of sea and river creatures. There is no reason why they should languish in the shade of their terrestrial cousins.

Herring	
Salmon fillet or steak, farmed	16g (wild salmon is half as oily as farmed, but rarer and more expensive)
Eel	15g
Smoked salmon	13g
Mackerel	11.6g
Trout	11.6g
Fresh tuna	6.2g
Sardines, fresh	4.5g
Sardines, tinned: . in lemon and basil . in olive oil	6g 35g
Turbot	3.7g
Sea bass	3g
Sea bream	2.8g
Langoustine, Dublin Bay prawns and US jumbo shrimp	2g
Lobster	2g
Fresh anchovy	2g
Mussels	2g
Coley	1.8g
Tinned yellow fin tuna (in its own juice)	1.6g
Shrimps/small prawns	1.4g
Sole	1.4g
Skate	1g
Squid	1g
Pollock	0.7g
Monkfish	0.7g
Whiting	0.6g
Cod	0.5g
Crabmeat	0.3g
Scallops	0.2g

Minimising your use of fat

I always recommend the use of non-stick frying pans (skillets) and saucepans. These are wonderful for the healthy low-calorie regime because they do not require the use of fat to prevent food from sticking. Using a good-quality non-stick frying pan, you can even sear a very rare or rare steak without adding any fat. (People who cannot do without the taste of olive oil or butter on their steak can add it after cooking: that way the purity of the oil or butter will be retained.)

However, this 'magic' utensil will never give food the scrumptious, characteristic taste of sautéed food that is associated with the good old iron pan, which does require a minimum amount of fat.

It is also important to select a frying pan (skillet) or other cooking utensil, according to the size of the food to be cooked – and no bigger. There are several reasons for this, the most important of which is the fact that you will use less fat. It is tragic – and above all dangerous – to see a small steak looking like a desert island afloat in the middle of an ocean of fat, in a frying pan four sizes too big.

Sauces and dressings

Health professionals frequently advocate an increase in consumption of fresh vegetables as a way to better health for most people. But without appropriate seasoning, some vegetables can be rather dull. This raises the issue of dressing and in particular, the traditional vinaigrette: why should we continue to stick to the usual, high-calorie formula of 1 tablespoon of vinegar to 3 or 4 tablespoons of oil? Remember, 1 tablespoon of oil contains 90 calories.

In this book, the Vinaigrettes (see pages 64–73) acquire their seductive lightness and their aromatic flavour through the sparing use of Flavoured Oils (see pages 55–63) and Stocks (see pages 41–54). What is more, with the addition of spices

and herbs, the Vinaigrettes can be transformed into exquisite sauces and served warm, as we shall see in the Essential Cuisine Minceur Recipes (pages 116–325).

The ever-popular traditional mayonnaise, hollandaise and béarnaise sauces are based on egg yolks (so they are rich in lecithin, which is to say, lipids) and a good deal of fat (butter and oil). As any health-conscious person can see, these are the drawbacks. Happily, it is possible to produce very acceptable, healthy versions, thanks to the discerning use of substitutes, such as yogurt, fromage blanc, petit-suisses and unsweetened evaporated milk (pages 23–4). A little fat might be added for flavour but it will amount to about 10% of the amount normally used in the classic versions.

The reputation of French cuisine owes much to its sauces. In fact, the sauce chef is the magician of the professional kitchen. In the game of alchemy that he or she plays, stocks are what allow sauces to flower and come to life, and that permit the thickening agents, or liaisons as they known, to blossom. Here at Eugénie-les-Bains, in order to make sauces that reduce or cut out altogether the use of thickening fats, we have devised new and original liaisons based on purées of vegetables or fruits. These cleverly allow us to safeguard the grand French tradition of serving dishes accompanied by sauces (see Puréed Liaisons and their Sauces, pages 83–9).

Cooking methods

In my approach to this book and to healthy gastronomy as a whole, I have decided, first and foremost, to limit the single cooking method which all specialists agree may be dangerous for health: frying. I will start by discussing frying and other traditional, but questionable, methods before moving on to looking at healthy methods that are better adapted to my approach.

But before I start, I must draw your attention to the very significant Maillard Reaction that sometimes occurs during the cooking process.

The Maillard Reaction

We all have slightly different ideas about what constitutes a culinary delicacy. Some people's fancy is a piece of meat or fish fried to the point that its crust acquires some crunch and a slightly caramelized flavour resembling toasted hazelnuts. This effect is due to a process known as the Maillard Reaction, after the French chemist Louis-Camille Maillard, who first described it in 1912. It is also simply referred to as the 'browning reaction'.

Caused by a complex chemical reaction between sugars and amino-acids, the tantalizing aroma of the Maillard Reaction is associated with crusty bread, toasted cereals, coffee, roast potatoes, barbecued meat, and so on. However, the reaction has a dark side: if temperatures in excess of 180°C (355°F) are reached, carcinogens such as acrylamides can be produced.

To prevent overcooking, you should avoid leaving food too long in the pan. This means choosing pieces of fish or meat that are thin enough to cook through fairly quickly, at a moderate temperature. Escalopes are a good example. Simply cook such pieces on both sides to the desired colour. Thicker pieces of meat and poultry might lend themselves to being flattened slightly between two sheets of clingfilm (plastic wrap).

Chef's tip

if you are frying or sautéing thick pieces of food that do not lend themselves to being flattened and so need a relatively long time in the pan, you can prevent the build-up of heat as follows: as soon as the food items are browned on both sides, add a few tablespoons of cold water or stock to the pan. This will allow you to complete the cooking and, at the same time, produce some flavoursome cooking juices. Another option is to proceed in stages: if the recipes calls for one tablespoon of oil, use one-third to coat the food and brown it, then add the rest in two stages. That way, you avoid overheating the oil at each stage.

Questionable cooking methods

Deep-frying

Deep-frying is mostly associated with the frying of chips. There are two stages involved in this process:

- Stage 1, the cut potatoes are plunged into an oil bath at 150°C (300°F) to 'poach' them. During this stage, they absorb fat like blotting paper even if, after cooking, a good deal of this oil drains out and can be mopped up with absorbent kitchen paper.
- Stage 2, they are plunged again into oil at 170°C (325°F). This makes them golden and crispy.

Apart from the fact that the potatoes absorb an enormous quantity of unhealthy, calorie-laden oil, frying a potato chip to a crisp finish requires that the oil be heated to a temperature at which the oil smokes and produces carcinogens.

Chef's tip

Stage 1, which is particularly harmful, can be replaced by a more natural method involving steaming the chip-cut potatoes in stock, either in a steamer or in a microwave oven. This prevents the potatoes from absorbing excessive fat. Health-conscious readers may be relieved to know there is now an appliance on the market, the Actifry by Seb, which fries at 90°C (194°F) and at low pressure, thereby reducing the health risks.

Rapid pan-frying and sautéing

This very simple method involves cooking food rapidly in a frying pan (skillet) or sauté pan of some kind. With its emphasis on speed, it suits fairly flat, thin pieces of food. The heat can penetrate to the centre without overcooking the outside and the short cooking time is, more or less, the time it takes for the outside to become coloured or browned.

For that reason, this method lends itself particularly well to trimmed, prime, cuts of meat that require little cooking at medium to high heat – for example, steaks of beef and lamb, especially when destined to be eaten rare.

Veal and chicken escalopes and fillets of fish call for gentler heat and must be cooked through evenly using this method. Thicker breasts of chicken and duck fare well, but their skin should be left intact to prevent the flesh from drying out.

For this type of cooking, I recommend you use a non-stick frying pan (skillet), the base of which should be lightly oiled using absorbent kitchen paper. The great advantage of this type of pan is that food cooked in it does not stick and, at the same time, you can keep your use of oil to an absolute minimum.

Wok cookery

There are similar issues surrounding high temperatures and the possibility of the oil producing carcinogens when it comes to wok cookery. Several studies have found a correlation between wok cookery, which calls for food to be tossed in hot, smoking oil, and the high levels of lung cancer in Asian women, who favour this method of cooking. It appears that the emanations from the oil have a lot to answer for. However, rather than foregoing this interesting and speedy method of cooking, I suggest the following: as soon as the food (meat, fish or vegetable) has taken on a light colour, and before the oil burns, add half a glass of the stock of your choice. The liquid will not only prevent the oil from smoking, it will also evaporate slowly during cooking and create a smooth, syrupy sauce that gives the food an attractive coating.

Slower pan-frying and braising techniques

A slower method of pan-frying and sautéing over a medium or a low heat can be used for thicker pieces of fish and chicken and also for cheaper, tougher, often gelatinous, cuts of meat that would toughen and shrink if cooked rapidly over high heat.

Roasting

This involves subjecting poultry, game, meat and fish to the dry heat of an oven. The item to be cooked is either set in a roasting pan or put on a spit. It is a method that accounts for the succulence of dishes such as leg of lamb, roast beef and roast chicken. Yet it is also an excellent method for cooking large, whole fish. The item destined for the oven should be trimmed of all fat (and, in the case of fish, the fins should be removed) and coated with an absolute minimum of oil. An aromatic garnish can be added before roasting.

As a general guide, chicken and meat cuts that are slightly fatty, such as shoulder of lamb and most pork joints, should be roasted at 160°C–170°C (320°F–325°F, gas mark 3). When the item is almost cooked, it makes sense to brown the surface by increasing the oven temperature to 200°C (400°F, gas mark 6). By contrast, much-prized leg of lamb and prime cuts of beef, veal and pork are best roasted at the higher temperature of 200°C (400°F, gas mark 6) throughout the entire cooking process.

During the course of roasting, baste the cut frequently with its juices to which you have added some stock. At the end of cooking, you should skim away all the fat before adding a little more stock, then boiling it down to a sauce or gravy of a syrupy consistency. Note that food cooked in this way loses 25%–40% of its water-soluble vitamins, due to the evaporation of the food's natural water content.

Chef's tip

Cooked at high heat, meat shrinks and its muscles tighten, leading to a hardening of its fibres. In turn, the blood runs to the centre and the juiciness vanishes from the surrounding areas. When the meat is carved, the blood – now concentrated in the centre – pours out, while the surface of the meat appears cooked. If this happens, it is not necessarily a failure in the cooking, but rather, that the meat has not been rested. Resting or relaxing the roasted meat in a warm place gives the blood time to be distributed and reabsorbed evenly throughout the meat. In this way, the whole piece of meat will be rare or medium-rare, as required. For all direct heat methods, including the grill (broiler), the barbecue or the plancha, the resting time should be at least as long as the cooking time. Generally speaking, though, meat for a hot roast should rest for 15–30 minutes, depending on its size. During this time, the cook can take the opportunity to deglaze the roasting pan and make a sauce.

Grilling (broiling)

The method involves direct, radiant heat, the source of which can be above or below the food. The utensil that the food sits on can vary: it can be a ridged griddle (broiler) pan, a wire grill rack or a flat plate known as a plancha. Depending on the thickness of the food being cooked and its distance from the heat source, grilling is a relatively quick cooking method that gives the outside of the food a good colour and crust, while ensuring tenderness on the inside. However, if the food is exposed to excessively high temperatures, then a Maillard Reaction (page 29) can take place. For this reason, therefore, we advise grilling at a moderate heat.

To avoid subjecting the food to excessively high temperatures, choose small, relatively thin, pieces of poultry, fish, meat or vegetables, which will cook quickly. Bring them to room temperature and oil them very lightly using kitchen paper, before grilling. Before you cook them, you can, if you like, dip them quickly into some stock to which you have added a little soy sauce. This will counteract the hot dry heat as well as adding flavour. Certain vegetables, such as sliced courgettes (zucchini) and aubergines (eggplants) respond very well to this treatment.

Note that food cooked in this way loses 20% of its water-soluble vitamins, due to the evaporation of the food's natural water content.

Grilling (broiling) red meat and testing for doneness

- To grill to a very rare (blue) stage, place the meat on a preheated griddle or grill rack, just long enough for it to be seared on one side and get grill marks. Turn the meat over and repeat the process. When pressed with your forefinger, blue meat will feel soft and will yield to very slight pressure – just as if it were raw. The meat is now sufficiently cooked but you need to keep it fairly close to the heat for several minutes more so that the meat warms through right to the centre.
- To grill to a rare stage, cook as for very rare (above). However, when you have seared the second side of the meat, continue grilling, watching the meat carefully: when small red beads of juice appear on the surface, remove it from the heat source. When pressed with your forefinger, the meat will be slightly resistant but will still maintain its springiness.
- To grill to a medium-rare stage, cook as for rare (above) but once you have removed it from the direct source of heat, leave it on the griddle pan or grill rack in a warm place until the beads of juice that appear on the surface are pink rather than red. They will also be more numerous. When pressed with your forefinger, the meat will be firm to the touch.
- To grill to a well done stage, sear the meat on both sides as when cooking to a rare stage. Increase the distance of the meat from the direct heat source and turn the meat again. Leave it on the griddle pan or grill rack until the beads of juice that appear on the surface coagulate and become light brown. When pressed with your forefinger, the meat will be very firm to the touch.

Grilling on a chimenea or barbecue

The golden rule for this type of grilling is that the food should not come into contact with the flames, which can reach a temperature of 500°C (932°F). To avoid this happening, prepare and light the chimenea or barbecue, using either wood or charcoal. As soon as the embers are red, you can be sure that the metal grill is sufficiently hot. Push the embers to the back and put the food on the front of the grill, where there is no risk of the flames reaching it. Cook to a golden colour without burning, thus avoiding any harmful carbonisation.

Healthy cooking methods

The following methods are those that are best suited to the healthy cooking that is in keeping with the spirit of Essential Cuisine Minceur.

Poaching

This is a very versatile, moist-heat cooking method, which suits almost every kind of food, from fish to poultry, meat and vegetables. The basic principle is that the food is immersed in a cooking liquid of some kind, such as stock or water, and is then cooked in a covered or partially covered saucepan, over very gentle heat on top of the stove.

The cold-start method

When food begins its poaching process in a cold liquid, the cooking process is longer and gentler than when cooking starts in a hot liquid. As the cold liquid heats up, the flavours of the ingredients are drawn out and blend gradually and thoroughly, so that the food being poached is enriched by the flavour of cooking liquid. Naturally, the flavour will be enhanced if the liquid consists of an aromatic stock.

The gentleness of this method is well suited to the delicate flesh of fish. It also suits cheaper, tough, cuts of meat: these have large amounts of connective tissue, cartilage and muscle, all of which take time to become tender.

Poaching temperatures can vary slightly. Very gentle poaching is ideally carried out at temperatures of 71°C–80°C (160°F–175°F), so below simmering point. If you do not have a thermometer, just watch the surface of the liquid: it should ripple gently without bubbling. If you find it difficult to lower the heat sufficiently, use a heat-diffusing mat. Often the terms poaching and simmering are used interchangeably but, when simmering, the cooking liquid rises and forms bubbles on the surface, indicating a temperature of 82°C–96°C (180°F–205°F).

In the case of a boiled beef 'pot-au-feu', cold-start poaching produces a particularly flavoursome broth, or stock, due to the prolonged exchange between the liquid and the meat. Once cooled, the fat can be skimmed off. The cold-start method is also the accepted way of cooking dried pulses such as lentils and beans.

The hot-start method

This method is better reserved for prime, tender, cuts of meat. It is used to cook the Poached beef with barley (page 268). The immersion of the meat in the hot, simmering liquid seals in the flavour and preserves the taste and aroma. The hot-start method Is also associated with cooking fish 'au bleu': trout is a great example.

The majority of green vegetables are also cooked in this way, uncovered, so as to preserve their bright green colour. If the cooked vegetables are not to be used straight away, they are refreshed in cold water to stop them cooking and preserve their colour. Vegetables pre-cooked in this way can be reheated conveniently either in a steamer or a microwave, or in a saucepan with a minimal amount of fat to prevent sticking.

Note that food cooked in this way loses some of its natural water and water-soluble vitamins. However, you can minimise this by avoiding cutting the food into small pieces.

Steaming

Convenient, and well suited to healthy cooking and special diets, this is a form of cooking that takes place in an atmosphere saturated with very hot steam. Sometimes the liquid generating the steam is flavoured; sometimes plain water is used. (You can buy special steaming utensils or you can create your own, using a rack set over simmering liquid.) Because steaming does not need any fat, it is a pure cooking method, that is reputed to retain a food's essential flavour and vitamins. Virtually all food can be steamed but it is particularly appropriate for fish, vegetables and poultry.

Braising or stewing

The method of slow, moist cooking in a closed container, is known variously as braising and stewing. The technique involves an initial browning of the meat – so the process starts in a similar way to the slow-frying method (page 30). The difference is that a deep saucepan or casserole dish with a well-fitting lid is used so that stock can be added after browning. The meat is then bathed in moisture during its gentle cooking in a technique that resembles steaming.

Once the ingredients are ready and in the covered pan, the whole thing is placed either in a low to medium oven, or on top of the stove over a gentle heat. The cooking time for braises and stews varies widely, from one to six hours, depending on the exact type of cut being employed and how tender you want it to be. This is the way to make a classic stew such as a beef bourguignon or a navarin of lamb.

So-called 'white' stews, or fricassées, of bite-sized pieces of veal or chicken, are prepared in a similar way, except that these pale, delicate, morsels of food are not browned before braising. Neither are large, whole pieces of meat usually browned prior to braising because they are often too unwieldy to turn and brown on all their surfaces.

Naturally, meat – and also some poultry and fish – exudes a certain amount of fat during cooking. That is why braised dishes are at their best if prepared the day before and chilled: the fat then forms a solid layer that can easily be skimmed off before reheating and serving.

Braising in a natural crust of salt or in a clay brick (see photo on page 35)

This is similar to poaching and steaming in that it is a moist-heat method that does not require any browning. The natural water content of the ingredients is preserved because the food is cooked in a semi-hermetic shell – usually of salt or clay. This preserves the natural flavour and ensures that the flesh is incomparably tender. There is a sense in which baking a fish in its skin in the oven, without first removing the scales, comes close to this method of cooking.

Usually, food encased in a shell of salt is cooked in the dry heat of an oven preheated to 220°C (425°F, gas mark 7). Temperatures for roasting fish can vary while clay bricks, often used for chicken, are put into ovens at about 180°C (350°F, gas mark 5).

Braising in paper or foil parcels (en papillote)

In this method, the food is cooked in a steamy atmosphere in a paper or foil parcel with an airtight seal. A double layer of parchment paper works best, but greaseproof or aluminium foil will do. It is a simple method: you lay the ingredients on the paper – for example, a fillet of salmon, which you might combine with a julienne (Terms and Techniques, page 327) of garnish vegetables, so that you can cook the two elements simultaneously. You then add a little aromatic stock. Some of this liquid will be converted to steam and will help with the cooking, but the rest will become the accompanying juices. You should take care to bring the edges of the paper or foil together neatly and fold them over several times to make a good seal, before transferring the parcel to the oven. In this way, the sealed-in flavour becomes very concentrated until the parcel is opened – and a delightful burst of fragrance greets the diner.

Slow, enclosed cooking is the best way of preserving food's water-soluble vitamins. Indeed, there is very little loss of water from the food itself using these semi-hermetic methods and a gentle heat.

Vacuum-sealed low-temperature cookery

The interest in this technique is mostly confined to professional caterers. It can be used for all types of meat, poultry, fish, vegetables and fruit; in fact, its use is practically universal. Vacuum-sealed cookery calls for the food to be wrapped in a special cellophane cooking bag that is then made airtight to ensure the even cooking and conservation of the food concerned. A special gadget is often used to help create the required vacuum by extracting a certain quantity of air. The bag is then heated in a temperature-controlled bain-marie or in a special steam-oven, for a given time, at a temperature ranging from 55°C to 85°C (131°F–185°F), depending on the type of food, the precise method and the equipment.

With this method, professionals are able to cook with a precision of one degree, which prevents sudden changes in temperature. This method also means that you do not have to worry about the resting times associated with roasted joints of meat and poultry.

Vacuum-sealed cookery is of interest for several reasons: firstly, because it preserves the food's nutritional and sensory qualities, notably vitamins, minerals, taste, aroma and texture. Secondly, because food cooked in this way retains its original weight. I feel it would be profitable if this method were to be adopted more widely throughout the food and health industries as a whole.

Chef's tip

Professor of Medicine, Jean-Philippe Derenne, who is also a cookery writer, has developed a practical household version of vacuum-sealed cookery, which I feel bound to pass on to you. Slip the food you want to cook (say, a piece of fish, poultry or meat) into a zip-lock freezer bag. Season to taste and, if you wish, add two tablespoonfuls of aromatic stock and a drop of oil or sliver of butter. Close the bag and plunge it into a bowl of cold water. This will push against the sides of the bag and force out the air. You can help by squeezing the bag with the flat of your hand. Put the closed bag into an empty container or saucepan. Submerge the bag completely in boiling water. Cooking times will vary. As a rough guide, it will take just 3 or 4 minutes to cook a fillet of sea bream in this way.

The multi-functional whipper

The use of what we, in France, call the siphon was originally confined exclusively to making whipped chantilly cream: the use of siphon technology was the almost exclusive territory of commercial foodstuff manufacturers. It is what made possible those whipped cream dispensers with nozzles that dispense great bursts of swirled cream. It was also associated with the making of soda water and fizzy drinks.

That was, of course, until the celebrated Catalan chef, Ferran Adrià, arrived on the scene. He revolutionized the technique of adding air and adapted the siphon to seemingly a million other uses in the kitchen. Hence, foams and froths – often called espumas – were born, along with a whole new spectrum of exceptionally light sauces, mousses and purées.

One of the advantages of incorporating air mechanically into an intensely flavoured sauce or preparation in this way, is that the flavour expands and becomes light and sumptuous, while the volume doubles. With some of these creations, a small amount of gelatine may be added so that the resulting foam, mousse or aerated purée, holds its shape on the plate.

Of course, the extension of the scope of the siphon beyond making whipped cream or soda for drinks, has also resulted in new categories of siphon and a change of name: in some parts of the world, notably the UK and the USA, the tool that I and other chefs use nowadays is known to consumers as a multi-functional whipper.

It really does not matter too much what you put into the whipper: it can be savoury or sweet, a hot mixture or a cold one, it can be mixed with a gelling agent or not, it can be a soup, a cream or a purée. Whatever you use, the magic is always what comes out – the original preparation is aerated and takes on a mousse-like consistency.

Unfortunately, the effect does not last long, which is not always convenient when it comes to serving. A mousse will keep its volume for 2–3 minutes, after which it gradually falls.

Adding a little gelatine (page 22) helps it keep its shape a little longer, say, 5–6 minutes. This slight disadvantage takes nothing from the silky texture that simply slips into the mouth. The effect is magical. It's like biting into a cloud!

Desirable though these whippers are, you can make the dishes in this book perfectly well without one. You can obtain a very similar effect – though the foam will be wispier – if you use a hand-held stick blender. Of course, this method lacks the convenience of the whipper, which is a particular boon to professional cooks.

The uses of the multi-functional whipper in dessert cookery
One of the advantages of a whipper for low-calorie dessert cookery is its power to give volume to a range of preparations that include only a small amount of beaten egg white. It also allows the creation of low-calorie mousses that tantalize the palate with their ethereal lightness. And although you need cream with a fat content of 30%–35% in order to be able to whip it successfully, when you use the whipper, you will only require a small amount because it will expand in volume.

When it comes to simply whipping cream, a basic cream whipper will do the job perfectly well, but this cannot be used for any of the other more innovative applications. For these you need a multi-functional whipper – or simply whip by hand with a hand-held stick blender.

Using a multi-functional whipper

Models and sizes of whippers vary according to the manufacturer, so methods of use vary slightly. For this reason, it is always important to follow the manufacturer's instructions carefully.

Generally speaking, a whipper can take a charge of between one and three nitrogen (N_2O) gas cartridges.

Some models allow you to use an extra cartridge to achieve an extra degree of lightness, which can be appropriate for certain desserts.

The instructions will inevitably tell you, however, not to overfill the container. Other tips include storing spare cartridges in a cool place and passing the preparation through a fine sieve before loading it in the whipper – small food particles can clog the valves.

Note

The multi-functional whipper employs cartridges of nitrogen gas (N_2O) and not cartridges of carbon dioxide (CO_2). The latter are used mostly for fizzy drinks. Carbon dioxide should never be used for food, partly because it does not produce the desired volume and, most importantly, because it results in a very disagreeable taste. I recall blunders with cartridges occurring even in quite grand restaurants.

THE ESSENTIAL CUISINE MINCEUR TOOLKIT

This specially created Toolkit is a wonderful asset for any cooks who want the key elements of a low-calorie gastronomic meal ready and waiting, to be used at their convenience. Unlock the Toolkit and you will find the low-calorie, innovative culinary tools that underpin the minceur eating regime.

These culinary tools include a range of minceur-inspired Master Stocks and Stock Variations, whose lively flavours reflect today's culinary borrowings from the East. Other tools include heavenly-scented Flavoured Oils and must-have Vinaigrettes, which will lift salads to new levels of taste without weighing them down with calories. Then there are my reinvented Classic Sauces and Condiments, as well as my special low-calorie vegetable and fruit purées, which are the crucial elements for making super-light Liaisons, Sauces and Cold Coulis.

The tools are all preparations in their own right, yet they also act as stepping stones to the creation of other assemblies and sauces. They are versatile enough to allow you to be creative and to mix and match according to your individual needs and whims; the permutations are almost endless. What is more, these tools are conducive to advance preparation, so you can store them away, ready to be unlocked when needed. This makes them well suited to home cooks, particularly those with limited time to spend in the kitchen, yet who still want to eat well in a calorie-controlled way. At the same time, the convenience and ease of storage of the tools, and their role as stepping stones to other assemblies, also makes them very practical for commercial catering enterprises.

Making these preparations in advance may require a little effort, but it is well worth it because they last well: several days in the refrigerator, a week when vacuum-sealed, and up to a year in a freezer. It makes sense to store them in quantities most appropriate for their use, for instance 150ml (¾ US cup), 250 ml (1⅛ US cups) or 500ml (2⅛ US cups).

Home cooks with busy professional lives might have to use a long weekend to put some tools in their culinary Toolkit, but the result will be delicious, readily available food on returning home from work and some decent lunches to take to the office. Many readers may also feel inspired by having the crucial elements of a sophisticated meal at their fingertips. It is, after all, a wonderful incentive for entertaining friends.

Some examples from the Toolkit

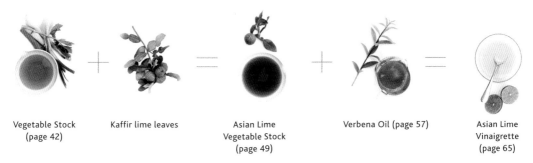

| Vegetable Stock (page 42) | Kaffir lime leaves | Asian Lime Vegetable Stock (page 49) | Verbena Oil (page 57) | Asian Lime Vinaigrette (page 65) |

Serve with, for example, Herb-scented prawn skewers (page 182).

| Chicken Stock (page 44) | Plants and condiments | Thai Stock (page 52) | Coconut Oil (page 60) | Thai Vinaigrette (page 68) |

Serve with, for example, Warm chicken salad with potatoes (page 204) or Thai-flavoured wing of skate with Chinese cabbage (page 206).

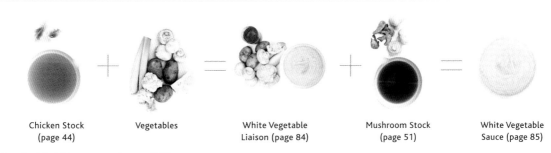

| Chicken Stock (page 44) | Vegetables | White Vegetable Liaison (page 84) | Mushroom Stock (page 51) | White Vegetable Sauce (page 85) |

Use hot for Veal blanquette (page 103).

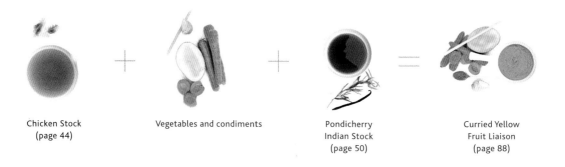

Chicken Stock
(page 44)

Vegetables and condiments

Pondicherry
Indian Stock
(page 50)

Curried Yellow
Fruit Liaison
(page 88)

Use hot for Lamb curry (page 104).

Chicken Stock
(page 44)

Vegetables

White Vegetable
Liaison (page 84)

breadcrumbs or
Parmesan

Pear and White
Vegetable Gratin
(page 106)

Use to make a pretty golden topping for a gratin!

Master Stocks and Stock Variations

Stocks, or bouillons, lie at the heart of my approach to healthy cooking. I have divided them into Master Stocks (based on the great classics) and Stock Variations. Together they form the keystone to the wide range of recipes and sauces in this book, either as an integral part the dish itself or contributing to an accompanying sauce.

Stocks play a crucial role in poached dishes, bathing the food in moisture and helping to bring about an intermingling of flavours. With braises and stews, a similar exchange of flavours takes place between the main ingredients and the stock.

Stocks have other uses, too. Their moisture creates a steamy atmosphere for food cooked en papillote – loosely wrapped in paper or foil parcels, then transferred to the oven. They are also the ideal liquid with which to deglaze a sauté or roasting pan so that the crusty deposits can be incorporated and dissolved into a sauce.

When it comes to soups, a stock might form the entire basis of a thin soup, to which pieces of vegetable or pasta, poultry or meat might be added, as in a minestrone. Stocks can also be combined with purées to make thick, smooth soups.

For my Stock Variations (pages 49–54), I have built on the Master Stocks, adding to them a wide range of aromatic elements so as to modify their flavour in ways that are sometimes subtle, sometimes more dynamic. Kaffir lime leaves, lemongrass, coconut and Indian spices are among the contemporary favourites used to update and broaden the range of flavours associated with the traditional stocks of the French kitchen.

These uses of stock form part of the classical French tradition. However, in this new approach to healthy cooking, I have also used stocks in innovative ways. For example, I use them to replace, or at least minimize, the use of oil in the creation of my new generation of low-calorie Vinaigrettes (pages 64–73). Sometimes, I combine a stock with a vegetable or fruit purée – to make what I call a Puréed Liaison (pages 83–9) – that can,

in its turn, become a sauce to accompany and transform a very simply prepared piece of food, such as a poached or grilled chicken breast or fillet of fish.

Historical titbit

Until approximately the middle of the eighteenth century, stocks – or bouillons as they are known in France – were regarded as a health-restoring drink, or broth that was given to a patient following an illness. Understandably, such stocks were described as 'restaurant', meaning 'restorative'. Then, in 1765, a Parisian soup-vendor named Boulanger (which, confusingly, means Baker) put up a sign outside his shop, saying: 'Venite ad me vos qui stomach laboratis et ego restaurabo vos' (come to me all who labour in the stomach, and I will restore you). This led to the use of the word 'restaurant' to describe a place where people could relax and enjoy a meal on the premises in exchange for payment.

- 2kg (4½lb) vegetables, washed and trimmed or peeled and sliced, for example:
- 500g (1lb 2oz) fennel
- 500g (1lb 2oz) carrots
- 300g (11oz) onions
- 300g (11oz) leeks
- 250g (9oz) celery
- 150g (5½oz) shallots
- 4 litres (17 US cups) cold water
- ½ bottle dry white wine

For the aromatics
- 2 long strips orange peel, white pith removed
- 3 star anise
- 50g (1¾oz) finely chopped garlic
- 10 long sprigs of flat-leaf parsley
- 1 sprig of thyme
- 1 bay leaf, fresh or dried
- 120g (scant 4½oz) orange slices, peel and pith removed
- 40g (scant 1½oz) lemon slices, peel and pith removed
- 25g (scant 1oz) peeled and chopped fresh ginger
- 15g (about 2 tsp) salt
- pinch of ground pepper

VEGETABLE STOCK

Cooking and preparation: 3 hours
Makes 2 litres (8½ US cups)

1. Put the vegetables into a stockpot, large saucepan or casserole (Dutch oven).

2. Pour in the water and white wine. Add the strips of orange peel and all the aromatics except the orange and lemon slices and the fresh ginger. Season with salt and pepper.

3. Bring the stock slowly to the boil. With the saucepan uncovered, adjust the heat so that the surface of the liquid murmurs and makes only very small bubbles for about 2 hours, or until the stock has reduced by half.

4. Add the orange and lemon slices and the ginger. Cover the saucepan, remove from the heat and leave the ingredients to infuse for 30 minutes. Taste and adjust the seasoning with salt.

5. Pour the stock through a fine sieve – ideally a chinois – set over a large bowl. When the stock is cold, store it in convenient quantities in airtight containers, in the refrigerator or freezer.

- 2kg (4½lb) of stewing beef, trimmed of fat: chuck, shoulder, shin, cheek, 7-bone steak, short ribs plus some veal or beef shank, bones or calf's foot (An assortment of different cuts of meat will add an extra layer of complexity to the flavour of the stock.)
- 4 litres (17 US cups) cold water

For the aromatics
- 300g (11oz) carrots, peeled and coarsely chopped
- 300g (11oz) onions, coarsely chopped
- 300g (11oz) leeks, coarsely chopped
- 100g (3½oz) celery, coarsely chopped
- ½ onion, cut in half and well browned in a frying pan (skillet)
- 2 garlic cloves, unpeeled and crushed
- 1 fresh bouquet garni
- 3 cloves
- about 25g (scant 1oz) coarse salt

BEEF STOCK

Cooking and preparation: 4 hours
Makes 2 litres (8½ US cups)

1. Put the meat and bones into a stockpot, large saucepan or casserole (Dutch oven). Pour in the cold water and bring the liquid slowly to the boil. Use a skimmer or small ladle to carefully remove the impurities that will float to the surface of the stock. Let the stock boil briefly then lower the heat to maintain a simmer. Continue to skim the stock for a further 5–8 minutes or until no more impurities rise to the surface.

2. Add the remaining ingredients – all the aromatics and the coarse salt. Return to the boil briefly, then reduce the heat. With the saucepan uncovered, maintain the gentlest possible simmer for 3–4 hours, or until the liquid has reduced by half and you can insert a skewer easily into the meat. This slow cooking, with the surface of the liquid forming only the smallest of bubbles, will produce a stock that is clear.

3. Once the stock has reduced sufficiently, remove it from the heat. Lift out the meat and vegetables using a skimmer or slotted spoon. Taste and adjust the seasoning with salt.

4. Transfer the stock to a bowl, preferably of glass, and put it in the refrigerator. The stock may appear a little fatty at this stage but the fat will solidify and rise to the surface, at which point you should lift it away with a spoon. As the stock cools and settles, some sediment will fall to the bottom and this will probably become visible.

5. Pour or ladle the degreased stock through a fine-meshed sieve – preferably a chinois – set over a bowl, taking care to stop pouring as soon as you reach any sediment or impurities that may have settled at the bottom of the liquid; discard these impurities. Store the stock in convenient quantities in airtight containers, in the refrigerator or freezer.

- 2kg (4½lb) whole chicken (or two smaller ones), split in half along the backbone, with giblets
- 4 litres (17 US cups) cold water

For the aromatics
- 300g (11oz) carrots, peeled and coarsely chopped
- 300g (11oz) onions, coarsely chopped
- 300g (11oz) leeks, coarsely chopped
- 100g (3½oz) celery, coarsely chopped
- 1 onion, cut in half and well browned in a frying pan (skillet)
- 2 garlic cloves, unpeeled and crushed
- 1 fresh bouquet garni
- 3 cloves
- about 25g (scant 1oz) coarse salt

CHICKEN STOCK

Cooking and preparation: 4 hours
Makes 2 litres (8½ US cups)

1. Preheat the oven to 220°C (425°F, gas mark 7). Using a fork, prick the skin of the chicken so the fat will be released during cooking. Put the chicken halves, skin side up, along with the giblets, in a baking dish. Roast the chicken until the skin is golden – usually about 20 minutes.

2. Remove the chicken from the baking dish, draining off the fat and transferring the chicken to a stockpot, large saucepan or casserole (Dutch oven). Pour in the cold water and bring the liquid slowly to the boil. Use a skimmer or small ladle to carefully remove the impurities that will float to the surface of the stock. Let the stock boil briefly then lower the heat to maintain a simmer, and continue to skim the stock for a further 5–8 minutes or until no more impurities rise to the surface.

3. Add the remaining ingredients. Return to the boil briefly, then reduce the heat. With the saucepan uncovered, maintain the gentlest possible simmer for 3–4 hours. This slow cooking, with the surface of the liquid forming only the smallest of bubbles, will produce a stock that is clear. The stock will be ready when you can insert a skewer or larding needle into the chicken without meeting resistance.

4. Use a slotted spoon or skimmer to remove the chicken and vegetables from the stock. Taste and adjust the seasoning with salt. Transfer the stock to a bowl, preferably of glass, and put it in the refrigerator. The stock may appear a little fatty at this stage but the fat will solidify and rise to the surface, at which point you should lift it away with a spoon. As the stock cools and settles, some sediment will fall to the bottom and this will probably become visible.

5. Pour or ladle the degreased stock through a fine-meshed sieve – preferably a chinois – set over a bowl, taking care to stop pouring as soon as you reach any sediment or impurities that may have settled at the bottom of the liquid; discard these impurities. Store the stock in convenient quantities in airtight containers, in the refrigerator or freezer.

Variation
You can replace the chicken in this recipe with duck, guinea fowl or rabbit.

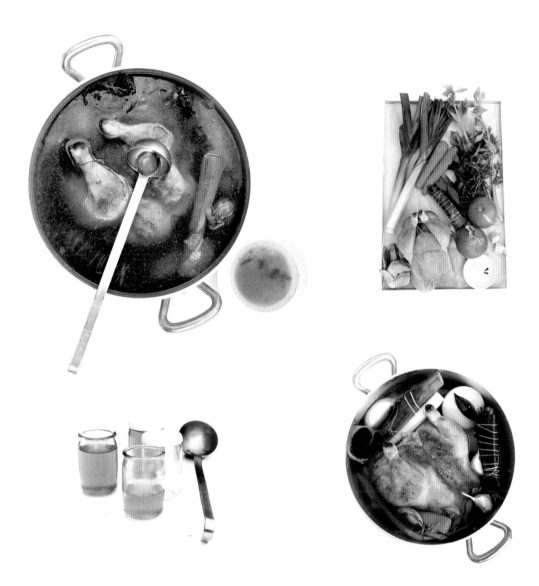

Any stock that is not used immediately can be put into suitable airtight containers and stored in the freezer for up to one year. In this way, you can create a reserve and draw on it as required. You might use the Chicken Stock, for example, as a bouillon, or light soup, in its own right. Or you might use some stock to make a Vinaigrette or a Liaison, or to impart flavour and moisture to a variety of fish, vegetable, poultry and meat dishes.

- 2kg (4½lb) meaty veal trimmings including, if possible, a veal shank bone sawn into 5cm (2in) pieces
- about 4 litres (17 US cups) cold water

For the aromatics
- 300g (11oz) carrots, peeled and cut into large chunks
- 300g (11oz) onions, cut into large chunks
- 300g (11oz) leeks, cut into large chunks
- 100g (3½oz) celery, cut into large chunks
- 2 cloves of garlic, unpeeled and crushed
- 1 fresh bouquet garni
- 3 cloves
- about 25g (1 oz) coarse salt

VEAL STOCK

Cooking and preparation: 4 hours
Makes 2 litres (8½ US cups)

1. Put the meat and bones into a stockpot or large saucepan (or Dutch oven). Add enough cold water to cover the ingredients by about 5 cm (2 inches). Bring the liquid slowly to a boil. Use a skimmer or small ladle to carefully remove the impurities that will float to the surface of the stock, adding cold water to keep the meat covered. Let the stock boil briefly then lower the heat to maintain a simmer, and continue to skim the stock for a further 5–8 minutes or until no more impurities rise to the surface.

2. Add the remaining ingredients – all the aromatics and the coarse salt. Return the stock to a boil briefly. Reduce the heat to a very low setting and cook, uncovered, at a bare simmer for 3 to 4 hours or until the liquid has reduced by half, skimming occasionally.

3. Strain the stock through a colander set over a large bowl, preferably of glass. Discard the solids. Taste and adjust seasoning. Cool the strained stock then transfer it to the refrigerator. After several hours, degrease the stock by lifting away any solidified surface fat with a spoon.

4. If there is any residue at the bottom of the bowl, strain it out using a very fine sieve, such as a chinois or a sieve lined with muslin. If you have used a gelatine-rich veal shank bone, and therefore created a jellied stock, you will have to warm the stock gently to make it liquid enough to strain. Chill the strained stock for up to 3 days or freeze it.

- 1kg (2.2lb) fish heads, bones and trimmings, rinsed and broken into convenient sizes
- about 2 litres (8½ US cups) cold water

For the aromatics
- 1 onion, sliced
- 1 carrot, peeled and sliced
- 1 leek, sliced
- 1 celery stick (stalk), coarsely diced
- 1 fresh bouquet garni
- 500ml (2⅛ US cups) dry white wine
- salt to taste

FISH STOCK

Cooking and preparation: about 45 minutes
Makes 2 litres (8½ US cups)

1. Put the fish, vegetables and herbs into a stockpot, large saucepan or casserole (Dutch oven). Add the water and season lightly to taste with salt. Bring the liquid slowly to a boil. Use a skimmer or small ladle to skim off the scum that rises to the surface as the liquid reaches a simmer. Continue to skim until no more scum rises.

2. Cover the pan and simmer for 15 minutes. Add the wine and simmer, covered, for a further 15 minutes.

3. Pour the stock through a colander set over a large bowl, in order to remove the large pieces of solid matter. Do not press the solids when straining otherwise they will cloud the liquid. To make the stock as pure and limpid as possible, strain it again using a fine sieve, such as a chinois, or a sieve lined with muslin. Chill the strained stock for up to 24 hours or freeze it.

- 2kg (4½lb) raw heads or shells of langoustines, Dublin bay prawns or Jumbo shrimp (or the same weight in lobster or crab shells), crushed (ask your fishmonger)
- 4 litres (17 US cups) cold water
- ½ bottle dry white wine

For the aromatics
- 2 oranges, peel and pith removed, and cut into slices ½cm (¼in) thick
- 1 grapefruit, peel and pith removed, and cut into slices ½cm (¼in) thick
- 1 lemon, peel and pith removed, and cut into slices ½cm (¼in) thick
- 1 lime, peel and pith removed, and cut into slices ½cm (¼in) thick
- 250g (9oz) fennel, coarsely chopped
- 150g (5½oz) onions, coarsely chopped
- 150g (5½oz) shallots, coarsely chopped
- 150g (5½oz) carrots, peeled and coarsely chopped
- 1 celery stick (stalk), coarsely chopped
- 1 garlic clove, unpeeled and crushed
- 1 fresh bouquet garni
- 2 star anise
- salt to taste

SHELLFISH STOCK

Cooking and preparation: 1 hour
Makes 2 litres (8½ US cups)

1. Put the crushed shells and heads into a stockpot, large saucepan or casserole (Dutch oven). Pour in the water and wine and bring the liquid slowly to the boil. Use a skimmer or small ladle to carefully remove the impurities that will float to the surface of the liquid. Let the liquid boil briefly then lower the heat to maintain a simmer, and continue to skim the surface for a further 5–8 minutes or until no more impurities rise.

2. Add the remaining ingredients – all the fruit and aromatics, and salt to taste. Return to the boil briefly, then reduce the heat. With the saucepan uncovered, maintain the gentlest possible simmer, with the surface of the liquid forming the smallest of bubbles, for 45 minutes. This slow cooking will yield a clear stock.

3. Remove the stock from the heat. When it is cool enough to handle, pour or ladle it through a fine-meshed sieve – preferably a chinois – set over a bowl, taking care to stop straining the stock as soon as you reach any sediment or impurities which may have settled at the bottom of the saucepan. Check that you have 2 litres (4½ US cups) of stock. If you have more, return it to a saucepan and continue to simmer it until it reduces to the required quantity. Taste and adjust the seasoning when the stock is completed.

4. Store the stock in convenient quantities in airtight containers, in the refrigerator or freezer.

Chef's tip
This stock is delicious served as a light consommé garnished with small pieces of seafood. It is also a wonderful cooking agent for a variety of fish and seafood dishes.

- 1 litre (4¼ US cups/1 quart) Vegetable Stock (page 42)
- 2 kaffir lime leaves, chopped
- salt to taste

ASIAN LIME VEGETABLE STOCK

Cooking and preparation: 30 minutes
Makes 1 litre (4¼ US cups/1 quart)

1. Pour the Vegetable Stock into a large saucepan and bring slowly to the boil. Add the kaffir lime leaves, cover the saucepan and remove it from heat. Allow the leaves to infuse in the stock for 15 minutes.

2. To make the stock perfectly clear, strain it through a fine-meshed sieve — preferably a chinois — set over a bowl; discard the leaves. Taste and adjust the seasoning with salt.

3. When the stock is cold, store it in convenient quantities, in airtight containers, in the refrigerator or freezer.

Chef's tip

This stock marries well with all manner of fish, seafood and white meats. Garnished with vegetables or a vegetable ravioli, the Asian Lime Vegetable Stock makes an delicious consommé.

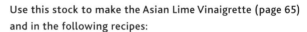

Use this stock to make the Asian Lime Vinaigrette (page 65) and in the following recipes:
- Terrine of skate in a market garden jelly (page 168)
- Coley stars with an Asian-inspired sauce (page 222)
- Vegetable pot-au-feu sauced with asian lime vegetable stock (page 49)

- 1 litre (4¼ US cups/1 quart) Beef Stock
  (page 43) or Chicken Stock (page 44)
- 3g (1¾ tsp) Pondicherry Indian Spice Blend
  (see below)
- 20g (¾oz) concentrated tomato paste
- ¼ vanilla pod (bean), split lengthways
- sprig of tarragon
- salt to taste

**For the Pondicherry Indian Spice Blend
(Makes 18g/just over ½oz)**
- 3g (1½ tsp) ground cumin
- 3g (1½ tsp) curry powder
- 3g (1¾ tsp) tandoori spices
- 4g (2 tsp) dried thyme
- 5g (2 tsp) ground black pepper

PONDICHERRY INDIAN STOCK

Cooking and preparation: 45 minutes
Makes 1 litre (4¼ US cups/1 quart)

1. Pour the cold Beef or Chicken stock in a large saucepan and whisk in the concentrated tomato paste until it is completely blended. Add the Pondicherry Spice Blend, the vanilla bean and the tarragon. Bring the stock slowly to the boil.

2. Remove from the heat, cover the saucepan and allow the stock to infuse until it has cooled.

3. Strain the stock through a fine-meshed sieve – preferably a chinois – and discard the solids. Taste and adjust the seasoning with salt.

4. Store the stock in convenient quantities in airtight containers, in the refrigerator or freezer.

Chef's tip
This stock subtly enlivens a range of dishes based on poultry, lamb, pork and veal.

**Use this stock to make the Pondicherry Indian Vinaigrette (page 67)
and in the following recipes:**
- Cod steamed in fig leaves (page 213)
- Calamari in a curry-scented velouté (page 134)

- 1 litre (4¼ US cups/1 quart) Beef Stock (page 43)
- about ⅓ a chicken or beef stock cube, crumbled
- 100g (3½oz) white button mushrooms, wiped and finely chopped
- 4g (a little less than ¼oz, a small handful) dried ceps (porcini) or other dried wild mushrooms
- salt to taste

MUSHROOM STOCK

Cooking and preparation: 45 minutes
Makes 1 litre (4¼ US cups/1 quart)

1. Pour the Beef Stock into a large saucepan and bring it slowly to the boil. Stir in the fresh and dried mushrooms. Return the liquid briefly to the boil then adjust the heat to maintain a gentle simmer for 5 minutes. Remove from the heat, taste and adjust the seasoning with salt as required.

2. When the stock is cool enough to handle, strain it through a fine-meshed sieve – preferably a chinois – set over a bowl. Remove the mushrooms and ceps. Either discard these or use them in soups.

3. When the stock is completely cold, store it in convenient quantities in airtight containers, in the refrigerator or freezer.

Chef's tip
With its earthy aroma, this stock is the ideal choice for dishes of beef and game.

Use this stock to make the Mushroom Vinaigrette (page 66), other sauces with a mushroom base, and in the following recipes:
- Soft-boiled eggs with a green sauce (page 153)
- Tartare of tomatoes with basil (page 162)

- 1 litre (4¼ US cups/1 quart) Chicken Stock (page 44)
- 1 garlic clove, finely chopped
- 25g (scant 1oz) lemongrass, tough outer layers removed and the rest finely chopped
- 25g (scant 1oz) peeled and finely chopped fresh ginger
- 4 sprigs of coriander (cilantro)
- 60g (2oz) desiccated coconut
- skin of a pineapple (optional), preferably the extra-sweet Victoria variety (exclusive to Réunion and Mauritius)
- 1 tbsp teriyaki sauce
- salt to taste

THAI STOCK

Cooking and preparation: 1 hour
Makes 1 litre (4¼ US cups/1 quart)

1. Pour the Chicken Stock into a large saucepan. Add the garlic, lemongrass, ginger, coriander (cilantro), desiccated coconut and the pineapple skin, if used. Bring slowly to the boil.

2. Reduce the heat, cover the saucepan and simmer gently for 10 minutes. Remove from the heat, keep the lid closed and leave the ingredients to infuse until the stock is cold.

3. Strain the cold stock through a fine-meshed sieve – preferably a chinois. Discard the solids. Add the teriyaki sauce. Taste and adjust the seasoning with salt if necessary.

4. Store the stock in convenient quantities, in airtight containers, in the refrigerator or freezer.

Use this stock to make the Thai Vinaigrette (page 68), various other sauces, and in the following recipe:
- Thai-flavoured wing of skate with Chinese cabbage (page 206)

Chef's tip
Thai stock lends a subtle but exotic flavour to recipes with fish, shellfish, chicken, pork and beef.

- 1 litre (4¼ US cups/1 quart) Beef Stock (page 43), cold
- ½ beef stock cube, crumbled
- 2g (1 tbsp) finely chopped thyme
- 2g (1 heaped tbsp) finely chopped marjoram
- 2g (1 heaped tbsp) finely chopped coriander (cilantro)
- 2g (1 tbsp) finely chopped sage
- 2g (1 tbsp) finely chopped rosemary
- 2g (1 tbsp) finely chopped savory (optional)
- 2g (1 tbsp) finely chopped basil
- 1 fresh bay leaf, finely chopped
- salt to taste

HERBY BEEF STOCK

Cooking and preparation: 45 minutes
Makes 1 litre (4¼ US cups/1 quart)

1. In a saucepan, mix the herbs and the crumbled stock cube into the cold Beef Stock. Bring the stock to the boil very slowly, uncovered.

2. Remove the saucepan from the heat, cover it and leave the ingredients to infuse until the stock is completely cold.

3. Strain the stock through a fine-meshed sieve – preferably a chinois. Discard the solids. Taste the stock and salt if desired.

4. Store the stock in convenient quantities in airtight containers, in the refrigerator or freezer.

Chef's tip

If you add some smoked pork (but not bacon because it is too fatty) to the stock when it begins to boil, you will give it a smoky aroma. This herb-infused stock is an excellent cooking companion for beef recipes. Use it, for example, when cooking a pot-au-feu or as the deglazing agent for a sauce to serve with fillet steak or roast beef.

Use this stock to make the Herby Beef Vinaigrette (page 69).

My home-made flavoured oils, heady in their aroma and evoking a sense of warm, fragrant gardens, have been created thanks to the technical advice of my friend and fellow chef, Michel Trama. His own olive oil is world-famous.

In this book, the following oils are frequently blended with our Stocks to make our Vinaigrettes. These are an innovative advance on traditional vinaigrettes.

The oils, which can be used in a variety of different ways, keep reasonably well, stored in a bottle in a cool room or cupboard. However, keeping them in a freezer prolongs their life and is recommended. If you wish, you can put the chilled oil in an ice-tray, freeze it and use it cube by cube.

Note that the Vinaigrette recipes (pages 64–73) use one-quarter of the amount of oil produced by the following recipes.

- 750ml (3¼ US cups) olive oil
- 250ml (1⅛ US cups) grapeseed oil
- 100g (3½oz) thyme leaves, torn into small pieces
- 10g (¼oz) salt

THYME OIL

90 CALORIES PER 10G (¼OZ) OR PER 1 TBSP
Cooking and preparation: 1 hour 30 minutes
Makes 1 litre (4¼ US cups/1 quart)

For the home cook
Combine the ingredients in a saucepan, mixing bowl or large jar. Cover the container with clingfilm (plastic wrap), then put it in a bain-marie, such as a deep roasting pan or stock-pot, filled with enough hot water to immerse the container by at least one-third. Set the bain-marie over very gentle heat or put it in a low oven. Every 10 minutes or so, peel back the clingfilm (plastic wrap) and check the temperature of the oil, using a thermometer. When the temperature reaches 80°C (176°F), remove the container from the bain-marie and leave the oil to infuse for 1 hour. At the end of this infusion time, the oil will probably have returned to room temperature but if it has not, leave it to cool a little longer. Strain the oil through a fine sieve, preferably a chinois, then pour it through a funnel into an airtight bottle and store it in a cool place. Alternatively, store the oil in ice-cube trays, wrapped in a freezing or cooking bag, in the freezer.

For the professional cook
Mix together the ingredients and put them into a vacuum-sealed, boilable cooking bag. Using a special machine, sterilise the bag at 80°C (176°F) for 1 hour. Plunge the bag into iced water and when it is cold, strain the contents through a fine sieve, preferably a chinois. Pour the strained oil through a funnel into an airtight bottle and store it in a cool place. Alternatively, store the oil in ice-cube trays, wrapped in a freezing or cooking bag, in the freezer.

- 1 litre (4¼ US cups/1 quart) groundnut oil or sunflower oil
- 100g (3½oz) chopped verbena leaves
- 10g (¼oz) salt

VERBENA OIL

90 CALORIES PER 10G (¼OZ) OR PER 1 TBSP

Cooking and preparation: 1 hour 30 minutes
Makes 1 litre (4¼ US cups/1 quart)

For the home cook

Combine the ingredients in a saucepan, mixing bowl or large jar. Cover the container with clingfilm (plastic wrap), then put it in a bain-marie, such as a deep roasting pan or stock-pot, filled with enough hot water to immerse the container by at least one-third. Set the bain-marie over very gentle heat or put it in a low oven. Every 10 minutes or so, peel back the clingfilm (plastic wrap) and check the temperature of the oil, using a thermometer. When the temperature reaches 80°C (176°F), remove the container from the bain-marie and leave the oil to infuse for 1 hour. At the end of this infusion time, the oil will probably have returned to room temperature but if it has not, leave it to cool a little longer. Strain the oil through a fine sieve, preferably a chinois, then pour it through a funnel into an airtight bottle and store it in a cool place. Alternatively, store the oil in ice-cube trays, wrapped in a freezing or cooking bag, in the freezer.

For the professional cook

Mix together the ingredients and put them into a vacuum-sealed, boilable cooking bag. Using a special machine, sterilise the bag at 80°C (176°F), for 1 hour. Plunge the bag into iced water and when it is cold, strain the contents through a fine sieve, preferably a chinois. Pour the strained oil through a funnel into an airtight bottle and store it in a cool place. Alternatively, store the oil in ice-cube trays, wrapped in a freezing or cooking bag, in the freezer.

Note: When fresh verbena is not available, a similar-tasting lemon-scented oil can be made using lemongrass: for every 1 litre (4¼ US cups/1 quart) of oil, use 8 chopped fresh or frozen stalks or, alternatively, 4 heaped tablespoons of dried lemongrass shavings, which are found in jars at the spice counter of most supermarkets.

- 750ml (3¼ US cups) olive oil
- 250ml (1⅛ US cups) grapeseed oil
- 100g (3½oz) rosemary leaves, chopped
- 10g (¼oz) salt

ROSEMARY OIL

90 CALORIES PER 10G (¼OZ) OR PER 1 TBSP
Cooking and preparation: 1 hour 30 minutes
Makes 1 litre (4¼ US cups/1 quart)

For the home cook
Combine the ingredients in a saucepan, mixing bowl or large jar. Cover the container with clingfilm (plastic wrap), then put it in a bain-marie, such as a deep roasting pan or stock-pot, filled with enough hot water to immerse the container by at least one-third. Set the bain-marie over very gentle heat or put it in a low oven. Every 10 minutes or so, peel back the clingfilm (plastic wrap) and check the temperature of the oil, using a thermometer. When the temperature reaches 80°C (176°F), remove the container from the bain-marie and leave the oil to infuse for 1 hour. At the end of this infusion time, the oil will probably have returned to room temperature but if it has not, leave it to cool a little longer. Strain the oil through a fine sieve, preferably a chinois, then pour it through a funnel into an airtight bottle and store it in a cool place. Alternatively, store the oil in ice-cube trays, wrapped in a freezing or cooking bag, in the freezer.

For the professional cook
Mix together the ingredients and put them into a vacuum-sealed, boilable cooking bag. Using a special machine, sterilise the bag at 80°C (176°F) for 1 hour. Plunge the bag into iced water and when it is cold, strain the contents through a fine sieve, preferably a chinois. Pour the strained oil through a funnel into an airtight bottle and store it in a cool place. Alternatively, store the oil in ice-cube trays, wrapped in a freezing or cooking bag, in the freezer.

- 1 litre (4¼ US cups/1 quart) groundnut oil or sunflower oil
- 250g (9oz) freshly grated coconut or commercial desiccated coconut
- 10g (¼oz) salt

COCONUT OIL

90 CALORIES PER 10G (¼OZ) OR PER 1 TBSP
Cooking and preparation: 1 hour 30 minutes
Makes 1 litre (4¼ US cups/1 quart)

For the home cook
Combine the ingredients in a saucepan, mixing bowl or large jar. Cover the container with clingfilm (plastic wrap), then put it in a bain-marie, such as a deep roasting pan or stock-pot, filled with enough hot water to immerse the container by at least one-third. Set the bain-marie over very gentle heat or put it in a low oven. Every 10 minutes or so, peel back the clingfilm (plastic wrap) and check the temperature of the oil, using a thermometer. When the temperature reaches 80°C (176°F), remove the container from the bain-marie and leave the oil to infuse for 1 hour. At the end of this infusion time, the oil will probably have returned to room temperature but if it has not, leave it to cool a little longer. Strain the oil through a fine sieve, preferably a chinois, then pour it through a funnel into an airtight bottle and store it in a cool place. Alternatively, store the oil in ice-cube trays, wrapped in a freezing or cooking bag, in the freezer.

For the professional cook
Mix together the ingredients and put them into a vacuum-sealed, boilable cooking bag. Using a special machine, sterilise the bag at 80°C (176°F) for 1 hour. Plunge the bag into iced water and when it is cold, strain the contents through a fine sieve, preferably a chinois. Pour the strained oil through a funnel into an airtight bottle and store it in a cool place. Alternatively, store the oil in ice-cube trays, wrapped in a freezing or cooking bag, in the freezer.

- 1 litre (4¼ US cups/1 quart) groundnut oil or sunflower oil
- 60g (2oz) Pondicherry Indian Spice Blend (see below)
- 10g (¼oz) salt

For the Pondicherry Indian Spice Blend
- 30g (1oz) powdered cumin
- 30g (1oz) curry powder
- 30g (1oz) tandoori spices
- 40g (scant 1½oz) dried thyme
- 50g (1¾oz) ground pepper of your choice

Finely blend these quantities in a mixer or a coffee grinder. Use 60g (2oz) of the blended mixture in the main recipe. Store the remainder in an airtight jar.

INDIAN SPICED OIL

90 CALORIES PER 10G (¼OZ) OR PER 1 TBSP
Cooking and preparation: 1 hour 30 minutes
Makes 1 litre (4¼ US cups/1 quart)

For the home cook

Combine the ingredients in a saucepan, mixing bowl or large jar. Cover the container with clingfilm (plastic wrap), then put it in a bain-marie, such as a deep roasting pan or stock-pot, filled with enough hot water to immerse the container by at least one-third. Set the bain-marie over very gentle heat or put it in a low oven. Every 10 minutes or so, peel back the clingfilm (plastic wrap) and check the temperature of the oil, using a thermometer. When the temperature reaches 80°C (176°F), remove the container from the bain-marie and leave the oil to infuse for 1 hour. At the end of this infusion time, the oil will probably have returned to room temperature but if it has not, leave it to cool a little longer. Strain the oil through a fine sieve, preferably a chinois, then pour it through a funnel into an airtight bottle and store it in a cool place. Alternatively, store the oil in ice-cube trays, wrapped in a freezing or cooking bag, in the freezer.

For the professional cook

Mix together the ingredients and put them into a vacuum-sealed, boilable cooking bag. Using a special machine, sterilise the bag at 80°C (176°F) for 1 hour. Plunge the bag into iced water and when it is cold, strain the contents through a fine sieve, preferably a chinois. Pour the strained oil through a funnel into an airtight bottle and store it in a cool place. Alternatively, store the oil in ice-cube trays, wrapped in a freezing or cooking bag, in the freezer.

- 1 litre (4¼ US cups/1 quart) groundnut oil or sunflower oil
- 1kg (2.2 lb) crushed shells from lobster or crab, or heads and upper shells of langoustines, Dublin Bay prawns, scampi or Jumbo shrimp
- 50g (1¾oz) peeled and chopped carrot
- 50g onion coarsely chopped
- 1 fresh bouquet garni
- 10g (¼oz) salt

SHELLFISH OIL

90 CALORIES PER 10G (¼OZ) OR PER 1 TBSP
Cooking and preparation: 1 hour 30 minutes
Makes 1 litre (4¼ US cups/1 quart)

1. In a saucepan or frying pan (skillet) sauté the shells and/or heads in 100ml (⅜ US cup) of the groundnut oil until they take on some colour. Add the onion, carrot and bouquet garni, and continue to sauté for a few minutes or until the vegetables are lightly coloured. Transfer to a clean saucepan or a heatproof container, and add the remaining oil and the salt. Cover securely with clingfilm (plastic wrap) or with a lid.

2. Put the container in a bain-marie, such as a deep roasting pan or stock-pot, filled with enough hot water to immerse the container of shells by at least one-third. Set the bain-marie over very gentle heat or put it in a low oven. Adjust the heat so that the water in the bain-marie maintains a gentle simmer for 1 hour, with its surface barely moving, adding more water as necessary. Remove the container from the bain-marie and let it cool. Strain the oil through a fine sieve, preferably a chinois, then pour it through a funnel into an airtight bottle and store it in a cool place. Alternatively, store in ice-cube trays, wrapped in a freezing or cooking bag, in the freezer.

Note: the shells of lobster and baby crab contain a red-coloured oil, and so give a better colour than other varieties of shellfish. You can crush sturdy shells and heads using a pestle and mortar. Alternatively, you can crush them with a rolling pin after laying them flat on a work counter and covering them with a cloth or clingfilm (plastic wrap).

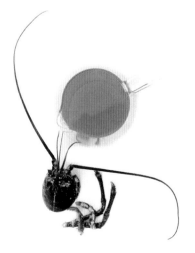

Using the Essential Master Stocks and Flavoured Oils as building blocks, we can now embark on an entirely new approach to the concept of the vinaigrette. We can rid it of its unnecessary calories and we can heighten its flavour with aromatic seasonings that are far more alluring and innovative than anything found in the traditional versions. The new Essential Vinaigrettes will suit your personal tastes and preferences as well as proving the ideal partners to a wide range of salads and fish, vegetable, poultry and meat dishes. They will also flatter relatively humble food and leftovers. The following vinaigrettes can be stored in airtight containers for up to a week in the refrigerator.

- 350ml (scant 1½ US cups) Asian Lime
  Vegetable Stock (page 49) or Vegetable Stock
  (page 42)
- 50ml (¼ US cup) lime juice
- 15g (1 tbsp) cornflour (cornstarch), mixed with
  a little cold water
- 100ml (⅜ US cup) Verbena Oil (page 57)
- salt and pepper to taste

ASIAN LIME VINAIGRETTE

ABOUT 19 CALORIES PER 1 TBSP
Cooking and preparation: 10 minutes
Makes 500ml (2⅛ US cups)

1. In a small saucepan, bring the stock to the boil and whisk in the cornflour (cornstarch). Let it boil for about 1 minute, stirring continuously, so that the stock acquires a syrupy consistency. Remove from heat and allow to cool.

2. Once the stock is cold, pour it into the bowl of a food processor or blender, add the lime juice and Verbena Oil and blend the ingredients until they have emulsified. Taste, and adjust the seasoning.

Note: The volume of the stock must always be close to 350ml (scant 1½ US cups) and should not be reduced by boiling it down, either before or after blending with the cornflour (cornstarch). If this happens, there will be an undesirable change in the consistency of the mixture.

Chef's tip
With its delicate hint of lime, this vinaigrette lends a refreshing note to poultry, fish, shellfish and vegetable dishes. Its character is particularly well expressed when it is served warm with a simply prepared fillet of fish.

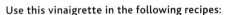

Use this vinaigrette in the following recipes:
- Grilled red mullet with a carrot confit (page 186)
- Coley stars with an Asian-inspired sauce (page 222)
- Ceviche of white fish with mango and ginger (page 143)
- Roasted tomatoes stuffed with goat's cheese and vegetables (page 172)
- Spicy salmon with coffee sauce (page 161)
- Herb-scented prawn skewers (page 182)

- 350ml (scant 1½ US cups) Mushroom Stock (page 51)
- 15g (1 tbsp) cornflour (cornstarch), mixed with a little cold water
- 50ml (¼ US cup) Xeres vinegar or other sherry vinegar of your choice
- 50ml (¼ US cup) Thyme Oil (page 56)
- 50ml (¼ US cup) walnut oil or cep (porcini) oil pinch of fructose or the sweetener of your choice (pages 16–20)
- salt and pepper to taste

MUSHROOM VINAIGRETTE

ABOUT 19 CALORIES PER 1 TBSP
Cooking and preparation: 10 minutes
Makes 500ml (2⅛ US cups)

1. In a small saucepan, bring the Mushroom Stock to the boil and whisk in the cornflour (cornstarch). Let it boil for about 1 minute, stirring continuously, so that the stock acquires a syrupy consistency. Remove from heat and allow to cool.

2. When the stock is cold, pour it into the bowl of a food processor or blender. Add the Xeres vinegar, the Thyme Oil, the walnut oil and the fructose, and blend the ingredients until they have emulsified. Taste, and adjust the seasoning.

Chef's tips

The volume of the stock must always be close to 350ml (scant 1½ US cups) , and should not be reduced by boiling it down, either before or after blending with the cornflour (cornstarch). If this happens, there will be an undesirable change in the consistency of the mixture.

Served warm, this vinaigrette, with its flavour of mushrooms, goes particularly well with dishes of beef, pork, ham, game, and offal.

Use this vinaigrette in the following recipes:
- Spaghetti salad with grilled vegetables (page 100)
- Salad of white beans, mango, mushroom and pear (page 202)
- A salad of mushrooms, celeriac, tomato and apple (page 106)
- Mushroom terrine (page 166)
- Soft-boiled eggs with a green sauce (page 153)
- Tartare of tomatoes with basil (page 162)
- Aromatic grilled mackerel (page 228)

- 350ml (scant 1½ US cups) Pondicherry Indian Stock (page 50)
- 50ml (¼ US cup) lime juice
- 15g (1 tbsp) cornflour (cornstarch), mixed with a little cold water
- 100ml (⅜ US cup) Verbena Oil (page 57) or Indian Spiced Oil (page 62)
- salt and pepper to taste

PONDICHERRY INDIAN VINAIGRETTE

ABOUT 19 CALORIES PER 1 TBSP
Cooking and preparation: 10 minutes
Makes 500ml (2⅛ US cups)

1. In a small saucepan, bring the Pondicherry Indian Stock to the boil and whisk in the cornflour (cornstarch). Let it boil for about 1 minute, stirring continuously, so that the stock acquires a syrupy consistency. Remove from heat and allow to cool.

2. When the stock is cold, pour it into the bowl of a food processor or blender. Add the lime juice and Verbena Oil and blend the ingredients until they have emulsified. Taste, and adjust the seasoning.

Chef's tips
The volume of the stock must always be close to 350ml (scant 1½ US cups) , and should not be reduced by boiling it down, either before or after blending with the cornflour (cornstarch). If this happens, there will be an undesirable change in the consistency of the mixture.

Inspired by the cuisine of Pondicherry in India, this vinaigrette served warm is a spicy accompaniment to a wide range of chicken, fish and vegetable dishes.

Use this vinaigrette in the following recipe:
- Brochettes of monkfish with carrot and apricot quenelles (page 212)

- 350ml (scant 1½ US cups) Thai Stock (page 52)
- 15g (1 tbsp) cornflour (cornstarch), mixed with a little cold water
- 50ml (¼ US cup) rice vinegar or white wine vinegar
- 50ml (¼ US cup) Coconut Oil (page 60)
- 50ml (¼ US cup) toasted sesame oil
- pinch of fructose or the sweetener of your choice (pages 16–20)
- 1 tbsp teriyaki sauce
- salt and pepper to taste

THAI VINAIGRETTE

ABOUT 29 CALORIES PER 1 TBSP
Cooking and preparation: 10 minutes
Makes 500ml (2⅛ US cups)

1. In a small saucepan, bring the Thai Stock to the boil and whisk in the cornflour (cornstarch). Let it boil for about 1 minute, stirring continuously, so that the stock acquires a syrupy consistency. Remove from heat and allow to cool.

2. When the stock is cold, pour it into the bowl of a food processor or blender. Add the rice vinegar, the coconut oil, the sesame oil, the fructose and the teriyaki sauce, and blend the ingredients until they have emulsified. Taste and adjust the seasoning.

Chef's tips

The volume of the stock must always be close to 350ml (scant 1½ US cups) , and should not be reduced by boiling it down, either before or after blending with the cornflour (cornstarch). If this happens, there will be an undesirable change in the consistency of the mixture.

With its tangy flavours of the Orient, this vinaigrette – served warm or cold – will give a complex edge to a range of simply prepared dishes, whether based on chicken, fish, vegetables or meats.

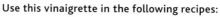

Use this vinaigrette in the following recipes:
- Beef salad with red onion and red cabbage (page 191)
- Warm chicken salad with potatoes (page 204)
- Oriental pasta shells with vegetables (page 102)
- Carpaccio of salmon with olives and tapioca (page 139)
- Terrine of carrots with orange and cumin (page 167)
- Terrine of ratatouille vegetables (page 164)
- Thai-flavoured wing of skate with Chinese cabbage (page 206)

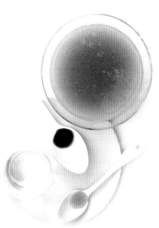

- 350ml (scant 1½ US cups) Herby Beef Stock (page 54)
- 15g (1 tbsp) cornflour (cornstarch), mixed with a little cold water
- 50ml (¼ US cup) Xeres vinegar or other sherry vinegar of your choice
- 100ml (⅜ US cup) Rosemary Oil (page 58)
- salt and pepper to taste

HERBY BEEF VINAIGRETTE

ABOUT 19 CALORIES PER 1 TBSP

Cooking and preparation: 10 minutes
Makes 500ml (2⅛ US cups)

1. In a small saucepan, bring the Herby Beef Stock to the boil and whisk in the cornflour (cornstarch). Let it boil for about 1 minute, stirring continuously, so that the stock acquires a syrupy consistency. Remove from heat and allow to cool.

2. When the stock is cold, pour it into the bowl of a food processor or blender. Add the Xeres vinegar and the Rosemary Oil, and blend the ingredients until they have emulsified. Taste, and adjust the seasoning if necessary.

Chef's tips

The volume of the stock must always be close to 350ml (scant 1½ US cups), and should not be reduced by boiling it down, either before or after blending with the cornflour (cornstarch). If this happens, there will be an undesirable change in the consistency of the mixture.

With its intoxicating aroma of fresh herbs, this vinaigrette is an excellent alternative to the Light Vinaigrette (page 70). Served cold, it can accompany a multitude of dishes from vegetables to meats. Served warm, it is a natural partner for roast beef or steak.

- 500ml (2⅛ US cups) Chicken Stock (page 44) or 10g (¼oz) crumbled chicken stock cube dissolved in 500ml (2⅛ US cups) boiling water
- 15g (1 tbsp) cornflour (cornstarch), mixed with a little cold water
- 2 tbsp mustard of your choice
- ½ tsp fructose or the sweetener of your choice (pages 16–20)
- 6 tbsp lemon juice
- 1 tbsp Xeres vinegar or other sherry vinegar of your choice
- 120ml (½ US cup) grapeseed oil (or canola oil)
- 100ml (⅜ US cup) olive oil
- ½ tsp fine salt
- ground pepper of your choice

LIGHT VINAIGRETTE

ABOUT 26 CALORIES PER 1 TBSP
Cooking and preparation: 10 minutes
Makes 750ml (3¼ US cups)

1. In a small saucepan, bring the Chicken Stock to the boil and whisk in the cornflour (cornstarch). Let it boil for about 1 minute, stirring continuously, so that the stock acquires a syrupy consistency. Remove from heat and allow to cool.

2. In a medium-sized bowl, mix the mustard with the salt, pepper and the fructose. Gradually stir in the lemon juice and the Xeres vinegar. Whisk in the grapeseed oil and the olive oil a little at a time, ensuring the oil is incorporated smoothly. Stir in the cooled stock and continue mixing until the ingredients have emulsified. Taste, and adjust the seasoning.

Use this vinaigrette in the following recipes:
- Crunchy vegetable spring rolls with a spicy sauce (page 158)
- Greek-style sweet-and-sour chicory (page 152)
- Celeriac mousse with a garden of crispy vegetables (page 144)
- Spiced crab on pink grapefruit jelly with a citrus mousse (page 149)
- Artichoke custards and artichoke hearts (page 157)
- Terrine of skate in a market garden jelly (page 168)
- Langoustines with a grapefruit and potato salad (page 174)
- Cold beef salad with a mustard sauce (page 192)
- Spatchcocked quail with mushroom mousse (page 188)
- Ceps and pear in a passion-fruit dressing (page 193)
- Catalan-style squid salad with sweet red peppers (page 197)
- A warm salad of orange-scented scallops and lamb's lettuce (page 203)
- Tuna steaks with ribbon vegetables and a herb vinaigrette (page 220)
- Lemon sole grenobloise (page 224)
- Escalopes of monkfish with saffron (page 232)
- Steamed white fish with sauce vierge (page 230)
- Tandoori-spiced white fish (page 240)

- 350ml (scant 1½ US cups) Shellfish Stock (page 48)
- 50ml (¼ US cup) Xeres vinegar or other sherry vinegar of your choice
- 15g (1 tbsp) cornflour (cornstarch), mixed with a little cold water
- 100ml (⅜ US cup) Shellfish Oil (pages 63)
- pinch of fructose or the sweetener of your choice (pages 16–20)
- salt and pepper to taste

SHELLFISH VINAIGRETTE

ABOUT 19 CALORIES PER 1 TBSP

Cooking and preparation: 10 minutes
Makes 500ml (2⅛ US cups)

In a small saucepan, bring the Shellfish Stock to the boil and whisk in the cornflour (cornstarch). Let it boil for about 1 minute, stirring continuously, so that the stock acquires a syrupy consistency. Remove from heat and allow to cool.

When the stock is cold, pour it into the bowl of a food processor or blender. Add the Xeres vinegar, the shellfish oil and the fructose, and blend the ingredients until they have emulsified. Taste, and adjust the seasoning if necessary.

Chef's tips

The volume of the stock must always be close to 350ml (scant 1½ US cups) and should not be reduced by boiling it down, either before or after blending with the cornflour (cornstarch). If this happens, there will be an undesirable change in the consistency of the mixture.

This vinaigrette is delicious served cold, with virtually any sort of shellfish or seafood salad. Served warm, it is a delightful accompaniment for grilled or poached fish.

Use this vinaigrette in the following recipes:
- Prawns with frisée, banana and grapefruit (page 98)
- Red mullet with a pocketful of fruit (page 238)
- Prawn salad with crunchy crab-filled biscuits (page 198)

Sauces, including emulsified sauces such as mayonnaise and hollandaise, have long been an indispensable element in French cuisine. They have existed in an abundance that the French have always taken to be the norm. This assumption of plentiful variety was underlined by Talleyrand on his return to France from the USA in 1796. He expressed his shock at having found so few sauces outside his homeland, saying: 'I have found a country with thirty-two religions, but only one sauce.' Of course, the same could certainly not be said of the USA today!

In order to meet the demands of today's health-conscious gourmets, the continuation of the French tradition calls for new versions of many of the calorie-laden classic sauces. To this end, I have produced healthy, light versions of the richer counterparts. These new sauces include Béarnaise, Mayonnaise and Hollandaise. This section also includes recipes for Tomato Confit and Garlic Flakes.

- about 6ml (½ tbsp) orange blossom water
- 1 tsp olive oil
- 1 tbsp finely chopped shallot
- 50g (1¾oz) carrots, peeled and cut into julienne strips, 4cm x 3mm (1½in x ⅛in)
- 20g (¾oz) fresh ginger, peeled and cut into 3mm (⅛in) dice
- 20ml (2 tbsp) white port
- 5g (1¼ tsp) green curry paste
- 2g (½ tsp) red curry paste
- 2g (½ tsp) turmeric
- 90ml (scant ⅜ US cup) orange juice
- pinch of vadouvan (page 330), a mix of Indian spices (optional)
- salt to taste

ORANGE BLOSSOM SAUCE

6 CALORIES PER SERVING
Cooking and preparation: 30 minutes
Serves 20

1. In a medium-sized saucepan, heat the olive oil, add the shallots and gently sweat them for 2–3 minutes without colouring. Stir in the carrots and the ginger, cover and continue to sweat gently for a further 2–3 minutes.

2. Once the carrots become translucent, add the white port and deglaze the saucepan, raising the heat, stirring well and scraping up the deposits of vegetable from the bottom. After deglazing, simmer the port and vegetable mixture until most of the port has evaporated and the vegetables are almost dry. Add the curry pastes and the turmeric. Stir well and cook for a further 2 minutes.

3. Stir in the orange juice and the vadouvan, if used, bring to a simmer and let the sauce cook gently for 5 minutes or until the texture resembles a coarse marmalade. Remove from the heat. When the sauce is cool, add the orange flower water. Taste and add more orange flower water until the sauce is to your liking. Mix well and keep chilled until you are ready to serve it.

Chef's tip
This spicy sauce is a wonderful accompaniment to shellfish and white meats such as chicken, rabbit and pork.

This sauce is used in the following recipes:
Langoustines with a grapefruit and potato salad (page 174)
A warm salad of orange-scented scallops and lamb's lettuce (page 203)

- 150ml (¾ US cup) white wine vinegar
- 40g (scant 1½oz) very finely chopped shallots
- 2 tsp very finely chopped tarragon
- 100g (3½oz) cold unsweetened evaporated milk
- 3 egg yolks
- ½ tsp freshly ground pepper
- 1 tbsp finely chopped parsley
- salt to taste

BÉARNAISE SAUCE

68 CALORIES PER SERVING
Cooking and preparation: 20 minutes
Serves 6

1. In a medium-sized saucepan, combine the vinegar, shallots, ground pepper and one teaspoons of the fresh tarragon. Bring to the boil, lower the heat slightly and reduce the vinegar to three-quarters of its original volume. Remove from the heat and allow to cool.

2. Pour the cold evaporated milk into the bowl of an electric mixer and beat the milk on medium speed to a soft peak stage. Alternatively, beat the milk by hand with a whisk. Reserve the whipped milk in the refrigerator.

3. Transfer the cooled shallot and vinegar reduction to a bowl and stir in the egg yolks. Suspend the bowl over a saucepan of simmering water to form a bain-marie (the bottom of the bowl should not touch the water). Whisk the sauce until the yolks coagulate into a creamy mixture that forms a trail or 'ribbon' across the surface when it falls from the whisk. Remove the bowl from the heat.

4. Incorporate the reserved whipped milk a little at a time. To help thicken the sauce to a coating consistency, whisk it in brief bursts over gently simmering water. Whisk in the parsley and the remaining teaspoon of fresh tarragon. Taste and adjust the seasoning. Remove the sauce from the heat, pour it into a warmed sauceboat and serve.

Chef's tips
Egg yolks coagulate at 65°C (150°F) and you can, if you like, use a thermometer to check this stage. As a rougher guide, dip the back of your finger into the sauce: it should feel comfortably warm.

This sauce goes extremely well with red meat dishes such as Poached beef with barley (page 268)

- 100g (3½oz) cold unsweetened evaporated milk
- 3 egg yolks
- 2 tbsp cold water
- 1 tbsp lemon juice
- salt to taste

HOLLANDAISE SAUCE

54 CALORIES PER SERVING
Cooking and preparation: 20 minutes
Serves 6

1. Pour the cold evaporated milk into the bowl of an electric mixer and beat the milk on medium speed to a soft peak stage. Alternatively, beat the milk by hand with a whisk. Reserve the whipped milk in the refrigerator.

2. Add the egg yolks and the cold water to a bowl. Suspend the bowl over a saucepan of simmering water to form a bain-marie (the bottom of the bowl should not touch the water). Whisk until the yolks coagulate into a creamy mixture that forms a trail or 'ribbon' across the surface when it falls from the whisk. Remove the bowl from the heat.

3. Incorporate the reserved whipped milk a little at a time. To help thicken the sauce to a coating consistency, whisk it in brief bursts over gently simmering water. Whisk in the lemon juice, taste and adjust the seasoning. Remove the sauce from the heat, pour it into a warmed sauceboat and serve.

Chef's tip
This slightly acidic sauce pairs well with white fish, asparagus and poached eggs.

- 130g (scant 5oz) fat-free fromage blanc or Greek yogurt
- 1 egg yolk
- 1 heaped tsp mustard
- 1 tbsp white wine vinegar
- 100ml (⅜ US cup) olive oil or other healthy oil of your choice (page 25)
- salt and pepper to taste

LIGHT MAYONNAISE

75 CALORIES PER 20G (¾OZ) OR PER 1 TBSP

Cooking and preparation: 10 minutes
Serves 6–8

1. Put the egg yolk and mustard in a bowl. Add salt and pepper to taste. Stand the bowl on a damp cloth to prevent it from slipping then use a small whisk to beat the mixture smooth. Whisk in the vinegar.

2. Whisking constantly, add the oil drop by drop to begin with. When the sauce starts to thicken, pour in the remaining oil in a thin, steady stream, whisking rhythmically.

3. Once all of the olive oil has been incorporated, slowly mix in the fromage blanc, taste and adjust the seasoning. Keep the mayonnaise cool until you are ready to use it.

Chef's tip

Mayonnaise is a classic accompaniment for salmon, chicken, eggs and tuna. It can also be used as a dip for raw vegetable crudités. As a liaison, this mayonnaise can be combined with garlic, fresh herbs, gherkin and capers and purées of green vegetables.

This sauce is used in the following recipes:
- Crunchy vegetable spring rolls with a spicy sauce (page 158)
- Crab cannelloni with a passion-fruit sauce (page 140)
- Spiced crab on pink grapefruit jelly with a citrus mousse (page 149)
- Quenelles of white fish with horseradish sauce (page 156)
- Cold beef salad with a mustard sauce (page 192)
- Prawn salad with crunchy crab-filled biscuits (page 198)

- ½ tsp freshly ground black pepper
- 100ml (⅜ US cup) red wine
- 1 tsp olive oil
- 1 tbsp finely chopped shallot
- 200ml (⅞ US cup) veal stock
- 1 tsp cornflour (cornstarch), mixed with a little warm water
- salt to taste

PEPPERCORN AND RED WINE SAUCE

29 CALORIES PER SERVING
Cooking and preparation: 20 minutes
Serves 4

1. In a small saucepan, heat the olive oil. Add the shallots and gently sweat them, uncovered, without letting them colour, for 1 minute or until soft. Pour in the red wine, add the pepper and bring to a low boil. Simmer briskly until the liquid has reduced to three-quarters of its original volume.

2. Add the veal stock and simmer for 5 minutes. Whisk in the cornflour (cornstarch). Taste and adjust the seasoning. If desired, pass the sauce through a fine sieve, such as a chinois, to remove the shallots and peppercorns.

Chef's tip
This autumnal sauce pairs well with all manner of game and red meat. It is especially good with steak and duck breasts.

- 3 medium tomatoes, peeled, cut in half, cored and deseeded (Terms and Techniques, page 328)
- pinch of fructose or the sweetener of your choice (pages 16–20)
- 1 tbsp olive oil
- 2 sprigs of thyme, leaves only, finely chopped
- 1 fresh bay leaf, sliced
- 1 garlic clove, unpeeled and crushed
- salt and pepper to taste

TOMATO CONFIT

175 CALORIES PER 100G (3½OZ)
Cooking and preparation: 1 hour 45 minutes
Makes 100g (3½oz)

1. Preheat the oven to 120°C–150°C (248°F–300°F, gas mark ½–2). Place the 6 tomato halves in a roasting pan, cut side down. Season with the fructose, salt and pepper. Drizzle the tomatoes with the olive oil, add the garlic clove, and sprinkle with the leaves of fresh thyme and the chopped bay leaf.

2. Roast in the oven for 1½ hours, checking on the tomatoes from time to time. The tomatoes are ready when they have flopped, and most of their juices have evaporated.

Chef's tip
This confit of tomatoes can be used in a variety of ways. You can also dice them and use them in a sauce or add them whole to salads and mixtures of fresh vegetables.

Tomato Confit is used in the following recipes:
- Courgette quenelles with black olive coulis (page 142)
- Salad of white beans, mango, mushroom and pear (page 202)
- Sea bream with thyme, savory and a medley of vegetables (page 214)

• large, fat garlic cloves
• olive oil

GARLIC FLAKES

4 CALORIES PER 3G
Cooking and preparation: 20 minutes

1. Preheat the oven to 120°C (250°F, gas mark ½–1). Peel the garlic cloves and cut them in half lengthways. Pick out any green shoot from the centre and discard it. With a very sharp knife, slice the garlic lengthways into paper-thin slices.

2. Spread out the garlic slices on a baking sheet in a single layer. Use a pastry brush to coat them lightly with a little olive oil. Roast the slices in the oven until they become crisp and acquire a pretty golden colour, checking their progress every few minutes.

3. Allow the crisped flakes to cool at room temperature. If you are not going to use them immediately, store them in an airtight container and use within a few days. Above all, they must be kept dry or they will lose their crispness.

Note: These crispy flakes add a lively crunch and bite to salads. They are also an effective garnish for many simple grilled fish or meat dishes.

Garlic flakes are used in the following recipes:
• Poached sea bass with garlic, teriyaki, vegetables and herbs (page 208)
• Braised loin of pork with lemongrass and tropical fruit (page 250)

In developing the new minceur range of low-calorie, gastronomic sauces that follow, I started by considering the role of the traditional thickening agent in many sauces. This is known as the liaison. In classic French cuisine, the most common liaisons were based on flour and butter (the classic roux), or on egg yolks and heavy cream – all of which were excessively rich and laden with calories.

I wanted to create an entirely new type of liaison – light and in keeping with modern cuisine, which often looks towards the East for new flavours. To this end, I explored the possibilities of certain types of vegetables and fruits and their performance when puréed. As you will see from the following recipes, I discovered purées that are capable of taking on the role of the liaison beautifully, bringing exquisite flavour and essential body to an otherwise thin stock or cooking liquid.

When I experimented further, with variations on the purées as well as with variations on coulis and stocks, a whole spectrum of low-calorie minceur sauces emerged from my endeavours. These liaisons, coulis and sauces are not only light and healthy but are also enticing to discerning palates. The Curried Yellow Fruit Liaison, for example, is a playful yet well-balanced blend of mango, lemongrass, ginger and curry. It bears all the hallmarks of contemporary trends.

But I have not overlooked the classic flavourings and all-time favourites. The White Vegetable Liaison recalls the classic béchamel sauce. Just like its heavier predecessor, the White Vegetable Liaison is very versatile: you can use it as a sauce in its own right, as the perfect accompaniment to chicken, as a smooth coating for vegetables and pasta, and as a topping for gratins.

You can even use it to replace the traditional egg-bound velouté liaison associated with Veal blanquette (page 103).

In fact, all the Vegetable Liaisons can be used in a variety of useful ways: accompanying poultry, fish or meat; partnering vegetables or coating all manner of food ready to be finished gratin-style.

Vegetables and fruit express flavours, both on their own and in combination, of infinite variety. The following chapters are just an indication of what is possible.

- 200g (7oz) leeks, chopped
- 200g (7oz) white button mushrooms, wiped and chopped
- 150g (5½oz) potatoes, peeled and chopped
- 100g (3½oz) onions, chopped
- 100g (3½oz) celeriac, chopped
- 60g (2oz) cauliflower, trimmed and chopped
- 5g (¼oz) chopped garlic
- 1 tbsp olive oil
- 500ml (2⅛ US cups) Chicken Stock, either home-made (page 44) or from a cube
- pinch of nutmeg (optional)
- salt and pepper of your choice

WHITE VEGETABLE LIAISON

4 CALORIES PER 10G (¼OZ) OR 19 CALORIES PER PORTION
Cooking and preparation: 30 minutes
Makes about 1kg (2.2lb) or 20 portions

1. Heat the olive oil in a large saucepan on medium heat. Add the vegetables, cover and sweat gently for 2 minutes without colouring. Add the garlic and the chicken stock. Season, cover and allow to simmer gently for 20 minutes or until flavours have combined.

2. Transfer the sauce to the bowl of a food processor and blend to a smooth, fine, purée. Taste and adjust the seasoning if needed.

Chef's tip

This light purée of pale vegetables is a particularly good accompaniment for white meats – chicken, veal and pork. Its hints of leek and mushrooms also make it an excellent choice for white fish, while its smooth texture and glazing ability make it an ideal topping for gratins.

Thinned with a combination of milk and flavourful stock (see below), the White Vegetable Liaison is transformed into a suave, new-style, White Vegetable Sauce.

WHITE VEGETABLE SAUCE

26 CALORIES PER SERVING
Cooking and preparation: 5 minutes
Serves 4

1. Blend 100g (3½oz) of White Vegetable Liaison (left) with 150ml (¾ US cup) of semi-skimmed (2%) milk and 50ml (¼ US cup) of a stock variation of your choice (Herby Beef, Pondicherry Indian, Mushroom, Shellfish, Thai or Asian Lime Vegetable Stock). You could also use chicken stock from a cube or stock bought from the chilled counter of a supermarket. Pass the blended mixture through a very fine sieve, preferably a chinois.

2. Heat the sauce and adjust the seasoning to taste.

Chef's tips

When this sauce is made with Mushroom Stock (page 51), it becomes a well-matched accompaniment for chicken breast or escalope of veal, replacing traditional heavy cream-based sauces with its understated elegance.

To increase the aromatic complexity of the sauce, you can reduce the amount of potato to 100g (3½oz) and add 50g (1¾oz) of cooked white beans, such as cannellini beans or navy beans.

Use this sauce in the following recipes:
• Chicken breasts stuffed with lemony herbs (page 244)
• Veal blanquette (page 103)

- 500g (1lb 2oz) leeks, washed, trimmed and chopped
- 500g (1lb 2oz) courgettes (zucchini), chopped
- 200g (7oz) watercress (leaves and stalks), chopped
- 16 tarragon leaves, torn
- 200ml (⅞ US cup) Chicken Stock, either home-made (page 44) or from a cube
- salt and pepper of your choice

GREEN VEGETABLE LIAISON

2 CALORIES PER 10G (¼OZ) OR 11 CALORIES PER PORTION
Cooking and preparation: 20 minutes
Makes about 1kg (2.2lb) or 20 portions

1. Bring a large saucepan of lightly salted water to the boil. Add the leeks and courgettes (zucchini). Return to a light boil for 2 minutes, then add the watercress and simmer for a further 3 minutes. Add the tarragon leaves and simmer just long enough to soften them – about 30 seconds.

2. Strain through a large sieve or colander, then set the sieve over a bowl and leave the vegetables for a few minutes for any remaining liquid to drain away. Transfer the drained vegetables to the bowl of a food processor. Add the chicken stock and blend to a smooth, fine, purée.

Notes: You can use this exquisite vegetable purée just as it is. Without further additions, it makes an exceptionally pure, low-calorie accompaniment for simply prepared dishes of fish, poultry, veal or pork. It also works well as a topping for gratins.

Thinned with a combination of milk and stock, the Green Vegetable Liaison can be transformed into Green Vegetable Sauce (see opposite) – a low-calorie version of the rich sauce verte of old. The earlier version was bound with butter and cream; it brings back memories of French grandmothers and their vegetable gardens.

GREEN VEGETABLE SAUCE

22 CALORIES PER SERVING
Cooking and preparation: 5 minutes
Serves 4

1. Blend 100g (3½oz) of Green Vegetable Liaison (see left) with 150ml (¾ US cup) of semi-skimmed (2%) milk and 50ml (¼ US cup) of a Stock Variation of your choice (Herby Beef, Pondicherry Indian, Mushroom, Shellfish, Thai or Asian Lime Vegetable Stock). You could also use chicken stock from a cube or stock bought from the chilled counter of a supermarket. Pass the blended mixture through a very fine sieve, preferably a chinois.

2. Heat the sauce and adjust the seasoning to taste.

Chef's tip

Laced with Asian Lime Vegetable Stock, the Green Vegetable Sauce delivers a delicious fresh-tasting edge to very simply cooked fillets of fish. Combined with Herby Beef Stock, the sauce can equally well accompany a sauté of spring lamb or veal.

Use this sauce in the following recipe:
• Soft-boiled eggs with a green sauce (page 153)

- 250g (9oz) carrots, peeled and chopped
- 60g (2oz) onions, chopped
- 1 tsp olive oil
- 2 tbsp finely chopped fresh lemongrass, tough outer layers removed first
- 1 tsp finely chopped fresh ginger
- 50g (1¾oz) fresh apricots, halved and pitted
- 50g (1¾oz) fresh mango flesh
- 1½ tsp curry powder
- 400ml (1¾ US cups) chicken stock, either home-made (page 44) or from a cube
- 500ml (2⅛ US cups) semi-skimmed (0%) milk, mixed with 1 tbsp cornflour (cornstarch)
- salt and pepper of your choice

CURRIED YELLOW FRUIT LIAISON

5 CALORIES PER 10G (¼OZ) OR 25 CALORIES PER PORTION
Cooking and preparation: 1 hour
Makes about 500g (1.1lb) or 10 portions

1. Heat the olive oil in a large saucepan on medium heat. Add the carrots and onions, cover and gently sweat for 3 minutes without colouring. Add the lemongrass, the ginger and the curry powder. Stir the ingredients and let them sweat for a further 2 minutes. Stir in 250ml (1⅛ US cups) of the chicken stock. Season to taste. Cover the saucepan and simmer gently for 20 minutes.

2. Add the apricots and mango to the saucepan and continue to simmer gently, covered, for 10 minutes, stirring occasionally.

3. Transfer the fruit and sauce to the bowl of a food processor and blend to a smooth, fine, purée. Blend in the milk mixed with cornflour (cornstarch), then incorporate the remaining chicken stock. Taste and adjust the seasoning if needed.

Chef's tip
With its tangy flavouring of fruit and curry, this Curried Yellow Fruit Liaison makes a delicious, light alternative to more traditional types of curry sauce. It is especially good with chicken, white fish and vegetables.

Use this liaison in the following recipes:
- Vegetable curry with basmati rice (page 272)
- Lamb curry (page 104)

- 100g (3½oz) red beetroots (beets), cooked, peeled and finely chopped
- 90g (scant 3½oz) shallots, finely chopped
- 3 bay leaves, fresh or dried
- 1.5 litres (6½ US cups) veal stock, either home made or from a cube, or Chicken Stock (page 44) or Vegetable Stock (page 42)
- 5g (about 1 tsp) fructose or the sweetener of your choice (pages 16–20)
- 750ml (3¼ US cups) red wine
- 1 tbsp olive oil
- salt and pepper of your choice

RED BEET LIAISON
5 CALORIES PER 10G (¼OZ) OR 25 CALORIES PER PORTION
Cooking and preparation: 30 minutes
Makes about 1kg (2.2lb) or 20 portions

1. Heat the olive oil in a large saucepan set over gentle heat. Add the shallots and sweat them, without colouring them, for 1 minute. Add the red wine and the bay leaves. Raise the heat and simmer the wine briskly until it has reduced by at least half and the mixture resembles a loose marmalade.

2. Add the stock, the beetroot and the fructose, and season lightly to taste. Simmer the ingredients for 10 minutes. At the end of the cooking, remove the bay leaves if you do not want their strong flavour to be included in the finished sauce.

3. When the beetroot mixture is cool enough to handle, transfer it to the bowl of a food processor and blend it to a smooth, fine, purée. For an extra fine sauce, pass it through a fine-meshed sieve – preferably a chinois – to remove any remaining vegetable fibres. Taste and adjust the seasoning as desired.

Chef's tip
Beetroot sauces were once associated with the 'return from the hunt', because they accompanied the traditional game and red-meat dishes served on such occasions. This modern iron-rich sauce will bring similar dishes to life – and boost your energy levels into the bargain. Try it in an assembly that includes cold roast beef, duck or game, plus some walnuts and goat's cheese.

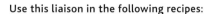

Use this liaison in the following recipes:
- Quick-cook quality beef with peppercorns and Puy lentils (page 271)
- Body skirt of veal with a celeriac and apple purée (page 252)

The Coulis that follow are cold emulsified sauces made from vegetables and/or fruit, sometimes with an Asian flavouring. They are based on the same culinary principle as the Puréed Liaisons (pags 83–9) – that is to say they are essentially a fine purée. The difference is that the Coulis are generally intended to be served cold and used as you might a mayonnaise. What they bring to the food they accompany is a real burst of vegetable and fruit flavour.

- 300g (11oz) carrots, peeled and chopped or fairly finely sliced
- 1 tsp olive oil
- ½ tsp cumin seeds
- pinch of fructose or the sweetener of your choice (pages 16–20)
- 150ml (¾ US cup) water
- 100ml (⅜ US cup) orange juice
- 3 tbsp Light Vinaigrette (page 70)
- salt and pepper of your choice

CARROT COULIS

10 CALORIES PER 10G (¼OZ) OR PER 1 TBSP
Cooking and preparation: 45 minutes
Makes about 320g (12oz)

1. In a saucepan, heat the olive oil together with the cumin seeds for 30 seconds. Add the carrots and stir in the fructose. Season to taste with salt and pepper. Sweat the carrots, uncovered, over gentle heat for 2 minutes. Add the water, cover the saucepan, and cook over medium heat for 15 minutes. Add the orange juice and continue to cook the carrots uncovered for about 10 minutes, or until the orange juice has reduced. Remove from the heat.

2. When the mixture is cool enough to handle, transfer it to a food processor and blend it to a fine purée. Pass the purée through a fine sieve, preferably a chinois. Whisk in the Light Vinaigrette.

3. Adjust the seasoning. Serve slightly chilled.

Chef's tip
The Carrot Coulis makes a delicious dip for all kinds of crudités or vegetable platters. It also makes a wonderful base for a highly original savoury cake – or better still, small individual cakes for the canapé tray. You can also slightly increase the amount of liquid you use to make the coulis so that you get a looser version that can be used as a dressing for salads of cold chicken and white fish.

- 100g (3½oz) beetroot, cooked, peeled and diced
- 1 tsp olive oil
- 50g (1¾oz) red onions, finely chopped
- sprig of thyme
- ½ bay leaf, fresh or dried
- good pinch of finely chopped garlic
- 50g (1¾oz) concentrated tomato paste
- 100ml (⅜ US cup) red wine
- 10g (1 tbsp) coconut milk
- 20g (2 tbsp) beetroot juice
- salt and pepper of your choice

BEET AND RED WINE COULIS

8 CALORIES PER 10G (¼OZ) OR PER 1 TBSP
Cooking and preparation: 40 minutes
Makes about 220g (8oz)

In a saucepan, heat the olive oil and add the onions, thyme, bay leaf and garlic. Sweat, uncovered, over gentle heat for 2 minutes. Add the concentrated tomato paste along with the red wine. Simmer briskly, uncovered, for 5 minutes or until the mixture resembles a loose marmalade. Add the beetroot and season to taste. Cover the saucepan, reduce the heat and cook gently for about 10 minutes. Remove from the heat.

Remove the thyme and bay leaf and, when the mixture is cool enough to handle, transfer it to a food processor. Blend it to a fine purée, gradually incorporating the coconut milk and then the beetroot juice. Taste and adjust the seasoning.

Chef's tip
Served cold, this Beet and Red Wine Coulis is a natural companion for a beetroot salad. Served warm, the coulis can be shaped into vibrant quenelles that look and taste wonderful with breast of duck, pigeon or pheasant. This is a coulis that also goes well with salads of cheese, especially goat's cheese.

- 240g (8½oz) ripe mango flesh
- 4 tbsp fromage blanc or Greek yogurt (0% or low-fat)
- 4 tsp coconut milk
- 4 tsp soy sauce
- 4 tbsp prepared expresso coffee
- 4 tsp hazelnut oil
- salt and pepper of your choice

MANGO AND COFFEE COULIS

12 CALORIES PER 10G (¼OZ) OR PER 1 TBSP

Cooking and preparation: 10 minutes
Makes about 360g (13oz)

1. Blend the mango to a smooth purée in a food processor. Add the fromage blanc, the coconut milk, the soy sauce, the expresso coffee and the hazelnut oil. Blend again to distribute the ingredients evenly. Taste, and adjust the seasoning as desired.

2. Transfer the coulis to a container and keep it chilled until ready to use.

Chef's tip

This exotic coulis is marvellous with a salad of grilled poultry. It works equally well as a moistening liaison in, say, an Asian noodle salad. Try it, too, instead of mayonnaise in a chicken sandwich.

- 200g (7oz) frozen petits pois
- 40g (scant 1½oz) of rocket (arugula) leaves or mesclun salad leaves
- 40g (scant 1½oz) flat-leaf parsley, leaves only
- 100ml (⅜ US cup) water
- pinch of fructose or the sweetener of your choice (pages 16–20)
- 1 tsp salt

PEA AND ROCKET COULIS
4 CALORIES PER 10G (¼OZ) OR PER 1 TBSP
Cooking and preparation: 20 minutes
Makes about 400g (14oz)

1. Blanch the leaves of the flat-leaf parsley and the rocket for 30 seconds in a saucepan of boiling salted water. Drain and refresh in cold water. Drain again and set aside.

2. Blend the peas in a food processor for 30 seconds; reserve the mixture in the bowl of the processor. In a small saucepan, bring the water to the boil with the fructose and the salt and pour it over the peas. To complete the coulis, blend again for about 2 minutes, gradually incorporating the blanched leaves, until you have a smooth purée.

3. Taste and adjust the seasoning. For an extra fine coulis, pass it through a fine-meshed sieve, preferably a chinois. Keep the coulis chilled until ready to use.

Variation
To reinforce the aromatic complexity of this coulis, add some basil leaves to the purée.

Chef's tip
This vibrant green coulis can be used in the same way as a pesto sauce – so it is delicious with tagliatelle and shavings of Parmesan, for example. It also makes a great partner for scallops, grilled, steamed or sautéed briefly. Pretty in colour and fresh in taste, the coulis will also give a new lease of life to leftovers of chicken and rabbit.

Thanks to the Essential Cuisine Minceur Toolkit (pages 38–95), you have at your disposal all you need to put together rapidly assembled healthy meals for every day. Our Master Stocks and Variations, Vinaigrettes, Liaisons and Sauces, and our Cold Coulis – all are invaluable tools for transforming simply prepared main ingredients into elegant dishes with complex flavours. For example, when you want to steam, poach or microwave fish, poultry, meat or vegetables, you can use the stock of your choice as a cooking liquid and simply leave it to impart its unique flavour to the food. You can then complement the resulting dish with a vinaigrette, an easily assembled sauce or a coulis. Ever ready to adapt to your needs, the same vinaigrette, sauce or coulis will also flatter virtually any type of food that has been simply sautéed or grilled.

- 100g (3½oz) lamb's lettuce, washed and dried
- 80g (scant 3oz) white button mushrooms, wiped and sliced
- 8 medium red radishes, sliced into thin rounds
- 1 small red onion (about 80g/scant 3oz), sliced into thin rounds
- 4 tbsp Light Vinaigrette (page 70)
- 80g (scant 3oz) beetroot, cooked and peeled
- fresh seasonal herbs, chopped (optional)
- salt and pepper of your choice

LAMB'S LETTUCE SALAD

60 CALORIES PER PERSON
Preparation: 10 minutes
Level of difficulty: *
Serves 4

1. Have ready the lamb's lettuce, mushroom, radish, onion and Light Vinaigrette.

2. Just before serving, cut the beetroot into thin batons about 5cm x 3mm (2in x ⅛in).

3. Put the lamb's lettuce, mushroom, radish, and onion into a large salad bowl or mixing bowl. Add the beetroot and dress the salad with the vinaigrette, turning the ingredients gently but thoroughly to coat them. Season to taste with salt and pepper.

4. Divide the salad between 4 serving plates and, if you wish, scatter over chopped seasonal herbs.

Chef's tip

You can either use red or yellow beetroot. Red is pretty with the radish. However, the yellow variety bleeds far less than its red counterpart, which means the salad will stay looking fresh for longer.

- 16 raw scampi or Dublin Bay or Jumbo prawns (shrimp) on the shell
- 120g (scant 4½oz) frisée salad leaves
- 1 tbsp snipped or chopped chives
- 2 tbsp Shellfish Vinaigrette (page 73)
- 80g (scant 3oz) banana, sliced into thin rounds
- 12 segments of grapefruit, pith and membrane removed
- 1 tsp oil
- salt and pepper of your choice

For the sauce (optional)
- 2 tbsp fromage blanc or Greek yogurt (0% fat or low-fat)
- 2 tbsp semi-skimmed (2%) milk
- 1 tsp traditional French mustard or other grainy mustard

PRAWNS WITH FRISÉE, BANANA AND GRAPEFRUIT

130 CALORIES PER PERSON with the prawn sauce
115 CALORIES PER PERSON without the sauce
Cooking and preparation: 20 minutes
Level of difficulty: *
Serves 4

1. Open up each prawn (shrimp) to resemble butterfly wings: pull the head and legs off, then peel away the shell, leaving the last big segment of shell and the tail firmly intact. With a small sharp knife, score lightly along the back of the prawn (shrimp) in a straight line, stopping just before the segment of shell. If there is a long black intestinal vein, pick it out and discard it. Cut deeper into the flesh to open the prawn (shrimp) to make two wings, which remain joined together at the last segment of shell and tail (see illustration below). Cover the prawns and set aside in the refrigerator until you are ready to cook them.

2. Put the frisée salad leaves in a large mixing bowl. Add the chives. Dress the salad with the Shellfish Vinaigrette, turning the leaves gently to coat them. Season to taste with salt and pepper. Divide the salad between 4 serving plates. Scatter with the banana and grapefruit.

3. For the sauce, if used, mix together the fromage blanc, milk and mustard in a small bowl. Add salt and pepper to taste.

4. Cook the prawns, either in a steamer or in a non-stick frying pan (skillet), for 1½ minutes, seasoning them with salt, pepper and a little oil. Arrange 4 prawns on each plate. If you are serving the sauce, use it to coat the prawns lightly. Serve straight away.

Note
You can find other recipes for salads on pages 188–205.

frisée salad leaves

banana rounds

grapefruit

prawns

Ideas for simple salads using my Vinaigrettes (pages 64–73)

• Lightly cooked haricot verts mixed with batons of pear and peach.

• Diced peeled tomatoes and diced cucumber, sprinkled with finely chopped shallot and fines herbes (served as a first-course 'tartare').

• Julienne strips or batons of vegetables (carrots, white button mushrooms, courgettes (zucchini), celeriac) mixed with a few leaves of Little Gem lettuce.

• Cooked red or yellow beetroot, cut into rounds and combined with sliced radish and thinly sliced red onion. Add the mixture to frisée salad leaves.

• A mixture of raw, finely sliced, cauliflower, broccoli, fennel and white onion.

• Lightly cooked haricots verts, mixed with small pieces of red pepper (bottled, raw or grilled and skinned), a few chopped capers, rocket (arugula) leaves and some diced, boiled, waxy, potato.

• Batons of chicory (Belgian endive), cooked beetroot, celery and apple, tossed over lettuce hearts.

- 2 small courgettes (zucchini), sliced lengthways into strips about ½cm (¼in) thick
- 200g (7oz) white button mushrooms, wiped and sliced
- 6 small new white onions, cut into small wedges, about ½cm (¼in) thick
- 4 pimientos del piquillo, bottled (Terms and Techniques, page 328) or other grilled sweet red peppers
- 1 tbsp olive oil
- about 150g (5½oz) dried spaghetti
- 8 tbsp Mushroom Vinaigrette (page 66)
- 1 tbsp finely chopped flat-leaf parsley
- salt and pepper of your choice

SPAGHETTI SALAD WITH GRILLED VEGETABLES

245 CALORIES PER PERSON
Cooking and preparation: 30 minutes
Level of difficulty: * *
Serves 4

1. Have ready the prepared courgettes (zucchini), mushrooms and onions. If you are using bottled pimientos del piquillo, open up 4 of them like a book and rinse away the seeds; drain them on kitchen paper. Alternatively, cut 2 small fresh red peppers in half, then grill or oven-roast them until the skin blisters; remove the skin and seeds and cut the peppers into strips.

2. You can grill or sauté the vegetables. If you opt to grill them, preheat the grill and grill pan about 15 minutes before you want to serve the dish. If you have one, a ridged grill pan can also be used over direct heat; it will mark the vegetables in an attractive way, but you can sauté the vegetables equally well in a regular non-stick frying pan (skillet). Before you cook the vegetables, brush them lightly with the olive oil and season with salt and pepper.

3. For the spaghetti, bring a large saucepan of lightly salted boiling water to the boil. Gradually add the spaghetti, return the water to the boil and cook the spaghetti until al dente – about 8 minutes.

4. While the spaghetti is simmering, cook the vegetables as follows on each side: the onions for about 4 minutes, the courgettes (zucchini) for 3 minutes, the mushrooms for 2 minutes, and the pimientos del piquillo for 1 minute – other red peppers take slightly longer.

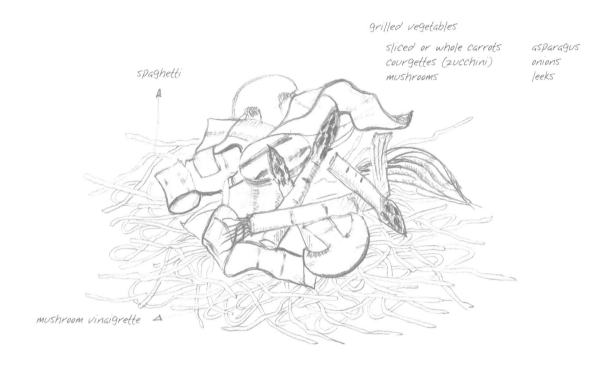

grilled vegetables

sliced or whole carrots   *asparagus*
courgettes (zucchini)   *onions*
mushrooms   *leeks*

spaghetti

mushroom vinaigrette

To serve

Drain the pasta, then return it to the dry saucepan. Immediately toss the spaghetti in just 4 tablespoons of the Mushroom Vinaigrette, reserving the rest. Adjust the seasoning and stir in the parsley. Transfer the spaghetti to 4 warm serving plates and arrange the cooked vegetables on top. Drizzle over the remaining vinaigrette and serve.

Chef's tip

In terms of health and diet, cooking pasta until al dente is beneficial because it allows the pasta to retain its starch, which encourages complex carbohydrates and glucose to be absorbed into the blood slowly and over a long period. The result is a steady blood-sugar level and the slow and sustained release of energy. These factors are particularly helpful for diabetics who must avoid sharp drops in their blood-glucose levels and should instead cultivate good glycaemic control (page 11). The same principle applies to rice, cereals and complex starchy carbohydrates in general.

- 150g (5½oz) cauliflower, cut into ½cm (¼in) slices
- 150g (5½oz) courgettes (zucchini), cut into 1cm (⅜in) dice
- 2 hearts of Little Gem lettuce or other sweet lettuce hearts, cut into 8 small wedges
- 120g (scant 4½oz) white button mushrooms, wiped, cut in half and thinly sliced
- 1 large tomato, peeled, cored and deseeded (Terms and Techniques, page 328), then cut into 12 pieces
- 150g (5½oz) small dried pasta shells
- 1 tbsp olive oil
- ½ tbsp balsamic vinegar
- 8 tbsp Thai Vinaigrette (page 68)
- 1 tbsp snipped coriander (cilantro) leaves
- salt and pepper of your choice

ORIENTAL PASTA SHELLS WITH VEGETABLES

220 CALORIES PER PERSON
Cooking and preparation: 30 minutes
Level of difficulty: *
Serves 4

1. Have ready the vegetables and lettuce, cut up appropriately.

2. To cook the pasta shells, bring a large saucepan of lightly salted boiling water to the boil. Add the pasta shells, return the water to the boil, then simmer until the shells are al dente – about 8 minutes, depending on size.

3. Meanwhile, heat the olive oil over a low heat in a non-stick frying pan (skillet), large enough to accommodate the vegetables and lettuce. Add the slices of cauliflower and the diced courgette (zucchini), stirring gently with a wooden spoon. Season to taste, then cover the frying pan (skillet) and sweat the vegetables gently for 1 minute or until they soften without colouring. Add the wedges of lettuce and the mushrooms. Adjust the seasoning, cover the pan again and sweat the vegetables for 1 minute more. Add the tomato and cook for a further 1 minute – this time uncovered.

4. Add the balsamic vinegar, increase the heat and stir the juices in the bottom of the pan to deglaze it. When the liquid has reduced almost completely, the vegetables will be ready.

To serve

Drain the pasta, then return it to the dry saucepan. Immediately toss the pasta in 4 tablespoons of the Thai Vinaigrette, reserving the rest. Adjust the seasoning. Transfer the pasta to 4 warm serving plates and scatter the vegetables on top. Drizzle over the remaining vinaigrette, sprinkle with coriander (cilantro) and serve.

- 1 litre (4¼ US cups/1 quart) cold water
- 1 chicken stock or veal stock cube
- 400g (14oz) shoulder of veal, stripped of fat and connective tissue and cut into 1.5cm (½in) cubes
- 500ml (2⅛ US cups) White Vegetable Sauce (page 85)
- salt

For the accompaniment

- 100g (3½oz) wholegrain wheat (wheat berries; page 112), or 75g (2½oz) pearl barley (page 111)
- Note: the uncooked quantity of cereal given here yields 240g (8½oz) of cooked cereal.

VEAL BLANQUETTE

365 CALORIES PER PERSON when served
with wholegrain wheat (wheat berries)
385 CALORIES PER PERSON when served with pearl barley
Cooking and preparation: 50 minutes
Level of difficulty: *
Serves 4

1. Cook the accompanying grain of your choice, according to pages 00–00 or following the packet instructions, soaking it first if required. You can start to cook the veal about 50 minutes before the accompanying grain is ready.

2. For the veal, bring the cold water to the boil in a large saucepan. Add the stock cube, stirring to dissolve it. Add the pieces of veal. When the liquid reaches a simmering point, partially cover the saucepan with a lid. Adjust the heat so that the liquid simmers gently for about 45 minutes or until the veal is tender.

3. While the veal simmers, reheat the White Vegetable Sauce.

To serve

Use a slotted spoon to transfer the veal to warm serving plates. Coat the veal with the sauce. Add the accompanying grain and serve with the vegetables of your choice.

- 500g (1lb 2oz) boned leg or shoulder of lamb, stripped of fat and connective tissue and cut into 1.5cm (½in) cubes
- 2 heaped tsp curry powder
- 500ml (2⅛ US cups) Curried Yellow Fruit Liaison (page 88)
- salt and pepper of your choice

For the accompaniment
- 80g (scant 3oz) bulgur (page 111) or 100g (3½oz) basmati rice (page 113)
  Note: the uncooked quantities of bulgur and basmati rice given here yield 240g (8½oz) of cooked bulgur or rice.

For the vegetable garnish
- 100g (3½oz) carrots, peeled and cut into batons, 3cm x ½cm (1¼in x ¼in)
- 200g (7oz) cauliflower florets, stalks removed
- 120g (scant 4½oz) broad beans (fava beans), podded and skins removed (Terms and Techniques, page 326)

LAMB CURRY

375 CALORIES PER PERSON when served with bulgur
420 CALORIES PER PERSON when served with basmati rice
Cooking and preparation: 30 minutes
plus 2 hours resting in the refrigerator
Level of difficulty: *
Serves 4

1. Coat the lamb evenly on all sides with the curry powder, then put it in a covered dish in the refrigerator for 2–3 hours.

2. About 20 minutes before you want to serve the dish, cook the accompaniment of your choice – either the bulgur or the basmati rice.

3. Cook the vegetables, in separate batches, in salted simmering water: about 10 minutes for the carrots, 7 for the cauliflower and 3 for the broad beans. Either keep the vegetables warm as you cook them, or refresh them in cold water for reheating later.

4. For the sauce, reheat the Curried Yellow Fruit Liaison. At the same time, sauté the lamb rapidly in a dry non-stick frying pan (skillet) over a medium heat. To ensure even cooking, keep the meat moving by shaking the pan and turning the meat using two wooden spoons. Add 1 or 2 tablespoons of water if the meat sticks. When the meat is done to your liking, after about 5 minutes, remove it from the heat.

To serve
Arrange the accompaniment in the middle of warm serving plates. Distribute the lamb on top and coat with the sauce. Add the vegetable garnish and serve.

Once a hallmark of traditional French cookery, gratins make fewer appearances nowadays. This is a pity. Thanks to their irresistible gratinéed topping, they have various advantages. One is that they can be prepared in advance and finished beneath the grill at the last moment. Another is that they offer a convenient way to entice children, and even adults, to eat vegetables that they might otherwise eschew.

Children can come to love eating vegetables as long as they are presented in imaginative ways, such as in a gratin. In fact, teenagers and adults alike regard the vegetable gratin as rather sophisticated. By bringing together multiple ingredients, and taking into account the balance of flavours and seasonings, you can easily devise an interesting and tasty dish. Whether simple or complex, a gratin topping can be readily assembled using one of the Essential Liaisons (pages 83–9). Just set it to bubble beneath a grill with a sprinkling of breadcrumbs and Parmesan on top.

Note

The health slogan recommending the consumption of 'five a day' fruit and vegetables has become one of the expressions of daily life. But it can be difficult to imagine what this represents in concrete terms: at a minimum, it is equivalent to 400g (14oz) of vegetables or fruit (fresh, frozen or bottled), which corresponds to 2 small plates of vegetables and 2 pieces of fruit.

- 2 pears (fresh or bottled)
- 500g (1lb 2oz) White Vegetable Liaison (page 84)
- 1 tsp olive oil
- 2 tbsp freshly grated Parmesan
- 2 tbsp breadcrumbs, made from day-old bread

Equipment
- 4 gratin dishes, 12cm (5in) in diameter

PEAR AND WHITE VEGETABLE GRATIN

95 CALORIES PER PERSON
Cooking and preparation: 5 minutes
Level of difficulty: *
Serves 4

1. Preheat the grill. Peel and core the pears and cut them into medium-sized chunks. Put them in the bowl of a food processor along with the White Vegetable Liaison. Blend to a coarse purée that retains some solid pieces of pear.

2. Brush a little of the olive oil over the surface of the gratin dishes. Add the blended purée. Sprinkle over the grated Parmesan and the breadcrumbs.

3. Put the dishes under the grill until the topping is a pretty golden colour.

- 1 fairly firm avocado pear
- 500g (1lb 2oz) Green Vegetable Liaison (page 86)
- 1 tsp olive oil
- 2 tbsp freshly grated Parmesan
- salt and pepper of your choice

Equipment
- 4 gratin dishes, 12cm (5in) in diameter

AVOCADO AND GREEN VEGETABLE GRATIN

50 CALORIES PER PERSON
Cooking and preparation: 5 minutes
Level of difficulty: *
Serves 4

1. Preheat the grill. Peel and stone the avocado and cut it into medium-sized chunks. Put them in the bowl of a food processor along with the Green Vegetable Liaison. Blend to a coarse purée that retains some solid pieces of avocado. Taste, and adjust the seasoning if necessary.

2. Brush a little of the olive oil over the surface of the gratin dishes. Add the blended purée. Sprinkle over the grated Parmesan.

3. Put the dishes under the grill until the topping is a pretty golden colour.

- 2 tsp olive oil
- 400g (14oz) Spanish onion or other sweet onion, finely sliced into small strips
- 1 sprig of fresh thyme or a good pinch of dried thyme
- pinch of fructose or the sweetener of your choice (pages 16–20)
- 100ml (⅜ US cup) water
- 100g (3½oz) celeriac, peeled and cut into 3mm (⅛in) slices
- 2 Golden Delicious or other sweet apples, peeled, cored and cut into ½cm (¼in) slices
- 200ml (⅞ US cup) Vegetable Stock (page 42)
- 120g (scant 4½oz) mango flesh, cut into ribbons about 3mm (⅛in) thick
- salt and pepper of your choice

Equipment
- 4 gratin dishes, 12cm (5in) in diameter

GRATIN OF ONION, APPLE, CELERIAC AND MANGO

110 CALORIES PER PERSON
Cooking and preparation: 45 minutes
Level of difficulty: * *
Serves 4

1. Heat 1 teaspoon of the olive oil in a small saucepan. Add the onion, thyme, fructose, and salt and pepper to taste. Leave the onion to cook, uncovered, over a low to medium heat until it softens and becomes golden in colour. Add the 100ml (⅜ US cup) of water. Cover the saucepan with a lid and sweat the onion over a very low heat for about 20 minutes or until it forms a compote; remove from the heat. Discard the sprig of fresh thyme, if used, and set the onion compote aside.

2. Simmer the slices of celeriac in lightly salted simmering water for 5 minutes or until al dente. Drain, refresh under cold water and drain again.

3. Heat a non-stick frying pan (skillet) over a gentle heat. Add the slices of apple to the dry pan and cook them – on one side only – until golden. Transfer them to a plate and set aside.

4. Preheat the oven to 160°C (310°F, gas mark 3). Have ready the Vegetable Stock, heated through. Brush the gratin dishes with the remaining olive oil. Assemble each dish with a layer of celeriac at the bottom. Use half of the onion compote to form the next layer, then add the mango. Spread the remaining onion compote on top. Season with salt and pepper if desired. Add a final layer of apple, coloured-side up. Gently spoon over the stock.

5. Cook in the oven for 20 minutes, then serve.

Chef's tip
This gratin is a particularly good accompaniment for breast of duck and a variety of game and pork dishes.

- 150ml (¾ US cup) semi-skimmed (2%) milk
  pinch of grated nutmeg
- 1 tsp olive oil
- 160g (5½oz) white button mushrooms, wiped
  and cut into 3mm (⅛in) slices
- 2 tbsp grated Parmesan
- 2 tbsp breadcrumbs
- salt and pepper to taste

For the mushroom duxelles
- Makes 450g (1lb) duxelles,
  containing **350 calories**
- Cooking and preparation: 30 minutes

- 500ml (2⅛ US cups) semi-skimmed (2%) milk
- 400g (14oz) white button mushrooms, wiped
  and cut into quarters
- ½ tbsp olive oil
- 2 tbsp finely chopped or snipped shallot
- ½ clove garlic, peeled and finely chopped
- 2 tbsp dry white wine
- pinch of grated nutmeg
- salt and pepper of your choice

Equipment
- 4 gratin dishes, 12cm (5in) in diameter

MUSHROOM GRATIN
150 CALORIES PER PERSON
Cooking and preparation: 40 minutes
Level of difficulty: * *
Serves 4

1. To make the duxelles, heat the milk in a saucepan and add the mushrooms. Add salt to taste. Cover the saucepan with a lid and adjust the heat to maintain a gentle simmer for about 10 minutes, or until the mushrooms are tender.

2. Strain the milk and mushroom mixture into a sieve set over a bowl. Reserve about 5 tablespoons of the milk and put this and the cooked mushrooms into the bowl of a food processor. Blend to a coarsely chopped mixture, taking care not to blend to a purée. Set the mixture aside.

3. Coat a saucepan with the olive oil. Set it over a low heat and sweat the shallot and garlic very gently for 2 minutes or until they have softened without colouring. Add the white wine and the chopped mushroom mixture. Add the nutmeg and season to taste with salt and pepper. Let this mixture cook over a very gentle heat, stirring occasionally, until the juices from the mushrooms have been reabsorbed and the pan is almost dry – about 10 minutes.

4. Adjust the seasoning and transfer the mixture to a bowl. The duxelles is now ready for you to use as you wish.

5. Measure out 400g (14oz) of duxelles and thin it with 150ml (¾ US cup) of milk. Stir in the nutmeg and adjust the seasoning. Distribute the mixture between 4 individual gratin dishes.

6. Gently heat the olive oil in a large non-stick frying pan (skillet). Add the sliced mushrooms, in a single layer, arranging them flat; season. Cook for 2 minutes or until lightly coloured on one side. Turn them with a spatula and cook on the reverse side for a further 2 minutes; remove from the heat. Arrange the sliced sautéed mushrooms on top of the duxelles; set aside.

7. About 12 minutes before you want to serve the gratins, preheat the grill. Sprinkle the gratins with the grated Parmesan and breadcrumbs. Put the dishes under the grill for 5–7 minutes, or until their topping is a pretty golden colour.

Chef's tip
The warm meaty flavour of this gratin makes it a good companion for Chicken breasts stuffed with lemony herbs (page 244) and for Veal with mushrooms and white sauce revisited (page 249). Generally, though, it will go well with a range of poultry dishes as well as with duck and pigeon.

For the health-conscious cook, grains are a great store-cupboard asset, always to hand to form the basis of a meal or to play a supporting role. Beyond this convenience and flexibility lie other advantages. One is that grains satisfy the appetite, creating an immediate feeling of fullness. They also release glucose gradually into the bloodstream, producing a slow release of energy. It is this gradual release that makes an often long wait from one meal to the next possible, without a snack in between. These factors are beneficial to the weight-conscious as well as to diabetics who require good glycaemic control, without sharp drops in their blood-glucose levels.

Grains offer the further benefit of being rich in fibre (page 11), just like fruit and vegetables, and so they promote gastrointestinal health. The fibres work to speed up intestinal transit time, thus countering constipation and, at the same time, contributing to body-weight management.

Medical studies have also shown that fibre lowers the risk of developing cancer of the colon by keeping the bowels moving and eliminating toxins. And grains have even more to commend them: their fibre prevents certain types of fats (lipids) and carbohydrates from being absorbed into the intestine. This, according to many scientific studies, helps to reduce cholesterol levels as well as reducing the risk of cardiovascular disease.

Note
The Glycaemic Index (GI) is a numerical index, using a scale of 0–100, that ranks foods based on their immediate effect on blood glucose (blood sugar) levels. It is essential data for diabetics. In short, carbohydrates that break down slowly, releasing glucose gradually into the blood stream, have a low GI, of 55 or under, while those that break down quickly have a high GI, of 70 and above.

Many commonly consumed foods fall into a middle range. As GI testing is very expensive, GI values have so far only been awarded to about 5% of foods, with the focus on those that are consumed widely, hence: spaghetti (40); wholegrain wheat/wheat berries (45); rice (50); peas, chick peas, split peas and dried haricot beans (30).

In this book we only consider those varieties of grains with a low or medium GI. Your local supermarket will stock most of them and your local health-food store will stock the less common varieties, such as spelt and buckwheat/kasha.

Once cooked, refreshed with cold water and drained, grains can be reheated in various ways: by steaming, by microwaving or by reheating gently in a saucepan with a small amount of oil to prevent sticking. To give the cooked grains a little tenderness and extra flavour, you can bind them with a Vegetable Liaison or a related sauce (pages 83–9).

Makes 320g/11½oz, cooked
- 1.5 litres (6½ US cups) water
- ½ bay leaf, fresh or dried
- 100g (3½oz) pearl barley
- pinch of salt

PEARL BARLEY

155 CALORIES PER 100G (3½OZ), COOKED

For cookery, the grains are processed to remove their outer casing of hull and bran. What is left is the inner 'pearl', which is then polished. It is a grain that is low in gluten and rich in Vitamin B, iron and zinc. With its appealing, mildly nutty flavour, pearl barley has recently caught the imagination of celebrity chefs in France, the UK and the USA alike. You can substitute pearl barley where you might normally use rice. Pearl barley has an extremely low GI – 25.

In a saucepan, bring the water to the boil. Add the bay leaf and a pinch of salt. Add the pearl barley, return the water to the boil, then reduce the heat and simmer the pearl barley, uncovered, over medium heat for about 1 hour or until tender. Drain and discard the bay leaf. Refresh under cold water and drain again.

Makes 300g/11oz, cooked
- 300ml (1¼ US cups) water
- ¼ chicken stock cube, crumbled
- 100g (3½oz) bulgur
- pinch of salt

BULGUR

85 CALORIES PER 100G (3½OZ), COOKED

Bulgur is a whole kernel of cereal grain, chiefly taken from durum wheat. Following minimal processing to remove its outer husk and most of its bran, it is then steamed, dried and, finally, crushed. Bulgur has roughly the same nutritional value as pasta and semolina. It is rich in iron, phosphorus and magnesium. With its low GI of 45, it permits the slow release of glucose into the blood and so reduces cravings for snacks in between meals.

In a saucepan, bring the water to the boil. Add the stock cube and stir to dissolve. Adjust the seasoning to taste. Add the bulgur, return to the boil, then reduce the heat and simmer over a gentle heat, uncovered, for about 20 minutes or until the liquid has evaporated and the bulgur is tender. The bulgur does not need to be refreshed under cold water and can be eaten straight away.

Makes 250g/9oz, cooked
• 1.5 litres (6½ US cups) water
• 100g (3½oz) wholegrain wheat
  (wheat berries)
• pinch of salt

WHOLEGRAIN WHEAT (WHEAT BERRIES)

120 CALORIES PER 100G (3½OZ), COOKED

Wholegrain wheat (often called wheat berries) refers to the kernels, or berries, on top of the wheat stalk. Harvested before the wheat matures, the berries retain the germ, bran and starchy endosperm; only the inedible hull is removed. The berries gain flavour from being smoked and dried at a temperature of 120°C–180°C (248°F–350°F), and they are a rich source of fibre (page 11), which promotes the elimination of waste and an efficient intestinal transit time. With a low GI of 45, wholegrain wheat produces slow-release energy. Additionally, its high levels of magnesium, phosphorus and iron give it an impressive nutrient profile.

In a saucepan, bring the water to the boil. Add a pinch of salt and the wholegrain wheat (wheat berries). Return the water to the boil, then reduce the heat and simmer over a medium heat, uncovered, for about 1 hour or until tender. Drain, refresh rapidly in cold water, and drain again. Soaking the wheat overnight will reduce the cooking time.

Makes 240g/8½oz, cooked
• 100g (3½oz) spelt
• 1.5 litres (6½ US cups) water
• pinch of salt

SPELT

140 CALORIES PER 100G (3½OZ), COOKED

Spelt is one of the earliest grains known to human beings and was eaten in abundance until Roman times, when it fell in popularity because of its low yield. With its distinctive nutty flavour, spelt is rich in iron and magnesium, and even richer in protein. Although spelt is derived from wheat, its gluten has a different structure from that of modern wheat – a factor that often makes spelt suitable for people with a wheat intolerance. It has a low GI of 45.

Rinse the spelt well. In a saucepan, bring the water to the boil. Add a pinch of salt and the spelt, return the water to the boil, then reduce the heat and simmer, uncovered, for about 40 minutes or until cooked to your liking. Refresh the spelt rapidly under cold water and drain. It is also possible, nowadays, to buy pre-cooked spelt, which reduces the cooking time to 20 minutes or so.

Makes 270g/9½oz, cooked
• 1.5 litres (6½ US cups) water
• 100g (3½oz) buckwheat/kasha
• pinch of salt

BUCKWHEAT

130 CALORIES PER 100G (3½OZ), COOKED

Originating in north-east Asia, buckwheat spread to Europe in the sixteenth century. In Brittany, buckwheat flour established itself as the essential ingredient for making galettes – the flat pancakes that are still much loved today. One of the chief characteristics of buckwheat – which incidentally is related to rhubarb and not to wheat – is that it is gluten-free. Flour aside, buckwheat is also sold in the form of kasha, which is hulled, whole, toasted buckwheat. This is consumed in much the same way as other cereal grains and makes a good alternative to porridge and rice. With a GI of 50, buckwheat contributes well to blood-sugar control. Its high fibre content aids intestinal transit, while its impressive list of nutrients is good for the cardiovascular system.

In a saucepan, bring the water to the boil. Add a pinch of salt and the buckwheat/kasha. Return the water to the boil, then reduce the heat and simmer, uncovered, over a medium heat for about 20 minutes or until tender. Refresh under cold water and drain.

Makes 230g/scant 8oz, cooked
• 1.5 litres (6½ US cups) water
• 100g (3½oz) basmati rice
• pinch of salt

BASMATI RICE

155 CALORIES PER 100G (3½OZ), COOKED

Basmati is a variety of long-grain rice that is traditionally grown in Nepal, India and Pakistan. The name basmati comes from Hindi meaning 'the queen of fragrance'. The rice is prized for its light, fluffy texture. It is assimilated into the body easily, is devoid of gluten and cholesterol, and contains almost no fat. It has a GI of 58.

In a saucepan, bring the water to the boil. Add a pinch of salt and the rice. Return the water to the boil and stir well. Reduce the heat to a brisk simmer and cook, uncovered, for 11 minutes or until cooked to your liking. Drain the rice in a sieve and allow it to stand for 5 minutes before fluffing it with a fork. If you do not want to use the rice immediately, refresh it rapidly under cold water, drain it and set aside.

Makes 220g/8oz, cooked
- 1.5 litres (6½ US cups) water
- 100g (3½oz) red Camargue rice
  pinch of salt

CAMARGUE RED RICE

175 CALORIES PER 100G (3½OZ), COOKED

Cultivated in the wetlands of the Camargue region of southern France, this reddish-brown rice is a short-grained, unmilled, variety with a nutty taste and a chewy texture. Cooking time can vary from 35–45 minutes, depending on the amount of 'bite' desired. Red rice can be cooked as below or like a risotto rice, in other words, by sautéing it in oil or butter first, then adding small amounts of water or stock until the liquid is absorbed. Red rice has more fibre than white rice and also contains vitamins B1, 2 and 3. It has a GI of 50–55.

In a saucepan, bring the water to the boil. Add a pinch of salt and the rice. Return the water to the boil and stir well. Reduce the heat, cover the saucepan and simmer for about 45 minutes, testing after 35 minutes. If you plan to eat the rice more or less straight away, turn off the heat and leave it to stand, covered, for a further 10 minutes or so. If you want to use the rice cold for a salad or set it aside for reheating later, then refresh it rapidly under cold water and drain it.

Makes 300g/11oz, cooked
- 100g (3½oz) quinoa
- 1.5 litres (6½ US cups) water
- pinch of salt

QUINOA

135 CALORIES PER 100G (3½OZ), COOKED

Cultivated on the plains of South America some 5000 years ago, and thought by the Incas to be the 'food of the Gods', quinoa has now become a contemporary 'superfood'. Strictly speaking, it isn't a grain but rather a seed related to the spinach family. However, it looks and tastes like a grain, and its light fluffy texture holds a wealth of proteins, minerals, anti-oxidants and amino acids similar in composition to those found in milk. Quinoa has a low GI rating of about 35.

Rinse the quinoa well in cold water to remove any trace of bitterness in its taste. In a saucepan, bring the water to the boil. Add a pinch of salt and the quinoa. Return the water to the boil, then reduce the heat and simmer, uncovered, for about 20 minutes or until cooked to your liking. Drain, refresh rapidly under cold running water and drain again.

Makes 360g/13oz, cooked
- 1.5 litres (6½ US cups) water
- ½ bay leaf, fresh or dried
- 120g (scant 4½oz) lentils
- pinch of salt

LENTILS
105 CALORIES PER 100G (3½OZ), COOKED

Not strictly a grain, lentils are a pulse and come from a leguminous plant grown for its flattened seeds. Slightly earthy in flavour, lentils contain high levels of protein, which often accounts for their popularity among vegetarians and vegans. They are also a rich source of magnesium, phosphorus, calcium, zinc and iron. With a low GI of between 25 and 30, lentils convert slowly to glucose in the body, which means they satisfy hunger over a long period. This makes them not only an obvious choice for diabetics but a good option for children and pregnant women, who also benefit from the trace elements that lentils contain.

There are various varieties of lentils, notably, green, red, yellow and brown. The much-acclaimed green Puy lentils, prized for their slightly peppery flavour, are cultivated in the Auvergne region of France, around the town of Puy-en-Velay – which is, incidentally, also celebrated for its lace.

Put the water in a saucepan along with the bay leaf and a pinch of salt. Bring the water to the boil and add the lentils. Return the water to the boil, then reduce the heat and simmer, uncovered, over a medium heat for about 35 minutes or until cooked to your liking. Drain and discard the bay leaf. Refresh under cold water and drain again.

PART TWO:
THE ESSENTIAL
CUISINE MINCEUR
RECIPES

- about 300g (11oz) young asparagus spears
- about 1 tsp olive oil
- 70g (2½ oz) onions, finely sliced or chopped
- 70g (2½ oz) white of leek, finely sliced
- 800ml (3½ US cups) chicken stock, either home-made (page 44) or from a cube
- 100ml (⅜ US cup) semi-skimmed (2%) milk
- salt and pepper of your choice

SPRINGTIME GREEN ASPARAGUS SOUP

60 CALORIES PER PERSON
Cooking and preparation: 40 minutes
Level of difficulty: *
Serves 3–4

1. Cut off and discard any tough woody stalks from the asparagus spears and cut the tips to a length of 3cm (1¼ in); set the tips aside. Chop the stalks finely. Heat the olive oil in a saucepan over a gentle heat. Sweat the onions and leeks, uncovered, for about 3 minutes or until they have softened without colouring.

2. Add the chopped asparagus stalks and sweat for a further 3 minutes. Stir in the chicken stock and adjust the seasoning. Cover the saucepan and allow the liquid to simmer gently over a low to medium heat for 25–30 minutes.

3. Remove the saucepan from the heat and, when the mixture is cool enough to handle, ladle it into a food processor and blend it to a smooth purée. Meanwhile, bring the milk to simmering point in a saucepan. Stir the purée and milk together to create the soup. For extra smoothness, pass the soup through a fine sieve. Adjust the seasoning. If the soup is not quite hot enough to serve, reheat it gently in a saucepan, without letting it boil, and keep it warm.

4. Meanwhile, simmer the reserved asparagus tips in lightly salted water for 4–5 minutes. Drain and refresh carefully in cold water, so as not to break them; drain again.

To serve
Transfer the soup to warm serving bowls and garnish with the asparagus tips.

Variation
You can also add a garnish of very thin ribbons of asparagus. To make them, use a very sharp small knife to slice one or two raw asparagus spears into paper-thin slices or ribbons, cutting from the tip to the end. To maintain the colour and shape of the ribbons, barely cover them with water and ice cubes for about 30 minutes. Scatter the ribbons on the soup before serving it.

- 800g (1¾ lb) ripe tomatoes, peeled, cored, deseeded (Terms and Techniques, page 328) and quartered
- 240g (8½ oz) strawberries, hulled
- 1 tsp concentrated tomato paste
- 1 tbsp Xeres vinegar or other sherry vinegar
- 1 tbsp balsamic vinegar
- 1 tsp olive oil
- salt and pepper of your choice

TOMATO AND STRAWBERRY GAZPACHO

75 CALORIES PER PERSON
Cooking and preparation: 20 minutes, plus 1 hour for chilling
Level of difficulty: *
Serves 4

1. Put the tomatoes, strawberries and tomato paste into the bowl of a food processor and blend to a fine purée. For an extra smooth consistency, pass the purée through a sieve – preferably a chinois – set over a mixing bowl.

2. To complete the gazpacho mixture, whisk the following into the tomato and strawberry purée: the sherry vinegar, balsamic vinegar, and the teaspoon of olive oil. Taste, and adjust the seasoning. Cover the gazpacho with clingfilm (plastic wrap) and transfer it to the refrigerator to chill for at least 1 hour.

To serve
Have ready 4 chilled soup bowls set on under-plates. Ladle the chilled gazpacho into the bowls. Garnish with sprigs of basil or the herbs of your choice, or even strawberry leaves. Drizzle over a few drops of olive oil. Finish the decoration with strawberries, either whole or cut in half, then serve.

Chef's tip
This simple but delicious gazpacho can be prepared up to a day in advance.

- about 1 tsp olive oil
- 120g (5oz) onions, finely chopped
- ½ clove of garlic, peeled and crushed
- 1 tsp coriander seeds
- 1 tsp finely chopped lemongrass, tough outer layers removed first
- 800ml (3½ US cups) chicken stock, either home-made (page 44) or from a cube
- 2 small pinches of ground turmeric about 400g (14oz) artichoke hearts, leaves and chokes removed, roughly chopped (frozen and thawed artichoke hearts may be substituted)
- 250ml (1⅛ US cups) semi-skimmed (2%) milk
- salt and pepper of your choice

For the coriander (cilantro) cream
- 1 tbsp fromage blanc or Greek yogurt (0% fat or low-fat)
- 1 tbsp semi-skimmed (2%) milk
- 1 tbsp chopped coriander (cilantro)

ARTICHOKE SOUP WITH LEMONGRASS AND CORIANDER CREAM

70 CALORIES PER PERSON
Cooking and preparation: 50 minutes
Level of difficulty: *
Serves 4

1. Heat the olive oil in a saucepan over gentle heat. Sweat the onions, uncovered, for about 1 minute. Add the garlic, the coriander seeds and the lemongrass, and continue to sweat for 1 minute more or until onions have softened without colouring.

2. Stir in the chicken stock, the turmeric and the artichoke hearts and adjust the seasoning. Bring the mixture to the boil, reduce the heat and simmer gently, covered, for 40 minutes or until the artichoke hearts are very soft and the flavours have combined.

3. While the soup is simmering, prepare the coriander (cilantro) cream for garnishing: in a small bowl, mix together the fromage blanc, the tablespoon of milk and the fresh coriander (cilantro). Stir well and season to taste with salt and pepper. Chill the cream until the soup is ready to serve.

4. When the soup is ready, remove it from the heat. When it is cool enough to handle, ladle it into a food processor and blend it to a smooth purée. Meanwhile, bring the 250ml (1⅛ US cups) of milk to simmering point in a saucepan. Stir the purée and milk together to create the soup. For extra smoothness, pass the soup through a fine sieve. Adjust the seasoning. If the soup is not quite hot enough to serve, reheat it gently in a saucepan, without letting it boil.

To serve
Transfer the soup to warm serving bowls and garnish each with a teaspoon of the coriander (cilantro) cream.

- about 1 tsp olive oil
- 100g (3½oz) onions, finely chopped
- 100g (3½oz) white of leek, finely chopped
- 60g (2oz) fennel, finely chopped
- 1 clove of garlic, peeled and crushed
- 50g (1¾oz) tomato, peeled, cored, deseeded (Terms and Techniques, page 328) and coarsely chopped
- 1 small fresh bouquet garni
- 500ml (2⅛ US cups) chicken stock, either home-made (page 44) or from a cube
- 60g (2oz) potatoes, peeled and chopped
- 200g (7oz) very white dried salt cod, soaked in several changes of cold water for 24 hours, drained on kitchen paper, then cut into large pieces
- pinch of powdered saffron
- salt and pepper of your choice

For the saffron cream garnish
- pinch of powdered saffron
- 1 tbsp semi-skimmed (2%) milk
- 1 tbsp fromage blanc or Greek yogurt (0% fat or low-fat)

A SALT COD SOUP

120 CALORIES PER PERSON
Cooking and preparation: 50 minutes, plus 24 hours to soak the salt cod
Level of difficulty: * *
Serves 4

1. To make the soup, heat the olive oil gently in a saucepan. Add the onion, leek and fennel. Cover the saucepan and sweat the ingredients very gently without colouring for 2–3 minutes. Add the garlic, the tomato, the bouquet garni and the chicken stock. Bring almost to the boil then partially cover the saucepan and simmer for 10 minutes.

2. Add the potatoes, cod and saffron and season lightly with freshly ground pepper. Partially cover the saucepan and let the soup mixture simmer gently for 15 minutes or until the pieces of fish and potato are tender.

3. While the soup mixture is simmering, prepare the saffron cream garnish: mix the saffron and the tablespoon of milk together in a bowl. Stir or whisk in the fromage blanc until all is well blended. Season to taste and set aside in a cold place.

4. Pour the soup mixture into the bowl of a food processor. Scald the 250ml (1⅛ US cups) of milk and remove from the heat. Blend the soup mixture to a purée on a low-speed setting, gradually adding the milk. Taste, and adjust the seasoning.

To serve
Ladle the soup into individual soup bowls. Add a garnish of saffron cream to each serving, floating it on top. Serve straight away.

Variation
You can serve this soup with thin slices of toasted, one-day old, bread, rubbed with the cut side of a piece of garlic and a thick slice of tomato.

- 1 ripe, fragrant, melon, such as a cantaloupe or charentais, weighing about 1kg (2¼lb) handful of basil leaves
- 300g (1⅓ US cups) ice cubes
- 3 tbsp sweet muscat wine, such as Beaumes de-Venise or Moscato
- 3 tbsp freshly squeezed lemon juice
- 2 tbsp olive oil
- salt and pepper of your choice

To garnish
- 5 sprigs of basil

CHILLED MELON AND BASIL SOUP

120 CALORIES PER PERSON
Cooking and preparation: 30 minutes
Level of difficulty: *
Serves 5

1. Cut the melon in half and use a sharp spoon to scrape out the seeds. Using a melon baller, scoop out 25 small balls and set these aside, covered, in the refrigerator, to use as garnish.

2. Preheat the oven to 150°C (300°F, gas mark 2). Remove the remaining flesh from the melon halves with a sharp spoon. Cut the flesh into large dice and transfer to a shallow oven dish. Bake the diced melon flesh in the oven for 15–20 minutes, then remove and set aside to cool.

3. Blend the cooled melon, the basil leaves and the ice cubes together in a food processor. Season to taste. Add the muscat wine, lemon juice and olive oil and adjust the seasoning if necessary. For a very smooth soup, wait until the ice has lost its grainy texture and pass the soup through a fine sieve – preferably a chinois – set over a bowl. Chill the soup until ready to serve.

To serve
Have ready 5 chilled soup bowls. Ladle the chilled soup into the bowls. Garnish each serving with 5 of the reserved melon balls and a sprig of basil. Serve straight away.

- about 1 tsp olive oil
- 60g (2oz) onions, finely sliced or chopped
- 50g (1¾oz) white of leek, split lengthways and sliced into 1cm (½in) lengths
- 180g (scant 6½oz) fresh ceps (porcini), wiped and roughly chopped, or about 90g (scant 3½oz) dried ceps (porcini) soaked in water for 20 minutes, then squeezed and chopped and water set aside (see Chef's tip below), or 180g (scant 6½oz) frozen ceps (porcini) – there is no need to defrost them
- 120g (scant 4½oz) white button mushrooms, wiped and quartered
- 400ml (1¾ US cups) chicken stock, either home-made (page 44) or from a cube
- 300ml (1¼ US cups) semi-skimmed (2%) milk
- salt and pepper of your choice

To garnish (optional)
- about 4 thin slices of cep or the mushroom of your choice, grilled or roasted briefly
- sprinkling of fresh, finely chopped herbs, such as chervil, flat-leaf parsley or chives

AUTUMNAL CEP AND MUSHROOM SOUP

75 CALORIES PER PERSON
Cooking and preparation: 45 minutes
Level of difficulty: *
Serves 4

1. Heat the olive oil in a saucepan over gentle heat. Add the onions and leek and sweat them, covered, for about 2 minutes or until they have softened without colouring. Add the ceps and button mushrooms. Stir for about 3 minutes or until they start to colour. Season but do so lightly, because you will season again after the reduction of the liquid.

2. Stir in the chicken stock (and soaking liquid if you are using dried ceps). Bring the liquid to the boil, then lower the heat, cover the saucepan and maintain a gentle simmer for 30 minutes.

3. Remove the saucepan from the heat and, when the mixture is cool enough to handle, ladle it into a food processor and blend it to a smooth purée. Meanwhile, bring the milk to simmering point in a saucepan. Combine the mushroom purée and the milk, stirring to mix. For extra smoothness, or if leek fibres are present, pass the soup through a fine sieve, preferably a chinois. Adjust the seasoning. If the soup is not quite hot enough to serve, reheat it gently in a saucepan, without letting it boil, and keep it warm.

To serve
Transfer the soup to warm serving bowls or individual small tureens. Garnish as desired and serve.

Chef's tip
If you use dried ceps (porcini), which are now widely available in supermarkets, you can strain the soaking liquid and use it to replace an equivalent quantity of stock.

- 1 whole Savoy cabbage, weighing about 1.5kg (3lb 3oz)
- about 1 tsp olive oil
- 240g (8½oz) duck necks, skin and fat removed
- 150g (5½oz) onions, finely chopped
- 80g (scant 3oz) turnips, finely chopped
- 2 large cloves of garlic, peeled
- 1 small fresh bouquet garni
- 2 litres (8½ US cups) chicken stock, either home-made (page 44) or from a cube
- 1 egg
- 2 tbsp truffle juice (optional)
- salt of your choice

For the truffle cream garnish
- 4 tbsp light whipping cream (30–35% fat)
- 1 tsp black truffle, very finely chopped (optional)

SAVOY CABBAGE SOUP WITH DUCK AND WHIPPED TRUFFLE CREAM

160 CALORIES PER PERSON
Cooking and preparation: 2 hours 45 minutes
Level of difficulty: ***
Serves 5

1. Remove and discard the outer leaves of the cabbage. Remove the remaining leaves, wash them, then cut out and discard the thick white core from each leaf. Set aside 250g (9oz) of the most tender green leaves. Chop the remainder of the leaves coarsely.

2. Heat the olive oil in a saucepan set over a medium heat. Add the duck necks and cook gently until they begin to brown, about 5–8 minutes. Stir in the onions, turnips and garlic along with the bouquet garni and chopped cabbage. Sweat the ingredients, covered, for 4–5 minutes or until the vegetables have softened without colouring.

3. Stir in the chicken stock and bring to a gentle boil. Cover the saucepan and allow the soup to simmer gently over a low to medium heat for about 2 hours, or until the duck meat is very soft and falls off the bone.

4. Remove the saucepan from the heat and carefully remove the duck necks from the soup with a slotted spoon. Use a fork to remove the meat from the bones. Discard the bones and set the meat aside on a plate; cover with clingfilm (plastic wrap). Remove the bouquet garni and cloves of garlic.

5. In a large saucepan of boiling salted water, cook the reserved 250g (9oz) of cabbage leaves for several minutes or until softened, then drain, refresh in iced water and drain again; set aside. When the soup is cool enough to handle, ladle it into a food processor. Add the drained cabbage leaves and blend until smooth.

6. Beat the egg and add it to the soup along with the truffle juice, if used. Blend again. For extra smoothness, pass the soup through a fine sieve, preferably a chinois. Taste, and adjust the seasoning. If the soup is not quite hot enough to serve, reheat it gently in a saucepan, without letting it boil, and keep it warm. Similarly, you can reheat the duck meat in a little stock if it is not hot enough to serve.

7. To prepare the truffle cream garnish, whip the cream to fairly firm peaks. Gently fold in the finely chopped truffle, if used. Season with salt as required.

To serve

Pass the truffle cream between 2 dessertspoons to make oval quenelle shapes. Transfer the soup to warm serving bowls and garnish with the shredded duck meat. Garnish the soup with the quenelles and serve straight away.

Variations

The duck necks can be replaced with duck legs, preferably the confit, preserved, variety that you can buy in jars and cans. Regular duck legs or oxtail can also be substituted. Whatever meat you use, the fat and skin must be removed.

- 450g (1lb) fresh petit pois, shelled (frozen and thawed may be substituted)
- 450ml (2 US cups) waterabout 1 tbsp coarse sea salt
- 1 tsp fructose or the sweetener of your choice (pages 16–20)
- salt and pepper of your choice

For the floating island garnish
- 125g (4½oz) unsweetened evaporated milk
- 2 sheets of leaf gelatine (soaked) or 1½ tsp powdered gelatine (page 22)
- 1 tbsp truffle juice

For the mushroom purée
- 100g (3½oz) white button mushrooms, wiped and coarsely chopped
- ½ tsp olive oil
- 1 tsp finely chopped shallots
- 100ml (⅜ US cup) semi-skimmed (2%) milk

For the vegetable garnish
- 6g (1½ tsp) haricots verts, cut into ½cm (¼in) pieces
- 10g (1 tbsp) small fresh peas (frozen and thawed may be substituted)
- 6g (1½ tsp) mangetout (snow peas), sliced diagonally into small pieces

To garnish (optional)
- few sprigs of fresh herbs such as fennel and chervil, and some tiny leaves of lamb's lettuce and rocket (arugula)

Equipment
- Multi-functional whipper with 2 gas cartridges
- 4 food rings or cutters, 5cm (2in) in diameter

PEA SOUP WITH A TRUFFLE-SCENTED FLOATING ISLAND

165 CALORIES PER PERSON
Cooking and preparation: 45 minutes
Level of difficulty: ***
Serves 4

1. Start by making the floating island garnish; gently heat 25g (scant 1oz) of the evaporated milk in a small saucepan. Once the milk is heated – but before it begins to boil – remove it from the heat. Dissolve and combine the gelatine of your choice with the warm milk. Whisk or stir the milk to ensure the gelatine is dissolved and evenly distributed. Stir in the remaining evaporated milk and the truffle juice. Season with salt. Pour the mixture into the multi-functional whipper, screw on the lid, insert the gas cartridges and chill until the soup is ready to serve.

2. For the soup, put the peas into a food processor and blend them to purée. In a small saucepan, bring to the boil the 450ml (2 US cups) of water, the salt and the fructose. Remove from the heat and, with the food processor on low speed, slowly add this flavoured water to the puréed peas. Blend again for 1 minute. Adjust the seasoning and pass the soup through a very fine sieve, preferably a chinois; set aside either at room temperature or in the refrigerator, depending on your personal taste.

3. For the vegetable garnish, simmer separately, in lightly salted water, the haricots verts for 8 minutes, and the peas and the mangetout (snow peas) for 3 minutes. Drain and refresh the vegetables in iced water and drain again; set aside.

4. For the mushroom purée, put the chopped mushrooms into a food processor and blend for about 10 seconds or until they resemble crumbs. Heat the olive oil gently in a saucepan, add the shallots and sweat them for about 30 seconds or until they have softened without colouring. Add the mushrooms, season, and cook for a minute or so, stirring with a wooden spoon. Stir in the milk and simmer gently for a further 5 minutes, uncovered. Remove the purée from the heat, adjust the seasoning and keep it warm, preferably in a bain-marie.

To serve

Ideally, use serving plates with a shallow bowl and a wide rim. Put a food ring in the middle of each plate and fill its centre with the creamy mixture from the whipper. Tap each ring to ensure that the mixture is evenly distributed, then smooth the top.

Distribute the vegetable garnish around each ring. Carefully ladle the pea soup over the vegetable garnish. If your serving plates have a rim, decorate the rims with fresh herbs and leaves. Just before serving, carefully lift away the food rings. At the table, delicately spoon some of the warm mushroom purée on top of each creamy island.

Chef's tip

This pea soup can be served chilled, hot or at room temperature, depending on personal taste. The mushroom purée, however, should always be served hot to make a delicious contrast to the chilled floating island.

- 1 celery stick (stalk), weighing about 20g (¾oz)
- 150g (5½oz) onion, finely chopped
- 2 cloves
- 5 black peppercorns
- 1 tsp olive oil
- 500ml (2⅛ US cups) chicken stock, either home-made (page 44) or from a cube
- ¼ vanilla pod (bean) split
- 850g (1¾lb) pumpkin (squash), such as acorn or butternut squash, peeled, deseeded and cut into chunks
- 1 litre (4¼ US cups/1 quart) semi skimmed (2%) milk
- pinch of freshly grated nutmeg
- salt and pepper of your choice

For the cream
- 2 tbsp fromage blanc or Greek yogurt (0% fat or low-fat)
- 3 tbsp semi-skimmed (2%) milk

To garnish (optional)
- few sprigs of coriander (cilantro), optional
- vanilla pods (beans) for decoration, optional

VANILLA-INFUSED PUMPKIN SOUP

130 CALORIES PER PERSON
Cooking and preparation: 45 minutes
Level of difficulty: *
Serves 6–7

1. To make the soup, remove and discard any tough fibres from the celery using a vegetable peeler. Finely chop the celery and set it aside briefly with the finely chopped onion.

2. Make a spice bag by putting the cloves and black peppercorns in a small piece of muslin and tying it with kitchen string; set aside.

3. Set a large saucepan over a low to medium heat, add the oil and, when this is warm, add the celery and onion. Sweat these ingredients, uncovered, for about 3 minutes or until soft without colouring. Add the chicken stock and the spice bag. Bring to a low boil, cover and simmer for 5 minutes, then remove from the heat and set aside.

4. Scrape the seeds from the vanilla pod (bean) and set them aside for the accompanying cream. Put the emptied vanilla pod (bean) in the saucepan along with the pumpkin, onion and celery. Add the milk, nutmeg, and salt to taste. Bring to the boil, reduce the heat and simmer, partially covered, for about 30 minutes, or until you can insert a small knife in the pumpkin without resistance.

5. While the pumpkin simmers, prepare the accompanying cream: mix together with a wooden spoon the fromage blanc (or Greek yogurt), the milk and the reserved vanilla seeds, until well blended. Season to taste and set aside in the refrigerator.

6. When the soup is ready, remove it from the heat. When it is cool enough to handle, discard the spice bag and the vanilla pod (bean). Using a food processor or blender, purée the soup in small batches. For an extra-smooth consistency, pass the soup through a very fine sieve, preferably a chinois. Taste, and adjust the seasoning. Return the soup to a saucepan and heat through before serving.

To serve
Have ready 4 warm soup bowls or cups, ideally on under-plates. Ladle the warm soup into the bowls and spoon the accompanying cream into the centre of each. If you like, garnish each under-plate with a few sprigs of coriander (cilantro) and a couple of vanilla pods (beans). Serve immediately.

- 1 tsp olive oil
- 200g (7oz) onion, sliced or cut into fine strips
- 500g (1lb 2oz) carrots, peeled and sliced into rounds
- 1½ litres (6⅓ US cups) chicken stock, either home-made (page 44) or from a cube
- 1 orange, peel and pith removed and segments separated from their membranes
- 1 small fresh bouquet garni
- 250ml (1⅛ US cups) semi-skimmed (2%) milk
- salt and pepper of your choice

For the orange cream
- 3 tbsp freshly squeezed orange juice
- 2 tbsp fromage blanc or Greek yogurt (0% or low-fat)
- 3 tbsp semi-skimmed (2%) milk

To garnish
- sprinkling of finely chopped fresh herbs, such as chervil or coriander (cilantro)

ZESTY CARROT AND ORANGE SOUP WITH AN ORANGE CREAM

95 CALORIES PER PERSON
Cooking and preparation time: 50 minutes
Level of difficulty: *
Serves 6

1. To make the soup, heat the olive oil in a large saucepan set over a low heat. Add the onion and sweat it, uncovered, for about 1 minute or until soft but not coloured. Add the carrots, stir them briefly, then cover the saucepan and cook for 4 minutes, stirring occasionally.

2. Add the chicken stock, the orange segments and the bouquet garni. Season lightly. Cover and simmer for about 40 minutes or until the carrots are soft.

3. While the soup is cooking, prepare the orange cream. In a small saucepan set over a low to medium heat, bring the orange juice to a fairly gentle simmer and reduce it by half. Transfer it to a bowl and when the juice is cold, whisk in the fromage blanc and the 3 tablespoons of cold milk until blended to a smooth cream. Season to taste, then cover the cream with clingfilm (plastic wrap) and chill it until you are ready to serve.

4. When the soup is almost ready, heat the milk gently in a small saucepan or in the microwave until very hot but not boiling. Remove the soup from the heat and remove and discard the bouquet garni. Using a food processor or blender, purée the soup in small batches, adding the milk a little at a time until it is incorporated. If the soup is not quite hot enough to serve, reheat it gently in a saucepan, without letting it boil.

To serve
Have ready 6 warm soup bowls or large cups set on under-plates. Ladle the soup into each and distribute the chilled orange cream on top. A sprinkling of fresh chopped herbs, such as chervil or coriander (cilantro), makes an attractive addition to the orange cream.

- about 1 tsp olive oil
- 150g (5½oz) onion, finely chopped or sliced
- ½ clove of garlic, peeled and crushed
- about 650g (1lb 7oz) aubergine (eggplant), peeled and sliced into ½cm (¼in) rounds
- 1 litre (4¼ US cups/1 quart) semi-skimmed (2%) milk
- 3 basil leaves
- salt and pepper of your choice

For the basil cream
- 1 tbsp fromage blanc or Greek yogurt (0% fat or low-fat)
- 2 tbsp semi-skimmed (2%) milk
- 3 basil leaves, chopped or finely snipped

VELOUTÉ OF AUBERGINE WITH A BASIL CREAM

115 CALORIES PER PERSON
Cooking and preparation: 50 minutes
Level of difficulty: *
Serves 6

1. To make the soup, heat the olive oil in a large saucepan. Add the onion and sweat it, uncovered, for 3 minutes or until it has softened without colouring. Add the crushed garlic and sweat it, stirring, for 1 minute. Stir in the sliced aubergine (eggplant), then season to taste.

2. Pour in the milk and add the basil leaves. Bring the liquid briefly to the boil and then reduce the heat to let the soup simmer gently, partially covered, for 30–40 minutes or until the aubergine (eggplant) is very soft without having fallen apart.

3. While the soup is cooking, prepare the basil cream. In a small bowl, mix together the fromage blanc, the milk, and the finely chopped basil leaves. Season and chill until the soup is ready to serve.

4. When the aubergines (eggplants) are tender, remove the mixture from the heat and, when it is cool enough to handle, ladle it into a food processor. To complete the soup, blend the mixture to a smooth purée. For extra smoothness, and to remove any remaining fibres, pass the soup through a fine sieve, preferably a chinois. Adjust the seasoning. If the soup is not quite hot enough to serve, reheat it gently in a saucepan, without letting it boil, and keep it warm.

To serve
Have ready 6 warm soup bowls. Ladle the soup into the bowls and garnish each with a little of the basil cream, swirling it on top. Serve straight away.

Variation
To add a different nuance to the soup, you might like to give the aubergines (eggplants) a smoky flavour prior to their being peeled and simmered. To do this, heat the grill to very hot. Slice the aubergines (eggplants) in half lengthways, then grill them, skin-side up, for 25 minutes, turning occasionally so the skin becomes evenly scorched. Or you might prefer the alternative method of skewering an aubergine (eggplant) and roasting it directly over the heat of the hob until the skin blisters.

- 500ml (2⅛ US cups) Pondicherry Indian Stock (page 50)
- 250ml (1⅛ US cup) semi-skimmed (2%) milk
- 1 tbsp cornflour (cornstarch), mixed with a little cold water
- seeds from ¼ vanilla pod (bean)
- pinch of curry powder
- 250g (9oz) small squid (calamari)
- salt and pepper of your choice

To garnish
- 1 tbsp finely snipped chives
- 20 small tarragon leaves, plus a few sprigs as desired

CALAMARI IN A CURRY-SCENTED VELOUTÉ

90 CALORIES PER PERSON
Cooking and preparation: 30 minutes
Level of difficulty: **
Serves 4

1. To make the velouté, bring the Pondicherry Indian Stock to the boil in a large saucepan. Lower the heat and add the milk, stirring to blend. Add the cornflour (cornstarch) and continue to stir until well combined. Pass through a fine sieve set over a bowl, then return the velouté to the saucepan.

2. Add the vanilla seeds and the curry powder and season with salt and pepper. Bring the velouté briefly to the boil then cover the saucepan and remove from the heat. Set aside to allow the flavours to infuse.

3. Meanwhile, prepare the squid by removing the tentacles from the body with a small sharp knife. Wash the squid under cold water and drain it in a colander. Cut the body of the squid into rings, 3–4cm (1¼–1½in) thick. If the tentacles are large, cut them in half.

4. Sprinkle a good pinch of fine salt on the bottom of a dry heavy-based frying or sauté pan. Set the pan over medium heat and, when it is hot, add the squid. Sauté the squid rapidly, shaking the pan to move the squid and cook them evenly. When, after 2–3 minutes, the rings begin to curl at the sides and become opaque, remove the squid from the heat, drain off the juices and set aside.

To serve
When you are almost ready to serve, reheat the velouté gently in its saucepan and adjust the seasoning. Remove it from the heat and, using a stick blender, blend the velouté until it is frothy. Divide it between 4 warm serving bowls. Arrange the squid in the centre of each bowl and scatter snipped chives and tarragon leaves on top.

- about 1 tsp olive oil
- 1 tbsp finely chopped onion
- 90g (scant 3½oz) white of leek, finely sliced
- 200ml (⅞ US cup) water
- 1 small fresh bouquet garni
- 175g (6oz) potatoes, peeled and finely chopped
- 150ml (¾ US cup) semi-skimmed (2%) milk
- 50g (1¾oz) herring or lumpfish roe
- 1 tbsp freshly squeezed lime juice
- salt and pepper of your choice

For the salmon tartare
- 225g (8oz) fresh salmon, cut into 5mm (¼in) dice
- 25g (scant 1oz) smoked salmon, cut into 5mm (¼in) dice
- 1 tbsp snipped chives
- ½ tsp finely chopped dill
- 1 tbsp freshly squeezed lime juice

To garnish
- 1 spear of asparagus, peeled and sliced lengthways into paper-thin ribbons
- 5 sprigs of salad burnet (Sanguisorba minor) or mint
- 5 sprigs of chervil or flat-leaf parsley
- 10 small frisée leaves
- 25g (scant 1oz) herring or lumpfish roe (optional)

Equipment
- 5 food rings, 6cm (2½in) in diameter

CHILLED VICHYSSOISE WITH A CAVIAR AND SALMON TARTARE

165 CALORIES PER PERSON
Cooking and preparation: 50 minutes
Level of difficulty: ***
Serves 5

1. To make the vichyssoise, heat the olive oil gently in a saucepan. Add the onion, stir it briefly, then add the leek. Sweat the ingredients, uncovered, for about 2 minutes or until soft but not coloured. Add the water and the bouquet garni, then simmer, covered, for about for 8–10 minutes. Add the potatoes and the milk, season lightly and simmer gently for a further 10 minutes or until you can easily insert a knife a knife into a piece of potato.

2. Remove the saucepan from the heat; discard the bouquet garni. When the mixture is cool enough to handle, ladle it into a food processor and blend to a smooth purée. To complete the vichyssoise, pour the purée into a bowl and chill it, either over ice or in the refrigerator. When the vichyssoise is very cold, gently stir in the herring roe and the lime juice. Taste the vichyssoise, adjust the seasoning, then transfer it to the refrigerator until you are ready to serve it.

3. To make the salmon tartare, combine the diced fresh and smoked salmon in a small bowl. Add the chives, dill and lime juice and stir together gently with a fork. Taste, adjust the seasoning, then transfer to the refrigerator.

4. To make the garnish, fill a small shallow dish with a few cups of cold water and some ice cubes. Add the paper-thin ribbons of asparagus, to preserve their colour and make them curl slightly. Add the herbs and leaves you are using for a garnish, to make them crisp and cold. Drain these items just before serving the vichyssoise.

To serve
Have ready 5 chilled soup plates with a food ring placed in the centre of each. Distribute the salmon tartare between the rings, filling them evenly. Ladle or spoon the chilled vichyssoise around the rings. Carefully lift away the rings and decorate the tartare with the chilled, drained garnish. For an additional flourish, you can, if you like, put a little extra herring or lumpfish roe on top of the tartare.

- 10g (¼oz) tapioca
- 15g (½oz) pitted green olives
- 1 tbsp finely chopped flat-leaf parsley
- 1 tbsp finely chopped basil
- 1 tbsp freshly squeezed lime juice
- 200g (7oz) fillet of salmon
- salt and pepper of your choice

To garnish
- about 5 tbsp Thai Vinaigrette (page 68)
- few small handfuls of mesclun salad leaves
  or other salad leaves of your choice
- fleur de sel
- 1 tbsp dill sprigs
- wedges of lemon

CARPACCIO OF SALMON WITH OLIVES AND TAPIOCA

105 CALORIES PER PERSON
Cooking and preparation: 30 minutes, plus 3 hours of resting
Level of difficulty: **
Serves 5

1. Cook the tapioca in simmering water for about 10 minutes, or for the time recommended on the packet instructions. Drain, refresh in cold water and drain again. Transfer the tapioca to a mixing bowl and add the olives, parsley and basil. Stir in the lime juice. Mix well and season to taste with salt and pepper; set aside.

2. To prepare the salmon, place it on a wooden board. Using a long, thin, well-sharpened knife, slice the salmon lengthways into the thinnest possible slices. Arrange the slices side by side – with the long edges towards you – on a sheet of aluminium foil, leaving a border of foil of about 4cm (1½in).

3. Season the salmon to taste with salt and pepper, then coat with the olive and tapioca mixture. Roll up the coated salmon tightly, using the aluminium foil to help you to fold the salmon over itself. Carefully close or twist the ends. Put the aluminium roll in the freezer for 2–3 hours.

To serve
Use about 1 tablespoon of the Thai Vinaigrette to brush the bottom of 5 serving plates. Remove the salmon roll from the freezer and undo the aluminium foil. Use an electric carving knife or a normal sharp knife to cut the salmon roll into thin slices. These should resemble petals of about 1mm (1/16in) thickness.

Transfer the 'petals' to each plate, arranging them in a circle and overlapping them slightly, to form a 'flower'. Use a little more of the Thai Vinaigrette to brush the salmon lightly; use the remainder to dress the salad leaves. Add a pinch of fleur de sel and scatter with the dressed salad leaves. Serve accompanied by the sprigs of dill and lemon wedges.

For the filling

- 1 tsp olive oil
- 10g (¼oz) onion, finely chopped
- 10g (¼oz) sweet green (bell) pepper, peeled and cut into 3mm (⅛in) dice
- 10g (¼oz) sweet red (bell) pepper, peeled and cut into 3mm (⅛in) dice
- 40g (scant 1½oz) courgette (zucchini), cut into 3mm (⅛in) dice
- 30g (1oz) tomato, peeled, cored, deseeded (Terms and Techniques, page 328) and cut into 3mm (⅛in) dice
- 25g (scant 1oz) Light Mayonnaise (page 79)
- 1 tsp finely chopped tarragon
- 1 tsp finely chopped chives
- drop of Tabasco sauce
- 2 tsp fromage blanc or Greek yogurt (0% fat or low-fat)
- 80g (scant 3oz) crabmeat (fresh, conserved in a jar, or frozen and thawed), flaked
- salt and pepper of your choice

For the dough

- 1 litre (4¼ US cups/1 quart) water about 20g (¾oz) pasta dough for ravioli in a sheet, about 15 x 15cm (6 x 6in), or pre-cut into rectangles

For the sauce

- 100g (3½oz) passion-fruit juice
- 2 black peppercorns
- ½ –1 tsp peeled and finely grated fresh ginger
- 1 tsp fructose or the sweetener of your choice (pages 16–20)
- 1 tsp cornflour (cornstarch), mixed with a little cold water

To garnish

- handful of small young salad leaves
- few sprigs of seasonal herbs

CRAB CANNELLONI WITH A PASSION-FRUIT SAUCE

150 CALORIES PER PERSON
Cooking and preparation: 30 minutes, plus 30 minutes chilling time
Level of difficulty: * *
Serves 3

1. To make the filling for the cannelloni, coat the bottom of a saucepan with the oil and, over a gentle heat, sweat the chopped onion, covered, for 30 seconds. Add the green and red (bell) peppers. After 1 minute, add the courgettes (zucchini). After 2 minutes, add the tomato. Sweat everything together for a further 1 minute. Season with salt and pepper, then transfer the vegetables to a small bowl and leave them to become completely cold.

2. In a separate large mixing bowl, stir together the Light Mayonnaise, the chopped tarragon and chives, the Tabasco sauce and the fromage blanc. Add the flaked crabmeat and the cold vegetable mixture. Stir with a fork until the ingredients form a well-blended mixture. Adjust the seasoning and set the filling aside in the refrigerator.

3. To prepare the sauce, put the passion-fruit juice, the black peppercorns, ginger and fructose into a small saucepan. Bring to the boil, stirring, then mix in the cornflour (cornstarch) blended with water. Season with salt to taste. Simmer the sauce for a few minutes then strain it through a fine sieve – preferably a chinois.

4. To prepare the dough, bring 1 litre (4¼ US cups/1 quart) lightly salted water to the boil. Add the pasta dough and simmer it according to instructions – usually for about 3 minutes. Drain and refresh the dough in cold water and drain again on kitchen paper. If the dough is not already cut to rectangles of a suitable size, then cut it now – ideally into 2 rectangles, each 15 x 7½cm (6 x 3in).

5. Cut 2 rectangles of clingfilm (plastic wrap) at least 10cm (4in) longer than the long edge of the dough. Lay these out on the work counter. Lay the rectangles of dough on top. Arrange the filling along the long edge of each rectangle, leaving a small border. Roll up the dough around the filling, using the clingfilm (plastic wrap) to help the rolling process and to hold the cannelloni together. Twist the ends of the clingfilm (plastic wrap) like a Christmas cracker and secure them, using string if needed. To firm the filling and make cutting easier, chill the cannelloni in the refrigerator for about 30 minutes.

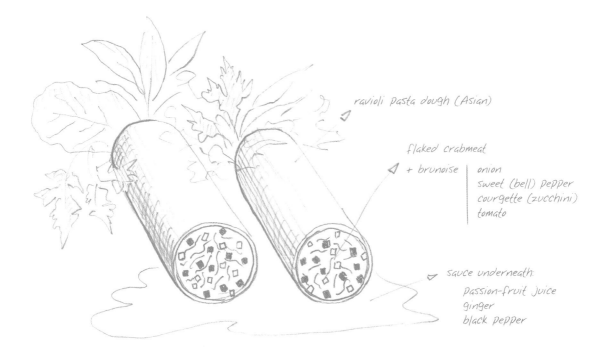

ravioli pasta dough (Asian)

flaked crabmeat

+ brunoise | onion
sweet (bell) pepper
courgette (zucchini)
tomato

sauce underneath:
passion-fruit juice
ginger
black pepper

To serve

Remove the clingfilm (plastic wrap) from the cannelloni and cut each one into 3 equal portions. Arrange 2 portions on each serving plate. Surround the portions with a little pool of the passion-fruit sauce. Garnish with some small young salad leaves and a few seasonal herbs.

Chef's tip

This recipe for cannelloni has been achieved using pasta dough intended for ravioli, which is finer and more delicate than the dough traditionally associated with cannelloni. You can make ravioli dough yourself, of course, or you can buy it, either from an Italian or an Asian grocer.

- 650g (1lb 7oz) courgettes (zucchini)
- 1 tsp olive oil
- sprig of thyme
- 1 bay leaf
- 1 clove of garlic, unpeeled and crushed
- 80g (scant 3oz) Tomato Confit (page 81)
- 8 basil leaves, snipped or chopped
- salt and pepper of your choice

For the black olive coulis
- 50g (1¾oz) unpitted black olives
- 40ml (scant ¼ US cup) water
- 60g (2oz) petits-suisses, fromage blanc
  or Greek yogurt (0% fat)

For the garnish and accompaniment
- 12 shavings of Parmesan
- few small salad leaves
- 4 slices of toasted bread

COURGETTE QUENELLES WITH BLACK OLIVE COULIS
135 CALORIES PER PERSON
Cooking and preparation: 45 minutes
Level of difficulty: *
Serves 4

1. To prepare the courgettes (zucchini), remove about half of their peel in long strips, working lengthways with a peeler or sharp knife to achieve a striped effect of alternating green peel and pale flesh.

2. Preheat the oven to 180°C (355°F, gas mark 4). Brush a gratin dish with olive oil. Arrange the courgettes (zucchini) in the dish in a single layer; add salt, pepper, thyme, bay leaf and the crushed garlic. Transfer the dish to the hot oven.

3. After 10 minutes, turn the courgettes (zucchini) over. After a further 10 minutes, turn them again and cover them with aluminium foil. After a further 10 minutes, test the courgettes (zucchini) for doneness: a knife inserted into them should meet no resistance. If they are not quite ready, continue to cook them, turning occasionally, until they are done, then remove them from the oven. Discard the herbs and garlic and set aside.

4. While the courgettes (zucchini) are being baked, prepare the black olive coulis: cut each olive in half and remove its stone (pit). Set the halves of olive flesh aside and put the stones (pits) in a small saucepan with the water. Bring to the boil then remove from the heat, cover, and leave the stones (pits) to infuse for at least 20 minutes.

5. Half-fill a separate small saucepan with water and bring it to the boil. Plunge the halves of olive flesh into the boiling water for few seconds, then drain them. Strain the infusion of olive stones (pits) and put the infused water in a food processor, along with the drained olives and the petits-suisses. Blend to a coulis, adjust the seasoning and set aside in the refrigerator.

6. Put the cooked courgettes (zucchini), in a mixing bowl and crush them with a fork. Stir in the Tomato Confit and the basil. Adjust the seasoning.

To serve
Divide the black olive coulis between 4 serving plates, preferably with a shallow bowl. Pass the courgette (zucchini) mixture between 2 dessertspoons to make oval quenelle shapes. Slide the quenelles onto each plate on top of the coulis. Add shavings of Parmesan and a few small salad leaves. Serve cold with toasted bread.

- 160g (5½oz) fillets of whiting (or brill, bass, plaice, halibut, salmon or red snapper), skinned
- 160g (5½oz) firm mango flesh
- 1 tbsp Asian Lime Vinaigrette (page 65)
- ¼ large Granny Smith apple or other firm-fleshed apple
- 1 tbsp chives, snipped into 2cm (¾in) lengths
- 1 tbsp snipped chervil leaves
- 2–3 mint leaves, finely chopped or snipped
- salt and pepper of your choice

For the marinade
- 2 tbsp freshly squeezed lime juice
- ½ tsp peeled and grated fresh ginger
- 3 drops of Tabasco sauce

To garnish
- few small mixed salad leaves or sprigs of lamb's lettuce.

Equipment
- 4 food rings, 6cm (2½in) in diameter

CEVICHE OF WHITE FISH WITH MANGO AND GINGER

70 CALORIES PER PERSON
Cooking and preparation: 20 minutes, plus chilling of at least 30 minutes
Level of difficulty: *
Serves 4

1. Cut the fillets of fish and the mango flesh into 1cm (½in) dice. Put the dice into a shallow ceramic, glass or porcelain dish that does not react to citrus juice. Spread the fish and mango in a single layer. If you are not serving the ceviche in the next 35 minutes or so, cover the dish and refrigerate it until it is time to add the marinade. (If you marinate the fish for too long, its texture will become flabby.)

2. About 35 minutes before you want to eat the ceviche, prepare its marinade: whisk together the lime juice, grated ginger and Tabasco sauce in a small bowl. Taste, and add salt if desired. Pour this marinade over the diced fish and mango, ensuring that the food is evenly coated. Cover the ceviche and chill it for 30 minutes before serving.

3. About 10 minutes before you want to serve, complete the elements of the assembly: have ready the Asian Lime Vinaigrette in a small bowl. Core the apple, leaving the skin on if you wish. Cut the flesh into small matchsticks of about 2 x ½cm (¾ x ¼in) and drop them immediately into the vinaigrette to prevent the apple from browning. Add the chives and chervil to the bowl and stir. Place a food ring in the centre of each serving plate.

4. About 5 minutes before you are ready to eat, remove the ceviche from the refrigerator and allow it to come to room temperature. Gently mix in the mint.

To serve
Spoon the ceviche into the rings. Top with the apple, herb and vinaigrette mixture. Carefully remove the rings. Decorate with a few salad leaves or sprigs of lamb's lettuce.

Variations
Just before you serve the ceviche, you can add a tablespoon of pomegranate seeds, which will lend a beautiful colour to the white fish. Many variations on the theme of ceviche are possible: for example, you can replace the whiting used here with plaice, brill, bass, halibut, salmon or scallops. Although you can dice the fish, as I have, you can also slice it very thinly, but if you do this, freeze the fish for about 10 minutes before attempting it, and slice it with an ultra-sharp knife.

A gastronomic titbit
A ceviche is essentially raw fish 'cooked' in a marinade of citrus juice. It is popular in coastal regions of the Americas, particularly Central and South America. It goes without saying that the freshness of the fish used in a ceviche is all-important.

- 200g (7oz) celeriac, cut into 1–2cm (⅜ –¾in) dice
- 100ml (⅜ US cup) semi-skimmed (2%) milk
- 1 sheet of leaf gelatine (soaked) or ¾ tsp powdered gelatine (page 22)
- 80g (scant 3oz) light whipping cream (30–35%) fat
- 1 large egg white, about 40g (scant 1½oz)
- salt and pepper of your choice

For the crispy vegetables
- 1 carrot, peeled
- ½ celery stick (stalk)
- 2 asparagus spears, tips removed
- 2 long radishes

For the dressing
- ½ beaten egg yolk
- 1 tsp Xeres vinegar or other sherry vinegar of your choice
- 2 tbsp Light Vinaigrette (page 70)
- 10g (1½oz) chopped herbs of your choice, or chopped black truffles
- about 1 tsp truffle juice (optional)

Equipment
- Steamer or couscoussier

CELERIAC MOUSSE WITH A GARDEN OF CRISPY VEGETABLES

CALORIE COUNT
Cooking and preparation: 50 minutes
Level of difficulty: **
Serves 4

1. To make the mousse, steam the diced celeriac in a steamer or couscoussier for 20–25 minutes or until tender. Transfer the celeriac to a food processor and blend to a smooth purée; set aside in a large mixing bowl.

2. In a saucepan, scald the milk without letting it boil. Remove from the heat; season with salt and pepper. Let the milk cool slightly. Dissolve and combine the gelatine of your choice with the warm milk, whisking to ensure the gelatine is incorporated smoothly. Stir the stiffened milk gradually into the celeriac purée, stirring well to blend. Set aside to cool while you prepare the remaining elements of the mousse.

3. In a bowl, beat the cream until it holds a soft but distinct peak on the whisk. In a separate bowl, beat the egg white to a soft peak stage. Incorporate the whisked cream into the celeriac purée, lifting the purée and folding it over the cream, until well blended. Fold in the egg white in a similar way. Taste, and adjust the seasoning. Make a bed of celeriac mousse in the bottom of 4 serving plates with a shallow bowl shape.

4. For the crispy vegetables, cut the carrot and celery into matchsticks 5cm (2in) long and ½cm (¼in) wide. With a very sharp small knife, cut the asparagus and radish lengthways into paper-thin ribbons and immerse these in iced water to make them crisp and firm.

5. For the dressing, mix the beaten egg yolk with the vinegar, the Light Vinaigrette and the herbs. For added luxury, you can replace the herbs with the same quantity of black truffle and add about 1 teaspoon of truffle juice.

To serve
Remove the plates of celeriac mousse from the refrigerator. Insert the raw vegetables into each bed of mousse, arranging them like a mini-garden. Drizzle over a spoonful of the dressing and serve the rest separately in a sauce boat.

- 1kg (2¼lb) mussels, scrubbed and debearded
- 1 litre (4¼ US cups/1 quart) water
- 30g (1oz) coarse sea salt
- 1 sheet of leaf gelatine (soaked) or 1 scant tsp powdered gelatine (page 22)
- salt and pepper of your choice

For the escabeche sauce
- about 1 tbsp olive oil
- 200g (7oz) shells taken from prawns, langoustines or Dublin Bay prawns (shrimp, crawfish or jumbo shrimp)
- 50g (1¾oz) onion, finely chopped
- 1 clove of garlic, unpeeled and crushed
- 5 black peppercorns
- ½ bay leaf
- pinch of chilli powder
- 50ml (¼ US cup or 6 tbsp) Xeres vinegar or other sherry vinegar of your choice
- 500ml (2⅛ US cups) water
- 1 tsp cornflour (cornstarch) mixed with 1 tbsp Xeres vinegar or other sherry vinegar of your choice

For the vegetable mixture
- 100g (3½oz) carrots, cut into ½cm (¼in) dice
- 100g (3½oz) young courgettes (zucchini), cut into ½cm (¼in) dice
- 50g (1¾oz) red (bell) pepper, stalk and seeds removed and cut into ½cm (¼in) dice
- about 1 tsp olive oil

ESCABECHE OF MUSSELS WITH AN OCEAN-SCENTED JELLY

105 CALORIES PER PERSON
Cooking and preparation: 50 minutes, plus 1 hour of resting
Level of difficulty: * *
Serves 5

1. To make the escabeche sauce, put the olive oil in a large saucepan set over a medium heat. Add the shells of the shellfish along with the onion and garlic, and cook for 5 minutes or until the shells are lightly coloured. Add the black peppercorns, bay leaf and chilli powder. Increase the heat, add the sherry vinegar and the 500ml (2⅛ US cups) of water. Bring to the boil and scrape the bottom of the saucepan to deglaze it.

2. Salt the mixture lightly then adjust the heat to maintain a gentle simmer for 20 minutes. Pass the mixture though a fine sieve – preferably a chinois – set over a saucepan. Stir in the cornflour (cornstarch) mixed with 1 tablespoon of the sherry vinegar. Adjust the seasoning. Leave the sauce to cool then set it aside in the refrigerator.

3. To prepare the vegetable mixture, bring lightly salted water to the boil and simmer the carrots and courgettes (zucchini) in separate batches until al dente – about 5 minutes for the carrots and about 3 minutes for the courgettes (zucchini). Drain and refresh the vegetables in cold water, then drain again and set aside in a cold place.

4. Put the red (bell) pepper in a separate saucepan coated with 1 tsp olive oil. Cover the pan and sweat the red (bell) pepper over very gentle heat for 5 minutes, shaking the pan or stirring frequently. Remove from the heat and set aside to cool.

5. To cook the mussels, put the 1 litre (4¼ US cups/1 quart) of water and the coarse sea salt in a large saucepan and bring it to the boil. Add the mussels in batches of 8–10 at a time, removing each batch when they open, after about 5 minutes.

6. Using a straining spoon, transfer the opened mussels to a dish, keeping the cooking liquid. When the mussels are cool enough to handle, remove them from their shells, taking care not to damage their flesh and reserving the juices. Set the mussels aside.

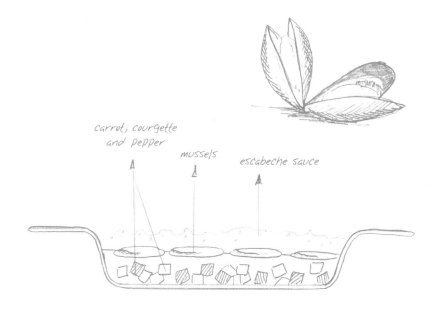

carrot, courgette and pepper

mussels

escabeche sauce

7. Measure out 100ml (⅜ US cup) of the mussel juices. Put this in saucepan with 100ml (⅜ US cup) of the cooking liquid. Warm the combined liquids over a very gentle heat, taking care not to overheat or boil it. Taste, and adjust the seasoning. Dissolve and combine the gelatine of your choice with the warm mussel liquid, whisking to ensure the gelatine is smoothly combined. Put the mixture in a bowl and chill it for about 1 hour or until it acquires a slippery consistency without setting completely.

8. To assemble the dish, have ready serving plates with shallow bowls. Combine the carrots, courgette (zucchini) and red (bell) pepper and distribute this mixture in the bottom of the plates. Add the stiffened mussel juice and arrange the mussels on top. Use a brush to coat the mussels with a little of the jelly. Put the plates to chill in the refrigerator for at least 1 hour.

To serve
Remove the escabeche sauce from the refrigerator and whisk it, preferably with a stick blender, to emulsify it. Put a little over each serving and offer the remainder in a sauce boat. If you put the serving plates on under-plates, you can decorate the under-plates with sprigs of lamb's lettuce and some chopped celery leaves.

A gastronomic titbit
Escabeche originated in Spain, where it refers to a wide range of marinades and pickling agents for various ingredients. Originally, it was closely associated with fresh fish – sardines, for example – which were put in a marinade as soon as their heads had been removed. Nowadays, an escabeche can just as easily refer to a vinegar-based sauce, sometimes flavoured with garlic, or it can even indicate a method of preparing fish whereby it is grilled first and then marinated afterwards.

- 60g (2oz) small courgettes (zucchini), cut into 3mm (⅛in) dice
- 2 tbsp Light Mayonnaise (page 79)
- 2 tbsp fromage blanc or Greek yogurt (0% fat or low-fat)
- 1 tbsp freshly squeezed lime juice
- 2 tbsp finely chopped flat-leaf parsley
- 3 drops of Tabasco sauce
- about ½ tsp wasabi paste, to taste
- pinch of curry powder
- 160g (5½oz) crabmeat (fresh or frozen and thawed; either spider or king crab, or the crabmeat of your choice)
- salt and pepper of your choice

For the pink grapefruit jelly
- 200ml (⅞ US cup) pink grapefruit juice
- 2 sheets of leaf gelatine (soaked) or 1½ tsp powdered gelatine (page 22)
- about ¼ Granny Smith apple peeled, cored, and cut into tiny matchsticks 2 x ½cm (¾ x ¼in)

For the citrus mousse
- 1 orange, peel and pith removed
- 1 lemon, peel and pith removed
- 1 tsp coriander seeds
- 1 large basil leaf
- 4 tbsp Light Vinaigrette (page 70)
- 1 sheet of leaf gelatine (soaked) or ¾ tsp powdered gelatine (page 22)

To garnish
- 16 long matchsticks of Granny Smith apple (optional)
- small sprigs of fresh seasonal herbs
- selection of small salad leaves
- few edible flowers such as pansies, borage, courgette (zucchini) or citrus blossom

Equipment
- Multi-functional whipper with 1 gas cartridge
- 4 food rings, 6cm (2½in) in diameter and 3cm (1¼in) high

SPICED CRAB ON PINK GRAPEFRUIT JELLY WITH A CITRUS MOUSSE

115 CALORIES PER PERSON
Cooking and preparation: 30 minutes, plus 2 hours of resting
Level of difficulty: * *
Serves 4

1. To make the pink grapefruit jelly, heat about 3 tablespoons of the pink grapefruit juice in a small saucepan, taking care not to allow it to boil. Dissolve and combine the gelatine of your choice with the warm juice. Whisk well to ensure the gelatine is completely dissolved. Season to taste.

2. Select 4 serving plates with a shallow bowl. Arrange about 10 small matchsticks of apple in the bottom of each bowl. Gently spoon over the setting, but still liquid, pink grapefruit jelly and put the serving plates in the refrigerator to chill for 2–3 hours or until the jelly has set.

3. To prepare the citrus mousse, dice the orange and lemon flesh. Transfer the fruit to a food processor along with the coriander seeds, basil leaf and Light Vinaigrette. Blend to a smooth purée. Pass it through a fine sieve – preferably a chinois – set over a bowl.

4. Put about one-third of the purée in a small saucepan and heat it without boiling. Dissolve and combine the gelatine of your choice with the warm purée, whisking to ensure the gelatine is smoothly combined. Season to taste. Pour the stiffened purée into a multi-functional whipper and set it aside in the refrigerator.

5. Blanch the courgettes (zucchini) for about 1 minute, then drain them, refresh in cold water and drain again; set aside briefly.

6. In a bowl, mix together the Light Mayonnaise, the fromage blanc, the lime juice and the parsley. Stir in the Tabasco sauce, wasabi paste and curry powder. Mix in the crabmeat and the drained, cooled courgettes (zucchini), using a fork to gently turn the ingredients. Taste, and adjust the seasoning.

To serve
Have ready some matchsticks of apple, if used. Remove the serving plates from the refrigerator. Rest a food ring gently on top of each jelly and fill it carefully with the courgette (zucchini) and crabmeat mixture, avoiding overcrowding.

Charge the whipper with a gas cartridge and pump a generous cloud of citrus mousse on top. Lift away the food rings with care. If appropriate, push the matchsticks of apple into the jelly. Add herbs, salad leaves and flowers according to seasonal availability.

- 8 portions rabbit, total weight 1.4kg (3lb)
- 2 litres (8½ US cups) chicken stock, either home-made (page 44) or from a cube
- 150g (5½oz) carrots, peeled and cut into 4mm (just over ⅛in) dice
- 80g (scant 3oz) celery, cut into 4mm (just over ⅛in) dice
- 200g (7oz) courgettes (zucchini), cut into 4mm (just over ⅛in) dice
- salt and pepper of your choice

For the marinade
- 100g (3½oz) onion, cut into 3mm (⅛in) dice
- 100g (3½oz) carrots, peeled and cut into 3mm (⅛in) dice
- 80g (scant 3oz) leeks, cut into 3mm (⅛in) dice
- 2 cloves of garlic, unpeeled
- sprig of tarragon
- small fresh bouquet garni
- 200ml (⅞ US cup) dry white wine

For the jelly
- 70g (3oz) onions, coarsely chopped
- 70g (3oz) leeks, coarsely chopped
- ¼ stick (stalk) celery, coarsely chopped
- 120g (scant 4½oz) tomatoes, coarsely chopped
- 20g (¾oz) white button mushrooms, wiped and coarsely chopped
- 200g (7oz) lean beef, chopped
- 2 tbsp coarsely chopped tarragon
- 3 egg whites, lightly beaten
- 8 sheets of leaf gelatine (soaked) or 6½ tsp powdered gelatine (page 22)

To garnish
- few small handfuls of mesclun salad leaves or other salad leaves of your choice, dressed
- few sprigs of seasonal herbs of your choice

Equipment
- Porcelain or enamelled cast-iron terrine mould, 18cm long x 9cm wide x 7cm high (7 x 3½ x 2¾in)

MORSELS OF RABBIT IN A VEGETABLE JELLY

165 CALORIES PER PERSON
Cooking and preparation: 1½ hours, plus half a day of chilling and overnight marinating
Level of difficulty: * *
Serves 8–10

1. The night before you cook the rabbit, marinate it: put all the ingredients for the marinade into a deep dish. Mix them so that they are evenly distributed. Add the pieces of rabbit, and turn them to ensure they are well coated.

2. The following day, remove the pieces of rabbit from the marinade using a slotted spoon; set the pieces of rabbit aside. Pour the marinade into a large saucepan and, over brisk heat, reduce the liquid by a half. Add the 2 litres (8½ US cups) of chicken stock, then add the pieces of rabbit. Cover the saucepan and adjust the heat to maintain a very gentle simmer for 50 minutes or until the rabbit meat is tender enough to pull away from the bone easily.

3. Once again, remove the pieces of rabbit using a slotted spoon. Detach the rabbit meat from the bone. Cut the meat into large 2cm (¾in) morsels. Set these aside in a cold place until you assemble the terrine. Measure out 1 litre (4¼ US cups/1 quart) of the cooking liquid and set this aside for the jelly.

4. To prepare the vegetables, simmer the carrots, celery and courgettes (zucchini) in lightly salted water, in separate batches, until they are just tender – the carrots will take about 10 minutes the celery about 5 minutes and the courgettes (zucchini) about 4 minutes. Drain and refresh the vegetables in cold water, then drain again; set these aside until you assemble the terrine.

5. To make the jelly, put the coarsely chopped onions, leeks, celery, tomatoes and mushrooms into a large saucepan. Add the chopped beef, tarragon, salt, pepper and lightly beaten egg whites. Add the reserved liquid from cooking the rabbit. Over a low heat, bring this bouillon to a gentle boil, whisking from time to time. Adjust the heat and simmer gently for 15–20 minutes.

6. Remove the saucepan from the heat. Dissolve and combine the gelatine of your choice with the warm bouillon, stirring to ensure that it is evenly combined. Line a sieve with a piece of damp muslin and set it over a large mixing bowl. Strain the jellied bouillon; discard the solids. Leave the jelly to cool, stirring it from time to time. When it acquires a slippery texture and starts to set, it is ready to use.

7. To assemble the terrine, spoon enough jelly into the bottom of the terrine mould to make a thin layer. Transfer it to the refrigerator for 15 minutes or until the jelly has set firmly. Add the reserved pieces of rabbit and the reserved vegetables. Cover with the remainder of the setting jelly. Transfer the terrine to the refrigerator and leave it to chill for at least half a day.

8. Have ready cold serving plates. The terrine can be served from its mould. If you want to unmould the terrine, run a small sharp knife around the edges to loosen the jelly, then, stand the terrine briefly in a little warm water, immersing it to about one-quarter of its depth. Alternatively, wrap it in a hot, damp tea towel, put a serving platter on top. Invert the terrine onto the platter and lift the mould away. If the terrine does not come away, repeat the procedure.

To serve

Cut the terrine into slices and transfer them to cold serving plates. Garnish with the salad leaves and herbs of your choice.

Variation

For a sweeter and more fragrant effect, you can add pieces of fresh fruit— such as pear, apricot or peach – to the vegetables.

- 4 large heads of chicory (Belgian endive), each 150–180g (5oz–scant 6½oz)
- 1.5 litres (6½ US cups) chicken stock, either home-made (page 44) or from a cube
- 4 long strips of orange zest, white pith removed
- 4 long strips of lemon zest, white pith removed
- 100ml (⅜ US cup) orange juice
- 50ml (¼ US cup or 6 tbsp) freshly squeezed lemon juice
- 1 tbsp coriander seeds
- 1 tbsp fructose or the sweetener of your choice (pages 16–20)
- sprig of fresh thyme
- 1 bay leaf, preferably fresh
- 2 tbsp Light Vinaigrette (page 70)
- salt and pepper of your choice

To garnish
- 2 tbsp chopped tomatoes
- 2 tbsp snipped coriander (cilantro) leaves

GREEK-STYLE SWEET-AND-SOUR CHICORY

80 CALORIES PER PERSON
Cooking and preparation: 50 minutes
Level of difficulty: *
Serves 4

1. Wash the chicory (Belgian endive) in cold water, then put it in a saucepan with the chicken stock, the orange and lemon zest, and a pinch of salt. To avoid the chicory (Belgian endive) discolouring, cut a round of greaseproof or parchment paper to the same diameter as the saucepan and place it on top.

2. Bring the stock briefly to the boil, then lower the heat to a very gentle simmer. Cook the chicory (Belgian endive) for about 25 minutes, or until the point of a knife can be inserted into it easily. Lift out the chicory (Belgian endive) with a slotted spoon and transfer it to a cutting board. Set aside 150ml (¾ US cup) of the stock. Cut each chicory (Belgian endive) lengthways into four strips and transfer them, preferably in a single layer, to a gratin dish or shallow oven dish; set aside.

3. Preheat the oven to 150°C (300°F, gas mark 2). Meanwhile, combine the orange and lemon juices, the coriander seeds, the fructose, thyme and bay leaf in a small saucepan. Bring to the boil and boil for 2 minutes, to concentrate the flavours. Stir in the reserved stock.

4. Spoon this mixture over the chicory (Belgian endive), then transfer it to the oven. Bake for about 20 minutes. Remove the dish and transfer it to a cool place. Discard the thyme and bay leaf, and allow the chicory (Belgian endive) to cool down completely in its juices.

To serve
Have ready 4 cold serving plates. Arrange 4 strips of chicory (Belgian endive) in a criss-cross pattern on each plate. Strain off the juices from the gratin dish and mix these with the Light Vinaigrette to make a dressing. Taste, and adjust the seasoning, then drizzle the dressing on top. Garnish with pieces of chopped tomato and coriander (cilantro) leaves, and serve.

- 200g (7oz) haricots verts
- 4 eggs
- 1 tbsp white wine vinegar
- 4 large firm white mushrooms, wiped and thinly sliced
- 1 tsp very finely chopped shallot
- 4 tbsp Mushroom Vinaigrette (page 66), plus a few extra drops for dressing the salad leaves
- 4 tbsp Green Vegetable Sauce (page 87)
- pinch of fleur de sel
- few turns of the pepper mill

To garnish
- few small handfuls of mesclun salad leaves or other salad leaves of your choice
- few sprigs of fresh herbs of your choice

SOFT-BOILED EGGS WITH A GREEN SAUCE

140 CALORIES PER PERSON
Cooking and preparation: 20 minutes
Level of difficulty: **
Serves 4

1. Simmer the haricots verts in lightly salted water for 4–8 minutes, depending on their size and your personal taste. Drain, refresh in iced water for a few seconds, then drain again and set aside on kitchen paper.

2. Put the eggs into a saucepan of boiling water and add the vinegar. Simmer the eggs for 5 minutes. Place them in cold water for a few minutes, then peel them carefully and set aside briefly.

3. Put the sliced mushrooms in a large bowl along with the shallot and cooked haricots verts. Add the 4 tablespoons of Mushroom Vinaigrette and turn the mixture to coat the vegetables evenly.

To serve
Have ready 4 cold serving plates. Make a nest of vegetables on each plate and place an egg in the middle. Coat each egg neatly with the Green Vegetable Sauce. Add a pinch of fleur de sel and a turn of the pepper mill to each egg. Dress the salad leaves in a few drops of Mushroom Vinaigrette and arrange them on top and around the edges. Decorate with the herbs of your choice and serve.

- 1 large orange
- freshly squeezed orange juice (optional)
- 6 large eggs
- 6 asparagus tips
- salt and pepper of your choice

For the carrot mousse
- 200g (7oz) carrots, peeled and cut into even-sized chunks
- 250ml (1⅛ US cups) chicken stock, either home-made (page 44) or from a cube
- ½ sheet of leaf gelatine (soaked) or ½ tsp powdered gelatin (page 22)
- 4 tbsp light whipping cream (30–35% fat)
- 1 tbsp fromage blanc or Greek yogurt (0% fat or low-fat)

Equipment
- An egg topper (optional)

EXTRAORDINARY EGGS WITH A CARROT MOUSSE

CALORIE COUNT
Cooking and preparation: 30 minutes
Level of difficulty: * * *
Serves 6

---

1. Peel one-quarter of the orange into long strips and scrape away the white pith to make pieces of zest. Blanch the zest for 3 minutes. Drain, refresh in cold water, then drain again. Trim away the ragged edges and cut the zest into very thin julienne strips 1½cm (about ½in) long; set aside for the garnish.

2. Working over a plate, peel the rest of the orange, using a small, sharp paring knife to remove the pith along with the peel. Cut along each side of the membrane to free the segments. Cut the segments into small dice and put the juice in a small bowl. Squeeze the membranes over the bowl to collect the last of the juice. You should now have at least 2 tablespoons of juice. If you have less, supplement it with additional juice. Set the juice and diced orange aside.

3. To prepare the eggs, take the tops off the 6 uncooked eggs, either using a special topper or a small sharp knife. Empty the contents of the shells into two mixing bowls, separating the whites from the yolks. (Reserve the whites for use in other recipes.) Poach the yolks in simmering salted water for 2 minutes. Remove them with a slotted spoon and drain them on kitchen paper. Rinse the eggshells and their 'hats' and drain them in the same way.

4. For the carrot mousse, simmer the carrots in the chicken stock in a covered saucepan for about 20 minutes, or until the stock has evaporated and the carrots are soft. Season, transfer to a food processor, add the orange juice and blend the mixture to a purée. Transfer the purée to a bain-marie set over gentle heat. When the purée is warm, remove it from the heat. Dissolve and combine the gelatine of your choice with the warm carrot purée. Stir the mixture well and transfer it to a mixing bowl. Leave it to cool slightly without setting.

5. To complete the carrot mousse, whip the cream until it holds a peak on the whisk, then combine it with the fromage blanc. Fold this mixture into the jellied carrot purée to make a mousse. Stir in the reserved diced orange and half of the reserved julienne zest.

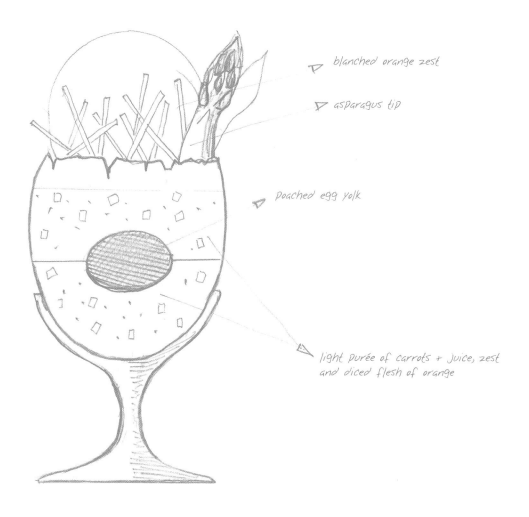

blanched orange zest

asparagus tip

Poached egg yolk

light purée of carrots + juice, zest
and diced flesh of orange

6. Put the drained eggshells in an empty egg carton. Fill them halfway with the carrot mousse. Add a cooked yolk to each, then cover with the remaining mousse. Transfer the egg carton to the refrigerator.

7. Just before serving, simmer the asparagus tips in lightly salted water for about 4 minutes or until al dente. Drain and refresh carefully in cold water so as not to break them, then drain again on kitchen paper.

To serve
Transfer the filled eggshells to pretty egg cups. Plant a few julienne strips of orange and an asparagus tip in each, and top with the little 'hat' set at a jaunty angle.

- 500ml (2⅛ US cups) fish stock, either home-made (page 47) or from a cube
- 200g (7oz) fillet of cod, hake, whiting or mackerel, skinned and cut into pieces about 3–4cm (1¼–1½in)
- 70g (3oz) courgette (zucchini), cut into ½cm (¼in) dice
- 30g (1oz) Tomato Confit (page 81)
- 1 tbsp finely chopped or snipped chives
- 1 tbsp chopped or snipped tarragon
- 1 tbsp Light Mayonnaise (page 79)
- 1 tbsp fromage blanc or Greek yogurt (0% fat or low-fat)
- few drops of Tabasco sauce
- 1 tsp freshly squeezed lemon juice
- salt and pepper of your choice

For the horseradish sauce
- 60g (2oz) fromage blanc or Greek yogurt (0% fat or low-fat)
- 20g (¾oz) creamed horseradish sauce
- 2 tbsp semi-skimmed (2%) milk
- 1 tsp freshly squeezed lemon juice

To garnish
- some radicchio leaves mixed with sprigs of dill or 4 hearts of Little Gem lettuces cut in half
- few drops of Light Vinaigrette (page 70)

QUENELLES OF WHITE FISH WITH HORSERADISH SAUCE

125 CALORIES PER PERSON FOR COD OR HAKE
(185 CALORIES FOR MACKEREL)
Cooking and preparation: 20 minutes
Level of difficulty: *
Serves 4

1. Bring the fish stock to the boil then add the pieces of fish and the salt and pepper. When the stock returns to the boil, remove the saucepan from the heat, cover it with a lid and leave the fish to continue cooking in the heat of the stock for about 8 minutes or until done. Remove the fish using a slotted spoon or a sieve and set aside to cool in a mixing bowl.

2. Meanwhile, blanch, refresh and drain the diced courgette (zucchini). When the fish is cool, flake it with a fork. Add the courgette (zucchini), the diced Tomato Confit and the chives and tarragon. Mix in the Light Mayonnaise, fromage blanc, Tabasco sauce and lemon juice. Stir delicately to distribute the ingredients evenly and form a light mixture that will hold its shape. Taste, and adjust the seasoning, then chill in the refrigerator for at least 20 minutes.

3. For the horseradish sauce, combine the fromage blanc with the creamed horseradish sauce, milk and lemon juice. Season to taste. Transfer the sauce to a sauce boat.

To serve
Have ready the serving plates. Pass the fish mixture between 2 dessertspoons to make oval quenelle shapes. Slide the quenelles onto the plates. Dress the salad leaves of your choice in the Light Vinaigrette and put them either side of the quenelles. Drizzle a little of the horseradish sauce onto the plates and serve the remainder separately in a sauce boat.

- 1 tsp olive oil
- 1 tbsp chopped or finely sliced onion
- 20g (¾oz) carrot, peeled and cut into small dice
- 1 clove of garlic, unpeeled and crushed
- 50ml (¼ US cup or 6 tbsp) white wine
- 300ml (1¼ US cups) vegetable stock or chicken stock, either home-made (pages 42 and 44) or from a cube
- 1 small fresh bouquet garni
- 6 purple poivrade artichokes or small globe artichokes, turned (Terms and Techniques, pages 328–9)
- 3 tbsp Light Vinaigrette (page 70)
- salt and pepper of your choice

For the artichoke custards
- 2 whole eggs
- 1 egg yolk
- 250ml (1⅛ US cups) semi-skimmed (2%) milk
- pinch of nutmeg
- 125g (4½oz) cooked artichoke hearts (fresh, frozen or bottled), blended to a purée

To garnish
- few small salad leaves
- 1 tbsp chopped or snipped chives

ARTICHOKE CUSTARDS AND ARTICHOKE HEARTS

120 CALORIES PER PERSON
Cooking and preparation: 45 minutes
Level of difficulty: * *
Serves 5

1. For the artichoke custards, preheat the oven to 95°C (203°F, gas mark ½ –1). Whisk together the whole eggs, the egg yolk and the milk. Season with nutmeg and salt and pepper to taste. Combine this with the purée of artichoke hearts, mixing well; adjust the seasoning. Spoon this mixture into 5 ovenproof glasses or cups and transfer them to the oven for 25–30 minutes. Remove the custards from the oven and set them aside in a cool place or refrigerator.

2. Coat the base of a small saucepan with the olive oil. Over low heat, sweat the onion for 1 minute. Add the carrot and garlic. Sweat for a further 2 minutes or until the vegetables soften without colouring. Add the white wine, increase the heat and reduce the wine to about 1 tablespoon. Add the vegetable stock and the bouquet garni. Bring the stock almost to the boil, then lower the heat, cover the saucepan and leave to simmer for 5 minutes; adjust the seasoning.

3. Add 5 of the 6 artichoke hearts – set aside one for decoration – to the gently simmering stock. Cover, and leave them to cook gently for 15 minutes or until tender. Transfer the cooked artichoke hearts to a plate using a slotted spoon.

4. Strain the stock through a fine sieve – preferably a chinois – into a clean saucepan; discard the solids. Over high heat, reduce the stock to about 3 tablespoons. When it is cool, mix it with the Light Vinaigrette.

To serve
Have ready the artichoke custards. Cut the cooked hearts into halves, quarters or wedges and arrange the pieces so they cover the custard. Slice the reserved uncooked artichoke into fine slivers and distribute them on top. Add the garnish of small young salad leaves. Drizzle over the vinaigrette. Sprinkle over the chopped chives and serve.

Variation
The small, purple, poivrade variety of fresh artichokes called for here are extra-tender and have a very distinctive flavour. They can, however, be replaced with regular globe artichokes or with frozen or bottled artichoke hearts.

- 60g (2oz) carrots, peeled
- 60g (2oz) celeriac, peeled
- 60g (2oz) radish, peeled
- 60g (2oz) celery
- 1 Little Gem lettuce, outer leaves removed
- 1 tbsp Light Mayonnaise (page 79)
- 1 tbsp fromage blanc or Greek yogurt (0% fat or low-fat)
- 1 tsp wasabi paste
- 4 sheets of nori (sushi) seaweed, ideally 20cm (8in) square
- 24 coriander (cilantro) leaves
- 12 small mint leaves
- salt and pepper of your choice

For the spicy sauce
- 4 tbsp white rice wine vinegar
- 1 tsp fructose or the sweetener of your choice (pages 16–20)
- pinch of powdered saffron
- pinch of powdered cumin
- pinch of very finely chopped fresh, hot chilli pepper
- pinch of finely chopped star anise
- 5 tbsp Light Vinaigrette (page 70)
- 2 tbsp semi-skimmed (2%) milk

To garnish
- few sections of Cos or Little Gem lettuce, or salad leaves of your choice
- few sprigs of mint and coriander (cilantro)

CRUNCHY VEGETABLE SPRING ROLLS WITH A SPICY SAUCE

70 CALORIES PER PERSON
Cooking and preparation: 30 minutes
Level of difficulty: * *
Serves 6

1. To prepare the vegetable filling, use a grater or a knife to make very fine julienne strips – about 1½cm (½in) long – from the carrots, celeriac and radish. Cut the celery and lettuce into similar julienne strips. In a large bowl, mix together the Light Mayonnaise, the fromage blanc and the wasabi paste. Add the julienne strips of vegetables and mix with a fork. Season to taste.

2. If you have a Japanese bamboo sushi mat lay it on the work counter, otherwise use a piece of dampened muslin or fine cloth. For even rolling, check that the bottom edge of the mat is parallel to the work counter.

3. Assemble the rolls one by one: put a sheet of nori (sushi) seaweed on top of the mat or muslin, leaving an edge of mat free along the bottom to allow you to hold it easily. At about 6cm (2½in) from the bottom edge of the seaweed sheet, distribute one-quarter of the vegetable filling and make it into a sausage shape about 2cm (¾in) thick. Carefully position 6 coriander (cilantro) leaves and 3 small mint leaves on top, alternating them.

4. Starting at the bottom edge, gently lift and roll the mat or muslin so that the seaweed sheet rolls over the filling. Tuck in the vegetables to keep the roll tight and neat, and press lightly with both hands. Finish the roll by sticking the edges of the last 3cm (1¼in) of seaweed sheet with a little water. Remove the roll from the mat and leave it to sit with the joined edges facing downwards. Repeat with the remaining 3 sheets. Set aside in the refrigerator or in a cool place until you are ready to serve.

5. To make the spicy sauce, mix together in a saucepan the white rice wine vinegar, the fructose, saffron, cumin, hot chilli pepper and star anise. Over a medium heat, boil this mixture until it reduces to about 1 teaspoon of syrupy glaze. Stir in the Light Vinaigrette and the milk. Return to the boil, check the sauce's seasoning, then strain it through a fine sieve into a small bowl. Set it aside to cool.

To serve
Cut each roll into 3 equal pieces and put 2 pieces on each serving plate. Decorate with salad leaves and sprigs of mint and fresh coriander (cilantro). Either drizzle a little sauce all around or serve the sauce in individual serving dishes placed on each plate.

- 200g (7oz) fillet of salmon, skinned and cut into a rough log shape about 25cm (9¾in) long and 3cm (1¼in) thick (ask your fishmonger to prepare this for you)
- salt and pepper of your choice

For the spice coating
- 1 tbsp green dill
- 1 tbsp coriander seeds
- 4 tbsp of five-peppercorn mix (comprising pink, green and white peppercorns, ground coriander and pimento)
- 1 tsp Indian long pepper (Piper longum) or ground black pepper
- 1 heaped tsp fleur de sel
- 2 tbsp toasted sesame seeds

For the coffee sauce
- 60g (2oz) firm mango flesh
- 1 tsp coconut milk
- 1 tsp soy sauce
- 1 tbsp fromage blanc or Greek yogurt (0% fat or low-fat)
- 1 tbsp ground expresso coffee
- pinch of Piment d'Espelette or other chilli powder
- 1 tbsp hazelnut oil

For the herb salad
- 12 sprigs of chervil
- 12 sprigs of dill
- 12 sprigs of coriander (cilantro)
- 4–6 tarragon leaves
- 8 chives
- 2 tbsp Asian Lime Vinaigrette (page 65)

SPICY SALMON WITH COFFEE SAUCE

150 CALORIES PER PERSON
Cooking and preparation: 20 minutes
Level of difficulty: *
Serves 4

1. For the spicy coating for the salmon, grind all of the spices except for the toasted sesame seeds in a coffee grinder or a blender. Stir in the toasted sesame seeds. Cover securely and set aside.

2. For the coffee sauce, blend all of the ingredients to a smooth purée using a blender. Transfer the sauce to a bowl, season to taste, then cover and chill until required.

3. For the herb salad, pick through the chervil, dill and coriander (cilantro) and remove any tough or bitter stalks. Tear the tarragon leaves into pieces. Leave the chives long or snip them as desired. Set aside a few coriander (cilantro) leaves for garnish and set the salad aside.

4. Just before you are ready to cook the salmon, preheat the grill and preheat a non-stick grilling pan. Spread the spice coating on a flat plate or tray. Roll the piece of salmon gently and evenly in the mixture, then tap the salmon to remove the excess spice. Use a long spatula to transfer the salmon to the heated grilling pan.

5. Grill the salmon just long enough for the spices to become roasted and for the colour of the salmon to lighten around the edge of the fillet, leaving the centre darker and uncooked. Leave the salmon to rest and become cold.

To serve
Cut the salmon log as desired, either into thickish steaks or into about 20 thin slices that you can overlap for presentation. Arrange the salmon on serving plates. Dress the salad with the Asian Lime Vinaigrette and divide it between the plates. Add blobs of the coffee sauce to the salmon pieces, decorate with the reserved coriander (cilantro) leaves, and serve.

- 4 large ripe tomatoes, peeled and cut in half
  (Terms and Techniques, pages 327–8)
- 60g (2oz) young courgettes (zucchini), cut into
  ½cm (¼in) dice
- 1 tbsp very finely chopped shallot
- 1 tbsp finely chopped basil leaves
- 1 tbsp finely chopped or snipped chives
- salt and pepper of your choice

For the dressing
- ½ tsp traditional French wholegrain mustard
  or other grainy mustard
- 3 drops of Tabasco sauce
- 3 tbsp Mushroom Vinaigrette (page 66)

To garnish
- 4 small handfuls of dressed mesclun
  salad leaves
- 1 tbsp Mushroom Vinaigrette (page 66)
- 12 thin shavings of Parmesan
- few sprigs of basil

Equipment
- 4 metal food rings or pastry cutters, 10cm
  (4in) in diameter

TARTARE OF TOMATOES WITH BASIL

45 CALORIES PER PERSON
Cooking and preparation: 20 minutes
Level of difficulty: *
Serves 4

1. Put the peeled tomato halves on a chopping board and flatten them with the back of your hand to squeeze out the juice and seeds. Cut the halves into ½cm (¼in) dice and put them in a strainer – preferably of nylon – set over a bowl. Lightly season with salt and set aside.

2. Blanch the diced courgettes (zucchini) in lightly salted boiling water for 2 minutes, then drain, refresh with iced water, and drain again; set aside.

3. Mix together the very finely chopped shallot, basil and chives. Put this mixture in a large bowl and add the reserved tomatoes and courgettes (zucchini). Combine the tartare ingredients gently.

4. In a separate small bowl, make a dressing by stirring together the mustard, Tabasco sauce and the Mushroom Vinaigrette. Add about half of this to the tartare mixture – just enough to moisten – and set aside the rest. Mix the tartare again and adjust the seasoning as desired.

To serve
Put a food ring on each of 4 cold serving plates. Spoon the tartare into each ring, making sure the edge is neat, then carefully lift away the ring. Drizzle over the remaining dressing or serve it separately. Season the mesclun salad with Mushroom Vinaigrette and add it to the plates, along with shavings of Parmesan and sprigs of basil.

Variations
Many variations are possible for this tartare. It looks lovely served in stemmed glasses, for example. You can also vary the size of the diced ingredients, making the tomato dice larger than the size given here. You can omit the shallot and you can vary the herbs – focusing exclusively on one herb, such as basil, mint or coriander (cilantro) if you want. If you prefer, you could also season the mesclun salad with the Thai Vinaigrette (page 68) or with the Light Vinaigrette (page 70). As for an accompanying sauce, why not try the low-calorie Pea and rocket coulis (page 95).

- 8 medium tomatoes, peeled, cut in half, cored and deseeded (Terms and Techniques, pages 327–8)
- about 2 tbsp olive oil
- 1 tsp fructose or the sweetener of your choice (pages 16–20)
- 4 sprigs of thyme
- 3 bay leaves (preferably fresh)
- 4 small shallots
- 2 cloves of garlic, peeled and cut in half
- 4 medium courgettes (zucchini)
- 2 small aubergines (eggplants)
- 1 tbsp Thai Vinaigrette (page 68)
- salt and pepper of your choice

To garnish
- 2 small handfuls of mesclun salad leaves or other salad leaves of your choice
- few sprigs of basil or seasonal herbs
- fleur de sel

Equipment
- Porcelain or enameled cast-iron terrine mould, 13cm long x 9cm wide x 6cm high (5¼ x 3½ x 2½in)
- To weight the mould: a thin piece of wood or stiff cardboard to fit inside the rim of the mould, plus a few weights to sit on top
- Electric carving knife (optional)

TERRINE OF RATATOUILLE VEGETABLES

110 CALORIES PER PERSON
Cooking and preparation: 1½ hours, plus 3 hours of chilling
Level of difficulty: * *
Serves 6

---

1. Preheat the oven to 170°C (325°F, gas mark 3). Arrange the cut halves of tomato, flat side up, on a baking sheet. Brush them with a little of the olive oil. Season them and sprinkle over the fructose. Crush or chop the leaves of one of the sprigs of thyme; scatter the pieces over the tomatoes. If you are using fresh bay leaves, chop one of them coarsely and distribute the pieces on top. If you are using dried bay leaf, crumble it over. Set the prepared tomatoes aside briefly.

2. Lay a sheet of aluminium foil about 30cm (12in) long on the work surface. Arrange on top of the foil, more or less in the middle, the shallots, the halved cloves of garlic, another sprig of thyme and half a bay leaf. Add 1 tablespoon of water and a pinch of salt. Draw up the edges of the foil and fold them to make a loose parcel. Put this parcel and the baking sheet of tomatoes in the oven for 45 minutes.

3. If you have a second oven, preheat it to 200°C (400°F, gas mark 6), otherwise wait until you have finished cooking the tomatoes and shallots, then raise the oven's temperature accordingly. Peel the courgettes (zucchini) lengthways, removing the tough ribs of peel but leaving the softer sections of peel in between; set aside. Peel the aubergines (eggplants) and cut them in half lengthways.

4. Put the remaining olive oil in a baking dish and heat it briefly in the oven. Add the courgettes (zucchini) and aubergines (eggplants) to the dish and return it to the oven until the vegetables have coloured lightly. Remove briefly from the oven, season, and add the remaining sprigs of thyme and bay leaves. Cover the dish with aluminium foil and return it to the oven for 35 minutes or until the vegetables are soft. During the course of cooking, lift the foil and add a little water to the dish to ensure the vegetables do not burn.

5. Leave all the cooked vegetables to cool. Meanwhile, line the inside of the terrine with clingfilm (plastic wrap), leaving a border all around so that one edge will fold over the other. The clingfilm (plastic wrap) will help with unmoulding the terrine.

6. To assemble the terrine, arrange the aubergines (eggplants) in the bottom. Use half the tomatoes to make a layer, arranging them flat side up. Put a row of shallots down the middle and, on each side, the halves of garlic. Use the remaining tomatoes to make another layer, this time putting the tomatoes flat side down. Finish by adding the courgettes (zucchini). Close the clingfilm (plastic wrap). Put the terrine on a plate to accommodate the juices that will flow.

7. Have ready a thin rectangle of wood or very stiff cardboard that sits very snugly just inside the rim of the terrine. Cover it in aluminium foil and put it on top of the terrine. Place weights on top. If you do not have weights, you can improvise. (My daughter uses pétanque balls but small tins of food may be more convenient.) Press down lightly on the weights for 30 seconds so the excess juice can escape onto the plate. Leave the terrine to rest, ideally at a cool, but not necessarily chilled, ambient temperature for 2–3 hours.

8. When you are ready to unmould the terrine, remove the weights and piece of wood. Set aside the excess juices. To unmould the terrine, stand it briefly in a little hot water, immersing it to about one-quarter of its depth. Alternatively, wrap it in a hot tea towel. Undo the clingfilm (plastic wrap) and place a flat serving platter on top. Invert the terrine onto the platter and lift the mould away.

9. Peel away the remaining clingfilm (plastic wrap). Mix the collected juices with the Thai Vinaigrette to make a sauce.

To serve

Cut the terrine in slices using a sharp knife or, better still, an electric carving knife. Transfer the slices to serving plates. Drizzle over a little of the sauce and serve the rest separately. Decorate the plate with the salad and seasonal herbs of your choice, and scatter with fleur de sel.

- about 1 tsp olive oil
- 25g (scant 1oz) shallot, finely chopped
- 500g (1lb 2oz) white button mushrooms, wiped and coarsely chopped
- ½ clove of garlic, peeled and finely chopped
- 100ml (⅜ US cup) semi-skimmed (2%) milk
- 100ml (⅜ US cup) single (light) cream
- 5 sheets of leaf gelatine (soaked) or 4 tsp powdered gelatine (page 22)
- 350g (12oz) seasonal mushrooms, such as ceps, chanterelles, enoki, shiitake, chestnut, oyster
- about 1 tsp olive oil
- 2 tsp chopped parsley
- 1 tbsp chopped chives
- salt and pepper of your choice

For the sauce
- 8 tbsp Mushroom Vinaigrette (page 66)
- 2 tbsp chopped flat-leaf parsley

To garnish
- 2 small handfuls of mesclun salad leaves or other salad leaves of your choice
- few sprigs of basil or seasonal herbs

Equipment
- Porcelain or enamelled cast-iron terrine mould, 15cm long x 9cm wide x 6cm high (6 x 3½ x 2½in)
- To weight the mould: a thin piece of wood or stiff cardboard to fit inside the rim of the mould, plus a few weights to sit on top

MUSHROOM TERRINE

105 CALORIES PER PERSON
Cooking and preparation: 20 minutes, plus overnight chilling
Level of difficulty: * *
Serves 8

1. Heat the oil in a large saucepan set over a low heat, add the shallot and sweat it gently, without colouring, for 1 minute. Add the coarsely chopped mushrooms, garlic, salt and pepper. Increase the heat and cook the mixture for 5 minutes, stirring all the time. Add the milk and the cream. Bring almost to the boil then adjust the heat to maintain a gentle simmer for 5 minutes.

2. Dissolve and combine the gelatine of your choice with the warm milk and mushroom mixture. Away from the heat, stir well to ensure the gelatine is evenly dispersed and fully dissolved; set this stiffened mushroom and cream mixture aside briefly.

3. Either slice, quarter or halve the mushrooms to make interesting shapes. Heat the olive oil in a non-stick frying pan (skillet) and sauté the mushrooms rapidly, turning them until they are lightly coloured. Season, then drain them in a sieve set over a bowl. Set aside the juices for later use in the sauce. Incorporate the drained mushrooms into the stiffened mushroom and cream mixture. Gently stir in the parsley and chives, and adjust the seasoning.

4. Line the inside of the terrine with clingfilm (plastic wrap), leaving a border all around so that one edge will fold over the other. The clingfilm (plastic wrap) will help with unmoulding the terrine. Transfer the terrine mixture to the mould, smoothing the top with a spatula. Close the clingfilm (plastic wrap) and put the terrine in the refrigerator (unweighted) overnight.

5. About 20 minutes before serving, let the terrine stand at room temperature. Make the sauce by mixing the Mushroom Vinaigrette with the reserved juices and the parsley. Undo the clingfilm (plastic wrap) and place a flat serving platter on top of the terrine. Invert the terrine onto the platter and lift the mould away. Peel away the remaining clingfilm (plastic wrap).

To serve
Cut the terrine into slices and transfer them to cold serving plates. Drizzle over the sauce. Garnish with the salad leaves and herbs of your choice.

- 500g (1lb 2oz) carrots, peeled
- about 1 tsp olive oil
- 1 clove of garlic, peeled and lightly crushed
- ½ tsp cumin seeds
- ½ tsp fructose or the sweetener of your choice (pages 16–20)
- 250ml (1⅛ US cups) orange juice
- 2½ sheets of leaf gelatine (soaked) or 2 tsp powdered gelatine (page 22)
- 1 tsp freshly squeezed lemon juice
- salt and pepper of your choice

For the orange sauce
- juice of 1 large orange
- 4 tbsp Thai Vinaigrette (page 68)

To garnish
- handful of small salad leaves of your choice
- few sprigs of coriander (cilantro) or the herbs of your choice

Equipment
- Porcelain or enameled cast-iron terrine mould, 13cm long x 9cm wide x 6cm high (5¼ x 3½ x 2½in)

TERRINE OF CARROTS WITH ORANGE AND CUMIN

105 CALORIES PER PERSON
Cooking and preparation: 45 minutes, plus overnight chilling
Level of difficulty: *
Serves 4–5

---

1. Cut the carrots into rounds about 3mm (⅛in) thick. Heat the olive oil gently in a heavy-based saucepan then add the carrots, garlic, cumin, fructose, salt and pepper. Partially cover with a lid and, over the lowest possible heat, sweat the ingredients without colouring them until the carrots are soft but keep their shape – up to 30 minutes. During this time, stir frequently and add a little water as required to prevent the ingredients from browning.

2. While the carrots are cooking, line the inside of the terrine with clingfilm (plastic wrap), leaving a border all around so that one edge will fold over the other. The clingfilm (plastic wrap) will help with unmoulding the terrine. To speed up the setting of the layers of jelly, sit the mould in an oval container containing ice cubes – ensuring that the mould is immersed to at least three-quarters of its depth; set aside in a cold place.

3. When the carrots are tender, add the orange juice and cook for a further 5 minutes, uncovered. Remove from the heat and discard the garlic. Dissolve and combine the gelatine of your choice with the carrot mixture, stirring to ensure that the gelatine is fully dissolved. Stir in the lemon juice, adjust the seasoning and leave the jellied carrot mixture to cool slightly.

4. To assemble the terrine, fill the chilled mould with the jellied carrot mixture in 3 or 4 successive stages, waiting for each layer to 'gel' before adding the next. Nudge the carrots into an attractive design using the back of a fork. If the jellied mixture becomes too stiff as you work, heat it very gently. When you have filled the terrine, close the clingfilm (plastic wrap) and chill overnight.

5. For the orange sauce, put the juice of the large orange in a small saucepan and, over high heat, reduce it to about 2 tablespoons. Let it get cold then mix it with the Thai Vinaigrette. Chill it until you are ready to serve the terrine.

To serve
Undo the clingfilm (plastic wrap) and place a flat serving platter on top of the terrine. Invert the terrine onto the platter and lift the mould away. Peel away the remaining clingfilm (plastic wrap). Cut the terrine into even-sized slices and transfer them to cold plates. Drizzle with the orange sauce and garnish with the salad leaves and herbs of your choice.

- 1 skate wing, about 700g (1lb 8oz)
- 5 sheets of leaf gelatine (soaked) or 4 tsp powdered gelatine (page 22)
- small handful of watercress leaves
- 2 tbsp capers

For the vegetables
- 2 bulbs of fennel
- 400ml (1¾ US cups) water
- ½ chicken stock cube, crumbled
- small pinch of powdered saffron
- pinch of fructose or the sweetener of your choice (pages 16–20)
- 100g (3½oz) broccoli florets
- 8 asparagus tips
- salt

For the court-bouillon
- 1.5 litres (6½ US cups) water
- 3 tbsp dry white wine
- 100ml (⅜ US cup) white wine vinegar
- 80g (scant 3oz) finely chopped onion
- 1 clove of garlic, peeled and crushed
- 1 fresh bouquet garni
- 1 tbsp coarse sea salt
- 1 tsp freshly ground pepper

For the sauce
- 50g (1¾oz) finely chopped shallot
- 6 tbsp Light Vinaigrette (page 70)
- 1 tbsp Xeres vinegar or other sherry vinegar of your choice
- few drops of Tabasco sauce
- 3–4 chives, snipped into longish strands
- 1 tbsp coarsely chopped or snipped flat-leaf parsley
- 1 tsp coarsely chopped tarragon

Equipment
- Porcelain or enamelled cast-iron terrine mould, 20cm long x 10cm wide x 6cm high (8 x 4 x 2½in)

TERRINE OF SKATE IN A MARKET GARDEN JELLY

200 CALORIES PER PERSON
Cooking and preparation: 2 hours, plus overnight chilling
Level of difficulty: * * *
Serves 6

1. To prepare the vegetables, cut off the green stalks and feathery tops from the bulbs of fennel. (Reserve these for use in other dishes.) Trim each bulb at its core end and discard any tough outer layers. Cut the bulbs in half lengthways and put the pieces in the bottom of a saucepan. Cover with the 400ml (1¾ US cups) water, then add the crumbled half chicken stock cube and the saffron and fructose. Season to taste.

2. Bring the mixture almost to the boil, stirring to dissolve the stock cube, then cover the saucepan, lower the heat and let the liquid simmer very gently for 30 minutes or until the fennel is tender. Drain the fennel and set it aside.

3. Simmer the broccoli in lightly salted water for 8 minutes, or until just tender. Simmer the asparagus tips for about 5 minutes. Drain and refresh the broccoli and asparagus tips in cold water, then drain again. Set aside in a cool place.

4. For the court-bouillon, put into a large saucepan the 1.5 litres (6½ US cups) of water, the white wine, vinegar, finely chopped onion, garlic, bouquet garni, coarse sea salt and ground pepper. Bring briefly to the boil, then adjust the heat to maintain a simmer for 15 minutes.

5. Wash the skate in cold water to remove the viscous substance covering the skin. Simmer the skate in the court-bouillon over gentle heat — preferably in a casserole dish (Dutch oven) made of enamelled cast iron. Transfer the skate to a plate. Set aside the court-bouillon.

6. When the skate is cool enough to handle, remove its white skin. Lift away the fillet of flesh that was beneath the white skin, then remove the black skin and lift away the second fillet of flesh. Divide these fillets into 2 equal portions and set aside. Measure out 500ml (2⅛ US cups) of the court-bouillon and strain it through a very fine sieve — preferably a chinois or a sieve lined with muslin.

7. To prepare the jelly for the terrine, bring the 500ml (2⅛ US cups) of the strained court-bouillon briefly to the boil then remove it from the heat. Dissolve and combine the gelatine of your choice with the warm court-bouillon, whisking well. Leave the jellified court-bouillon to cool to the point when the gelatine starts to 'take' and the court-bouillon acquires a slippery consistency. Meanwhile, line the inside of the terrine with clingfilm (plastic wrap), leaving a border all around so that one edge will fold over the other. The clingfilm (plastic wrap) will help with unmoulding the terrine.

8. Spoon about 50ml (¼ US cup or 6 tbsp) of the setting jelly into the bottom of the terrine to make a shallow layer then chill it in the refrigerator for 15 minutes to set firm. Cover this layer with the watercress leaves, add a second layer of jelly then chill the terrine again for 15 minutes. Continue to assemble the terrine, alternating a layer of jelly with a layer of the first portion of skate, then the asparagus tips trimmed to the width of the terrine, then the fennel, then the second portion of skate and the capers, and finally the broccoli. Finish with a layer of jelly. (If, while assembling the terrine, the jellied court-bouillon becomes too cold and stiff to use, put it in a bain-marie or in a bowl placed in a saucepan containing a little hot water, and heat it gently.) Close the clingfilm (plastic wrap) and chill the terrine in the refrigerator overnight.

9. Make the sauce just before serving the terrine: bring a small saucepan of water to the boil, add the chopped shallot and simmer for 15 seconds. Drain and refresh in cold water, then drain again. Put the shallot into a small bowl and add the Light Vinaigrette, sherry vinegar, Tabasco sauce and salt and pepper. Add a few of the chopped herbs, setting aside the rest. Stir to blend.

To serve
Undo the clingfilm (plastic wrap) and place a flat platter on top of the terrine. Invert the terrine onto the platter and lift the mould away. Peel away the remaining clingfilm (plastic wrap). Cut the terrine into slices 1.5cm (about ½in) thick and transfer them to cold plates. Make a little pool of sauce alongside each slice and sprinkle the remaining herbs over the sauce.

For the basil jelly
- 125ml (½ US cup) water
- 10 fresh basil leaves
- ½ sheet of leaf gelatine (soaked) or ½ tsp powdered gelatine (page 22)
- salt and pepper of your choice

For the tomato confit
- 6 ripe medium tomatoes, total weight about 1.2kg (2¾lb), peeled, cut in half, cored and deseeded (Terms and Techniques, pages 327–8)
- pinch of fructose or the sweetener of your choice (pages 16–20)
- large sprig of fresh thyme
- 1 clove of garlic, unpeeled and crushed
- 1 fresh bay leaf, broken into large pieces

For the cheese and herb mixture
- 100g (3½oz) fromage blanc or Greek yogurt (0% fat or low-fat)
- 200g (7oz) chèvre frais (very soft, fresh goat's cheese)
- 1 tsp freshly squeezed lemon juice
- 1 tbsp finely chopped flat-leaf parsley
- 1 tbsp finely chopped or snipped chives

For the garnish
- 6 small sprigs of green basil leaves
- 6 small sprigs of purple basil leaves

TIRAMISU OF TOMATO, FRESH GOAT'S CHEESE AND BASIL

75 CALORIES PER PERSON
Cooking and preparation: 1 hour 15 minutes
Level of difficulty:*
Serves 6

1. To make the basil jelly, bring the 125ml (½ US cup) of water to the boil in a small saucepan and season it with salt and pepper. Remove from the heat and add the basil leaves. Stir well, then cover with clingfilm (plastic wrap) and leave to infuse until completely cold.

2. Strain the infusion, reserving the water and squeezing the basil leaves; discard the basil leaves. Return the infused water to a saucepan and heat it until it is warm but not hot; remove from the heat. Dissolve and combine the gelatine of your choice with the warm basil-infused water, stirring or whisking well to ensure that the gelatine is evenly incorporated. Leave it to cool to room temperature then pour it into 6 serving glasses. Transfer the glasses to the refrigerator.

3. To prepare the tomato confit, preheat the oven to 150oC (300°F, gas mark 2). Select 6 of the 12 halves of tomato and arrange these on a baking sheet. Season with salt and pepper, sprinkle with the fructose, and add the thyme, crushed garlic and the bay leaf. Cook the tomatoes in the oven, turning them once, for about 1 hour, or until they shrivel to a confit. Leave to cool, then cut the tomato confit into ½cm (¼ in) dice.

4. Cut the remaining halves of fresh tomato into ½cm (¼in) dice. Season to taste. To drain any excess juice from the dice, put them in a sieve – preferably nylon – set over a bowl, and transfer it to a cool place or to the refrigerator.

5. For the cheese and herb mixture, combine the fromage blanc and the chèvre frais in a mixing bowl. Stir in the lemon juice and chopped parsley and chives, then season to taste. Stir or whisk well to create a smooth well-blended cream.

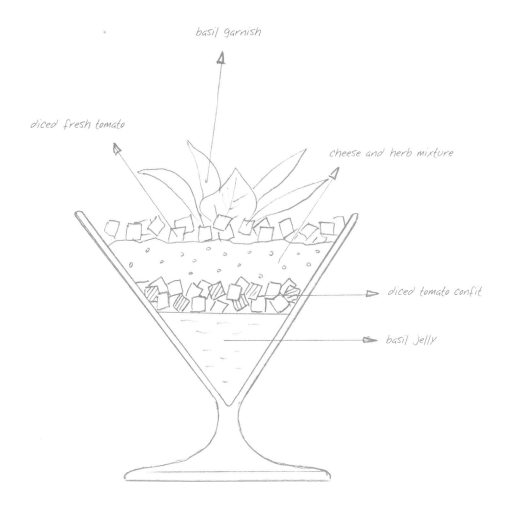

basil garnish

diced fresh tomato

cheese and herb mixture

diced tomato confit

basil jelly

To serve

Remove the serving glasses from the refrigerator, checking first that the basil jelly has set. On top of each jelly, arrange a layer of the diced tomato confit, smoothing it with the back of a spoon. Next, add a layer of the cheese mixture and, finally, a layer of the diced fresh tomato.

You can keep this assembly in the refrigerator for several hours until you are ready to serve. At the last moment, garnish the glasses with little bunches of green and purple basil.

- 5 small red tomatoes, about 5cm (2in) in diameter
- 5 small yellow tomatoes, about 5cm (2in) in diameter
- 10 small basil leaves
- 1 tbsp olive oil
- salt and pepper of your choice

For the filling
- 180g (scant 6½oz) carrots, peeled and cut into ½cm (¼in) dice
- 120g (scant 4½oz) haricot verts, cut into ½cm (¼in) pieces
- 80g (scant 3oz) broad beans (fava beans), shelled, but with inner skins left on; weight in pods about 140g (5oz)
- 110g (4oz) chèvre frais (very soft, fresh goat's cheese)
- 110g (4oz) fromage blanc or Greek yogurt (0% fat or low-fat)
- 1 tbsp freshly squeezed lemon juice
- 3 tbsp finely chopped fines herbes, such as flat-leaf parsley, chives, chervil and tarragon

For the dressing
- pinch of fructose or the sweetener of your choice (pages 16–20)
- 5 tbsp Asian Lime Vinaigrette (page 65)
- 1 tbsp balsamic vinegar
- 1 tsp of Worcestershire sauce

To garnish
- few sprigs of fresh herbs and some small salad leaves

ROASTED TOMATOES STUFFED WITH GOAT'S CHEESE AND VEGETABLES

170 CALORIES PER PERSON
Cooking and preparation: 45 minutes
Level of difficulty: **
Serves 5

1. Use a small knife to nick the skin of a tomato all around its circumference, about 2cm (¾in) from its stalk. Repeat with all the remaining red and yellow tomatoes. To loosen their skins, plunge the tomatoes – with stalks attached – in boiling water for a few seconds, then refresh in cold water. To separate the tomato bases from the 'hats', cut through each tomato at the level where you nicked the skin. Peel away and discard the skin from each base. Loosen the skin of each 'hat', curling it up to look pretty. Set aside the 'hats' on a plate, in a cold place.

2. Preheat the oven to 150o (300oF, gas mark 2). Separate the yellow tomato bases from the red. Use a small sharp spoon to scoop out the flesh and juice of the red tomatoes, and set this aside for later use in the vinaigrette dressing. Scoop out the flesh from the yellow tomatoes and use this in a different recipe or as extra garnish for this one.

3. Season inside all the emptied red and yellow tomato bases and put a basil leaf and a drop of olive oil at the bottom of each. Transfer the bases to a baking sheet or tray, and cook them in the oven for about 15 minutes or until they are tender but hold their shape. Remove and set aside to cool.

4. Meanwhile, prepare the dressing: chop the reserved red tomato flesh and transfer it, along with the juices, to a saucepan set over a medium heat. Reduce the mixture to a pulp. Season to taste and stir in the fructose. Pass the pulp through a sieve, preferably of nylon, to make a fine purée; set aside to cool completely. To complete the dressing, blend the cold purée with the Asian Lime Vinaigrette, balsamic vinegar and Worcestershire sauce.

5. To make the filling, bring a saucepan of lightly salted water to the boil and simmer, separately, the carrots for 10–12 minutes, the haricots verts for 7 minutes, and the broad beans in their skins for 2 minutes. Drain, refresh in cold water and drain again. Slip the broad beans free of their skins, chop the beans and combine them with the carrots and haricots verts.

6. To complete the filling, mix together in a bowl, the chèvre frais, the fromage blanc, the lemon juice and the fines herbes. Season. Add the cooked vegetables and mix gently, coating the vegetables evenly. Adjust the seasoning.

To serve

Have ready cold serving plates. Spoon enough of the filling mixture into each tomato base to make it sit slightly proud of the rim; keep the excess filling. Crown each base with a reserved tomato 'hat'. Spoon a few small rounds of the excess filling onto each plate. Flatten each round with the back of a spoon, and place one tomato of each colour on top.

Garnish the plates as you prefer, using the herbs and leaves of your choice. Either drizzle over some dressing or serve it separately in a sauce boat. If you like, you can also add a ribbon of reduced balsamic vinegar.

- 1 large potato, unpeeled
- 50g (1¾oz) fromage blanc or Greek yogurt (0% or low-fat)
- 2 tbsp Orange Blossom Sauce (page 75)
- 1 tsp fresh chives, snipped
- 25g (scant 1oz) grapefruit flesh, diced
- 15 medium uncooked langoustines (Dublin Bay Prawns), crawfish or jumbo prawns/shrimp
- about 1 tsp olive oil
- salt and pepper of your choice

For the garnish
- handful of small young frisée leaves
- handful of baby spinach, stems removed
- 1 tbsp finely chopped flat-leaf parsley
- 5 tbsp Asian Lime Vinaigrette (page 65)
- ½ Granny Smith apple, unpeeled
- 1 tbsp freshly squeezed lemon juice

Equipment
- 5 food rings, 5cm (2in) in diameter
- 5 small metal or wooden skewers, no longer than the base of the frying pan (skillet) (optional)

LANGOUSTINES WITH A GRAPEFRUIT AND POTATO SALAD

155 CALORIES PER PERSON
Cooking and preparation: 1 hour
Level of difficulty: ***
Serves 5

1. Bake the potato in an oven set at 180°C (350°F, gas mark 4) for 45 minutes or until you can easily slide a knife into it. Once the potato is cooked, use a small sharp knife to peel away the skin and discard it. Weigh out 75g (2½oz) of the potato and cut it into a small dice. Put the diced potato in a bowl and leave it to cool.

2. In a medium-sized bowl, mix together the fromage blanc, the Orange Blossom Sauce, the chives and the grapefruit. Gently stir in the diced potato with a fork. Adjust the seasoning and set this grapefruit potato salad aside in a cool place.

3. To prepare the garnish, combine the frisée and the spinach in a small bowl. Mix the parsley into the Asian Lime Vinaigrette and set aside. Remove the core from the apple, keeping the skin intact. Slice the apple into thin matchsticks, about 5cm x 3mm (2x ⅛in). To prevent the apple from browning, put the matchsticks in a small dish and just cover with lemon juice and water.

4. Remove the head and legs from each langoustine, then peel away the shell, leaving the last big segment of shell and the tail firmly intact. Discard the heads and shells. With a small sharp knife, score lightly along the back of the langoustine in a straight line, stopping just before the segment of shell. If there is a long black intestinal vein, pick it out and discard it. Put 3 langoustines on each skewer, curling them slightly to that the skewer passes through them twice and the langoustines lie flat. Set the skewers aside until you are ready to cook them.

5. A few minutes before you cook the langoustines, put a food ring in the centre of each serving plate and fill with the grapefruit potato salad, without packing it down. Remove the food rings.

6. Heat the olive oil in a non-stick frying pan (skillet) over a medium heat. Season the langoustine skewers and sauté them for 1 minute on each side or until they are pink and no longer transparent. Use the skewers to turn the langoustines; alternatively, forego the skewers and turn the langoustines with tongs. Remove the langoustines from the frying pan (skillet) and remove the skewers, if used.

To serve
Place 3 cooked langoustines on top of each grapefruit potato salad. Garnish the plates with the salad leaves. Drain the apple matchsticks and scatter them over. Drizzle each plate with a tablespoon of the vinaigrette and serve immediately.

- 8 whites of young leeks, about 2cm (¾in) in diameter
- 500ml (2⅛ US cups) Asian Lime Vegetable Stock (page 49), Mushroom Stock (page 51) or chicken stock, either home-made (page 44) or from a cube
- 1 tbsp fromage blanc or Greek yohgurt (0% fat or low-fat)
- 2 tbsp (⅜ US cup) semi-skimmed (2%) milk
- 1 tbsp wine vinegar
- 1 tbsp snipped chives
- 1 tbsp olive oil
- 1 tomato, peeled, core and deseeded (Terms and Techniques, page 327–8), then diced
- salt and pepper of your choice

To garnish
- few young salad leaves of your choice

SALAD OF WARM LEEKS WITH FROMAGE BLANC SAUCE

90 CALORIES PER PERSON
Cooking and preparation: 15 minutes
Level of difficulty: *
Serves 4

1. Simmer the leeks in lightly salted water for 10–12 minutes or until they are just done. A knife inserted into them should slide in easily. Drain the leeks and refresh in cold water, drain again and set aside on kitchen paper to dry. In a medium-sized saucepan, gently warm the stock of your choice until it comes to a gentle simmer. Remove from the heat, cover and keep it warm.

2. In a small bowl, mix together the fromage blanc, the milk, the wine vinegar and the chives until well blended. Season with salt and pepper and set this fromage blanc sauce aside.

3. Preheat a grill or ridged griddle pan. Using a pastry brush, lightly brush the leeks with olive oil. Grill the leeks on each side, turning them through 90 degrees to give them diamond-shaped grill marks. Remove the leeks from the heat and slice them on a diagonal into 5cm (2in) pieces.

To serve
Transfer the leeks to warm serving bowls and add the diced tomatoes. Gently pour some of the warmed stock on top of the leeks and tomatoes and, using a spoon, drizzle them with the fromage blanc sauce. Garnish with the salad leaves and serve immediately.

- 100g (3½oz) puff pastry, home-made or ready made, and thawed if frozen
- ½ bunch fresh basil, leaves only, sliced
- 1 tsp concentrated tomato paste
- 500g (1lb 2oz) medium tomatoes, peeled (Terms and Techniques, pages 327–8)
- pinch of thyme
- pinch of fructose or the sweetener of your choice (pages 16–20)
- salt and pepper of your choice

To garnish
- few fresh basil leaves

SKINNY TOMATO TARTS

130 CALORIES PER PERSON
Cooking and preparation: 30 minutes
Level of difficulty: **
Serves 4

1. Divide the puff pastry into 4 quarters and roll into balls. Using a rolling pin, roll out each ball into a circle 14cm (5½–6in) in diameter and 1mm (1/16in) thick. Put the circles onto a baking sheet lined with parchment paper and put into the refrigerator.

2. In a saucepan of lightly salted water, blanch the sliced basil leaves for 10 seconds. Drain the leaves and refresh in cold water; drain again. Chop the leaves finely and mix with the tomato paste.

3. Preheat the oven to 220°C (425°F, gas mark 7). Spread the tomato-basil mixture onto the chilled puff pastry, leaving a ½cm (¼in) border.

4. Cut the peeled tomatoes into 3–4mm (⅛in) slices. Tap them lightly to get rid of the seeds. Carefully lay the tomatoes on top of the tomato-basil mixture without overlapping and respecting the ½cm (¼in) border. If there are too many empty spaces due to the missing seeds, fill them with pulp from another tomato. Sprinkle the thyme and fructose onto the tarts and season with salt and pepper. Bake the tarts in the oven for 10–12 minutes or until the pastry is golden and slightly puffed.

To serve
Have ready 4 warm serving plates. When the tarts are done, put one on each plate and decorate with the fresh basil leaves. Serve immediately.

Chef's tip
Store-bought puff pastry often has a lower fat content than the home-made variety. This tart is most flavourful when tomatoes are ripe and in season.

- about 1 tsp olive oil, for brushing
- 5 egg whites
- salt and pepper of your choice

For the prawn sauce
- about 1 tsp olive oil
- 100g (3½oz) onion, cut into tiny dice about 3mm (⅛in)
- 50g (1¾oz) carrot cut into tiny dice about 3mm (⅛in)
- about 250g (9oz) small prawn (shrimp) shells taken from the prawn garnish (below)
- 1 tbsp concentrated tomato paste
- 1 tbsp port
- 1 tbsp Armagnac
- 200ml (⅞ US cup) dry white wine
- 1 small sprig of tarragon
- 1 small fresh bouquet garni
- 500ml (2⅛ US cups) fish stock, either home-made (page 47) or from a cube
- pinch of Cayenne pepper
- 50ml (¼ US cup or 6 tbsp) semi-skimmed (2%) milk
- 1 tsp cornflour (cornstarch), mixed with a little cold water

For the soufflé base
- 150g (5½oz) fillet of salmon, skin removed pinch of Cayenne pepper
- 1 whole egg
- 300g (11oz) unsweetened low-fat evaporated milk

For the prawn garnish
- 18 small prawns removed from their shells, and the shells reserved for the prawn sauce (above)
- about 1 tsp olive oil
- 1 tsp chopped tarragon

Equipment
- 6 porcelain moulds, 8cm (3in) in diameter and about 4cm (1½in) high

SALMON SOUFFLÉ FLECKED WITH PRAWNS

210 CALORIES PER PERSON
Cooking and preparation: 45 minutes
Level of difficulty: * *
Serves 6

1. To make the prawn sauce, coat the bottom of a large saucepan with the olive oil and sweat the finely diced onion and carrot over a gentle heat for 3–4 minutes or until the vegetables soften without colouring. Add the prawn shells and cook for 2 minutes, then add the concentrated tomato paste.

2. Mix the ingredients well. Stir in the port, Armagnac and white wine. Add the sprig of tarragon and the bouquet garni. Increase the heat, bring the liquid to the boil and reduce it until the bottom of the saucepan is almost dry. Add the fish stock and the Cayenne pepper and simmer for 15 minutes. Season to taste with salt.

3. Strain the mixture through a large sieve set over a small saucepan, crushing the shells with a pestle or spoon to extract the last of their juice. Discard the shells and other solids. Over a low heat, add the milk and cornflour (cornstarch). Stir to blend then strain the sauce again through a fine sieve – preferably a chinois – or a sieve lined with muslin. Set aside this prawn sauce until you are ready to use it.

4. For the soufflé base, chop the salmon into small pieces and put them in the bowl of a food processor, then blend for about 2 minutes. Add salt, pepper and Cayenne pepper, then blend again for about 30 seconds. With a spatula, push down the salmon flesh that clings to the sides of the bowl. Lightly beat the whole egg and stir it into the milk, then add this mixture to the food processor and blend again briefly to combine well. Transfer to a large mixing bowl and set it aside in a cold place.

5. To prepare the soufflé moulds, brush the insides lightly with a little olive oil and set them aside in a cool place.

6. To prepare the prawn garnish that will fleck the soufflé, cut the shelled prawns into ½cm (¼in) pieces and season them with salt to taste. Coat a small frying pan (skillet) with the olive oil and, over a medium heat, sauté the prawns for 30 seconds, shaking the pan to turn the prawns and cook them evenly. Stir in a tablespoon of the reserved prawn sauce and the tarragon. Transfer to a bowl and set aside to cool.

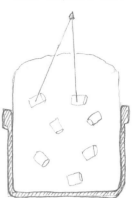

flecks of prawn garnish
coated in prawn sauce

7. When you are ready to complete the soufflé mixture, preheat the oven to 180°C (350°F, gas mark 4). Have the soufflé base, the prawn garnish and the moulds — arranged on a baking sheet — to hand. In a separate large bowl, whisk the egg whites together with a pinch of salt until they form stiff, but not dry, peaks. Mix about a quarter of the whisked egg white into the salmon base, then combine this with the remaining whites, repeatedly lifting the whites from the bottom of the bowl and folding them over the top of the soufflé mixture until all is well mixed.

8. Working quickly, fill the moulds with the soufflé mixture using a dessertspoon. Tap down the moulds gently on the work surface to settle their contents, then push the little pieces of prawn garnish into the mixture using your finger. Finally, rub your thumb around the rim of the mould to clear a path and help the soufflé to rise at the beginning of its cooking. Cook the soufflés for about 6 minutes or until they have risen. Meanwhile, bring the prawn sauce to serving temperature and warm a sauce boat.

To serve
Have ready 6 under-plates. Remove the soufflés from the oven. Use a sharp-edged teaspoon or a small knife to carefully make an opening in the top of each soufflé and pour a little of the prawn sauce inside. Transfer the soufflés to the under-plates. Put the rest of the sauce in the warmed sauce boat and serve immediately.

For the mushroom and ceps mixture
- about 1 tsp olive oil
- 300g (11oz) white button mushrooms, wiped and quartered
- 150g (5½oz) ceps (porcini), fresh or frozen, roughly chopped
- 1 clove of garlic, unpeeled
- 1 sprig of fresh thyme
- ½ bay leaf
- 3 tbsp Xeres vinegar or other sherry vinegar of your choice
- salt and pepper of your choice

For the mushroom sauce
- about 1 tsp olive oil
- 1 tbsp finely chopped shallot
- 1 clove of garlic, unpeeled
- 400g (14oz) white button mushrooms, wiped and roughly chopped
- 50ml (¼ US cup or 6 tbsp) Noilly Prat (vermouth)
- 300ml (1¼ US cups) semi-skimmed (2%) milk
- 1 sprig of fresh thyme
- ½ bay leaf

For the potato purée
- about 100g (3½oz) potato
- 100ml (⅜ US cup) semi-skimmed (2%) milk
- 30ml (2½ tbsp) single (light) cream
- 1 tbsp olive oil

To garnish (optional)
- 5 thin slices of black truffle
- few sprigs of chervil

Equipment
- Multi-functional whipper with 1 gas cartridge (optional)
- 5 food rings or cutters, 5cm (2in) in diameter

MUSHROOMS IN VERMOUTH WITH A POTATO PURÉE

130 CALORIES PER PERSON
Cooking and preparation: 45 minutes
Level of difficulty: ***
Serves 5

1. To prepare the mushroom and ceps mixture, heat the olive oil in a non-stick frying pan (skillet) over a medium-high heat and sauté the white button mushrooms and the ceps with the garlic, thyme, and bay leaf, stirring continually with a wooden spoon until the mushrooms have softened and become slightly golden. Season with salt and pepper.

2. Deglaze the frying pan (skillet) with the Xeres vinegar, then lower the heat and let the liquid simmer until it is reduced by three-quarters. Remove the frying pan (skillet) from the heat and transfer the mushrooms and their juices to a shallow bowl to allow to cool.

3. To prepare the mushroom sauce, heat the olive oil in a large saucepan over a gentle heat. Sweat the shallots and the clove of garlic for 1 minute before adding the white button mushrooms. Season with salt and pepper and stir well. Cook the mushroom mixture over a medium heat until the mushrooms have flopped and become slightly golden, about 10 minutes.

4. Deglaze the frying pan (skillet) with the Noilly Prat and allow the mushrooms to cook in the liquid until it has almost completely evaporated. Add the milk, thyme and bay leaf and bring to a gentle simmer. Cover the saucepan and simmer for about 15 minutes or until the flavours have combined. Remove the saucepan from the heat and, using a slotted spoon, remove the thyme, bay leaf and the clove of garlic and discard.

5. When the sauce is cool enough to handle, ladle it into a food processor and blend it into a coarse purée – some small chunks of mushroom should still be visible. Adjust the seasoning and keep the sauce warm, preferably in a bain-maire, until you are ready to serve it.

6. To prepare the potato purée, boil the potato in lightly salted water for 15 minutes or until soft. Drain it, peel it and mash it to a fine purée. For an extra-smooth purée, pass it through a ricer or food mill. Put the puréed potato into a medium-sized saucepan and add the milk, the cream and the olive oil. Beat well over a low to medium heat until all the ingredients are smoothly blended and the mixture starts to bubble; remove from heat and set aside briefly.

To serve

Have ready 5 warm serving plates with a shallow bowl that can accommodate the mushroom sauce. Place a food ring in the centre of each plate and fill each ring with the mushroom and ceps mixture. Spoon the warm mushroom sauce carefully around the rings, then lift them away.

Distribute the warm potato purée on top of the mushroom and ceps mixture. If you like, add a garnish of truffle and chervil. Serve immediately.

Chef's tip

If you have a multi-functional whipper, blend the warm potato purée with 2g (1 tsp) agar-agar, soaked, and transfer the potato mixture to the whipper. Insert the cartridge and keep it warm, not above 60°C (140°F), in a bain-marie.

- 20 medium-large prawns (shrimp), uncooked
- 4 stems of verbena or rosemary, to be used
  as skewers, about 20cm (8in) long
- about 1 tsp olive oil
- 8 tbsp Asian Lime Vinaigrette (page 65)
- salt and pepper of your choice

To garnish
- 1 tbsp torn chervil leaves
- 1 tbsp snipped dill

Equipment
- Metal skewer

HERB-SCENTED PRAWN SKEWERS

115 CALORIES PER PERSON
Cooking and preparation: 15 minutes
Level of difficulty: *
Serves 4

1. Open up each prawn (shrimp) to resemble butterfly wings: pull the head and legs off the prawn (shrimp), then peel away the shell, leaving the last big segment of shell and the tail firmly intact. With a small sharp knife, score lightly along the back of the prawn (shrimp) in a straight line, stopping just before the segment of shell. If there is a long black intestinal vein, pick it out and discard it. Cut deeper into the flesh to open up the prawn (shrimp) into two wings, which remain joined together at the last segment of shell and tail.

2. Strip away and discard the leaves from the verbena stems. If you substitute rosemary, strip away the needle-like leaves and gently straighten the natural curve of the stem. Blanch the stripped stems in a saucepan of boiling salted water for 30 seconds. Drain and refresh in cold water. Using a metal skewer, make a small hole through the tail of each prawn (shrimp). Thread 5 prawns onto each herb-scented skewer through the pre-made holes. Season with salt and pepper.

3. Heat the olive oil in a non-stick frying pan (skillet) over a medium heat. Sauté the skewered prawns for 2 minutes on each side or until they are pink and are no longer transparent. Remove them from the frying pan (skillet) and drain them on kitchen paper.

To serve
Have ready the 4 warm serving plates of your choice, bearing in mind that rectangular plates would lend themselves to the shape of the skewered prawns. Place a skewer on each plate and dress with the Asian Lime Vinaigrette. Garnish with the chervil and dill.

verbena or
rosemary skewer

prawns ◁

asian lime
vinaigrette ▷

Variations

If you cannot obtain verbena or rosemary, you can use bamboo skewers. You can also replace the Asian Lime Vinaigrette with Pondicherry Indian Vinaigrette (page 67) or Thai Vinaigrette (page 68).

- 100g (3½oz) puff pastry, home-made or ready-made, and thawed if frozen
- 500g (1lb 2oz) white button mushrooms, wiped
- 750ml (3 US cups) semi-skimmed (2%) milk
- 200g (7oz) duxelles of mushroom (page 108)
- salt and pepper of your choice

To garnish
- 12 asparagus tips
- 1 tbsp fromage blanc or Greek yogurt (0% fat or low-fat)
- 2 tbsp snipped chives

MUSHROOM TARTS WITH ASPARAGUS TIPS

165 CALORIES PER PERSON
Cooking and preparation: 40 minutes
Level of difficulty: **
Serves 4

1. Divide the puff pastry in 4 quarters and roll into balls. Using a rolling pin, roll out each ball into a circle 14cm (5½–6in) in diameter and 1mm (1/16in) thick. Put the circles onto a baking sheet lined with parchment paper and put into the refrigerator.

2. Put the white button mushrooms in a large saucepan and cover with the milk. Season with salt and pepper and bring the mixture to a simmer over a medium heat. Let it simmer gently for 10 minutes or until the mushrooms are cooked. Drain the mushrooms, setting aside the milk. When the mushrooms are cool enough to handle, cut them into 3–4mm (⅛in) slices and set them aside.

3. Preheat the oven to 200°C (400°F, gas mark 6). Spread the duxelles of mushrooms onto the chilled puff pastry, leaving a ½cm (¼in) border. Carefully lay the slices of mushrooms on top of the duxelles in rows, slightly overlapping each row. Bake the tarts in the oven for 12 minutes or until the pastry is golden and slightly puffed.

4. While the tarts are baking, simmer the asparagus tips in lightly salted water for 3–4 minutes or until bright green and just tender or until al dente. Drain the asparagus gently so as not to break them, and refresh in cold water; drain again and set aside.

5. Pour 300ml (1¼ US cups) of the reserved milk into a medium-sized saucepan and bring to a gentle simmer. Allow the milk to simmer until it is reduced by half. Whisk in the fromage blanc and adjust the seasoning. Cover the sauce and keep it warm, preferably in a bain-marie, until ready to serve.

To serve
Have ready 4 warm serving plates. When the tarts are done, put one on each plate and decorate with the asparagus tips. Using a spoon, gently drizzle the sauce over the tarts and garnish with the fresh chives.

Variations
These tarts can be an attractive feature of a main dish when served with chicken breasts or cooked shellfish, such as clams or mussels.

A historical titbit
The duxelles of mushrooms was created by François Pierre de la Varenne (1618–1678), author of the celebrated book *Cuisinier Francois* and personal chef to the Marquis d'Uxelles, to whom he dedicated his culinary creation.

- 250g (9oz) carrots, peeled and cut into rounds about 3mm (⅛in) thick
- 100ml (⅜ US cup) freshly squeezed orange juice
- 1 tsp honey
- ½ tsp cumin seeds
- 1 egg, lightly beaten
- 4 tbsp Asian Lime Vinaigrette (page 65)
- 4 fillets of red mullet, scaled and small bones removed
- salt and pepper of your choice

For the garnish
- 1 tbsp torn or snipped chervil leaves
- 1 tbsp coriander (cilantro) leaves, some left whole and some snipped
- 1 tbsp snipped flat-leaf parsley
- few small salad leaves (optional)

GRILLED RED MULLET WITH A CARROT CONFIT

160 CALORIES PER PERSON
Cooking and preparation: 45 minutes
Level of difficulty: * *
Serves 4

1. Make a carrot confit. Bring a saucepan of lightly salted water to the boil, add the cut rounds of carrots and simmer for 3 minutes. Drain, refresh in cold water, then drain again; set aside.

2. Off the heat, put the orange juice, honey and cumin seeds into a saucepan or sauté pan with deep sloping sides. Stir to mix, then gently stir in the carrots. Season and cover with a close-fitting round of parchment paper to trap steam and speed up the cooking. Set the saucepan over a low heat and cook the carrots for 20–30 minutes, or until the carrots are tender but retain their shape. You can also cover the saucepan with a lid instead of the parchment paper but the cooking will take longer.

3. Meanwhile, mix together the ingredients for the garnish; set aside in a small dish. When the carrot confit is cooked, use a slotted spoon to transfer it carefully to a plate; set aside to cool. Set aside the cooking liquid.

4. Pour the carrot cooking liquid into a food processor, add the beaten egg and Asian Lime Vinaigrette, then blend together until these ingredients emulsify into a slightly frothy sauce. Set the sauce aside until you are ready to serve.

5. When you are almost ready to cook the fish, preheat the grill to 200°C (400°F, gas mark 6), and heat a grill or griddle pan. Season the fillets of red mullet with salt and pepper.

6. At the last moment, put the fillets on the grill or griddle pan and place under the grill for 2–3 minutes maximum.

To serve
Arrange the carrot confit in a circle of slightly overlapping slices on cold serving plates. Drizzle the sauce on top and around the circle and arrange a fillet of red mullet in the centre. Garnish with the herb salad and serve straight away.

Chef's tip
If you double the ingredients, this recipe can equally well become an attractive main course.

- 2 quail, each about 160g (5½oz), cleaned and spatchcocked (ask your butcher or poulterer)
- about 1 tsp olive oil
- salt and pepper of your choice

For the mushroom mousse
- 160g (5½oz) white button mushrooms, wiped and cut into about 6 pieces
- 100ml (⅜ US cup) semi-skimmed (2%) milk
- 1 tbsp fromage blanc or Greek yogurt (0% fat or low-fat)

For the salad
- 300g (11oz) haricots verts
- 40g (scant 1½oz) white button mushrooms, wiped and cut into small matchsticks
- 100g (3½oz) fresh peach, peeled, stone removed, and cut into small matchsticks
- 1 tsp very finely chopped shallot

For the salad dressing
- 4 tbsp Light Vinaigrette (page 70)
- 2 tbsp passion-fruit juice
- 1 tsp Worcestershire sauce

To garnish (optional)
- few small salad leaves
- few sprigs of chervil or the fresh herbs of your choice

SPATCHCOCKED QUAIL WITH MUSHROOM MOUSSE

170 CALORIES PER PERSON
Cooking and preparation: 30 minutes
Level of difficulty: * *
Serves 4

1. To prepare the mushroom mousse, put the mushroom pieces in a saucepan along with the milk and simmer over a medium heat for about 10 minutes or until the mushrooms are very tender. Drain the mushrooms and transfer them to a food processor with the liquid that clings to them. Blend them to a smooth purée and gradually incorporate the fromage blanc. Taste, and adjust the seasoning of the mousse; set it aside in a cool place.

2. For the salad, cook the haricots verts in lightly salted simmering water for 6–8 minutes, depending on their size. Drain, refresh in cold water, drain again and transfer to a mixing bowl. Add the remaining salad ingredients – the mushroom and peach matchsticks and the shallot. Mix gently to distribute the ingredients; set aside. In a separate bowl, make the salad dressing by mixing together the Light Vinaigrette, the passion-fruit juice, the Worcestershire sauce and the salt and pepper; set aside.

3. When you are almost ready to cook the quail, preheat the grill to its hot setting or preheat the oven to 200°C (400°F, gas mark 6). Season the quail, brush them with a little olive oil and cook them beneath the grill or in the oven for 3–4 minutes on each side, or until done to your liking.

To serve
Turn the salad in the dressing and divide it between 4 serving plates. Pass the mushroom mousse between two teaspoons to make oval quenelle shapes.Gently place a quenelle alongside each salad. Cut each quail once through its back and then across its breast and thighs to make 4 pieces. Place 2 pieces of quail on top of each salad arrangement. If you like, add a few small salad leaves and the herbs of your choice.

Chef's tip
Spatchcocking is an old Irish term meaning to make a butterfly shape, usually with a bird. If you want to try to do it yourself, it is easy: lay the bird on a board, breast-side down. Cut along the spine on both sides and remove it. You will now be able to lay the bird flat and open it up like a book.

- 500ml (2⅛ US cups) water
- 1 tbsp white wine vinegar
- 40g (scant 1½oz) finely sliced red cabbage
  about 2 tsp olive oil
- 60g (2oz) courgette (zucchini) peel in long
  strips, with a thin layer of flesh attached
- 30g (1oz) mangetout (snow peas), cut into thin
  julienne strips about 4cm (1½in) long
- 30g (1oz) red onion, chopped
- 360g (13oz) piece of sirloin, fillet or rump steak
  (top sirloin, sirloin, filet mignon or round steak),
  trimmed of fat and connective tissue
- salt and pepper of your choice

For the raw onion garnish
- 30g (1oz) red onion, finely sliced
- 2 tbsp coriander (cilantro) leaves

To garnish
- 2 hearts of Little Gem or cos lettuce,
  leaves separated
- 6 tbsp Thai Vinaigrette (page 68)
- fleur de sel

BEEF SALAD WITH RED ONION AND RED CABBAGE

185 CALORIES PER PERSON
Cooking and preparation: 30 minutes
Level of difficulty: * *
Serves 4

1. Start by preparing the raw onion garnish: soak the onions and the coriander (cilantro) leaves in cold water containing a few ice cubes for 30 minutes – this will increase their flavour and crispness.

2. Meanwhile, prepare the vegetables: bring 500ml (2⅛ US cups) water and the white wine vinegar to the boil. Blanch the red cabbage for 3 minutes then drain, refresh in cold water and drain again; set aside.

3. If you intend to grill the beef and eat it warm, preheat the grill to a hot setting about 20 minutes before you want to serve the dish.

4. Complete the cooked vegetables by heating 1 tbsp of the olive oil in a non-stick frying pan (skillet). Lightly sauté the courgette (zucchini) peel and the mangetout (snow peas) for 2 minutes, all the time stirring and shaking the pan. Season and set aside on a plate in a warm place.

5. Add the remaining olive oil to the frying pan (skillet), and sweat the chopped red onion for several minutes or until soft without browning; set aside in a warm place.

6. Grill or pan-fry the beef to the degree of doneness you like, without using additional fat. When the beef is cooked, cover it loosely with foil and set aside to rest for 7 minutes in a warm place.

To serve
Drain the raw onion garnish and dress the lettuce leaves in about half of the Thai Vinaigrette. Arrange half the leaves on the bottom of 4 serving plates. Add the prepared red cabbage, the courgettes (zucchini), mangetout (snow peas) and onions, and then add the remaining salad leaves.

Carve the beef into thin slices. Season them and coat them lightly in the remaining Thai Vinaigrette. Drape the slices on top of the lettuce leaves and arrange the drained raw onion garnish over the beef. Add a touch of fleur de sel and serve.

- 160g (5½oz) cold cooked beef, trimmed and cut into 1cm (½in) dice
- 1 apple (Golden Delicious, Bramley, Pink Lady, Ja77, Adam's Pearmain or Cox), peeled, cored and cut into 1cm (½in) dice
- 50g (1¾oz) Tomato Confit (page 81), cut into ½cm (¼in) dice
- 20g (¾oz) capers, coarsely chopped
- 1 tbsp chopped flat-leaf parsley
- 1 tbsp chopped chives
- 2 tbsp Light Mayonnaise (page 79)
- 2 tbsp fromage blanc or Greek yogurt (0% fat or low-fat)
- few drops of Tabasco sauce
- ½ tbsp Xeres vinegar or other sherry vinegar of your choice
- salt and pepper of your choice

For the sauce
- 2 tbsp fromage blanc or Greek yogurt (0% fat or low-fat)
- 1 tbsp semi-skimmed (2%) milk
- 1 tsp traditional French wholegrain mustard
- 1 tsp Xeres vinegar or other sherry vinegar of your choice
- 1 tbsp chopped or snipped chives

To garnish
- handful of lamb's lettuce or mesclun salad leaves
- 1 tbsp Light Vinaigrette (page 70)
- ½ Granny Smith apple, cored, left unpeeled and cut into matchsticks 3mm x 5cm (⅛in x 2in)

Equipment
- 4 metal or silicone food rings

COLD BEEF SALAD WITH A MUSTARD SAUCE

250 CALORIES PER PERSON
Cooking and preparation: 15 minutes
Level of difficulty: * *
Serves 4

1. In a large mixing bowl, combine the diced cold beef, the diced apple, the Tomato Confit and the chopped capers, parsley and chives. Gradually stir in the Light Mayonnaise, the fromage blanc, the Tabasco sauce and the vinegar. Use a fork to mix gently until the ingredients are evenly distributed. Taste, and adjust the seasoning. Cover and chill this beef salad in the refrigerator.

2. For the sauce, in a separate bowl mix together the fromage blanc, milk, mustard, vinegar, chives and seasoning; set this aside in the refrigerator until you are ready to serve the salad.

To serve
Dress the lamb's lettuce or mesclun salad leaves in the Light Vinaigrette and arrange them in a circle on each serving plate. Put a food ring on top and fill it with the beef salad. Leave the salad to settle for at least a few minutes, then, just before serving, lift away the rings. Garnish with the matchsticks of apple, standing them upright in the beef salad. Drizzle a ribbon of sauce around the circle of leaves and serve.

Chef's tip
The beef salad tastes even better if it is prepared the night before.

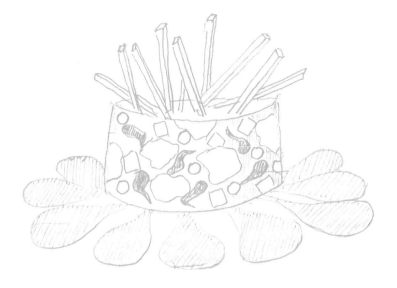

- 600g (1lb 5oz) fresh ceps, or frozen and thawed
- 1 tbsp olive oil
- 1 tbsp finely chopped shallot
- 1 firm pear, about 220g (8oz)
- about 3 tbsp Light Vinaigrette (page 70)
- 2 tbsp meat juices left over from a roast, or good-quality stock, home-made or from a cube
- 2 tbsp passion-fruit juice
- 4 very small sprigs of mesclun salad leaves
- salt and pepper of your choice

To garnish
- 20g (¾oz) lamb's lettuce or other very small leaves
- 1 tbsp finely chopped fresh herbs, such as flat-leaf parsley, tarragon and chives
- 1–2 tbsp julienne strips of lemon zest (Terms and Techniques, page 327)

Equipment
- 4 food rings, 10cm (4in) in diameter

CEPS AND PEAR IN A PASSION-FRUIT DRESSING

150 CALORIES PER PERSON
Cooking and preparation: 30 minutes
Level of difficulty: *
Serves 4

---

1. Wipe the ceps clean and separate the caps from the stalks. Cut the caps into thin 3mm (⅛in) slices. Cut the stalks into ½cm (¼in) dice. Heat half of the olive oil in a non-stick frying pan (skillet). Add the sliced caps and colour them lightly on each side, adding salt and pepper. Drain them on kitchen paper and set aside.

2. Add the remaining oil to the frying pan (skillet) and sauté the diced stalks rapidly for about 30 seconds, shaking the pan to keep them moving. Add the finely chopped shallot. Season to taste and sweat for a minute or two until the shallot softens without colouring. Use a slotted spoon to transfer the ingredients to kitchen paper to drain.

3. Peel and core the pear, then cut the flesh into ½cm (¼in) dice. (If you are not going to use the diced pear immediately, put it into a little water and lemon juice to prevent browning.) In a mixing bowl, combine the diced stalks of the ceps and the pear. In a separate bowl, mix together 2 of the tablespoons of Light Vinaigrette, the meat juices or stock, and the passion-fruit juice. Taste, and adjust the seasoning, then pour it over the ceps and pear; mix gently.

4. Dress the slices of cep and the mesclun salad leaves, separately, in the remaining Light Vinaigrette.

To serve

Arrange the lamb's lettuce in a circle, about 12cm (5in) in diameter, on each serving plate. Put a food ring on top. Fill it with the dressed diced stalks of ceps and pear, flattening the surface lightly with the back of a spoon to leave a small space between the salad and the rim of the food ring. Arrange the slices of ceps in this space.

Sprinkle the chopped herbs and julienne strips of lemon zest over the entire arrangement. Lift off the rings. Add a small bunch of dressed mesclun salad leaves alongside the ceps and serve.

- 1 large orange or 2 small ones
- pinch of powdered cinnamon
- few drops of orange flower water (also called orange blossom water)
- 1 tbsp olive oil
- 250g (9oz) carrots
- ½ clove of garlic, peeled and sliced wafer-thin
- 500ml (2⅛ US cups) water
- 2g (1 tsp) ground cumin
- 2 tbsp freshly squeezed lemon juice
- 1 tbsp torn coriander (cilantro) leaves
- salt and pepper of your choice

To garnish
- 2 hearts of Little Gem or cos lettuce, washed, dried and cut into quarters
- 4–8 pitted black olives, whole or sliced into small rings
- 8 small sprigs of chervil or a few mint leaves
- few sprigs of coriander (cilantro)
- fleur de sel (optional)

SPICED CARROT AND ORANGE SALAD

75 CALORIES PER PERSON
Cooking and preparation: 30 minutes
Level of difficulty: *
Serves 4

---

1. Peel the orange using a knife to cut away the white pith along with the peel. Using a plate to collect the juice, cut the orange in half, then slice it into half-rounds, then into quarters to make fan shapes about ½cm (¼in) thick. Sprinkle with the cinnamon, salt, orange flower water and half of the olive oil. Set aside in a cool place.

2. Peel and slice the carrots into thin 2mm (about ⅛in) rounds, using a canelle knife (Terms and Techniques, page 326) if possible to create grooves that give the slices a pretty edge. Put the slices in a saucepan with the garlic, the remaining olive oil and the water. Season and bring to the boil. Adjust the heat and simmer the carrots for 10 minutes or until they are tender but retain their shape.

3. Strain through a sieve set over a bowl to catch the cooking liquid. Set the carrots aside, spread out on a plate, to become cold. Over a high heat, reduce the cooking liquid to about 1 tablespoon of syrupy glaze; set it aside in a small dish to cool.

4. Sprinkle the cold carrots evenly with the cumin, the cooled glaze, the lemon juice and the coriander (cilantro) leaves. Turn the carrots to coat them. Taste, and adjust the seasoning.

To serve

Arrange the carrots and orange among the lettuce hearts. Drizzle over any remaining juices from the orange. Add the black olives and sprigs of chervil or mint and a few coriander (cilantro) leaves. If you like, finish with a pinch of fleur de sel.

Variation

By adding a few scallops or slices of grilled chicken to this salad, you can very easily transform it into a main course.

- 160g (5½oz) white button mushrooms, wiped carefully so as not to remove the skin
- 50g (1¾oz) celeriac, peeled and grated
- 50g (1¾oz) tomatoes, peeled, cored and deseeded (Terms and Techniques, pages 327–8), then cut into small dice or 50g (1¾oz) Tomato Confit (page 81), cut into small dice
- 1 tbsp chopped or snipped chives
- 1 tbsp traditional French wholegrain mustard
- 4 tbsp Mushroom Vinaigrette (page 66)
- 4 tbsp fromage blanc or Greek yogurt (0% fat or low-fat)
- salt and pepper of your choice

To garnish
- handful of lamb's lettuce or mesclun salad leaves
- ½ Granny Smith apple, unpeeled

Equipment (optional)
- 4 food rings, 10cm (4in) in diameter

A SALAD OF MUSHROOMS, CELERIAC, TOMATO AND APPLE

75 CALORIES PER PERSON USING FRESH TOMATO;
90 CALORIES USING TOMATO CONFIT
Cooking and preparation: 15 minutes
Level of difficulty: *
Serves 4

1. Cut each mushroom in half lengthways. For neat slices, turn each half onto its cut side and slice it thinly. Put the slices in a bowl and add the grated celeriac, the diced tomato or Tomato Confit, and the chives. Mix these ingredients together gently so as not to break the mushrooms.

2. In a separate bowl, mix together the mustard, salt and pepper, the Mushroom Vinaigrette and the fromage blanc. Add this mixture to the vegetables and turn them gently to coat them. Taste, and adjust the seasoning.

To serve
Arrange the salad leaves on 4 serving plates. If you are using food rings, put them on the plates and fill them with the mushroom salad. Grate the Granny Smith apple at the last moment so that the flesh does not brown, and scatter the grated apple on top of the salad. Lift away the food rings and serve.

- 300g (11oz) very small squid, with tentacles, cleaned, washed in cold water and dried
- 4 pimientos del piquillo, bottled (Terms and Techniques, page 328)
- salt

For the marinade
- 1 clove of garlic, unpeeled and crushed
- 2 sprigs of thyme
- 1 bay leaf, preferably fresh
- 3 tbsp Light Vinaigrette (page 70)
- 1 tbsp Xeres vinegar or other sherry vinegar of your choice

To garnish
- 4 bunches of mesclun salad leaves
- 2 tbsp Light Vinaigrette (page 70)
- 1 tbsp chervil, leaves only
- fleur de sel

CATALAN-STYLE SQUID SALAD WITH SWEET RED PEPPERS

160 CALORIES PER PERSON
Cooking and preparation: 20 minutes, plus 24 hours of resting in the refrigerator. This recipe is to be started the day before.
Level of difficulty: * *
Serves 4

1. Prepare the squid; if you have not been able to buy very small squid, slice larger ones into rings. Set a heavy-based frying pan (skillet) over a medium heat. When it is hot, add the squid and the salt but no fat or oil. Sauté the squid, making sure they move – or jump – all the time by stirring and shaking the frying pan (skillet). When, after about 2–3 minutes, the squid are lightly coloured, transfer them to a bowl.

2. Add the marinade ingredients – the crushed garlic, thyme, bay leaf, the 3 tablespoons of Light Vinaigrette and the sherry vinegar. Mix together, ensuring that the squid are thoroughly and evenly coated in the marinade, then cover and chill in the refrigerator for 24 hours.

3. Cut the pimientos del piquillo in half lengthways, then rinse them carefully under cold running water to remove the pips. Pat them dry on kitchen paper. Using, ideally, a ridged griddle pan to give the peppers scorch lines, grill or pan-fry the peppers on one side only for several minutes.

To serve
Dress the mesclun salad leaves in the 2 tablespoons of Light Vinaigrette and divide them between the 4 serving plates. Add two halves of the pimientos del piquillo to each plate.

Remove the bowl of marinated squid from the refrigerator and discard the garlic, thyme and bay leaf. Use a slotted spoon to lift the squid out of the marinade and arrange them on the plates. Drizzle over a little of the marinade. Scatter over the chervil leaves and a little fleur de sel and serve.

- 15 large uncooked prawns (large or jumbo shrimp), on the shell
- 1 large sheet of filo (phyllo) pastry
- salt and pepper of your choice

For the crab filling
- 100g (3½oz) crabmeat (fresh or frozen and thawed)
- 1 tbsp freshly squeezed lime juice,
- 2 tbsp Light Mayonnaise (page 79)
- 1 tbsp fromage blanc or Greek yogurt (0% fat or low-fat)
- 2 drops of Tabasco sauce
- 1 tbsp finely chopped or snipped coriander (cilantro) leaves

For the salad
- 40g (scant 1½oz) small frisée leaves
- 30g (1oz) watercress leaves
- 10 small basil leaves
- 5 small mint leaves
- 10 small tarragon leaves
- 3 segments of grapefruit, cut into small, even dice
- 3 segments of orange, cut into small, even dice
- 3 tbsp Shellfish Vinaigrette (page 73)

For the sauce
- 2 tbsp fromage blanc or Greek yogurt (0% fat or low-fat)
- 1 tbsp traditional French wholegrain mustard or other grainy mustard
- 2 tbsp semi-skimmed (2%) milk

To garnish (optional)
- ½ Granny Smith apple, cut into fine julienne strips

PRAWN SALAD WITH CRUNCHY CRAB-FILLED BISCUITS

160 CALORIES PER PERSON
Cooking and preparation: 30 minutes
Level of difficulty: * *
Serves 5

1. To butterfly the prawns (shrimp), open up each prawn (shrimp) to resemble butterfly wings: pull the head and legs off, then peel away the shell, leaving the last big segment of shell and the tail firmly intact. With a small sharp knife, score lightly along the back of the prawn (shrimp) in a straight line, stopping just before the segment of shell. If there is a long black intestinal vein, pick it out and discard it. Cut deeper into the flesh to open the prawn (shrimp) to make two wings, which remain joined together at the last segment of shell and tail. Cover and set aside in the refrigerator until you are ready to cook them.

2. For the filo (phyllo) pastry biscuits, preheat the oven to 150°C (300°F, gas mark 2). Lay the sheet of filo (phyllo) pastry carefully on a marble slab or work counter. To keep the filo (phyllo) moist while you work, cover it with a layer of greaseproof or waxed paper and put a damp tea towel on top. Working quickly, use a 4cm (1½in) pastry cutter or an upside-down coffee cup and a small sharp knife, to cut 30 circles. Lift these with a spatula and transfer them carefully to a baking sheet. Bake them in the oven for 15 minutes, or until dry and lightly coloured. Set them aside in a cool dry place.

3. For the crab filling, put the crabmeat in a bowl and flake it with a fork. Add the lime juice, the Light Mayonnaise, the fromage blanc, Tabasco sauce, coriander (cilantro), salt and pepper. Use the fork to mix the ingredients until they are distributed evenly; set aside until ready to use.

4. To prepare the salad, combine the frisée with the leaves of watercress, basil, mint and tarragon. In a separate bowl, mix the diced grapefruit and orange with the Shellfish Vinaigrette. For the sauce, mix together the fromage blanc, the mustard and the milk. Season to taste and set aside the salad and sauce separately until you are ready to serve.

5. About 10–15 minutes before serving, use a small coffee spoon to distribute a little of the crab filling onto 15 of the filo (phyllo) pastry biscuits. Top these with the remaining 15 biscuits. Steam or poach the prawns for 2 minutes or until pink and cooked to your liking.

To serve

Have ready the serving plates. On one side of each plate, arrange 3 crab-filled biscuits in a row with 3 blobs of sauce in an adjoining row. On the other side, make a little pile of the dressed citrus fruit with the salad leaves on top. Sprinkle with the julienne of apple. Add 3 prawns with their tails pointing upwards.

- 200g (7oz) carrots
- 100g (3½oz) celeriac
- 150g (5½oz) courgettes (zucchini)
- 150g (5½oz) cauliflower or broccoli
- 150g (5½oz) celery sticks (stalks)
- 1 leek
- 150g (5½oz) fennel
- 1 head of chicory (Belgian endive)
- 100g (3½oz) white button mushrooms
- 4–5 small new onions
- 4–5 small purple poivrade artichokes
- 50g (1¾oz) mangetout (snow peas)
- ½ tbsp coarse sea salt and freshly
  ground pepper
- 1 tsp coriander seeds
- 1 tsp fructose
- 4 sprigs of thyme
- 1 bay leaf, preferably fresh
- 2 cloves of garlic, unpeeled and crushed
- 120ml (½ US cup) dry white wine
- 1 tbsp olive oil
- 4–5 tomatoes, ideally a mixture of round and
  plum shapes

To garnish
- few very small salad leaves, ideally with some
  colour, such as radicchio
- 8–10 sprigs of fresh seasonal herbs

CRUNCHY VEGETABLES WITH CORIANDER SEEDS

100 CALORIES PER PERSON
Cooking and preparation: 45 minutes (can be started the night before)
Level of difficulty: * *
Serves 4–5

1. Scrape or peel and wash the vegetables. Cut them as follows: the carrots, celeriac and courgettes (zucchini) into matchsticks about 3cm (1¼in) long x ½cm (¼in) wide; the cauliflower or broccoli into little florets; the sticks of celery and the leek widthways into ½cm (¼in) pieces; the fennel into small quarters or wedges; the chicory (Belgian endive) lengthways into quarters; and the mushrooms into halves or quarters, depending on size. Peel the small new onions and leave them whole. Turn the purple poivrade artichokes and remove the choke (Terms and Techniques, pages 328–9). Cut the hearts and the attached part of the stalk in half. Trim the mangetout (snow peas), then cut them diagonally, either into halves or thirds, depending on size.

2. Put all the vegetables – except the courgettes (zucchini), mangetout (snow peas) and tomatoes – into a large saucepan. Season with salt, pepper, the coriander seeds, fructose, thyme, bay leaf and garlic. Add the white wine and olive oil, cover and simmer briskly for 12–15 minutes, stirring frequently. Remove the saucepan from the heat. Leave the vegetables to cool in their cooking liquid – overnight if you wish. Drain them in a sieve set over a bowl. Set the vegetables aside and keep the cooking liquid.

3. Just before serving, cook the courgettes (zucchini) and mangetout (snow peas) in a saucepan of lightly salted water for 6 minutes or until al dente. Drain and refresh in cold water, then drain again. Peel the tomatoes by nicking their skin and dropping them into very hot water for up to 1 minute, then plunging them into cold water and pulling back the skin. If you like, leave the stalks of any small tomatoes intact. Depending on size and shape, cut the tomatoes into halves, quarters or wedges. Combine the cooled courgettes (zucchini) and mangetout (snow peas) with the tomatoes and the drained cooked vegetables.

To serve
If possible, use serving plates with shallow bowls. Arrange the vegetables in a pretty piled-up design on each plate. Drizzle over a little of the reserved cooking liquid. Garnish with a few small, colourful salad leaves and herbs. Small leaves of radicchio, purple basil, chervil and coriander (cilantro) are all good choices.

Variations

This delicious salad of mixed vegetable shapes lends itself to a variety of uses and presentations. The version here makes an excellent first course. However, with the addition of a poached or boiled egg, it becomes a light and simple main-course salad. It also partners well with a main course of fish.

- 200g (7oz) Coco de Paimpol beans or other dried white beans
- 1 tsp olive oil
- 50g (1¾oz) ceps or white button mushrooms, wiped and cut into 1cm (½in) dice
- 2 tbsp Mushroom Vinaigrette (page 66)
- 1 tbsp passion-fruit juice
- 1 tsp Worcestershire sauce
- 50g (1¾oz) mango, cut into 1cm (½in) dice
- 50g (1¾oz) pear flesh, cut into 1cm (½in) dice
- 1 tbsp very finely chopped or snipped new white onion
- 50g (1¾oz) Tomato Confit (page 81), cut into
- 1cm (½in) dice
- 1 tbsp finely chopped flat-leaf parsley
- salt and pepper of your choice

To garnish
- 5 small bunches of frisée lettuce, lamb's lettuce or mesclun salad leaves
- 2 pears, peeled, cored and thinly sliced (optional)

SALAD OF WHITE BEANS, MANGO, MUSHROOM AND PEAR

100 CALORIES PER PERSON
Cooking and preparation: 10 minutes
Level of difficulty: *
Serves 5

---

1. To cook the dried white beans, simmer them in a saucepan of water for about 45 minutes or until tender. Check the packet instructions in case they must be soaked overnight before cooking. Drain, refresh in cold water and drain again.

2. Heat the olive oil in a non-stick frying pan (skillet) and sauté the diced mushroms for 2–3 minutes, shaking the pan and stirring. Season the mushrooms then set them aside.

3. Mix together in a small bowl the Mushroom Vinaigrette, the passion-fruit juice and the Worcestershire sauce to make a dressing. Taste, and adjust the seasoning.

4. In a large salad bowl, combine the white beans, the mango, the diced pear and the onion. Add the Tomato Confit, the parsley and the dressing, then mix gently to distribute the ingredients evenly. Taste, and adjust the seasoning.

To serve
Place a little bunch of frisée or the leaves of your choice in the centre of each serving plate and surround it with the white bean salad. If you like, you can lightly colour slices of pear in a non-stick frying pan (skillet) and add these just before serving.

- 6 tbsp Light Vinaigrette (page 70)
- 15g (½oz) Orange Blossom Sauce (page 75)
- 200g (7oz) scallops, off the shell
- 5 bunches of lamb's lettuce
- few small young salad leaves of your choice
- 2 tsp olive oil
- few orange blossoms (optional)
- pinch of fleur de sel
- salt and pepper of your choice

A WARM SALAD OF ORANGE-SCENTED SCALLOPS AND LAMB'S LETTUCE

140 CALORIES PER PERSON
Cooking and preparation: 15 minutes
Level of difficulty: *
Serves 5

1. To prepare the sauce, put the Light Vinaigrette and the Orange Blossom Sauce in a small saucepan. Stir, and add salt and pepper to taste. Set the saucepan aside, ready to be heated through just before serving.

2. With a sharp knife, slice horizontally through each scallop to make 2 or 3 thin rounds. Cover the rounds and set them aside in the refrigerator until you are ready to cook them.

3. When you are almost ready to serve the salad, put the bunches of lamb's lettuce and the other salad leaves in a mixing bowl. Turn the leaves in one of the teaspoons of olive oil. Season with salt as required. Divide the lamb's lettuce between 5 serving plates, setting aside the other salad leaves.

4. Put the saucepan containing the sauce over a low heat. Heat the remaining teaspoon of olive oil in a non-stick frying pan (skillet) over a medium heat. Add the scallops to the pan, season to taste, and cook them for about 1 minute – on one side only to avoid over-cooking them.

To serve
Drizzle a little of the sauce onto each plate. Use a spatula to lift the scallops and place them on top of the sauce. Decorate with the remaining salad leaves and orange blossom, if used. Add a pinch of fleur de sel and serve.

- 300g (11oz) new potatoes, unpeeled and washed
- 7 tbsp Thai Vinaigrette (page 68)
- 1 tbsp soy sauce
- 2 chicken breasts, skin removed and trimmed free of connective tissue and fat
- 450ml (2 US cups) chicken stock, preferably home-made (page 44) or from a cube
- 3 Little Gem lettuces, leaves separated, rinsed and dried
- julienne strips from the zest of 1 lemon (Terms and Techniques, page 327)
- 1 tsp peeled and julienned or grated fresh ginger
- 1 tbsp chopped coriander (cilantro) leaves
- 1 tbsp chopped chervil leaves
- salt and pepper of your choice
- fleur de sel (optional)

WARM CHICKEN SALAD WITH POTATOES

140 CALORIES PER PERSON
Cooking and preparation: 30 minutes
Level of difficulty: **
Serves 6

1. Cook the potatoes in lightly salted boiling water for about 20 minutes or until tender; drain. When they are cool enough to handle, slice them into rounds, peeling them first if you wish. Season with 4 tbsp of the Thai vinaigrette and the soy sauce. Taste the potatoes for seasoning and add salt and pepper if required. Use the potatoes straight away or, if you like, leave them to marinate at room temperature for at least 20 minutes and up to 2 hours. The longer they marinate, the more intense their flavour.

2. About 20 minutes before you want to serve the salad, poach the chicken breasts in gently simmering stock for 8–10 minutes or until cooked. Remove them with a slotted spoon and transfer them to a cutting board. Leave them to cool for a few minutes.

To serve

Arrange the potatoes in a flat layer on each plate. Slice the chicken breasts into long, slender strips and lay them over the potatoes. Pile the lettuce leaves on top.

Combine the julienne of lemon and ginger with the chopped coriander (cilantro) and chervil, then sprinkle this mixture over the salads. Drizzle over the remaining 3 tbsp of Thai Vinaigrette and, if you like, add a pinch of fleur de sel.

- 1 skate wing, about 800g (1¾lb)
- 1 small Chinese cabbage, about 600g (1lb 5oz)
- 1 tsp olive oil
- 8 tbsp Thai Vinaigrette (page 68)
- salt and pepper of your choice
- fleur de sel

For the garnish
- 2 small new white onions
- 2 tbsp coriander (cilantro) leaves

Equipment
- Steamer or couscoussier

THAI-FLAVOURED WING OF SKATE WITH CHINESE CABBAGE

235 CALORIES PER PERSON
Cooking and preparation: 30 minutes
Level of difficulty: *
Serves 4

1. To prepare the skate wing ready for cooking, cut it into 4 equal pieces and wash in cold water to remove the viscous material covering their skin; set aside, covered, in the refrigerator.

2. To prepare the garnish, peel the white onions and slice them very thinly. Immerse the slices in a bowl of iced water to make them taste milder. Add the coriander (cilantro) leaves. Cover the bowl and transfer it to a cold place.

3. Separate the leaves of the Chinese cabbage and wash and drain them. Cut away the white rib from each leaf, then slice the rib widthways into pieces about ½cm (¼in) wide. Slice the leaves into strips about 3cm (1¼in) long. Heat the olive oil in a non-stick frying pan (skillet) and sauté the white rib pieces for 4–5 minutes over a medium heat. Season, then add the green strips of leaf and cook for a further 1–2 minutes. Adjust the seasoning and keep the cabbage warm.

4. In a small saucepan set over a low heat, warm the Thai Vinaigrette.

5. Put the pieces of skate into a steamer or couscoussier and season to taste. Cover the steamer and set it to cook for about 10 minutes. When the fish is cooked, lift away the skin from each section then gently lift away the fillets from the cartilaginous skeleton. Keep the fillets warm in a covered dish.

To serve
Arrange a bed of cabbage on each plate and lay the pieces of skate on top. Drizzle over the warm Thai Vinaigrette. Drain the onions and coriander (cilantro), then drape curls of onion on top and sprinkle with the coriander (cilantro) leaves. Finish with a pinch of fleur de sel.

- 2 fillets of sea bass, skin left on, taken from a fish weighing 800g—1kg (1¾—2¼lb)
- 500ml (2⅛ US cups) vegetable stock, preferably home-made (page 42) or from a cube
- 2 garlic flakes (page 82)
- 1 tbsp teriyaki sauce
- salt and pepper of your choice

For the vegetables
- 40g (scant 1½oz) carrots, peeled or scrubbed
- 2 new white onions
- 4 small potatoes, preferably Charlotte, unpeeled
- 12 small asparagus spears, peeled
- 150g (5½oz) green cabbage leaves, white core removed and cut into strips
- 75g (2½oz) whites of leek, cut into julienne strips 4cm (1½in) long

To garnish
- fleur de sel
- 4 slices of lemon, pith and peel removed
- about 8 tarragon leaves
- about 8 sprigs of chervil
- 4–8 sprigs of dill

POACHED SEA BASS WITH GARLIC, TERIYAKI, VEGETABLES AND HERBS

330 CALORIES PER PERSON
Cooking and preparation: 45 minutes
Level of difficulty: * * *
Serves 4

1. Use tweezers to remove any small bones remaining in the 2 fillets of sea bass. Trim each fillet and cut it in half lengthways, to make 4 equal-sized smaller fillets. Cover these and set them aside in the refrigerator.

2. Put half of the vegetable stock in a saucepan, adding the garlic flakes and the teriyaki sauce. Bring this stock to the boil, then remove it from the heat and leave it to infuse, covered, at room temperature.

3. Prepare the vegetables: for a pretty effect when the carrots are sliced, cut grooves down their sides using a canelle knife (Terms and Techniques, page 326). Slice the carrots widthways into thin rounds no more than 3mm (⅛in) thick; set aside. Slice the peeled onions into very thin rounds; set aside. Cook the potatoes in lightly salted simmering water for about 20 minutes or until just cooked.

4. Meanwhile, heat the remaining vegetable stock in a saucepan large enough to accommodate all the vegetables. Drain the potatoes and, when cool enough to handle, peel them. Transfer them to the warm stock, cover and set aside in a warm place, such as a very low oven.

5. In separate saucepans of lightly salted water, simmer the carrots, asparagus spears, strips of cabbage, julienne strips of leek and sliced onions briefly until al dente — allowing no more than 6 minutes for the carrots, 5 for the asparagus, 4 for the cabbage and leeks, and 3 for the onions. Drain the vegetables, refresh in cold water and drain again. Cut off the tips of the asparagus spears to a length of about 5cm (2in); cut the stalk section into tiny dice of about ½cm (¼in). Transfer all these vegetables to the saucepan of warm stock containing the potatoes and continue to keep the stock warm.

6. Select a roasting pan or baking dish (preferably of enamelled cast-iron) that you can put over direct heat. Season the fillets of bass and lay them in the bottom. Add the garlic-infused stock. Over a slow to medium heat, bring the stock to the boil, then remove the roasting pan from the heat and cover it with aluminium foil. Set it aside in a warm place, so that the fish can continue to cook in its own heat. After 5 minutes, test the fish for doneness, preferably using a digital probe thermometer which should read 49°–50°C (120°–122°F). If the fish isn't ready, leave it a few minutes longer.

To serve

Have ready 4 warm shallow-bowled serving plates that can accommodate the juices. Use a spatula to transfer the fillets of bass to the plates. Either peel off the fish skin completely or, for a decorative effect, peel away about half of it and fold it back on itself (see photograph).

Retrieve the vegetables from the stock and distribute them around the fish, ladling over some of the stock as well. Taste, and adjust the seasoning, adding fleur de sel as required. Garnish with the slices of lemon and sprigs of chervil and dill, and serve immediately.

- 12 scallops
- 80g (scant 3oz) young spinach leaves, unwashed, stems and main ribs removed
- little olive oil, for brushing
- 2 tbsp tomatoes, peeled, cored and deseeded (Terms and Techniques, pages 327–8), then cut into ½cm (¼in) dice
- salt and pepper of your choice

For the sauce

- 1 tbsp very finely chopped shallot
- 5 tbsp Noilly Prat (vermouth)
- 300ml (1¼ US cups) fish stock, either home-made (page 47) or from a cube
- 200ml (⅞ US cup) semi-skimmed (2%) milk
- ½ tsp peeled and chopped fresh ginger
- 5g (¼oz) green cardamom pods, lightly crushed
- 1 tsp cornflour (cornstarch), mixed with a little cold water

To garnish

- salad leaves from the heart of a Little Gem, or the leaves of your choice
- 2 tbsp chervil, leaves only
- fleur de sel (optional)

Equipment

- 4 individual flameproof porcelain or enamelled cast-iron shallow-sided oven-to-table dishes

CARDAMOM-SCENTED SCALLOPS WITH TOMATOES AND SPINACH

120 CALORIES PER PERSON
Cooking and preparation: 50 minutes
Level of difficulty: * *
Serves 4

1. For the sauce, put the shallot and Noilly Prat in a saucepan and bring the liquid to the boil. Adjust the heat to maintain a brisk simmer until the shallot is soft and the liquid has reduced to the consistency of runny jam. Add the fish stock and reduce the liquid by half.

2. Stir in the milk, ginger and cardamom, and simmer for a further 5 minutes. Remove the sauce from the heat; Taste, and adjust the seasoning. Cover with a lid or clingfilm (plastic wrap) and leave to infuse for about 30 minutes.

3. Bring the infusion briefly back to the boil, then remove it from the heat. After a minute or so, gradually stir in the cornflour (cornstarch) blended with a little water. Stir well then strain the sauce through a fine sieve. Check the seasoning once more and keep the sauce hot, preferably in a bain-marie.

4. Slice each scallop horizontally into 2 or 3 rounds, depending on the thickness of the scallops; set these aside briefly in a cold place. When you are almost ready to serve the scallops, heat the flameproof dishes and preheat the grill to its highest setting.

5. Wash and drain the spinach leaves. Do not dry them but leave the water that clings to them. Chop the leaves coarsely. Arrange the spinach in the bottom of each dish, then put the scallops – brushed with a little oil – on top, and scatter over the diced tomato. Season with salt and pepper.

6. Put the dishes under the hot grill for about 2 minutes. Meanwhile, over heat, quickly whisk the sauce to a smooth emulsion – preferably using a stick blender. Make sure the sauce is hot.

To serve

Remove the dishes from the grill and sit each one on a large unheated serving plate. Coat the scallops with the sauce. Accompany the scallops with a few dressed leaves of a slightly sweet lettuce, such as Little Gem. Add a few leaves of chervil and, if you like, a little fleur de sel.

- 8 fillets of red mullet, skin left on and scaled
- 1 tsp finely chopped shallot
- 200ml (⅞ US cup) fish stock, either home-made (page 47) or from a cube
- small bunch of mint leaves or verbena leaves, tied with kitchen string
- salt of your choice

For the sauce
- 1 tbsp chopped or snipped mint leaves or verbena leaves
- ½ tsp coarsely ground mixed peppercorns of your choice
- 2 egg yolks
- 3 tbsp cold water

RED MULLET WITH A FROTHY MINT AND PEPPER SABAYON

250 CALORIES PER PERSON
Cooking and preparation: 20 minutes
Level of difficulty: * *
Serves 4

1. Preheat the oven to 180°C (350°F, gas mark 4). Remove any remaining scales from the fillets of red mullet and use tweezers to pick out any small bones. Rinse and pat dry. Choose a roasting pan or baking dish big enough to accommodate the fillets in a single layer and distribute the chopped shallot in the bottom. Lay the fillets on top and season them with salt.

2. Heat the fish stock and drizzle it over the fish. Add the bunch of mint or verbena leaves. Cover the roasting pan with aluminium foil. Put it in the hot oven for 3 minutes then take it out. Remove the fillets and transfer them to a warm covered dish in a warm place while you prepare the sauce.

3. To make the sabayon sauce, strain the cooking juices from the roasting pan through a fine sieve set over a saucepan; discard the bunch of leaves. Add to the juices the chopped mint leaves or verbena leaves and the ground peppercorns, then reduce the juices by one-third over a high heat and set it aside.

4. While the juices are reducing, beat the egg yolks vigorously using a balloon or electric whisk and a bowl, preferably of metal. When the yolks turn pale and form a ribbon, gradually add 3 tbsp cold water, continuing to whisk until the mixture expands and froths.

5. To complete the sauce, gradually whisk about a quarter of the hot, reduced cooking juices into the whisked yolks, and, when these are smoothly combined, turn the mixture into the remaining cooking juices, whisking all the time to create a frothy sabayon sauce. If the sauce is slow to thicken, you can whisk it over a low heat, but you must remove it from the heat as soon as the sauce starts to 'grab' the whisk, otherwise the yolks will curdle.

To serve
Arrange the fillets of red mullet on warm serving plates and spoon the sabayon sauce around them. This dish is particularly delicious served with a few lightly cooked carrots sprinkled with lemon juice.

For the brochettes
- 360g (13oz) filleted monkfish, skin removed
- 16 fresh bay leaves
- 16 cherry tomatoes
- about 1 tsp olive oil
- salt and pepper of your choice

For the carrot and apricot purée
- 300g (11oz) carrots, peeled or scrubbed, then finely diced or sliced
- 150ml (¾ US cup) semi-skimmed (2%) milk
- ½ chicken stock cube, crumbled
- 6 fresh mint leaves, torn
- 40g (scant 1½oz) apricot halves (fresh or conserved in a jar), finely diced

For the sauce
- about 4 tbsp Pondicherry Indian Vinaigrette (page 67)
- ¼ tbsp finely chopped fresh tarragon
- ¼ tbsp finely chopped flat-leaf parsley

Equipment
- 4 metal or wooden skewers, about 25cm (9¾in) long
- Steamer (optional)

BROCHETTES OF MONKFISH WITH CARROT AND APRICOT QUENELLES

140 CALORIES PER PERSON
Cooking and preparation: 40 minutes
Level of difficulty: *
Serves 4

---

1. To assemble the brochettes ready for cooking, cut the monkfish into 16 even-sized pieces each weighing about 20g (¾oz). Have ready 4 skewers. Thread each skewer by alternating (4 times) a piece of the monkfish, a bay leaf and a cherry tomato. Set the brochettes aside, covered, in a cool place.

2. To prepare the carrot and apricot purée for the quenelles, put the carrots, milk, crumbled chicken stock cube, mint leaves and a pinch of salt in a bowl suitable for use in a microwave; cover with clingfilm (plastic wrap). Microwave the ingredients at full power for about 15 minutes or until the carrots are soft. Let the mixture cool a little then blend it to a smooth purée. Add the diced apricots and blend briefly again. Taste, adjust the seasoning and keep this purée warm, ideally in a bain-marie over a low heat.

3. To assemble the sauce, heat the Pondicherry Indian Vinaigrette, then add the chopped tarragon and parsley and adjust the seasoning. Keep this sauce warm.

4. When you are almost ready to cook the brochettes, preheat the oven to 200°C (400°F, gas mark 6) and warm a shallow or flat rectangular baking dish. (Alternatively, you can cook the brochettes in a hot steamer for 4–5 minutes.) Brush the baking dish and the brochettes lightly with olive oil. Lay the brochettes on the dish, season to taste, then transfer them to the upper part of the preheated oven.

5. After 3 minutes, turn the brochettes over and cook for a further 2–3 minutes. Transfer the brochettes to a warm serving dish and leave them briefly in a warm place – such the oven, turned off and with the door slightly open – while you finish the quenelles.

To serve
Have ready 4 warm serving plates. Pass the carrot purée between 2 dessertspoons or 2 teaspoons, depending on your preference, to make oval quenelle shapes. Slip a knife underneath the quenelles to release them. Arrange 2 or 3 quenelles on each plate, placing them slightly off-centre. Lay a brochette down the middle of the plate. You can remove the food from the skewer first, if you wish, Pour a thin stream of the sauce around the edge and serve immediately.

- 7 fresh fig leaves (or cabbage or banana leaves)
- 4 thick pieces of cod fillet, each about 90g (scant 3½oz)
- 100g (3½oz) mangetout (snow peas)
- 8 large prawns, butterflied (Terms and Techniques, page 326)
- salt and pepper of your choice

For the sauce
- 150ml (¾ US cup) Pondicherry Indian Stock (page 50)
- 50ml (¼ US cup or 6 tbsp) concentrated jus (such as jellied chicken juices left over from a roast) or concentrated chicken stock, either home-made (page 44) or from a cube
- 1 tsp cornflour (cornstarch), mixed with a little cold water
- 1 tsp freshly squeezed lemon juice

To serve
- fleur de sel (optional)
- little fresh tagliatelle, cooked until al dente (optional)

Equipment
- Steamer or couscoussier

COD STEAMED IN FIG LEAVES

140 CALORIES PER PERSON
Cooking and preparation: 40 minutes
Level of difficulty: *
Serves 4

1. To make the parcels of cod, blanch 6 of the 7 fig leaves (or leaves of your choice) in lightly salted boiling water for 15 seconds. Refresh them in cold water and dry them flat on kitchen paper. Season the pieces of cod and wrap each in a fig leaf to make a neat parcel. Cut the remaining 2 blanched leaves into a total of 8 strips and set these aside for decoration. Chop or cut the remaining unblanched leaf into small pieces for use in the sauce.

2. For the sauce, put the Pondicherry Indian Stock, the chicken jus or stock and the unblanched chopped fig leaf in a small saucepan. Set it, uncovered, over a medium heat. When the liquid comes to the boil, remove the saucepan from the heat and cover it with a lid. Set the mixture aside for 10 minutes so that the flavours can intermingle, then pass the mixture through a fine sieve set over a bowl. Blend the cornflour (cornstarch) and water into the strained liquid. Add lemon juice and salt and pepper to taste. Keep this sauce hot, preferably in a bain-marie.

3. Blanch the mangetout (snow peas) for 5 minutes. Drain, refresh in cold water, drain again and set aside.

4. Steam the cod parcels in a steamer or couscoussier for 4–5 minutes, then add the butterflied prawns and cook for a further 2 minutes. Finally, add the reserved mangetout (snow peas) and the strips of blanched fig leaf. When these have warmed through, turn off the heat.

To serve
Put each cod parcel on a warm serving plate. Open up each parcel and add 2 strips of blanched fig leaf, 2 butterflied prawns and the mangetout (snow peas). Coat with the reserved hot sauce. If you wish, add a sprinkling of fleur de sel. A little fresh tagliatelle, cooked until al dente and drizzled with some of the sauce, makes a lovely accompaniment.

- 2 tsp olive oil
- 240g (8½oz) onions, finely chopped
- pinch of fructose or the sweetener of your choice (pages 16–20)
- 240g (8½oz) white button mushrooms, wiped and thinly sliced
- ½ clove of garlic, peeled and finely chopped
- about ½ tsp crushed thyme flowers
- about ½ tsp finely chopped savory
- 100g (3½oz) Tomato Confit (page 81)
- ½ tbsp Lemon Confit (Terms and Techniques, page 327), cut into small dice (optional)
- 4 tbsp dry white wine
- 200ml (⅞ US cup) water
- 4 fillets of sea bream, each about 600g (1lb 5oz)
- about 12 slices of lemon (optional)
- salt and pepper of your choice

To garnish
- about 1 tbsp finely chopped flat-leaf parsley
- 4 little bunches consisting of a mixture of fresh thyme, savory and a bay leaf

SEA BREAM WITH THYME, SAVORY AND A MEDLEY OF VEGETABLES

340 CALORIES PER PERSON
Cooking and preparation: 40 minutes
Level of difficulty: * *
Serves 4

1. Coat a non-stick frying pan (skillet) with a tablespoon of the olive oil and sweat the onions, uncovered, over a gentle heat. Season, and add the pinch of fructose. In a separate frying pan (skillet), sauté the mushrooms in about ½ tablespoon of the oil until they flop; season to taste.

2. In a large saucepan, combine the onions, mushrooms, garlic, thyme, savory, Tomato Confit and the Lemon Confit, if used. Add the white wine and water, then stir to mix. Bring the mixture to the boil, uncovered, over a medium heat, the lower the heat to maintain a simmer for 10 minutes. Meanwhile, preheat the oven to 200°C (400°F, gas mark 6). Transfer the simmered vegetable mixture to a baking dish or roasting pan.

3. Season the fillets of sea bream and lay them, skin-side up, on top of the vegetable mixture. Brush them with a little of the oil. Add 3 slices of lemon, if used, to each fillet and transfer the baking dish to the preheated oven for 7–8 minutes or until the fish is cooked. Remove the baking dish from the oven and transfer the fillets to a separate warm dish, reserving the lemon slices, if used, for garnish. Set aside the fillets in a warm place while you dress the plates.

4. Strain off the excess cooking juices from the vegetable mixture, adjust their seasoning and set them aside briefly.

To serve
Arrange the vegetables on 4 warm serving plates. Drizzle over the strained cooking juices and sprinkle with the parsley. Lay a fillet of sea bream on top. You can either peel away the skin for presentation or you can leave it intact. If you like, garnish with the slices of lemon used in cooking, or use fresh slices if you prefer. A little bunch of fresh thyme, savory and bay leaf makes an ideal garnish that enhances the flavours of the dish.

- about 150g (5½oz) small new potatoes (preferably La Ratte or Russian Banana fingerling potatoes), unpeeled
- 200g (7oz) courgettes (zucchini), preferably small
- 12 medium langoustines (Dublin Bay prawns), peeled
- 240g (8½oz) fresh crabmeat
- salt and pepper of your choice

For the sauce
- 1 tsp olive oil
- 1 tbsp finely chopped shallot
- 50g (1¾oz) white button mushrooms, wiped and finely chopped
- 100ml (⅜ US cup) dry white wine
- 500ml (2⅛ US cups) fish stock, either home-made (page 47) or from a cube
- 200ml (⅞ US cup) semi-skimmed (2%) milk
- ½ tbsp vadouvan (Terms and Techniques, page 329) or curry powder of your choice
- 1 tbsp passion-fruit juice

To garnish
- 4 sprigs of parsley dried in the oven, or 1 tbsp finely chopped fresh parsley

SEAFARER'S BRAISED CRAB AND LANGOUSTINES

155 CALORIES PER PERSON
Cooking and preparation: 45 minutes
Level of difficulty: * *
Serves 4

1. To make the sauce, coat the bottom of a saucepan with a little olive oil and, over a low heat, sweat the shallot and mushrooms, uncovered, for several minutes, or until they have softened. Add the wine, increase the heat and scrape the bottom of the saucepan with a wooden spoon to deglaze it. When the liquid has reduced so that the pan is almost dry, add the fish stock and, over a high heat, reduce it again by half.

2. Add the milk, salt and pepper to taste, and the vadouvan or curry powder. Simmer the mixture, without boiling it, for 5 minutes, then remove it from the heat. When it is cool enough to handle, transfer it to a food processor and blend it finely. Strain it through a fine sieve – preferably a chinois – or a sieve lined with muslin. Set this sauce aside, covered, in a warm place.

3. Simmer the unpeeled potatoes in lightly salted water for about 15 minutes or until cooked; strain. When they are cool enough to handle, peel them and cut them into small rounds or half-rounds. If the courgettes (zucchini) are small, cut them into 1cm (½in) rounds; if they are large, cut them into half-rounds about 1cm (½in) thick. Blanch and refresh the courgettes (zucchini). Set these vegetables aside.

4. When you are almost ready to serve the dish, transfer the sauce to a saucepan large enough to contain the seafood and ensure the sauce is hot. To warm through the potatoes and courgettes (zucchini), put them in a sieve set over a saucepan of simmering water.

5. Cook the langoustines by plunging them into the hot sauce and simmering them for about 1 minute. Add the crabmeat and bring the sauce back to simmering point.

To serve
Have ready 4 warm shallow-bowled serving plates that can accommodate the sauce. Distribute the potatoes and courgettes (zucchini) in the bottom of the plates and put the seafood on top, lifting it from the sauce with a slotted spoon and putting 3 langoustines on each plate. Over heat, stir the passion-fruit juice into the sauce and check its seasoning. Pour the sauce over the seafood, add the garnish of parsley and serve immediately.

- 1 tsp olive oil
- 1 fillet of coley, about 450g (1lb), cut into 4 equal pieces
- 100ml (⅜ US cup) rich chicken or veal juices, ideally left over from a roast, or 100ml (⅜ US cup) chicken stock, either home-made (page 44) or from a cube
- salt and pepper of your choice

For the grapefruit and potato purée
- 1 pink grapefruit
- 400g (14oz) potatoes suitable for mashing, scrubbed or peeled
- 100ml (⅜ US cup) semi-skimmed (2%) milk
- 1 tbsp freshly squeezed lime juice
- 1 tsp lime zest

To garnish
- few pinches of chopped savory or mint
- 4 sprigs of savory or mint

COLEY FILLETS WITH QUENELLES SPIKED WITH PINK GRAPEFUIT

230 CALORIES PER PERSON
Cooking and preparation: 45 minutes
Level of difficulty: *
Serves 4

1. To prepare the grapefruit and potato purée, remove the peel and white pith from the grapefruit. Cut along each side of the membranes to free the segments. Cut the segments into ½cm (¼in) dice, put them in a nylon sieve to drain, and set aside.

2. Simmer the potatoes in lightly salted water for about 20 minutes until done; drain. If you cooked the potatoes in their skins, peel them when cool enough to handle. Crush the potatoes with a masher and have ready the milk, heated in a saucepan. Add the mashed potatoes to the milk, beating with a whisk until smooth. Keep this purée warm, preferably in a bain-marie.

3. To cook the fish, heat the olive oil in a large non-stick frying pan (skillet) and add the fish, skin-side down. Cook over a medium heat for about 2 minutes. Reduce the heat to a minimum, cover the frying pan (skillet) with a lid and leave the fish to cook gently for a further 5 minutes.

4. Meanwhile, heat the chicken or veal juices or stock in a small saucepan. Leave to simmer gently and reduce slightly while you finish the dish. Add the drained grapefruit dice and the lime juice and zest to the potato purée. Mix together gently and season to taste.

To serve
Have ready 4 warm serving plates. Pass the grapefruit and potato purée between 2 dessertspoons to make oval quenelle shapes. Slip a knife underneath each quenelle to release it. Arrange 2 quenelles on each plate and add a piece of fish alongside. Add a trickle of reduced stock along the edge. Sprinkle the quenelles with the chopped savory or mint. Add a sprig of the same to each plate and serve immediately.

- 4 tuna steaks, each about 100g (3½oz)
- 2 tbsp olive oil
- 2 or 3 long carrots, peeled
- 2 or 3 small courgettes (zucchini)
- 1 aubergine (eggplant)
- 4 asparagus tips (optional)
- 1 new onion, peeled and cut into 12 petal shapes about ½cm (¼in) thick
- 4 medium white button mushrooms, wiped and cut into ½cm (¼in) slices
- salt and pepper of your choice

For the vinaigrette
- 6 tbsp Light Vinaigrette (page 70)
- 2 tbsp white wine vinegar
- 4 tbsp rich jus or chicken stock, either home-made (page 44) or from a cube
- 1 tbsp coarsely chopped parsley
- 1 tbsp coarsely chopped chervil
- 1 tsp finely chopped tarragon

To garnish
- 4 sprigs of flowering thyme or savory, or the herbs of your choice
- fleur de sel (optional)
- freshly ground pepper (optional)

TUNA STEAKS WITH RIBBON VEGETABLES AND A HERB VINAIGRETTE

360 CALORIES PER PERSON
Cooking and preparation: 45 minutes
Level of difficulty: * * *
Serves 4

---

1. Put the tuna steaks in a dish and coat them with 1 tablespoon of the olive oil; set them aside at room temperature.

2. Using a mandolin or a sharp knife, cut the carrots lengthways into 12 thin ribbon-like slices, no more than 2mm (about 3/8in) thick. Cut the courgettes (zucchini) into similar ribbons and the aubergines (eggplants) into 8 slightly thicker slices of 5mm (¼in thick).

3. In separate batches, blanch these vegetables – and the asparagus tips, if used – for about 1 minute in boiling, lightly salted water, then refresh them in cold water and drain them flat on kitchen paper.

4. Have ready a frying pan (skillet) or a grill pan, preferably with a ribbed base.

5. When you are almost ready to serve the dish, either grill or sauté the vegetables. To grill them, brush the grill or griddle pan with the remaining tablespoon of olive oil. Alternatively, coat a non-stick frying pan (skillet) with the oil.

6. Cook the onions and aubergines (eggplants) for 2 minutes on each side, and the carrots, courgettes (zucchini) and mushrooms for 1 minute each side. Cook the asparagus tips, if used, for 30 seconds. Season the vegetables and keep them warm.

7. Mix together all the ingredients for the vinaigrette in a small saucepan. Heat the mixture without allowing it to boil, then keep the vinaigrette warm.

8. Season the tuna steaks and cook them rapidly for about 3 minutes on each side, either using the hot grill pan or the non-stick frying pan (skillet). The steaks should remain pink on the inside.

To serve

Divide the vinaigrette between 4 warm serving plates. Add the tuna steaks and the vegetables. Garnish with sprigs of thyme or savory or the herbs of your choice. If you like, add a touch of fleur de sel and freshly ground pepper. Serve immediately.

- 2 tsp olive oil
- 300g (11oz) coley, skin and small bones removed, then cut into slender fillets no more than 2mm (⅛in) thick
- salt and pepper of your choice

For the sauce
- 1 tbsp finely chopped shallot
- ½ bay leaf
- ½ clove of garlic, peeled and finely chopped
- ½–1 stalk of lemongrass, tough outer layers removed and the rest finely chopped
- 3g (1 tsp) peeled and grated fresh ginger
- pinch of coarsely chopped flowering thyme
- good pinch of crumbled chicken stock cube
- 150ml (¾ US cup) fish stock, either home made (page 47) or from a cube, or 150ml (¾ US cup) Asian Lime Vegetable Stock (page 49)
- 1 tbsp dry white wine
- 300g (11oz) tomatoes, peeled, cored and deseeded (Terms and Techniques, pages 327–8) then cut into ½cm (¼in) dice
- 1 tbsp finely snipped chives
- 1 tsp finely chopped tarragon
- 1 tsp finely chopped flat-leaf parsley

To garnish
- 12 broccoli florets

COLEY STARS WITH AN ASIAN-INSPIRED SAUCE

140 CALORIES PER PERSON
Cooking and preparation: 45 minutes
Level of difficulty: * *
Serves 4

1. Cut four 17cm (6¾in) squares of greaseproof or parchment paper and brush them lightly with one of the teaspoons of the olive oil. Put the paper squares on a flat baking sheet or tray. On each piece of paper, arrange the filleted strips of coley so that they radiate from the centre to form a star shape about 15cm (6in) in diameter. Cover the fish with clingfilm (plastic wrap) and transfer it to the refrigerator while you make the sauce.

2. To prepare the sauce, heat the remaining olive oil in a saucepan over a low heat and gently sweat the shallot, together with the bay leaf, garlic and lemongrass. When these ingredients have softened, stir in the ginger, thyme and crumbled chicken stock cube. Add the fish stock and white wine and bring the liquid to the boil, then lower the heat to maintain a simmer for about 3 minutes.

3. Add the diced tomatoes and simmer for at least 3–5 minutes more, or until the flavours have mingled. Taste, and adjust the seasoning. Either set this sauce aside until you are ready to cook the fish or, if you are cooking the fish straight away, keep the sauce warm, preferably in a bain-marie.

4. In a separate saucepan, simmer the broccoli garnish in lightly salted water for about 7 minutes. Drain and refresh in cold water, then drain again and set aside in a sieve, ready to be reheated.

5. About 5–10 minutes before you are ready to cook the fish, preheat the grill and a grill tray. Remove the fish from the refrigerator and season it with salt and pepper. Have ready 4 warm serving plates. Reheat the broccoli over simmering water and ensure the sauce is heated through. When the grill is hot, transfer the fish on its squares of paper to the heated grill tray and cook on one side only for about 2 minutes.

To serve
Pick up each piece of paper – steadying it between 2 wide spatulas if necessary – and turn it over directly onto each serving plate; lift away the paper. Complete the sauce by adding the chives, tarragon and parsley. Drizzle the sauce over the fish. Add 3 broccoli florets in the centre or around the edge of each coley star and serve straight away.

- 180g (scant 6½oz) fillet of salmon
- 90g (scant 3½oz) peeled langoustines
  (Dublin Bay prawns, scampi or Jumbo shrimp)
- 90g (scant 3½oz) peeled prawns (shrimp)
- ½ egg white, about 15g (½oz)
- 35g (1¼oz) natural yogurt (0% fat)
- 1½ tsp finely grated lime zest
- 1½ tsp coarsely ground or crushed
  green peppercorns
- 25g (scant 1oz) salmon roe, Avruga herring roe
  or lumpfish roe
- 1 tsp olive oil
- salt and pepper of your choice

To garnish (optional)
- 3 wedges of lemon
- 3 sprigs of watercress or some small
  salad leaves

Equipment
- 3 food rings, 9–10cm (3½–4in) in diameter

SALMON BURGER
200 CALORIES PER PERSON
Cooking and preparation: 20 minutes
Level of difficulty: *
Serves 3

1. Cut the salmon, the langoustines and the prawns into ½cm (¼in) dice.

2. In a large mixing bowl, whisk the egg white until it forms very soft peaks, then whisk in the yogurt, the lime zest and the green peppercorns. Add the diced fish and seafood and mix with a fork. Add the fish roe of your choice and mix again gently to distribute the ingredients. Taste, and adjust the seasoning, then stir again briefly.

3. Put 3 food rings on a baking sheet or tray, covered with some greaseproof or parchment paper. Spoon the fish mixture into the rings and level it. Transfer the baking sheet to a refrigerator for 1 hour, to allow the burger mixture to firm slightly.

4. When you are ready to cook the burgers, remove them from the refrigerator. Heat the olive oil in a non-stick frying pan (skillet). Carefully lift away the food rings, then lift each burger with a spatula and carefully slide it into the frying pan (skillet), easing it off the spatula with a knife if necessary. Cook the burgers for 2 minutes on each side – turning carefully with the spatula.

To serve
Transfer the burgers to 3 warm serving plates. If you like, you can add a garnish of lemon wedges and some sprigs of watercress or a few dressed salad leaves.

- croûtons made with 1–2 thick slices
  of one-day bread
- 4 fillets of lemon sole, skin removed, totalling
  about 400g (14oz)
- salt and pepper of your choice

For the sauce
- 4 fillets of anchovies preserved in salt
- 7 tbsp Light Vinaigrette (page 70)
- 1 tbsp soy sauce

For the accompaniment
- 1 large lemon or 2 small ones
- 20g (¾oz) capers
- 1 tsp olive oil
- 100g (3½oz) girolles or other mushrooms,
  wiped and cut in half or in quarters
- 2 baby cabbages, cut in half
- 1 tbsp finely chopped flat-leaf parsley

Equipment
- Steamer or couscoussier

LEMON SOLE GRENOBLOISE

230 CALORIES PER PERSON
Cooking and preparation: 35 minutes
Level of difficulty: * *
Serves 4

1. If you are making croûtons from scratch, preheat the oven to 150°C (300°F, gas mark 2).

2. For the sauce, briefly soak the fillets of anchovy in cold water to remove their salt; drain and pat them dry. Chop them, then transfer to a food processor along with the Light Vinaigrette and the soy sauce; blend to make a sauce. Pass the sauce through a fine sieve to ensure smoothness, then set it aside, covered, in a warm place.

3. For the croûtons, cut off and discard the crusts from the bread and cut it into even-sized small cubes. Spread these out on a baking sheet and bake for about 20 minutes or until crisp and slightly golden.

4. While the croûtons are being baked, make the accompaniment: remove the peel and pith from the lemon using a small sharp knife. Cut along each side of the membranes to free the segments. Cut the segments into ½cm (¼in) dice. Combine the diced lemon with the capers in a small bowl or cup covered with a splash of hot water; keep this garnish warm. Sauté the girolles in the olive oil until they flop; season and keep warm.

5. Prepare a steamer or couscoussier for the fish and, at the same time, bring lightly salted water to the boil in a large saucepan for the cabbage. Simmer the cabbage halves for about 5 minutes and steam the sole for about 4 minutes.

To serve
Have ready 4 warm serving plates. Arrange a fillet of sole along the centre of each plate. Drizzle a little of the sauce over part of each fillet. Scatter the drained lemon dice and capers, the croûtons and the chopped parsley over the other part. Add a portion of girolles and a cabbage half. Serve immediately.

A gastronomic titbit
The term grenobloise refers to the region around Grenoble where combinations of capers, lemon and croûtons are common – and usually bound in a brown butter sauce.

- 24 small pieces of peeled potato, turned, if wished, into the shape of fat cloves of garlic 4–5cm (1½–2in) long (Terms and Techniques, pages 328–9)
- 2 small sprigs of fresh thyme
- 2 fresh bay leaves
- 300g (11oz) white button mushrooms, wiped and thinly sliced
- about 3 tsp olive oil
- 12 small onions
- 150ml (¾ US cup) chicken stock, either home-made (page 44) or from a cube
- 1 tsp freshly squeezed lemon juice
- 1 tsp cornflour (cornstarch), mixed with a little water
- 4 pieces of brill, skin removed, each about 100g (3½oz)
- salt and pepper of your choice

To serve
- 4 wedges of lemon

Equipment
- 4 circles of parchment paper or greaseproof paper, about 40cm (16in) in diameter

STEAMED BRILL EN PAPILLOTE

230 CALORIES PER PERSON
Cooking and preparation: 45 minutes
Level of difficulty: * *
Serves 4

1. Put the potatoes, together with one of the sprigs of thyme and one of the bay leaves, in a large saucepan filled with about 1.5 litres (6½ US cups) of lightly salted water. Bring the water to the boil, adjust the heat to maintain a brisk simmer and cook the potatoes for about 15 minutes or until just cooked. Strain; discard the herbs and set aside the potatoes in a warm place.

2. Using a non-stick frying pan (skillet), sauté the mushrooms lightly in about 1 teaspoon of the olive oil; set aside.

3. Simmer the onions in lightly salted water for about 10 minutes or until just tender; drain and set aside in a warm place.

4. Bring the chicken stock to the boil along with the lemon juice and the remaining sprig of thyme and the bay leaf. Remove it from the heat, discard the herbs and gradually stir in the cornflour (cornstarch) mixed with water. Adjust the seasoning and keep this stock warm, preferably in a bain-marie.

5. In a non-stick frying pan (skillet), heat another teaspoon of the oil and colour the pieces of brill on one side only; season.

6. Preheat the oven to 180°C (355°F, gas mark 4). Spread out the circles of parchment paper on a flat work surface and brush them with the remaining teaspoon of the olive oil. Leaving half of each circle free, put a little bed of mushrooms towards the centre of the other half. Put a piece of the brill on top of each, with its coloured side uppermost.

7. Distribute the potatoes and onions around the brill. Divide 2 tablespoons of the reserved chicken stock between each parchment circle. To close each parcel and make a leakproof seal, bring together the edges of the paper and fold them over twice to make a narrow seam all along the edge, like an apple turnover. Transfer these little parcels – papillotes – to a lipped baking sheet and put the sheet in the oven. Cook for 8–10 minutes.

To serve
Have ready 4 warm serving plates. Remove the baking sheet from the oven and transfer the papillotes to the plates. Divide the wedges of lemon between the plates. Serve the papillotes closed so that guests can have the surprise of opening them at the table. Serve the remaining flavoured stock in a sauce boat and offer it separately.

Variations
You can replace the brill with halibut, salmon or striped bass if you prefer.

- 4 fillets of mackerel, skin left on, each about 200g (7oz)
- 1 tsp olive oil
- salt and pepper of your choice

For the sauce
- 50g (1¾oz) shallot, finely chopped
- about 1 tsp julienne strips of peeled fresh ginger
- about 1 tsp julienne strips of peeled garlic
- 15g (½oz) pimientos del piquillo, bottled (Terms and Techniques, page 328), cut into ½cm (¼in) dice
- 1 tbsp dry white wine
- 3 tbsp Xeres vinegar or other sherry vinegar of your choice
- 2 tbsp soy sauce
- 2 tbsp concentrated tomato paste
- 3 tbsp Mushroom Vinaigrette (page 66)

For the rougail leeks
- 500g (1lb 2oz) leeks, trimmed to give about ⅔ white and ⅓ green parts
- 1 tsp olive oil
- 15g (½oz) fresh ginger, peeled and chopped
- 40g (scant 1½oz) mango, cut into ½cm (¼in) dice
- 10g (¼oz) lemon zest, blanched and refreshed 3 times (Terms and Techniques, page 328), then cut into 2mm (⅛in) dice
- 2 tbsp finely chopped or snipped fresh coriander (cilantro)
- 2 tbsp dry white wine
- pinch of ground chili pepper, preferably the Espelette variety

To garnish
- few julienne strips of lemon zest (optional)
- few leaves of coriander (cilantro)

AROMATIC GRILLED MACKEREL

350 CALORIES PER PERSON
Cooking and preparation: 40 minutes
Level of difficulty: * *
Serves 4

1. Run your finger gently over the fillets of mackerel and, if you feel any remaining small bones, remove them with tweezers. Set aside the fillets in the refrigerator until you are ready to cook them.

2. For the sauce, put the shallot, ginger, garlic and diced pimientos del piquillo – the aromatics – into a bowl. In a saucepan, stir together the white wine, sherry vinegar, soy sauce and the concentrated tomato paste. Bring this liquid to the boil, maintaining a brisk simmer for 30 seconds, then add it to the bowl of aromatics. Cover with clingfilm (plastic wrap) and set aside.

3. For the rougail leeks: cut the leeks into rounds about ½cm (¼in) thick. Blanch them in simmering salted water then drain them, refresh in cold water and drain again in a small sieve that you can use to reheat them.

4. Heat the teaspoon of olive oil in a saucepan over a gentle heat and sweat the ginger for a few minutes without colouring it. Add the leeks, the mango, the lemon zest and the chopped coriander (cilantro). Mix gently, then stir in the wine and chili pepper. Taste, and adjust the seasoning and keep the mixture warm, preferably in a bain-marie.

5. You can cook the mackerel either over direct heat, using a heavy sauté pan with a ribbed base – in which case make sure this is hot – or you can grill it. If you are going to use the grill, preheat it to a high heat.

6. The mackerel is cooked quickly and on one side only to ensure the flesh remains moist, so make sure all the other elements are ready: heat the sauce through, adding the Mushroom Vinaigrette to complete it; keep this hot. Heat the leek mixture through and have ready 4 warm serving plates.

7. Season the mackerel and lightly brush the skin side with olive oil. Arrange the fillets with their skin towards the heat. Cook rapidly, for as little as 12 seconds or so, depending on how strong the heat is.

To serve

Distribute the hot rougail leeks between 4 hot serving plates. Add a fillet of mackerel to each plate, laying it skin-side up so that the uncooked side can continue to cook in the heat of the leeks. This also helps to keep the fish moist. Drizzle the hot sauce around the fish or over it. Scatter with a few coriander (cilantro) leaves and, if you like, some julienne strips of lemon zest. Serve straight away.

A gastronomic titbit

'Rougail' refers to a popular sauce found in Mauritius, Reunion, Madagascar and the Seychelles. It usually contains fresh ginger, tomato, garlic, chilli, garlic, wine and herbs.

- 4 pieces of lean, firm-textured fish, such as dogfish, cod, gurnard (catfish, sculpin, grouper), each about 100g (3½oz)

For the sauce vierge
- 400g (14oz) tomatoes, peeled, cored and deseeded (Terms and Techniques, page 327–8), then cut into ½cm (¼in) dice
- 1 tsp very finely chopped shallot
- flesh of 1 lemon, cut into ½cm (¼in) dice
- 8 tbsp Light Vinaigrette (page 70)
- 1 tbsp finely chopped or snipped chives
- 1 tbsp finely chopped flat-leaf parsley
- 1 tsp finely chopped tarragon
- salt and pepper of your choice

For the garnish
- 1 medium leek, white part only
- 1 celery stick (stalk)
- 1 bulb of fennel, about 300g (11oz)

Equipment
- Steamer or couscoussier

STEAMED WHITE FISH WITH SAUCE VIERGE

280 CALORIES PER PERSON
Cooking and preparation: 50 minutes
Level of difficulty: * *
Serves 4

---

1. Start by preparing the sauce vierge: put the tomatoes, shallot, diced lemon flesh and the Light Vinaigrette into a saucepan. Stir to mix and season with salt and pepper. Add the finely chopped chives and parsley. Cover and set this uncooked sauce vierge aside briefly at room temperature, to allow the ingredients to macerate.

2. To prepare the garnish, cut the white of leek lengthways into 2 bevelled logs. Cut these widthways to make little half-moons about 1cm (½in) wide. Cut the stick of celery at 2cm (¾in) intervals to make similar shapes. Cut the fennel in half and discard the tough core. (You can reserve the feathery leaves for another dish if you like.) Cut the fennel in 8 even-sized pieces.

3. Cook each vegetable separately in a saucepan of lightly salted simmering water, starting with the fennel, for about 20 minutes, then the leek for 15 minutes and finally, the celery for about 8 minutes. After cooking the vegetables, refresh them in cold water and drain in a sieve set over a saucepan of water, so they are ready to reheat later.

4. When you are almost ready to cook the fish, prepare the steamer or couscoussier. While this heats, simmer the vierge sauce until the shallot is tender. Season the fish and steam it for 4–6 minutes. At the same time, reheat the vegetables over simmering water.

To serve
Have ready 4 warm serving plates. Put a little pool of sauce vierge on the bottom of each plate. Place a piece of fish in the centre and surround it with the vegetable garnish. Serve straight away.

A gastronomic titbit
'Sauce vierge' means, literally, 'virgin sauce' and is made, usually, from olive oil, lemon juice, chopped tomato and chopped basil. It can also include coriander seed and herbs other than basil. This sauce became popular in the 1980s and is now regarded as a classic.

- 8 pimientos del piquillo, bottled (Terms and Techniques, page 328)
- 2 thick fillets of hake (or whiting or ling), totalling about 750g (1lb 10oz), skin left on and scaled
- ½ bunch of basil, leaves only
- 1 tsp olive oil
- salt and pepper of your choice

For the sauce
- 150g (5½oz) pimientos del piquillo, bottled (see above)
- 100g (3½oz) coconut milk
- 1 tbsp Japanese mirin (rice wine)
- 1 tbsp tamarind juice or 1 tsp tamarind paste mixed with 1 tbsp water

AN UNUSUAL FISH STEAK FILLED WITH SWEET PEPPERS

180 CALORIES PER PERSON

Cooking and preparation: 30 minutes (can be started the night before)
Level of difficulty: *
Serves 8

1. Open the pimientos del piquillo – sweet red peppers – and hold them under cold running water to rinse away any seeds. Drain on kitchen paper and set aside.

2. In order to make the fish steaks, you have to assemble a 'sandwich' that uses the fillets of fish to hold a filling of sweet red pepper and basil. If you like, you can do this the night before. Start by cutting the fillet of hake (or whiting or ling) lengthways into two equal-sized fillets; season. Lay one of the fillets flesh-side up on a work surface.

3. Arrange 4 of the opened-up red peppers side by side on the fillet, overlapping them slightly to make a solid layer, then put the basil leaves on top. Use the remaining 4 red peppers to add another layer. Top with the remaining fillet, skin-side up. Use fine kitchen string to tie this long assembly at 8 equally spaced points, as if it were a rolled cut of meat. Wrap in clingfilm (plastic wrap) and transfer to the refrigerator for at least several hours or until firm.

4. For the sauce, rinse away the seeds from the 150g (5½oz) of pimientos del piquillo, as previously described. Chop the red peppers coarsely and put them in a food processor along with the coconut milk, the Japanese mirin and the tamarind. Blend to make a fine-textured sauce. Season to taste and, for an extra-smooth finish, pass the sauce through a very fine sieve, preferably a chinois. Set the sauce aside, preferably in a bain-marie, ready to be heated when required.

5. When you are almost ready to cook the fish, cut the tied assembly of fish into 8 even-sized steaks, leaving the string in place so as to preserve the shape during cooking. Heat the olive oil in a non-stick frying pan (skillet) and cook the steaks for 3 minutes on each side, using a wide flexible spatula to turn them over carefully. At the same time, reheat the sauce.

To serve
Have ready 4 warm serving plates. Transfer 2 steaks to each plate and remove the string. Surround each steak with a trail of drizzled sauce.

Chef's tip
Excellent partners for these fish steaks include a helping of lightly cooked young spinach or some matchsticks of cucumbers, peeled, blanched and sautéed briefly.

- 400g (14oz) fillets of monkfish
- 4 fillets of anchovy preserved in oil, drained
- 12 small tarragon leaves
- 12 small flat-leaf parsley leaves
- 12 small sprigs of chervil, leaves only
- 2 pinches of powdered saffron
- 1 tsp olive oil
- salt and pepper of your choice

For the sauce and vegetables
- 200ml (⅞ US cup) fish stock, either home-made (page 47) or from a cube
- 12–16 small threads of saffron
- 12 coriander seeds and a pinch of either fresh or dried thyme, tied in a little muslin bag
- 1 tsp olive oil
- 250g (9oz) small young courgettes (zucchini), cut into 1cm (½in) dice
- 100g (3½oz) small well-flavoured mushrooms such as chanterelles, shiitake or wild edible mushrooms of your choice, wiped
- 200g (7oz) tomatoes, peeled, cored and deseeded (Terms and Techniques, pages 327–8), then cut into ½cm (¼in) dice
- 1 tbsp julienne of lemon zest (Terms and Techniques, page 327)
- 2 tbsp Light Vinaigrette (page 70)
- 2 tbsp finely chopped fines herbes, such as flat-leaf parsley, tarragon and chervil

To garnish
- few sprigs of chervil

ESCALOPES OF MONKFISH WITH SAFFRON

165 CALORIES PER PERSON
Cooking and preparation: 40 minutes
Level of difficulty: * *
Serves 4

1. Using a sharp flexible knife – preferably a filleting knife – lift away the thin membrane of skin that covers the fillets of monkfish. Cut the fillets into 12 small escalopes, about 1¼cm (½in) thick. Season lightly. Make a horizontal incision in each escalope to form a small pocket. You may season inside each pocket if you wish but bear in mind that the anchovy filling will add salt.

2. Cut each fillet of anchovy into 3 pieces, making 12 in all. Fill each pocket with a piece of anchovy, a tarragon leaf, a parsley leaf and a sprig of chervil. Close the pockets, sprinkle with powdered saffron, cover and set aside in a cold place.

3. For the accompaniment – which combines a sauce with vegetables – put the fish stock into a small saucepan. Add the saffron threads and the muslin bag containing the coriander seeds and thyme. Bring the liquid to the boil and let it simmer briskly for 1 minute. Remove from the heat, adjust the seasoning and set the sauce aside, covered.

4. For the vegetables that go into the sauce, heat the olive oil in a non-stick frying pan (skillet) and sauté the diced courgettes (zucchini) for 2 minutes, then add the mushrooms and sauté for a further 2 minutes. Remove from the pan, drain briefly in a sieve and season. Remove the muslin bag from the reserved sauce and discard it.

5. Add to the sauce the following: the drained courgettes (zucchini) and mushrooms, the diced tomatoes, the julienne of lemon, the Light Vinaigrette and the fines herbes. If you are going to serve the dish straight away, slowly warm this sauce through while you cook the fish; otherwise set it aside.

6. When you are almost ready to serve the dish, season the escalopes. Heat a little olive oil in a non-stick frying pan (skillet) and cook the escalopes for about 2 minutes on each side. Drain on kitchen paper.

To serve
Have ready 4 warm serving plates, preferably shallow-bowled plates to collect
the juices. Use a ladle to transfer the sauce and vegetables to the plates, then
add 3 escalopes to each and drizzle the juices on top. Scatter with a few sprigs
of chervil and serve.

Variation
If you can buy mussel juice or if you have some mussel juice left over from a
dish of Moules Marinières, you can use it in place of the fish stock. The result will
be delicious.

- 12 pimientos del piquillo, bottled
  (Terms and Techniques, page 328)
- 200g (7oz) potatoes for mashing
- 750ml (3⅛ US cups) semi-skimmed (2%) milk
- 1 clove of garlic, unpeeled
- 1 large sprig of fresh thyme
- 1 fresh bay leaf
- 240g (8½oz) very white dried salt cod, soaked
  in several changes of cold water for 24 hours,
  drained on kitchen paper, then cut into
  large pieces
- about ½ tbsp olive oil
- 2 tbsp snipped chives
- 1 tsp cornflour (cornstarch), mixed with
  a little cold water
- few tbsp black squid ink (optional)
- salt and pepper of your choice

To garnish
- few sprigs of fresh chervil
- few sprigs of fresh basil

Equipment
- Steamer or couscoussier

SWEET RED PEPPERS WITH A FILLING OF SALT COD AND POTATO

180 CALORIES PER PERSON
Cooking and preparation: 40 minutes, plus 24 hours to soak the salt cod
Level of difficulty: *
Serves 4

1. Hold the pimientos del piquillo – sweet red peppers – under cold running water and rinse away any seeds. Drain on kitchen paper and set aside until you are ready to fill them with the salt cod and potato mixture.

2. For the mashed potatoes, peel old potatoes before cooking and young ones after cooking. Simmer the potatoes in lightly salted water for about 20 minutes, depending on their size, then drain them. When they are cool enough to handle, mash them smoothly, either with a masher or with a vegetable mouli fitted with a fine disc. Set aside.

3. Put the milk, garlic, thyme and bay leaf into a saucepan. Bring the milk to simmering point, lower the heat and add the salt cod. Simmer gently over a low heat for about 8 minutes or until the fish is just cooked. Lift out the pieces of cod using a slotted spoon and transfer them to a bowl. Remove any pieces of black and white skin and any remaining bones. Break the fish into fine flakes. Strain the milk through a fine sieve – preferably a chinois – set over a bowl. Measure 200ml (⅞ US cup) of this milk into a jug and set it aside to make a white sauce. Use the remaining milk to make the filling.

4. For the filling, heat the olive oil gently in a heavy saucepan. Add the cod and the mashed potato. Beat the mixture quickly with a wooden spoon to blend it. Mix in the chives and gradually incorporate the milk that was set aside for the filling, beating all the time until you achieve the consistency of thick cream. Taste, and adjust the seasoning. Stuff the sweet red peppers with this filling and set aside.

5. For the white sauce, mix the cornflour (cornstarch) into the measured 200ml (⅞ US cup) of milk. Heat through and add seasoning. If using the black squid ink, remove 2 soup spoonfuls of the white sauce and mix it with the squid ink in a small bowl. Reheat the stuffed peppers in a steamer or couscoussier.

To serve

Have ready warm serving plates. Arrange the stuffed peppers in the centre of each plate and surround them with a little ribbon of the white sauce. Add some little trails of the squid ink and sauce mixture, if used, and a few sprigs of fresh chervil and basil. Serve immediately.

Variation

You can replace the salt cod with salted haddock, salted halibut or salted pollock.

- 2 bulbs of fennel, total weight about 350g (12oz)
- 4 fillets of salmon, each about 90g (scant 3½oz), skin left on and scaled
- 2 tsp olive oil
- salt and pepper of your choice
- fleur de sel (optional)

For the sorrel sauce
- 150ml (¾ US cup) semi-skimmed (2%) milk
- 1 level tbsp cornflour (cornstarch), mixed with a little cold water
- about 140g (5oz) sorrel, tough ribs and stalks removed, then washed and dried

SORREL SALMON WITH A NOD TOWARDS PIERRE TROISGROS

220 CALORIES PER PERSON
Cooking and preparation: 50 minutes
Level of difficulty: *
Serves 4

1. Trim the fennel of any tough outer layers. Cut the bulb in half and remove and discard the tough core. Lay the halves flat-side down in the bottom of a saucepan and cover with lightly salted water. Simmer very gently for about 40 minutes or until the fennel is tender, then drain on kitchen paper. Cut each half into 3 pieces, making 12 pieces in all. Set them aside.

2. For the sorrel sauce, scald the milk, remove it from the heat and stir in the cornflour (cornstarch) mixed with a little water. Leave to cool completely. Meanwhile, coarsely chop 100g (3½oz) of the sorrel – about two-thirds. Put it in a food processor, add the cooled, thickened milk, and blend smoothly to make a sauce. Season and set aside to be reheated just before use.

3. Chop the remaining sorrel into very fine even strips, chiffonade style, for later use as a garnish; set aside.

4. Just before you are ready to cook the salmon, preheat the oven to 150°C (300°F, gas mark 2). Pick over the salmon and remove any remaining small bones with tweezers. Season with salt. Heat 1 teaspoon of the olive oil in a non-stick frying pan (skillet) and, over a medium to high heat, cook the salmon, skin-side down, for 1 minute only.

5. Put the salmon in the frying pan (skillet) in the preheated oven for about 2 minutes, then transfer it carefully to a warm plate. Remove the salmon skin and put it back in the oven to become crisp. Cover the plate of salmon with aluminium foil and put it in a warm place for 5–6 minutes, allowing the salmon to continue cooking gently in its own heat, while remaining moist.

6. Meanwhile, heat the remaining teaspoon of olive oil in a non-stick frying pan (skillet) and rapidly sauté the pieces of fennel until they colour lightly. At the same time, reheat the sorrel sauce.

To serve

Have ready 4 warm serving plate and distribute the chiffonade of sorrel garnish in the centre of each. Place a fillet of salmon on top and arrange 3 pieces of sautéed fennel along one side. Spoon the sorrel sauce along the other side. Add the crispy salmon skin, twisting it into a decorative shape. If you like, add a pinch of fleur de sel. Serve immediately.

A gastronomic titbit

The Salmon with Sorrel Sauce invented by Pierre Trosgros, from which my recipe takes its inspiration, is legendary. His classic version achieves an unctuously creamy, yet light, sorrel sauce using crème fraiche and, sometimes, butter. The delicate sharpness of the sorrel is accentuated by the sharp edge of the local cream. Here, I have created a similar sauce, but using fewer calories.

- 4 red mullet, each weighing about 210g (7½oz), heads left on, gutted through the gills and filleted through openings made by cutting each side of the backbone (ask your fishmonger; see illustration)
- salt and pepper of your choice

For the filling

- about 1 tsp olive oil
- 1 clove of garlic, unpeeled
- 1 tsp finely chopped shallot
- 1 tsp finely chopped onion
- 1 tsp celery, cut into ½cm (¼in) dice
- 1 tbsp carrot, peeled and cut into ½cm (¼in) dice
- 1 tsp peeled and finely grated fresh ginger
- large sprig of thyme
- 1 fresh bay leaf
- 2 tomatoes, peeled, cored and deseeded (Terms and Techniques, pages 327–8), then cut into ½cm (¼in) dice
- 3 tbsp dry white wine
- 100ml (⅜ US cup) chicken stock, either home-made (page 44) or from a cube
- pinch of fructose or the sweetener of your choice (pages 16–20)
- 4 long strips of orange zest, blanched and refreshed
- 2 long strips of lemon zest, blanched and refreshed
- 1 tbsp mango, cut into ½cm (¼in) dice
- 1 tbsp finely chopped flat-leaf parsley

To garnish

- 6 tbsp Shellfish Vinaigrette (page 73)
- about 12 sprigs of fresh dill

RED MULLET WITH A POCKETFUL OF FRUIT

285 CALORIES PER PERSON
Cooking and preparation: 45 minutes
Level of difficulty: * * *
Serves 4

1. To make the filling, heat the oil gently in a heavy saucepan, adding the garlic, shallot, onion, celery, carrot, ginger, thyme and bay leaf. Add a little salt and sweat the mixture, covered, over a low heat for about 8 minutes or until the vegetables have softened without colouring.

2. Add all the diced tomatoes except for 1 tablespoon, which you should set aside. Increase the heat, add the white wine, the chicken stock and fructose. Bring to the boil then adjust the heat to maintain a brisk simmer, uncovered, until the mixture has reduced to the consistency of runny jam. Remove from the heat and allow to cool.

3. Cut the blanched citrus zest into tiny dice no more than about 3mm (⅛in) square. Add these to the filling, along with the diced mango, the reserved diced tomato and the parsley. Mix together and adjust the seasoning; set this filling aside.

4. When you are ready to cook the red mullet, preheat the oven to 200°C (400°F, gas mark 6). Line a baking sheet with greaseproof or parchment paper. Season the mullet and put them on the paper. Put the filling inside the pocket of each fish and distribute it evenly. Smooth the filling with a spatula. Transfer the baking sheet to the oven and cook the fish for 4–5 minutes or until cooked. Meanwhile, warm through the Shellfish Vinaigrette.

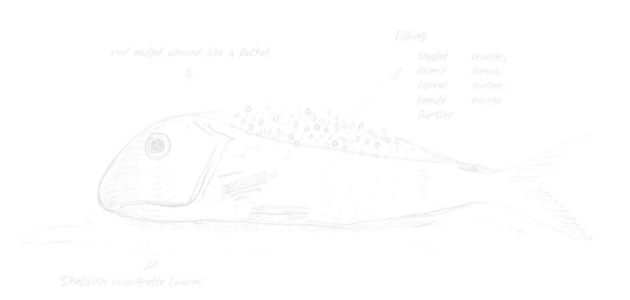

red mullet opened like a pocket

filling

shallot   orange,
celery   lemon,
carrot   ginger,
tomato   mango
parsley

Shellfish vinaigrette (warm)

To serve

Have ready 4 warm serving plates. Using a wide spatula, carefully transfer 1 red mullet to the centre of each plate. Pour a little vinaigrette all around and sprinkle with some sprigs of fresh dill. Serve immediately.

- 4 fillets of John Dory (for USA alternative, see Chef's tip, below), each 90–100g (scant 3½–3½oz)
- 1 tbsp tandoori spice powder
- 1 tsp olive oil
- salt and pepper of your choice

For the vegetable garnish
- 1 tbsp Light Vinaigrette (page 70)
- 1 tbsp fromage blanc or Greek yogurt (0%)
- pinch of curry powder
- about 120g (scant 4½oz) celeriac, peeled and cut into matchsticks about 4cm x 3mm (1½ x ⅛in)
- 1 tsp olive oil
- 150g (5½oz) young spinach leaves, tough ribs removed, then washed and drained

For the tandoori vinaigrette
- 6 tbsp Light Vinaigrette (page 70)
- 2 tsp tandoori spice powder

TANDOORI-SPICED WHITE FISH

225 CALORIES PER PERSON
Cooking and preparation: 30 minutes
Level of difficulty: *
Serves 4

1. Coat the fillets of fish on one side only with the tandoori spice powder. Cover the fish and set it aside in a cool place.

2. Prepare the first of the vegetables by mixing together in a bowl 1 tablespoon of Light Vinaigrette, the fromage blanc and the curry powder. Add the matchsticks of celeriac and turn them in the mixture to coat them evenly. Season to taste and set this celeriac garnish aside in the refrigerator until you are almost ready to serve the fish.

3. For the tandoori vinaigrette, put 6 tablespoons of Light Vinaigrette into a saucepan. Stir in 2 teaspoons of tandoori spice powder and bring the mixture to the boil. Remove from the heat, adjust the seasoning and keep this tandoori vinaigrette warm, preferably in a bain-marie, while you finish the dish.

4. Coat a non-stick frying pan (skillet) with 1 teaspoon of olive oil. Over a medium heat, cook the fillets of fish on the spiced side for 3 minutes, then turn them over and cook for a further 3 minutes on the other side.

5. Meanwhile, finish the vegetables by heating the second teaspoon of olive oil in a saucepan, adding the spinach and cooking it quickly until it wilts – about 30 seconds. Drain the spinach in a sieve over a bowl.

To serve
Have ready 4 warm serving plates and lay a fillet of fish, spice side up, along the centre of each plate. Drizzle over the warm tandoori vinaigrette. Arrange some spinach on one side and the celeriac garnish on the other.

Variations
The John Dory (St Pierre) fish used in this recipe is widely available in the UK but virtually impossible to find in the USA, except through internet sites. However, USA readers can substitute flounder or even swordfish steaks. Sole can also be used but its delicate flavour will be rather overwhelmed by the tandoori spice powder.

- 4 quails, plucked, cleaned and prepared
- 8 large green cabbage leaves (plus a few extra, as they are apt to tear)
- 150ml (¾ US cup) chicken stock, either home-made (page 44) or from a cube
- salt and pepper of your choice

For the filling
- 50g (1¾oz) pearl barley
- 1 tbsp onion, cut into very fine strips
- 1 tsp Lemon Confit (Terms and Techniques, page 327), cut into ½cm (¼in) pieces
- 1 tbsp tomato, peeled, cored, deseeded (Terms and Techniques, pages 327–8) and cut into ½cm (¼in) dice
- ½ tsp peeled and grated fresh ginger
- ½ tsp finely chopped tarragon
- 1 tbsp sweetcorn kernels
- 1 tbsp soy sauce
- 1 tbsp dry white wine

For the sauce
- 8 tbsp good-quality game or meat stock, such as the juices left over from a roast, mixed with 1 tbsp cornflour (cornstarch)

To garnish
- 4 sage leaves
- lightly cooked courgettes (zucchini) and carrots, made into matchsticks (optional)

Equipment
- Steamer or couscoussier

QUAIL-STUFFED CABBAGE LEAVES

225 CALORIES PER PERSON
Cooking and preparation: 1hr 30 minutes
Level of difficulty: * *
Serves 4

1. For the filling, simmer the pearl barley in lightly salted water for about 30 minutes, or until tender. Depending on the brand of pearl barley, the cooking time will vary and can sometimes take up to 1 hour – in which case you may have to add more water towards the end. Drain the cooked pearl barley and leave it to cool.

2. While the pearl barley is cooking, bring the chicken stock to a simmer in a saucepan. Use a small sharp knife to cut away the breast fillets and the thigh meat from the quails. Remove and discard the skin and plunge the quail meat into the gently simmering chicken stock, in batches, for 4–5 minutes. Lift the quail meat out with a slotted spoon and cut it into ½cm (¼in) pieces.

3. At the same time, blanch the cabbage leaves in lightly salted water for 2–3 minutes. Drain the cabbage leaves, refresh in cold water and drain flat on kitchen paper. Cut away the tough ribs.

4. To assemble the filling, put the pearl barley in a mixing bowl along with the flavourings for the filling: the onion, Lemon Confit, diced tomato, ginger, tarragon and sweetcorn kernels, and then the soy sauce and white wine. Add the quail meat and mix to distribute the ingredients evenly. Season the filling to taste and set aside briefly.

5. Cut 4 squares of clingfilm (plastic wrap) about 30 x 30cm (12 x 12in) square. On each square, arrange 2 cabbage leaves, head to tail and slightly overlapping. Put one-quarter of the filling in the centre, then pick up the 4 corners of the clingfilm (plastic wrap) and twist them to make a tight little ball. Secure the clingfilm (plastic wrap). either by tying it with kitchen string or by knotting it onto itself.

6. Heat the stuffed cabbage leaves in a steamer or couscoussier for about 10 minutes. At the same time, for the sauce, heat the game or meat stock mixed with cornflour (cornstarch) and keep it warm.

7. Transfer the stuffed cabbage leaves to a large flat plate or tray. When they are cool enough to handle, remove the clingfilm (plastic wrap). Mop up any excess cooking juices using kitchen paper.

To serve

Use a wide spatula to transfer the stuffed cabbage leaves to 4 warm serving plates. Garnish each with a sage leaf and a drizzle of the sauce. For an additional garnish, you can add simmered matchsticks of vegetables, such as courgettes (zucchini) or carrots.

Variations

In France, these stuffed cabbage leaves are called aumônières, or 'little purses'. They can be adapted to enclose other meats, such as rabbit, pheasant, pigeon or pork – or even a mixture of different meats if you prefer.

- 2 chicken breasts, skin removed
- 200g (7oz) fresh tagliatelle or fettuccine
- salt and pepper of your choice

For the filling
- 2 tbsp fromage blanc or Greek yogurt (0%)
- 1 tsp finely chopped chives
- 1 tsp finely chopped tarragon
- 1 tbsp finely chopped flat-leaf parsley
- 1 tsp Lemon Confit (Terms and Techniques, page 327) cut into ½cm (¼in) pieces

For the vegetables
- 120g (scant 4½oz) mangetout (snow peas)
- 2 artichoke hearts, fresh, preserved, or frozen and thawed and immersed in acidulated water to prevent discolouration
- 1 tsp olive oil
- 1 clove of garlic, unpeeled

For the sauce
- 300–400ml (1¼–1⅔ US cups) White Vegetable Sauce (page 85)
- 1½ tbsp finely chopped herbs, such as chives, flat-leaf parsley and tarragon (optional)

To garnish
- few sprigs of tarragon or savory

Equipment
- Steamer or couscoussier

CHICKEN BREASTS STUFFED WITH LEMONY HERBS

240 CALORIES PER PERSON
Cooking and preparation: 50 minutes
Level of difficulty: *
Serves 4

1. To make the filling for the chicken breasts, mix together the fromage blanc, the herbs and the Lemon Confit. Season to taste.

2. To fill the breasts, have ready a clean work surface and 2 pieces of clingfilm (plastic wrap), each large enough to wrap a breast comfortably. Use a small knife to ease open the natural lengthways-running pocket of each breast, leaving it closed at each end. Season the breasts inside and out. Divide the filling between the pockets and close them. Wrap the breasts tightly and set aside in the refrigerator.

3. Just before you want to serve the dish, prepare a steamer or couscoussier for the chicken and a saucepan of salted water for the pasta. Heat the White Vegetable Sauce through and keep it warm, preferably in a bain-marie.

4. To prepare and cook the vegetables, cut the mangetout (snow peas) diagonally at regular interval to make diamond shapes. Drain the artichoke hearts of their acidulated water and cut them into small dice. Sweat the diced artichoke, along with the clove of garlic, over a gentle heat in a saucepan coated with the olive oil, for about 2 minutes. Add the mangetout (snow peas) and cover with a lid. Sweat gently for about 10 minutes, shaking the saucepan or stirring occasionally to prevent the vegetables from sticking.

5. While the vegetables are sweating, steam the wrapped chicken breasts for about 6 minutes. Remove the chicken breasts with a spatula and leave to cool briefly. Meanwhile, plunge the fresh pasta into the simmering water for a few minutes, until al dente, then drain.

6. Remove and discard the garlic from the vegetables. Remove the clingfilm (plastic wrap) from the chicken breasts and cut each breast into 4–6 slices.

To serve

Have ready 4 warm serving plates. Make a nest of pasta on each plate and arrange slices of stuffed chicken breast alongside. Add the vegetable garnish and a small pool of White Vegetable Sauce. You can add some finely chopped mixed herbs to the sauce at the last moment if you wish. Decorate with a sprig of tarragon or savory and serve immediately.

Variation

You can replace the globe artichoke hearts with Jerusalem artichokes if you like. Scrub them well and simmer until tender, testing them for doneness after 10 minutes.

- 1 tbsp olive oil
- 100g (3½oz) carrots, peeled and cut into 3mm (⅛in) dice
- 80g (scant 3oz) onion, cut into 3mm (⅛in) dice
- 500g (1lb 2oz) beef cheek, in one piece, fat and skin removed
- 1 clove of garlic, unpeeled
- 1 small fresh bouquet garni
- salt and pepper of your choice

For the cooking liquid

- 300ml (1¼ US cups) red wine
- 6 cumin seeds
- 8 coriander seeds
- pinch of powdered saffron
- pinch of fructose or the sweetener of your choice (pages 16–20)
- 500ml (2⅛ US cups) veal stock, either home-made (page 46) or from a cube
- 1 tbsp cornflour (cornstarch), mixed with a little cold water

For the spicy carrot garnish

- 250g (9oz) carrots, peeled and cut into rounds 3–5mm (⅛–¼in) thick
- ¼ chicken stock cube, dissolved in 250ml (1⅛ US cups) hot water
- ¼ tsp cumin seeds
- pinch of fructose or the sweetener of your choice (pages 16–20)

For the crispy salad

- 1 small red onion, thinly sliced into rings
- 1 tbsp chervil, leaves only
- about 4 chives, cut into long strips (see illustration)
- 40g (scant 1½oz) Granny Smith or other tart apple, cut into matchsticks 3 x 5mm (⅛ x ¼in)

OVEN-BRAISED BEEF CHEEK WITH A CRISPY SALAD

265 CALORIES PER PERSON

Cooking and preparation: 3 hours (mostly of oven cooking)
Level of difficulty: * *
Serves 4

1. To prepare the cooking liquid, combine the red wine, the cumin seeds and coriander seeds, the powdered saffron and the fructose in a saucepan. Bring the liquid to the boil, then simmer briskly for 3–4 minutes. Add the veal stock, return to the boil briefly, then remove from the heat and set aside.

2. Preheat the oven to 150°C (300°F, gas mark 2). Select a heavy-based casserole dish (Dutch oven), preferably made of enamelled cast iron. Lightly coat the bottom of it with olive oil. Set it over a low heat and add the diced carrot and onion. Sweat the carrot and onion, uncovered, for a few minutes without allowing them to colour. Add the beef cheek and colour this lightly all over. Season then add the garlic and the bouquet garni.

3. Pour in the cooking liquid, bring to the boil, then adjust the heat to maintain a simmer. Using a large spoon, skim the surface to remove the fat and impurities. After about 5 minutes of skimming, cover the casserole dish (Dutch oven) with a lid and transfer it to the oven. Let the beef cheek braise for 2½ hours or until extremely tender.

4. About 30 minutes before you want to serve the beef cheek, prepare the spicy carrot garnish: put the thin rounds of carrot in a small saucepan along with the crumbled chicken stock cube dissolved in water. Add the cumin seeds and stir in the fructose. Cover the saucepan and leave the carrots to cook over a very low heat for 30 minutes or until tender.

5. Meanwhile, prepare the crispy salad: combine the red onion, chervil, chives and apple. Cover with iced water and set aside in the refrigerator.

6. When the meat is cooked, remove the casserole dish (Dutch oven) from the oven. Lift out the beef cheek, put it on a plate and cover it with clingfilm (plastic wrap) to prevent it from drying out.

7. To make the sauce, stir the cornflour (cornstarch) mixed with water into the cooking juices at the bottom of the casserole dish (Dutch oven). Adjust the seasoning. Strain through a very fine sieve – preferably a chinois – and discard the solids. Keep the sauce warm.

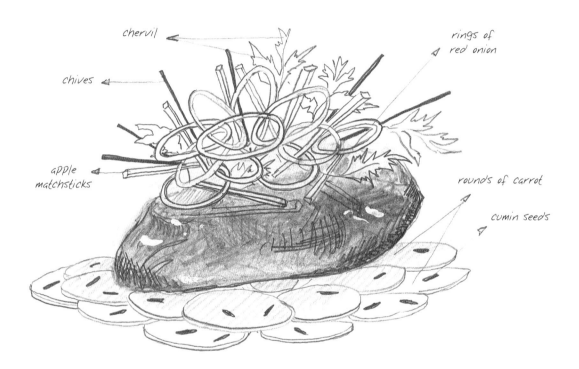

chervil

rings of
red onion

chives

apple
matchsticks

rounds of carrot

cumin seeds

To serve

Cut the beef cheek into 4 pieces. If they are not hot enough to serve, warm them
through in the sauce. Lay a bed of spicy carrots on each of 4 warm serving plates
and add a piece of beef cheek. Pour over the sauce. Drain the crispy salad and
arrange it prettily on top. Serve immediately.

- 2 large duck thighs, each about 250g (9oz), skin removed, trimmed of fat and cut in half to yield an upper and lower leg section
- 1 tbsp olive oil
- 40g (scant 1½oz) carrots, peeled and cut into 3mm (⅛in) dice
- 40g (scant 1½oz) onion, cut into 3mm (⅛in) dice
- 20g (¾oz) celery, cut into 3mm (⅛in) dice
- 300ml (1¼ US cups) young, slightly tannic red wine
- 300ml (1¼ US cups) home-made duck stock or game stock, or veal stock, home-made (page 46) or from a cube
- 1 small fresh bouquet garni
- ½ tbsp cornflour (cornstarch), mixed with a little cold water
- 1 tbsp port
- salt and pepper of your choice

For the vegetable accompaniment
- 150g (5½oz) carrots, peeled and cut into ½cm (¼in) dice
- 100g (3½oz) celeriac, peeled and cut into ½cm (¼in) dice
- 150g (5½oz) young courgettes (zucchini), cut into ½cm (¼in) dice

To garnish
- 4 small fresh bouquets garnis, each made with 1 small fresh bay leaf, 1 sprig of thyme and 1 sprig of savory, and tied with fine kitchen string:

Equipment (optional)
- Steamer or couscoussier

TENDER SLIVERS OF DUCK WITH YOUNG RED WINE

CALORIE COUNT
Cooking and preparation: 1 hour 15 minutes
Level of difficulty: *
Serves 4

1. To cook the duck, preheat the oven to 180°C (350°F, gas mark 4). Season the 4 portions of duck. Heat the oil gently in a small casserole dish (Dutch oven) – preferably made of enamelled cast iron – and lightly colour the portions of duck on both sides. Add the finely diced carrot, onion and celery and leave the ingredients to sweat, over a low heat, uncovered, for 5 minutes.

2. Spoon out and discard any excess fat from the bottom of the casserole dish (Dutch oven). Add the red wine, increase the heat and scrape the bottom of the casserole dish (Dutch oven) to deglaze the deposits. Bring the liquid to the boil and maintain a brisk simmer for 5 minutes. Add the stock and the bouquet garni. Season very lightly. Cover the casserole dish (Dutch oven) and transfer it to the oven. Cook for about 45 minutes or until the duck meat is tender enough to come away from the bone easily.

3. For the vegetable accompaniment, simmer each vegetable separately in lightly salted boiling water until just tender: about 10 minutes for the carrots, 8 minutes for the celeriac and 4 minutes for the courgettes (zucchini). Drain, refresh in cold water, then drain again. Set aside until you are almost ready to serve the dish.

4. Remove the casserole dish (Dutch oven) from the oven. With a slotted spoon, transfer the duck portions to a plate. Pull away and discard the bone. Break up the duck meat into slivers and set aside. Skim off any excess fat from the cooking liquid in the casserole dish (Dutch oven) and strain the cooking liquid through a fine sieve – preferably a chinois – set over a saucepan. Stir in the cornflour (cornstarch) mixed with water and the port. Taste, and adjust the seasoning. Strain the sauce again into a saucepan large enough to accommodate the duck as well.

5. When you are almost ready to serve the dish, put the duck in the sauce and heat it through. At the same time, reheat the vegetable accompaniment, preferably using a steamer or couscoussier.

To serve
Distribute the duck meat and its sauce evenly between 4 warm serving plates, arranging it in the centre of each. Arrange the vegetable accompaniment all around and garnish each with a fresh bouquet garni. Depending on personal taste and appetite, you might also add a little nest of tagliatelle, lightly cooked until al dente.

- 600g (1lb 5oz) boneless rump (or round) of veal, trimmed free of fat and connective tissue and tied with string
- about 2 tbsp olive oil
- 300g (11oz) seasonal mushrooms, such as girolles, ceps or shiitake, rinsed, dried and cut in half
- 1 tsp very finely chopped or snipped shallot
- 1 tbsp finely chopped flat-leaf parsley
- salt and pepper of your choice

For the white sauce
- 400ml (1¾ US cups) semi-skimmed (2%) milk
- 3 long strips of lemon zest, blanched and refreshed 3 times
- 2 long strips of orange zest, blanched and refreshed 3 times
- ½ chicken stock cube, finely crumbled
- 1 tbsp freshly squeezed lemon juice

For the accompaniment (optional)
- a little fresh tagliatelle cooked until al dente.

VEAL WITH MUSHROOMS AND WHITE SAUCE REVISITED

330 CALORIES PER PERSON
Cooking and preparation: 45 minutes
Level of difficulty: * *
Serves 4

1. To make the white sauce, combine the milk, lemon and orange zest, and the crumbled chicken stock cube in a saucepan. Bring almost to the boil, stir, then adjust the heat to maintain a simmer until the milk has reduced by half. Remove from the heat and when cool enough to handle, blend the mixture to a smooth sauce in a food processor. Pass through a very fine sieve set over a bowl. Add the lemon juice. Season to taste and set aside.

2. Season the tied veal. Gently heat one of the tablespoons of oil in a heavy-based oval casserole dish (Dutch oven) and cook the veal for about 8 minutes on each side or until lightly coloured all over. Transfer the veal to a plate, cover with aluminium foil and leave in a warm place to relax.

3. Meanwhile, heat a non-stick frying pan (skillet) and – without using any oil – add the mushrooms and sauté them rapidly for 30 seconds or so to draw out any excess liquid; drain. Add the remaining tablespoon of oil to the pan, then return the mushrooms to the pan along with the shallot. Sauté over a gentle heat until the shallot is soft and the mushrooms flop. At the last moment, stir in the parsley. Heat the white sauce through and emulsify it by whisking it with a stick blender or with a balloon whisk.

To serve
Remove the string from the veal and carve it into thin slices. Transfer the slices to 4 warm serving plates. Coat the veal lightly with the whisked white sauce and drizzle a little more sauce around each plate. Scatter with the mushroom mixture and, if you like, add a small nest of fresh tagliatelle, cooked until al dente.

- 800g (1¾lb) loin of pork, boned and trimmed free of connective tissue (ask your butcher) Note: if you intend to make stock for the recipe, retain the bones, along with the pork trimmings.
- 1 tbsp ground turmeric
- 1 heaped tsp peeled and finely grated fresh ginger
- 2 tbsp finely chopped fresh lemongrass, tough outer layers removed first
- 3 garlic flakes (page 82), dried and crushed into fine pieces
- 3 tbsp torn coriander (cilantro) leaves
- 1 tsp olive oil
- 1 medium carrot, peeled and cut into 1cm (½in) dice
- 1 medium onion, cut into 1cm (½in) dice
- ¼ stick (stalk) celery, cut into 1cm (½in) dice
- 1 small fresh bouquet garni
- ½ stalk lemongrass, tough outer layers removed
- 1 litre (4¼ US cups/1 quart) home-made pork stock, made with bones from the loin and some pork trimmings from the butcher, or 1 litre (4¼ US cups/1 quart) veal stock, home-made (page 46) or from a cube
- 2 tbsp soy sauce
- 1 tbsp cornflour (cornstarch), mixed with a little cold water
- salt and pepper of your choice

For the accompaniment
- 150g (5½oz) fine or coarse-grained couscous
- about ¼ chicken stock cube, crumbled
- 150ml (¾ US cup) water

For the garnish
- 200g (7oz) pineapple, cut into ½cm (¼in) dice
- 200g (7oz) mango, cut into ½cm (¼in) dice
- 200g (7oz) pear, peeled and cored and cut into ½cm (¼in) dice
- few coriander (cilantro) leaves (optional)

Equipment
- 6 food rings, 10cm (4in) in diameter

BRAISED LOIN OF PORK WITH LEMONGRASS AND TROPICAL FRUIT

380 CALORIES PER PERSON
Cooking and preparation: 3½ hours, plus overnight resting
Level of difficulty: * * *
Serves 6

1. Using a very large sharp knife, slice through the loin of pork lengthways, until it can be opened up like a book while still remaining in a single sheet of more or less even thickness; flatten the meat out slightly. Repeat this procedure twice more, so you create a large rectangle of pork of even thickness. Lay the pork on a sheet of clingfilm (plastic wrap) about 15cm (6in) bigger all around than the rectangle of pork. Meticulously cut away all of the fat, then flatten the trimmed pork with a rolling pin, making it a uniform thickness.

2. Sprinkle the surface of the pork with half of the turmeric. Lay another sheet of clingfilm (plastic wrap) on top and flip the loin over. Sprinkle the other side with the grated ginger and season with salt and pepper. Scatter the remaining turmeric evenly on top, along with the lemongrass, the garlic flakes and the coriander (cilantro) leaves.

3. Roll the loin up fairly tightly into a sausage shape, using the clingfilm (plastic wrap) to hold it together. Remove the clingfilm (plastic wrap) and tie the roll with string in 4 places.

4. Preheat the oven to 200°C (400°F, gas mark 6). Heat the olive oil in a casserole dish (Dutch oven), preferably made of enamelled cast iron. Add the rolled loin and colour it on all sides. Add the diced carrot, onion and celery, the bouquet garni and the half-stalk of lemongrass. Stir in the stock and the soy sauce. Bring the liquid briefly to the boil, then remove the casserole dish (Dutch oven) from the heat, cover it and transfer it to the oven for 2½ hours.

5. At the end of the cooking, the loin will have shrunk away from the string so the roll will need to be tightened. To do this, transfer the loin carefully to a sheet of clingfilm (plastic wrap) that is bigger than the meat. Let the meat cool a little, then cut off the string and roll up the loin tightly in the clingfilm (plastic wrap). Close the long edges and twist the ends tightly. Either secure the ends with string or knot them onto themselves. Transfer to a refrigerator for at least several hours but preferably overnight.

6. Strain the cooking juices through a fine sieve, ideally a chinois. To degrease the juices, chill them in the refrigerator until the fat solidifies, then skim off the fat.

7. When you are almost ready to serve the pork, preheat the oven to 180°C (350°F, gas mark 4). Warm the degreased cooking juices through and thicken them with the cornflour (cornstarch). Adjust the seasoning and keep the sauce warm.

8. Remove the clingfilm (plastic wrap) from the loin and cut it into 6 round slices. Arrange these on a shallow oven dish. Ladle over the sauce, allowing it to come halfway up the sides of the slices. Transfer to the oven for about 6 minutes, regularly basting the meat with the sauce to prevent it from drying out.

9. Meanwhile, complete the accompaniment and the garnish: put the fine-grained couscous in a saucepan. Pour over boiling chicken stock and stir. Season, then cover the saucepan with a lid. Leave the couscous to swell, without additional heat, for 5 minutes, then fluff it up with a fork. If you use large-grained couscous, simmer it according to the packet instructions. Warm through the fruit for the garnish, either in a small saucepan or on a plate in the oven.

To serve
Have ready 6 warm serving plates. Put a food ring in the centre of each plate. Fill the ring with couscous, then lift the ring away. Put a slice of pork on top of the couscous. Spoon the sauce over the pork and drizzle a little around the plate. Surround this arrangement with the fruit and add a few leaves of coriander (cilantro). Serve immediately.

- 4 body skirt steaks (also known as onglet steaks), totalling about 600g (1lb 5oz)
- 250g (9oz) cooked beetroot, coarsely diced
- 300ml (1¼ US cups) water
- 8 even-sized shallots, about 30g (1oz) each
- about 1 tsp olive oil
- 200ml (⅞ US cup) Red Beet Liaison (page 89)
- salt and pepper of your choice

For the purée
- 300g (11oz) celeriac, peeled and coarsely diced
- 100g (3½oz) potatoes, peeled and coarsely diced
- 100g (3½oz) Golden Delicious apple or other medium-sweet apple, peeled, cored and coarsely diced
- 5 tbsp semi-skimmed (2%) milk

Equipment
- Steamer or couscoussier

BODY SKIRT OF VEAL WITH A CELERIAC AND APPLE PURÉE

310 CALORIES PER PERSON
Cooking and preparation: 50 minutes
Level of difficulty: * *
Serves 4

1. Trim the skirt steaks free from any fat and fibrous connective tissue if the butcher has not already done so. Smooth out and flatten the steaks slightly; set these aside in a cold place.

2. Blend the beetroot and water in a food processor to make a juice, then strain the juice through a fine chinois or through a sieve lined with muslin.

3. Preheat the oven to 180°C (350°F, gas mark 4). Peel the shallots. Keep them whole and arrange them snugly in a small oven dish. Add the beetroot juice and cover with greaseproof paper, tucking the paper lightly around the shallots. Cook for 45 minutes or until the shallots are tender and tinted purple-pink. Season with salt and pepper.

4. While the shallots are cooking, start making the purée: steam the celeriac in a steamer or couscoussier, for about 5 minutes. Add the potato and cook for a further 15 minutes, then add the apple and cook for a further 5 minutes. Purée this mixture, ideally using a mouli with a fine disc. Bring the milk to a simmer then whisk it into the purée. Adjust the seasoning and keep this purée warm, preferably in a bain-marie, until you need it.

5. About 15 minutes towards the end of the shallots' cooking time, start cooking the veal: coat a non-stick frying pan (skillet) with the oil and cook the steaks for 3–4 minutes on each side over a low to medium heat. Transfer to a warm dish, cover with aluminium foil and leave the dish in a warm place for 8–10 minutes to allow the veal to relax. Heat the Red Beet Liaison through and keep it warm.

To serve
Have ready 4 warm serving plates. Arrange 2 shallots on each plate, slightly off-centre. Pass the purée between 2 dessertspoons to make oval quenelle shapes. Slip a knife underneath each quenelle to release it. Put 2 quenelles on each plate, towards the edge. Add a spoonful of Red Beet Liaison to the centre and place a steak on top. Spoon over a little Red Beet Liaison and serve the remainder in a sauce boat.

Chef's tip
Make sure your butcher takes these body skirt steaks, or onglet steaks, from inside the rib cage of the animal.

- 360g (13oz) rumpsteak, trimmed of fat and connective tissue
- 1 egg white
- 30g (1oz) fresh Parmesan, grated
- 6 basil leaves, finely snipped
- 5–6 tbsp good-quality beef jus, such as the degreased juices left over from a roast, or 5–6 tbsp beef stock, either home-made (page 43) or from a cube
- 1 tsp olive oil
- salt and pepper of your choice

To serve (optional)
- 4 bread rolls or buns of your choice
- tomato salad garnish with torn basil leaves
- handful of mesclun salad leaves or other salad leaves of your choice, dressed

Equipment
- 3 food rings or cutters, 10cm (4in) in diameter

ITALIAN-STYLE BEEFBURGERS WITH BASIL

215 CALORIES PER PERSON
Cooking and preparation: 20 minutes, plus 1 hour of chilling
Level of difficulty: *
Serves 3

1. Cut the steak into ½cm (¼in) dice. In a large mixing bowl, beat the egg white lightly until it foams, then stir in the grated Parmesan, the basil and the beef stock. Add the diced steak, season to taste with salt and pepper, then mix gently with a fork to distribute the ingredients evenly.

2. Select a small baking sheet or tray that will fit into the refrigerator. Line it with greaseproof or parchment paper and add the food rings. Spoon the steak mixture into the rings and tap the surface lightly with the back of the spoon to settle the contents. Transfer to the refrigerator for 1 hour.

3. When you are ready to cook the beefburgers, heat the olive oil in a non-stick frying pan (skillet). When the oil is hot, transfer each beefburger to the pan using a wide flexible spatula and carefully lifting away the food ring once the beefburger has slipped into the pan. Cook the beefburgers for 2 minutes on each side, turning them carefully with the spatula.

To serve
Transfer the beefburgers to 3 warm serving plates. If you like, you can serve the beefburger with a bread roll or bun. A tomato salad garnished with some torn basil leaves makes a good accompaniment, as does a dressed salad of mesclun leaves.

- 4 heads of chicory (Belgian endive), outer leaves removed
- 1 litre (4¼ US cups/1 quart) water
- 1 tbsp freshly squeezed lemon juice
- small pinch of fructose or the sweetener of your choice (pages 16–20)
- pinch of coarse salt
- salt and pepper of your choice

For the filling
- 25g (scant 1oz) bulgur
- 1 tsp olive oil
- 1 tbsp very finely chopped shallot
- 160g (5½oz) cooked chicken, cut into ½cm (¼in) dice
- ½ tsp peeled and grated fresh ginger
- about 2 small water chestnuts (tinned), drained and very finely diced to yield about 2 tbsp
- 1 tbsp dry white wine
- 1 tbsp soy sauce
- 1 tbsp oyster sauce
- 1 tbsp chopped coriander (cilantro) leaves

For the sauce
- Juice of 1 large orange
- 1 tsp fructose or the sweetener of your choice (pages 16–20)
- good pinch of peeled and grated fresh ginger
- 100ml (⅜ US cup) veal stock, either home-made (page 46) or from a cube, or 100ml (⅜ US cup) chicken stock, either home-made (page 44) or from a cube
- 1 tsp soy sauce

To garnish
- 12 mangetout (snow peas)
- 12 pith-free segments of orange
- 4 sprigs of chervil, leaves only
- few slices of pitted black olive or a sliver of black truffle (optional)

CHICKEN-FILLED CHICORY
140 CALORIES PER PERSON
Cooking and preparation: 1 hour 15 minutes
Level of difficulty: * *
Serves 4

1. Put the heads of chicory (Belgian endive) in a saucepan. Add the litre (4¼ US cups) of water, the lemon juice, the sweetener and a pinch of coarse salt. Cut a piece of greaseproof or parchment paper of the same diameter as the saucepan and lay this on the surface of the water, tucking it gently around the chicory (Belgian endive) to make a steamy cooking environment.

2. Bring the water to a gentle boil, then adjust the heat to maintain a very gentle simmer for up to 50 minutes, checking the chicory (Belgian endive) for doneness after 40 minutes. If the tip of a sharp knife meets no resistance when inserted in the chicory (Belgian endive), then it is cooked. Use a slotted spoon to transfer the chicory (Belgian endive) to kitchen paper to drain.

3. To make the filling, simmer the bulgur in lightly salted water for about 25 minutes or until cooked to your liking. Drain, refresh under cold water then drain again; set aside.

4. In a wok, or a frying pan (skillet) or sauté pan with sloping sides, heat the oil and add the shallot. Let the shallot sweat, stirring it all the time to prevent colouring. Continue to stir with a wooden spoon or a whisk while you add the chicken and ginger, then a little salt to taste. Stir in the water chestnuts, then the wine, soy sauce and oyster sauce. Remove from the heat. Stir in the reserved bulgur and the coriander (cilantro). Taste, and adjust the seasoning.

5. Press the heads of chicory (Belgian endive) gently between your hands to squeeze out the excess cooking liquid. Cut them in half lengthways so you have 8 halves. Lay the bulgur and the chicken filling on 4 of the halves, then top with the remaining 4 halves. The chicory (Belgian endive) 'sandwiches' are complete but will require reheating before you serve them. If you want to reheat them in a microwave, transfer them to a microwaveable dish and cover with suitable clingfilm (plastic wrap). Alternatively, you can reheat them in an oven, in which case, enclose each one loosely in aluminium foil.

6. To prepare the garnish, cook the mangetout (snow peas) in lightly salted simmering water for 3 minutes, then drain, refresh with cold water and drain again. Cut in half lengthways to make decorative shapes. Set them aside, preferably in a bain-marie, ready to reheat. Put the orange segments in a small covered dish, ready to be gently heated through just before serving.

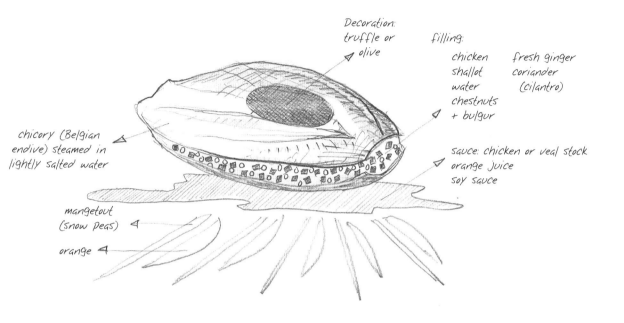

Decoration:
truffle or
olive

filling:

chicken
shallot
water
chestnuts
+ bulgur

fresh ginger
coriander
(cilantro)

chicory (Belgian
endive) steamed in
lightly salted water

sauce: chicken or veal stock
orange juice
soy sauce

mangetout
(snow peas)

orange

7. For the sauce, put the orange juice, the fructose and the grated ginger in a small saucepan, set over a medium to high heat. Bring the liquid to the boil and simmer briskly for a minute or so until it reduces slightly and becomes light brown in colour. Add the veal stock and the soy sauce. Bring the liquid to the boil, then simmer for about 2 minutes. Adjust the seasoning and set aside in a warm place.

8. Just before you are ready to serve the dish, reheat the chicory (Belgian endive) according to your preferred method. Bring the mangetout (snow peas), the orange segments and the sauce to serving temperature.

To serve
Have ready 4 warm serving plates. Arrange a filled head of chicory (Belgian endive) in the middle of each plate and top each one with a little sauce. If you like, decorate each with a slice of black olive or truffle. Drizzle a little more sauce around each head of chicory (Belgian endive). Position pieces of mangetout (snow peas) and orange along one side, alternating them. Add a sprig of chervil and serve straight away.

- 360g (13oz) duck breast, trimmed of fat and connective tissue
- 20g (¾oz) fresh ginger, peeled
- 3 tbsp fresh coriander (cilantro) leaves
- 1 egg white
- 30g (1oz) yogurt (0%)
- 2 tbsp soy sauce
- 1 tsp olive oil
- salt and pepper of your choice

To serve (optional)
- 4 bread rolls or buns of your choice
- handful of mesclun salad leaves or other salad leaves of your choice, dressed

Equipment
- 3 food rings or cutters, 10cm (4in) in diameter

EASTERN-INSPIRED DUCK BURGERS

260 CALORIES PER PERSON
Cooking and preparation: 20 minutes, plus 1 hour of chilling
Level of difficulty: *
Serves 3

1. Cut the duck breasts into ½cm (¼in) dice. Finely chop the fresh ginger. Finely chop or snip the coriander (cilantro) leaves. Set these ingredients aside briefly.

2. In a large mixing bowl, beat the egg white lightly until it foams, then whisk in the yogurt, the soy sauce, and the ginger and coriander (cilantro). Season very lightly with salt. Add the duck and mix very gently with a fork to distribute the ingredients evenly. Adjust the seasoning.

3. Select a small baking sheet or tray that will fit into the refrigerator. Line it with greaseproof or parchment paper and add the food rings. Spoon the duck mixture into the rings and tap the surface lightly with the back of the spoon to settle the contents. Transfer to the refrigerator for 1 hour.

4. When you are ready to cook the burgers, heat the olive oil in a non-stick frying pan (skillet). When the oil is hot, transfer each burger to the pan using a wide flexible spatula and carefully lifting away the food ring once the burger has slipped into the pan. Cook the burgers for 2 minutes on each side, turning them carefully with the spatula.

To serve
Transfer the burgers to 3 warm serving plates. If you like, you can serve the burger with a bread roll or bun and with a dressed salad of mesclun leaves.

- 220g (8oz) veal, cut from the upper part of the leg
- 140g (5oz) peeled King prawns or scampi (large shrimp)
- 1 egg white
- 30g (1oz) yogurt (0%)
- 15g (½oz) fresh ginger, peeled and grated
- 5g (¼oz) coriander (cilantro), finely chopped or snipped
- 1 tsp olive oil
- salt and pepper of your choice

To serve
- 4 bread rolls or buns of your choice (optional) handful of mesclun salad leaves or other salad leaves of your choice, dressed

Equipment
- 3 food rings or cutters, 10cm (4in) in diameter

VEAL AND PRAWN BURGERS VENETIAN STYLE

200 CALORIES PER PERSON

Cooking and preparation: 20 minutes plus 1 hour of chilling
Level of difficulty: *
Serves 3

1. Cut the veal and the prawns into ½cm (¼in) dice. Transfer to a large mixing bowl.

2. In a separate bowl, beat the egg white lightly until it foams, then whisk in the yogurt, the ginger and the coriander (cilantro). Add this mixture to the diced veal and prawns and stir well with a fork to distribute the ingredients evenly. Adjust the seasoning.

3. Select a small baking sheet or tray that will fit into the refrigerator. Line it with greaseproof or parchment paper and add the food rings. Spoon the veal and prawn mixture into the rings and tap the surface lightly with the back of the spoon to settle the contents. Transfer to the refrigerator for 1 hour.

4. When you are ready to cook the burgers, heat the olive oil in a non-stick frying pan (skillet). When the oil is hot, transfer each burger to the pan using a wide flexible spatula and carefully lifting away the food ring once the burger has slipped into the pan. Cook the burgers for 2 minutes on each side, turning them carefully with the spatula.

To serve

Transfer the burgers to 3 warm serving plates. If you like, you can serve the burger with a bread roll or bun and with a dressed salad of mesclun leaves.

- 2 shanks (fore-shanks) of lamb on the bone, each about 350g (12oz)
- 1 large grapefruit
- about 1 tsp olive oil
- 150ml (¾ US cup) veal stock, either home-made (page 46) or from a cube
- 60ml (¼ US cup or 6tbsp) red wine vinegar
- 3 tsp fructose or the sweetener of your choice (pages 16–20)
- salt and pepper of your choice

For the marinade
- 100g (3½oz) onion, finely chopped
- 1 clove of garlic, unpeeled and crushed
- 1 small fresh bouquet garni
- juice of 1 orange
- juice of 1 grapefruit

BRAISED LAMB SHANKS WITH GRAPEFRUIT

365 CALORIES PER PERSON

Cooking and preparation: 1½ hours, plus marinating overnight
Level of difficulty: * *
Serves 4

1. In a dish or shallow bowl, combine all the marinade ingredients. Add the lamb shanks and cover the dish loosely with aluminium foil. Leave the ingredients to marinate for 12 hours, or overnight, in a cold place or a refrigerator. Turn the shanks 2 or 3 times while they marinate.

2. While the lamb marinates, use a vegetable peeler to remove the peel of the grapefruit in strips and scrape away the white pith. Blanch and refresh the strips 3 times then cut them into julienne strips; set these aside in an airtight container.

3. Use a small sharp knife to trim the peeled grapefruit free of any remaining pith. Cut along each side of the membranes to free the segments. Cut the segments into ½cm (¼in) dice; cover tightly and set aside in the refrigerator.

4. When you are ready to cook the lamb shanks, preheat the oven to 180°C (350°F, gas mark 4). Remove the lamb from its marinade and pat it dry with kitchen paper; set aside the marinade. Heat the oil in a heavy casserole dish (Dutch oven), preferably made of enamelled cast iron. Over a low to medium heat, colour the shanks lightly all over. Add the marinade and, when it comes to a simmer, cover the dish and put it in the oven. After 30 minutes, add the veal stock. Cook for a further 30 minutes, or until the lamb is extremely tender and shrinks slightly from the bone.

5. In a small saucepan, bring the red wine vinegar to the boil. Lower the heat to maintain a simmer and stir in the fructose. Continue to stir until the liquid becomes syrupy and a light brown colour; set aside.

6. When the lamb is cooked, remove the shanks from the casserole dish (Dutch oven), and transfer them to a covered dish in a warm place. Discard the bouquet garni. Transfer the cooking juices to a food processor and blend to a smooth sauce. For extra smoothness, pass the sauce through a very fine sieve – preferably a chinois – set over a saucepan.

7. Complete the sauce by adding the red wine vinegar mixture, along with the diced grapefruit segments and the julienne strips. Heat the finished sauce to a serving temperature and keep it warm.

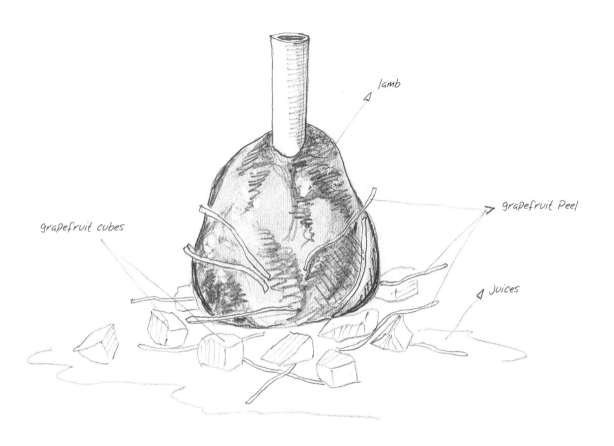

lamb

grapefruit peel

grapefruit cubes

juices

To serve

Have ready 4 warm serving plates. Remove the shank meat from the bone and cut it into slices about 3cm (1¼ in) thick. Coat with the sauce. The dish lends itself to various accompaniments including puréed potato, bulgur or tagliatelle. My favourites are Camargue Red Rice (page 114) or buckwheat (page 113).

- 1 tbsp olive oil
- 4 veal cheeks
- 40g (scant 1½oz) carrots, peeled and cut into 3mm (⅛in) dice
- 40g (scant 1½oz) onion, cut into 3mm (⅛in) dice
- 1 clove of garlic, unpeeled and lightly crushed
- ½ stalk lemongrass, tough outer layers removed and the rest finely chopped
- 30g (1oz) fresh ginger, peeled and finely chopped
- 1 small fresh bouquet garni
- 1 litre (4¼ US cups/1 quart) veal stock, either home-made (page 46) or from a cube
- salt and pepper of your choice

For the glaze
- 1 tbsp honey
- 2 tbsp Xeres vinegar or other sherry vinegar of your choice
- ½ tsp peeled and grated fresh ginger
- 1 tbsp soy sauce

To garnish
- 4 large prawns, butterflied (Terms and Techniques, page 326)
- handful of mixed fresh herbs and salad leaves

Equipment
- Steamer or couscoussier

VEAL CHEEK SPICED WITH GINGER AND LEMONGRASS

250 CALORIES PER PERSON

Cooking and preparation: 3 hours
Level of difficulty: * *
Serves 4

---

1. Preheat the oven to 150°C (300°F, gas mark 2). Choose a casserole dish (Dutch oven), preferably made of enamelled cast iron and with a good seal. Coat the bottom of it with the oil. Season the veal cheeks and colour them lightly in the casserole dish (Dutch oven), turning them frequently to ensure even cooking. Add the carrots, onion, garlic, lemongrass, ginger and the bouquet garni. Sweat the ingredients, uncovered, over a very gentle heat, for about 3 minutes or until the flavourings are soft. Stir with a wooden spoon to prevent sticking.

2. Add the veal stock and increase the heat. When the liquid comes to the boil, remove the dish from the heat, cover it and put it in the oven. Braise for 2½ hours, basting regularly with the stock, until the veal is tender. It is ready when the tip of a knife inserted into the veal meets no resistance.

3. Meanwhile, combine the ingredients for the glaze in a small saucepan set over a gentle heat. Stir until the ingredients have blended together smoothly, then remove the saucepan from the heat and set it aside.

4. When the veal is ready, preheat the grill if separate from the oven. Remove the casserole dish (Dutch oven) from the oven and transfer the veal cheeks to a gratin dish. Strain the cooking juices from the casserole dish (Dutch oven) through a fine sieve, adding a tablespoon of water if they are very thick; keep the cooking juices warm.

5. Coat the veal cheeks with the glaze, setting aside any excess for basting. Put the gratin dish under the hot grill for a few minutes, basting with the remaining glaze until the surface of the meat is lightly caramelized.

6. Steam the prawns for the garnish for 2–3 minutes in a steamer or couscoussier.

To serve

Have ready 4 warm serving plates. Add a veal cheek to each, positioning it slightly off-centre. Drizzle the reserved warm cooking juices around the meat. Arrange the herbs and leaves to one side and a prawn garnish to the other. If you like, serve some seasonal vegetables separately, for instance, lightly cooked spinach, carrots cooked until al dente, mangetout (snow peas) or new potatoes.

- 1 baron of young rabbit (saddle and hind legs) with the liver and kidneys (the baron should be prepared by the butcher and separated from the rest of the rabbit at the first rib)
- 1 tsp coarse sea salt
- salt and pepper of your choice

For the stuffing
- about 1 tbsp olive oil
- 1 tsp finely chopped shallot
- 1 tbsp Armagnac
- 50g (1¾oz) duxelles of mushrooms (page 108)
- 1 large fresh or preserved apricot, peeled and stone removed, or 1–2 dried and rehydrated pitted apricots, cut into small dice
- 1 egg yolk
- 50g (1¾oz) young spinach, stems and tough ribs removed, then washed and drained

For the cooking liquid
- 500ml (2⅛ US cups) Pomerol or other red wine
- 500ml (2⅛ US cups) chicken stock, either home-made (page 44) or from a cube
- 1 fresh bouquet garni
- pinch of nutmeg
- 1 tsp fructose or the sweetener of your choice (pages 16–20)
- 1 spice bag made by tying together in muslin: 8 crushed juniper berries, 1 clove, 1 unpeeled clove of garlic and 4 crushed peppercorns 250g (9oz) button mushrooms, wiped and quartered
- 1 tsp coarse sea salt

To garnish
- 2 courgettes (zucchini)

To serve
- lentils or the accompaniment of your choice

BONED AND STUFFED RABBIT IN RED WINE

200 CALORIES PER PERSON
Cooking and preparation: 3 hours
Level of difficulty: * * *
Serves 6

---

1. Put the baron on a wooden board so that the inside of the rabbit is facing you. With a small, sharp, flexible knife, detach the flesh from the bone on each side of the 'saddle' section – the backbone and the ribs on either side of it. To do this, make an incision along the backbone (from neck to tail end) on both sides of the vertebral column. Then, hold the knife blade flat against the ribs and detach the flesh from the ribs of each half-saddle section, keeping the flesh in a single piece attached to its adjoining leg.

2. When the saddle flesh is freed, carefully detach the backbone from the ribcage, leaving each leg attached to its saddle section. In this way, you will end up with 2 half-barons. If you like, set aside the stripped backbone and ribcage to make stock for another dish. Make a lengthways incision through the upper section of each leg And remove the thighbone, leaving the lower-leg bone in place.

3. Make an incision along the flaps of meat on each side of the saddle and open them out. Then, using the flat of a blade of a large knife, flatten the 2 half-barons at the point of the upper thigh section. Set these half-barons aside in a cold place while you make the stuffing – in which you will use the liver and kidneys.

4. To make the stuffing, wash and dry the liver and kidneys and remove and discard the membrane covering the kidneys. Chop the liver and kidneys and set them aside. In a non-stick frying pan (skillet), gently heat about half of the oil and sweat the shallots for several minutes without colouring them. Add the liver and kidneys. Season and cook for 1 minute. Add the Armagnac and let it boil while you deglaze the bottom of the frying pan (skillet), scraping up the meaty deposits.

5. Transfer the mixture to a mixing bowl. Add the duxelles of mushrooms, the diced apricot and the egg yolk. Stir to distribute the ingredients evenly; season to taste and set this stuffing aside. In a saucepan set over a medium heat, cook the spinach until it wilts – about 30 seconds – in the remaining olive oil. Drain the spinach and set aside to cool.

6. Lay the 2 half-barons flat on a work surface so that you have two rectangles of saddle and thigh flesh plus an attached lower-leg section on the bone. The lower-leg sections should be furthest away from you. Season with salt and pepper. Distribute the spinach over the surface, then spread the stuffing on top. Roll up the flesh of the saddle section to make 2 sausage rolls, each with its own leg attached. Tie each roll with kitchen string; set aside briefly in a cold place.

7. For the cooking liquid, put the red wine in a saucepan over a medium heat and boil for 5 minutes. Add the chicken stock, bouquet garni, salt, nutmeg, fructose, the muslin bag of spices, the button mushrooms and the sea salt. Stir and set aside.

8. Put the 2 rolls of rabbit In a casserole dish (Dutch oven), preferably made of enamelled cast iron. Add the cooking liquid and bring to a simmer over a low to medium heat. Cover with a lid and adjust the heat to maintain a very gentle simmer for about 2 hours, or until the rabbit is tender.

9. At the end of the cooking, lift out the rolls of rabbit, transfer them to a warm covered dish and set aside in a warm place. Remove the bouquet garni and the muslin bag of spices and reduce the cooking liquid over a high heat to one-third. Let it cool slightly then put it in a food processor and blend to a smooth sauce. For extra smoothness, pass the sauce through a fine sieve set over a saucepan. Check the seasoning and keep the sauce warm.

10. For the garnish, top and tail the courgettes (zucchini). Do not peel them unless the skin is particularly tough. Cut each courgette (zucchini) lengthways into 6 long strips. Blanch the strips for 30 seconds in lightly salted simmering water, then refresh in cold water and drain. Set aside ready to be reheated quickly when you serve the rabbit.

To serve
Transfer the rolls of rabbit to a carving board. Remove the string and cut them into slices about ½cm (¼in) thick. Cut each leg into 3 pieces. Distribute the meat between 6 warm serving plates and decorate each serving with 2 strips of courgette (zucchini). Coat the meat with a little of the reduced sauce and serve the remainder separately in a sauce boat. Serve with lentils or the accompaniment of your choice.

Chef's tip
If your butcher offers to bone the baron for you, do accept. It is a tricky job. Small holes in the skin must be avoided, otherwise the stuffing will seep through. If you prefer to do it yourself, follow the instructions above.

- 2 duck large duck breasts, skin removed and trimmed of fat and connective tissue
- about 1 tsp olive oil
- salt and pepper of your choice

For the sauce
- 1 tbsp green peppercorns, preferably canned and drained
- 2 tbsp Armagnac
- 5 tbsp dry white wine
- 100ml (⅜ US cup) home-made duck stock or 100ml (⅜ US cup) home-made veal stock (page 46) or from a cube
- 300ml (1¼ US cups) semi-skimmed (2%) milk
- 60g (2oz) white button mushrooms, wiped and finely chopped

For the purée
- 400g (14oz) spinach, stalks and tough ribs removed, then washed and drained
- 100g (3½oz) pears, peeled, cored and diced
- 60g (2oz) petit-suisse or other fromage frais (0%), or 60g (2oz) fromage blanc or Greek yogurt (0%)

DUCK BREASTS WITH SPINACH AND PEAR QUENELLES AND A MUSHROOM AND PEPPERCORN SAUCE

220 CALORIES PER PERSON
Cooking and preparation: 40 minutes
Level of difficulty: * *
Serves 4–6

1. To make the sauce, put the green peppercorns in a small cup and cover with about 1 tablespoon of cold water. Leave the peppercorns to soak for about 20 minutes, then strain off the water into a separate cup and set it aside.

2. Put the Armagnac and white wine in a saucepan over a high heat. Reduce the liquid to no more than 3 tablespoons. Add the stock and the water reserved from the soaked peppercorns. Bring this liquid very briefly to the boil, then lower the heat and let the mixture simmer very gently for 5 minutes. Add the milk and the chopped mushrooms and simmer very gently for 10 minutes or until the mushrooms are cooked.

3. Remove from the heat, cool slightly, season to taste with salt, then transfer to a food processor and blend to a smooth sauce. For extra smoothness, pass the sauce through a very fine sieve – preferably a chinois – set over a saucepan. Add the soaked green peppercorns, cover, and leave to infuse for about 15 minutes; adjust the seasoning.

4. While the sauce infuses, make the purée for the quenelles: blanch the spinach in slightly salted boiling water for 2 minutes, then drain, refresh in cold water and drain again. Chop the spinach coarsely.

5. Put the morsels of pear in shallow microwave dish, cover with 1 tablespoon of water and cook at a medium temperature in the microwave for 3 minutes; drain in a small sieve. Combine the spinach, pear and petit-suisse (or alternative) in a food processor and blend to a smooth purée. Taste, and adjust the seasoning.

6. To keep the purée warm while you cook the duck, transfer it to a bain-marie or a small bowl set over simmering water. Gradually bring the peppercorn and mushroom sauce to serving temperature over a low heat.

7. Choose a heavy-based frying pan (skillet) large enough to accommodate the duck breasts side by side. Season the duck breasts. Heat the oil in the pan and cook the duck breasts for 4 minutes on each side. Transfer them to a warm plate and cover with aluminium foil. Put the plate in a warm place and leave the duck to rest for 5 minutes.

To serve

Pass the purée between 2 lightly oiled dessertspoons to make oval quenelle shapes. Slip a knife underneath each quenelle to release it and distribute them between 4–6 warm serving plates. On a wooden board, carve the breasts – slightly on the bias – into slices about ½cm (¼in) thick. Arrange them on the serving plates and coat lightly with the mushroom and peppercorn sauce. Serve immediately.

- 2 pigeon, each about 525g (1lb 2oz), plucked, cleaned and prepared
- about 1 tsp olive oil
- 1 litre (4¼ US cups/1 quart) chicken stock, either home-made (page 44) or from a cube
- salt and pepper of your choice

For the marinade
- 6 juniper berries, crushed
- ½ tsp peppercorns, crushed
- 500g (1lb 2oz) coarse sea salt
- 1 tsp fructose or the sweetener of your choice (pages 16–20)
- sprig of thyme, crumbled or chopped
- 1 fresh bay leaf, cut into small pieces
- 10g (¼oz) fresh ginger, peeled and grated

For the sauce
- 100ml (⅜ US cup) meat juices, either home-made, left over from a roast; or 100ml (⅜ US cup) veal or chicken stock from a cube
- 1 tbsp capers, chopped
- 1 fillet of anchovy preserved in oil, drained and chopped
- 2½ tbsp coarsely chopped chervil
- 1 tbsp coarsely chopped flat-leaf parsley
- ½ tbsp finely chopped tarragon

For the garnish
- 1 large orange
- 4 tart apples,such as Granny Smith
- pinch of fructose or the sweetener of your choice (pages 16–20)

Equipment
- Steamer or couscoussier

MARINATED PIGEON WITH A HERB SAUCE

290 CALORIES PER PERSON
Cooking and preparation: 45 minutes, plus 16 hours resting
Level of difficulty: * * *
Serves 4

---

1. In a mixing bowl, combine all the ingredients for the marinade and stir. Put the pigeons, side by side, in a dish that is large enough to accommodate the marinade as well. Coat the pigeons with the marinade, then cover with clingfilm (plastic wrap). Transfer the dish to a refrigerator or cold place for 16 hours.

2. While the pigeons marinate, use a vegetable peeler to remove the peel of the orange in strips and scrape away the white pith. Blanch and refresh the strips 3 times then cut them into julienne strips – you should have about 2 tablespoons. Cut the peeled orange in half and squeeze out its juice. Set aside the julienne strips and the juice.

3. Remove the pigeons from the marinade and rinse them well in cold water, removing all traces of salt. Pat them dry with kitchen paper. Heat the oil in a non-stick frying pan (skillet) and colour the pigeons lightly on all sides. Set them aside.

4. To complete the cooking of the pigeons, put the chicken stock in the bottom of a steamer or couscoussier and bring the stock to the boil. Put the pigeons in the steaming container. Steam the over a medium heat for 13–15 minutes, or until they pigeons are cooked to a pink stage – corresponding to an internal temperature of 60°C (140°F). Transfer to a warm plate, cover with aluminium foil and leave to rest in a warm place – such as a warming oven – for 10–15 minutes.

5. For the sauce, heat the meat juices in a small saucepan. Add 100ml (⅜ US cup) of the chicken stock used to steam the pigeons. Reduce the combined liquid to one-third over a high heat. Add the capers and anchovy. Set this sauce aside.

6. To complete the garnish, peel the apples and core them using a coring tool. Slice the apples into rings about ½cm (¼in) thick. Transfer the apple rings to a non-stick frying pan (skillet) set over a low to medium heat. Sprinkle with the fructose and cook for 2 minutes on each side. Add the julienne strips and juice of the orange. Reduce the liquid so it almost evaporates completely, then remove from the heat and keep the fruit warm.

7. At the end of the pigeons' resting time, set them on a wooden board. With a sharp knife, remove the breasts and the thighs. Remove and discard the skin and put the breasts and thighs in a warm covered dish in a low oven to reheat gently. Meanwhile, bring the reserved sauce back to the boil and stir in the chopped chervil, flat-leaf parsley and tarragon. Adjust the seasoning.

To serve

Divide the apple rings between 4 warm shallow-bowled serving plates. Arrange
a pigeon breast and a thigh on top of each and scatter over the julienne strips.
Drizzle over the herb-scented sauce. Add extra sprigs of fresh herbs for decoration
if you wish, and serve immediately.

- 320g (12oz) beef tenderloin, fillet, rumpsteak or sirloin, trimmed of fat and connective tissue and cut into 4 pieces, each about 3cm (1¼in) thick
- 1 litre (4¼ US cups/1 quart) beef stock, either home-made (page 43) or from a cube
- fleur de sel
- salt and freshly ground pepper of your choice

For the garnish
- 1 carrot, peeled
- 1 turnip, preferably a long variety
- 1 stick (stalk) celery
- 1 white of leek
- 12 Brussels sprouts (optional)

For the accompaniments
- 70g (3oz) pearl barley
- 1 litre (4¼ US cups/1 quart) water
- 1 pot-au-feu flavour stock cube, or veal or chicken stock cube
- Béarnaise Sauce (page 76) or Dijon mustard

POACHED BEEF WITH BARLEY

235 CALORIES PER PERSON
Cooking and preparation: 50 minutes
Level of difficulty: * *
Serves 4

---

1. Use fine kitchen string to tie the pieces of beef individually, passing the string around the length and width of each piece – like a little parcel – and leaving a long end of string. Put the tied pieces in a cold place or a refrigerator until you are almost ready to cook them.

2. To prepare the garnish, cut the carrot in half lengthways then cut the halves into 4 chunks about 5cm (2in) long. If you are using a long turnip, cut it in the same way. If it is round, cut it into chunks about 4cm (1½in) wide. If you like, you can turn the carrot and turnip to make barrel shapes (Terms and Techniques, pages 328–9). Cut the celery widthways into 8 pieces. Cut the white of leek widthways into 4 round chunks.

3. In a fairly large saucepan of lightly salted simmering water, cook the vegetables in batches until al dente: about 12 minutes for the carrots, 10 minutes for the turnip and leek, 7 minutes for the celery and 5 minutes for the Brussels sprouts, if used. Remove the vegetables with a slotted spoon and refresh them quickly in ice-cold water; drain again and set aside, covered in a little vegetable stock or meat stock, until you are ready to reheat them.

4. About 40 minutes before you want to serve the beef, prepare the pearl barley: dissolve the stock cube of your choice in 1 litre (4¼ US cups/1 quart) boiling water in a saucepan set over a medium heat; add the pearl barley, bring the stock back to the boil then simmer until the pearl barley is just tender – about 40 minutes. Drain, and keep warm.

5. If you are accompanying the beef with Béarnaise Sauce, prepare it while the pearl barley simmers, allowing about 20 minutes to do so. Keep the sauce warm in a bain-marie.

6. To cook the beef, bring the beef stock to just below boiling point – about 90°C (194°F) – in a large saucepan. Lower the pieces of beef into the stock using the string. If you like, you can suspend then in the stock by tying the string to the handles of the saucepan, but you should ensure that the beef does not touch the sides of the saucepan. Cook the beef according to taste: allow 7 minutes for very rare (bleue), 9 minutes for rare (saignante) and 11 minutes for medium to well done (à point). Reheat the vegetables while the beef is cooking.

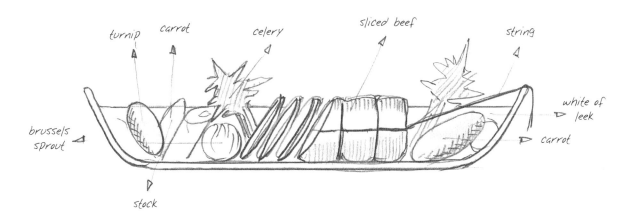

turnip   carrot   celery   sliced beef   string

brussels sprout

stock

white of leek

carrot

To serve

Have ready 4 warm shallow-bowled serving plates. Transfer the pieces of beef to a wooden board. Remove the string and carve each piece on a sharp bias into slices.

Put the pearl barley in the centre of each plate and arrange the beef on top. Place the garnish vegetables all around and drizzle over the cooking liquid from the beef. Sprinkle the meat with a little fleur de sel and add a few grinds of pepper. Serve the Béarnaise Sauce, if used separately in a sauce boat. Otherwise, serve with the Dijon mustard.

Variations

The beef could very well be replaced by quail or a fillet of turkey, or even – and why not? – some fish steaks.

A historical titbit

The use of the string is not strictly necessary but is nevertheless useful. The tradition was devised so that cooks could retrieve meat from hot liquids without burning their fingers.

- 4 breasts of guinea fowl, skin, tissue and fat removed
- 2 tsp tandoori spice powder or the curry powder of your choice
- 200ml (⅞ US cup) chicken stock, either home-made (page 44) or from a cube
- 100ml (⅜ US cup) semi-skimmed (2%) milk
- 1 tbsp cornflour (cornstarch), mixed with a little cold water
- 1 tsp olive oil
- salt and pepper of your choice

For the accompaniments
- 50g (1¾oz) basmati rice (page 113)
- 4–8 broccoli florets
- 120g (scant 4½oz) mangetout (snow peas), cut diagonally into diamond shapes

BREASTS OF GUINEA FOWL WITH A TOUCH OF TANDOORI

275 CALORIES PER PERSON
Cooking and preparation: 40 minutes
Level of difficulty: *
Serves 4

1. Use a brush to coat one side of the guinea fowl breasts with 1 teaspoon of the tandoori spice powder. Set the rest of the tandoori spice powder aside. Put the breasts on a plate, cover, and set aside in a refrigerator or a cold place until you are ready to cook them.

2. To prepare the sauce, put the chicken stock in a saucepan and reduce it by half over a high heat. Lower the heat, add the milk and season to taste. Bring the liquid briefly back to the boil then remove from the heat.

3. When the liquid has cooled slightly, stir in the cornflour (cornstarch) mixed with a little water. Transfer to a food processor, add the remaining tandoori spice powder and blend to make a smooth sauce. Transfer the sauce to a bain-marie or a saucepan, ready to be reheated quickly when the guinea fowl breasts are almost cooked.

4. To cook the guinea fowl breasts, coat a non-stick frying pan (skillet) with the olive oil and set it over a medium heat. Add the breasts, spiced-side down, and cook for 4 minutes, then turn them over and cook for a further 3–4 minutes. Transfer to a warm plate, cover with aluminium foil and put them to rest in a warm place, such as a very low oven or a warming oven for at least 15 minutes or until cooked to your liking.

5. Meanwhile , prepare the accompaniments: cook the basmati rice for about 11 minutes and keep it warm. Cook the broccoli florets in lightly salted, briskly simmering water for 5–6 minutes. Simmer the mangetout (snow peas) for 2–3 minutes. Drain and keep them warm. Heat the reserved sauce through.

To serve
Have ready 4 warm serving plates. Transfer the guinea fowl breasts to a wooden board and carve them on the bias into thin slices. Divide the cooked rice between the plates and arrange the slices of breast meat on top. Place the vegetable garnish all around and coat with the sauce. Serve straight away.

- 1 litre (4¼ US cups/1 quart) water
- 100g (3½oz) Puy lentils
- 1 small onion, cut in half
- 1 small carrot, peeled and cut in half
- 1 fresh bouquet garni
- 2 tbsp finely chopped flat-leaf parsley
- 200g (7oz) Red Beet Liaison (page 89)
- about 1 tsp olive oil
- 320g (11½oz) fillet of beef or rumpsteak, trimmed of fat and connective tissue and cut into 2cm (¾in) dice, or in pieces according to your taste
- 1 tbsp very finely chopped onion
- 1 heaped tsp mixed peppercorns (including black, pink and Sichuan), crushed
- salt and pepper of your choice

For the garnish
- 80g (scant 3oz) carrots, peeled and cut into matchsticks about 3 x 1cm (1¼ x ½in)
- 60g (2oz) haricots verts, cut into 3cm (1¼in) pieces
- 100g (3½oz) cauliflower florets
- few sprigs of fresh thyme and savory (optional)

QUICK-COOK QUALITY BEEF WITH PEPPERCORNS AND PUY LENTILS

225 CALORIES PER PERSON
Cooking and preparation: 40 minutes
Level of difficulty: *
Serves 4

1. To cook the lentils, bring the 1 litre (4¼ US cups/1 quart) of water to the boil. Add the lentils, the onion, the carrot and the bouquet garni. Bring the liquid back to the boil then simmer for 20–25 minutes. Season to taste. Strain the lentils through a sieve and discard the onion, carrot and bouquet garni. Put the lentils in a bain-marie or in a bowl that you can set over hot water. Stir in 1 tablespoon of the chopped flat-leaf parsley and keep the mixture warm.

2. About halfway through cooking the lentils, simmer the garnish vegetables in lightly salted simmering water in separate batches: the carrots for about 8 minutes, the haricots verts for about 6 minutes and the cauliflower florets for about 5 minutes. When they are ready, strain them and briefly keep them warm.

3. When you are almost ready to cook the beef, heat the Red Beet Liaison through.

4. To cook the beef, heat the olive oil in a non-stick frying pan (skillet). Add the diced beef. After about 30 seconds, turn the pieces of beef over and season the seared side to taste with salt. Turn again after about 30 seconds and, according to taste, season again. Continue to cook for 1 further minute, turning the beef frequently. Towards the end of cooking, add the very finely chopped onion, the remaining 1 tablespoon of chopped parsley and the crushed peppercorn mixture.

To serve
Have ready 4 warm serving plates. Put the lentils in the centre of each. Arrange the pieces of beef on top and coat them lightly in the Red Beet Liaison. Distribute the vegetable garnish around the edge. If you wish, you can also garnish with a few sprigs of fresh seasonal herbs, such as thyme and savory.

- 2 carrots, peeled
- 2 whites of young leeks
- 8 baby courgettes (zucchini)
- 8 small broccoli florets
- 8 small cauliflower florets
- 8 asparagus tips
- 12 cherry tomatoes, stems left on
- pinch of fructose or the sweetener of your choice (pages 16–20)
- 2 tsp olive oil
- 300g (1⅓ US cups) Curried Yellow Fruit Liaison (page 88)
- 200ml (⅞ US cup) chicken stock, either home-made (page 44) or from a cube
- 1 tbsp finely chopped onion
- 100g (3½oz) basmati rice
- salt and pepper of your choice

To garnish
- 12 shavings of Parmesan

Equipment
- 2 skewers that will fit into a large saucepan

VEGETABLE CURRY WITH BASMATI RICE

255 CALORIES PER PERSON
Cooking and preparation: 45 minutes
Level of difficulty: **
Serves 4

1. Cut each carrot in half lengthways, then cut each half-carrot into 6 pieces. Cut the whites of the leeks into 12 pieces, each about 3cm (1¼ in) long. To keep their shape during cooking, thread the leeks on skewers. Cut the baby courgettes (zucchini) lengthways into 8 pieces.

2. In a large saucepan of lightly salted simmering water, cook the vegetables separately, using the same water throughout: 18–20 minutes for the carrots, 15 minutes for the leeks, 8–10 minutes for the broccoli, 6–7 minutes for the cauliflower and courgettes (zucchini), and 6 minutes for the asparagus tips.

3. After each vegetable has finished cooking, drain and refresh in cold water, then drain again and set aside on a tea towel to dry. Remove the leeks from the skewers. Set aside the water that you used to cook the vegetables.

4. Preheat the oven to 150°C (300°F, gas mark 2). While the vegetables are cooking, season the tomatoes with salt, pepper and a pinch of fructose. Put the tomatoes in a shallow baking dish, drizzle with 1 teaspoon of the olive oil and toss to coat. Bake the tomatoes for 15 minutes or until they have softened.

5. Heat the Curried Yellow Fruit Liaison and keep it warm, preferably in a bain-marie. When you have removed the tomatoes from the oven, increase the temperature to 200°C (400°F, gas mark 6). In a small saucepan, gently bring the stock to a simmer and then cover, remove from the heat and keep warm.

6. Heat the remaining olive oil in a small heatproof casserole dish (Dutch oven). Gently sweat the onion in the oil for about 30 seconds without colouring. Add the basmati rice and cook 1 minute more or until the rice becomes translucent. Stir the warm stock into the rice mixture, cover, and place in the oven for 12 minutes. After that time, remove from the oven and let the rice finish cooking, covered, for 5 minutes more.

7. When you are ready to serve, reheat all of the vegetables, except the tomatoes, in the water that they were cooked in. To do so, gently put them into the hot water and allow them to heat through before carefully lifting them out again with a slotted spoon.

To serve

Transfer the warmed vegetables to 4 warm serving plates, making sure that there are a few pieces of each vegetable on each plate. Divide the baked tomatoes between the plates. Garnish the vegetables with the shaved Parmesan and drizzle the vegetables with the Curried Yellow Fruit Liaison. If you like, you can serve the rice in small bowls on the side or you may place the vegetables on top of it on the serving plates.

- 2 tomatoes, peeled, cored and deseeded
  (Terms and Techniques, pages 327–8),
  then each cut into 8 pieces
- pinch of fructose or the sweetener of your
  choice (pages 16–20)
- 2 sprigs of thyme
- ½ bay leaf
- 1 tbsp olive oil
- 160g (5½oz) carrots, peeled
- 160g (5½oz) courgettes (zucchini)
- 12 asparagus tips
- 4 small cauliflower florets
- 4 small broccoli florets
- 2 tbsp peas, fresh or frozen
- 8 mangetout (snow peas), cut diagonally
  to make diamond shapes
- 120g (scant 4½oz) fresh tagliatelle
- salt and pepper of your choice

For the basil sauce
- bunch of fresh basil
- 200ml (⅞ US cup) chicken stock, either home-
  made (page 44) or from a cube
- 200ml (⅞ US cup) semi-skimmed (2%) milk
- 60g (2oz) white button mushrooms, wiped
  and very finely chopped

To garnish
- 4 sprigs of basil
- 4 sprigs of flat-leaf parsley
- 4 sprigs of chervil

TAGLIATELLE WITH VEGETABLES AND BASIL SAUCE

210 CALORIES PER PERSON
Cooking and preparation: 45 minutes
Level of difficulty: **
Serves 4

1. Preheat the oven to 150°C (300°F, gas mark 2). Arrange the prepared tomatoes in a casserole dish (Dutch oven), season with salt and pepper and sprinkle with fructose. Add the sprigs of thyme and the ½ bay leaf. Using a pastry brush, lightly brush the tomatoes with olive oil and bake in the oven for 30 minutes or until the tomatoes are very soft.

2. Cut the carrots and courgettes (zucchini) into chunks about 4cm (1½ in) wide. If you like, you can turn the vegetable chunks to make barrel shapes (Terms and Technqiues, pages 328–9).

3. In a large saucepan of lightly salted simmering water, cook the vegetables separately, using the same water throughout: 5 minutes for the asparagus tips, 6–7 minutes for the cauliflower, 7–8 minutes for the broccoli, 10–12 minutes for the carrots, 5–6 minutes for the courgettes (zucchini), and 2–3 minutes for the peas and the mangetout (snow peas). After each vegetable has finished cooking, drain, refresh in cold water, then drain again and set aside on a plate. Set aside the water that you used to cook the vegetables.

4. To make the basil sauce, wash the basil thoroughly, remove the leaves from the stems and discard the stems. Bring the stock and the milk to a gentle boil in a medium-sized saucepan, then lower the heat to maintain a simmer. Season, add the mushrooms and simmer for 5 minutes. Stir in the basil leaves and cook for 2 minutes more.

5. Remove from the heat and when cool enough to handle, transfer to a food processor and blend until smooth. Pass the sauce through a fine sieve, such as a chinoi, and keep the sauce warm, preferably in a bain-marie.

6. Cook the tagliatelle until al dente in a saucepan of salted boiling water – about 2–3 minutes. Drain and toss with some of the basil sauce.

7. When you are ready to serve, reheat all of the vegetables, except the tomatoes, in the water that they were cooked in. To do so, gently put them into the hot water and allow them to heat through before carefully lifting them out again with a slotted spoon.

To serve

Place some of the tagliatelle on each of 4 warm serving plates. Divide the warmed vegetables between the serving plates, making sure that there are a few pieces of each vegetable on each plate. Divide the baked tomatoes, discarding the thyme and the bay leaf, between the plates. Spoon some basil sauce over the vegetables and tagliatelle and garnish with the fresh herbs.

- 4 litres (17 US cups) water
- 1 fresh bouquet garni
- 4 medium carrots, peeled
- 4 whites of young leeks
- 4 small cauliflower florets
- 2 celery sticks (stalks), each cut into 4 lengths
- 4 young turnips
- 4 spring onions
- 100g (3½oz) haricots verts
- 2 small courgettes (zucchini), sliced in half lengthways
- 50g (1¾oz) peas, fresh or frozen
- 4 tomatoes, peeled, cored and deseeded (Terms and Techniques, pages 327–8), then quartered
- 300ml (1¼ US cups) Asian Lime Vegetable Stock (page 49)
- pinch of ras el-hanout (Moroccan spice blend; Terms and Techniques, page 328)
- salt and pepper of your choice

To garnish
- small sprigs of seasonal herbs such as parsley or mint

VEGETABLE POT-AU-FEU WITH ASIAN LIME VEGETABLE STOCK

180 CALORIES PER PERSON
Cooking and preparation: 30 minutes
Level of difficulty: *
Serves 4

1. In a large saucepan, bring the water to a gentle simmer, add the bouquet garni, the carrots, the leeks and a pinch of salt, and simmer for 10 minutes, uncovered. Add the cauliflower, the celery, the turnips and the spring onions and simmer for 5 minutes before adding the haricots verts and the courgettes (zucchini). Continue simmering for 5 more minutes, then add the peas and the tomatoes. Remove from the heat after 2 minutes more.

2. While the vegetables are cooking, gently bring the stock to a simmer in a large saucepan and add the ras el-hanout.

To serve
When you are ready to serve, gently remove the vegetables from the hot water with a slotted spoon. Transfer the vegetables to 4 warm serving bowls, making sure that there are a few pieces of each vegetable in each bowl. Generously ladle the warm stock onto the vegetables and garnish with fresh herbs.

Variation
This dish can be served throughout the year, using whatever vegetables are in season.

- 200g (7oz) carrots, peeled
- 200g (7oz) courgettes (zucchini)
- 150g (5½oz) radishes, preferably a long variety, peeled
- 120g (scant 4½oz) broad beans (fava beans), fresh or frozen, shelled
- 1 fresh bouquet garni
- 2 litres (8½ US cups) water
- 12 small onions, preferably pearl onions
- 100g (3½oz) haricots verts
- 2 medium tomatoes, peeled, cored and deseeded (Terms and Techniques, pages 327–8), then each cut into 6 wedges
- salt and pepper of your choice

For the herby sauce
- 150ml (¾ US cup) semi-skimmed (2%) milk
- 1 tsp cornflour (cornstarch), mixed with cold water
- pinch of freshly grated nutmeg
- 1 tbsp finely chopped flat-leaf parsley
- 1 tbsp finely chopped fresh tarragon
- 1 tbsp finely chopped fresh dill

Equipment (optional)
Steamer

POACHED VEGETABLES WITH A HERB SAUCE

110 CALORIES PER PERSON
Cooking and preparation: 30 minutes
Level of difficulty: *
Serves 4

1. Cut the carrots, courgettes (zucchini) and radishes into chunks about 4cm (1½in) long. If you like, you can turn the vegetable chunks to make barrel shapes (Terms and Techniques, pages 328–9). If you are using fresh, shelled, broad beans, blanch them for a few minutes, refresh and drain again, then slip them free of their skins (Terms and Techniques, page 326).

2. Add the bouquet garni to a large saucepan containing the 2 litres (8½ US cups) of simmering water, lightly salted. Cook the vegetables separately in the simmering water, using the same water throughout: 10 minutes for the onions, 3 minutes for the haricots verts and the broad beans, and 2 minutes for the carrots, courgettes (zucchini) and radishes.

3. After each vegetable has finished cooking, drain, refresh in cold water, then drain again and set aside on a tea towel to dry. Set aside 100ml (⅜ US cup) of the water that you used to cook the vegetables.

4. To prepare the herby sauce, gently simmer the reserved vegetable cooking water with the milk. Whisk in the cornflour (cornstarch) that has been mixed with some water. Add the nutmeg and season with pepper. Keep the sauce warm, preferably in a bain-marie, until ready to serve. At the last moment before serving, whisk in the fresh herbs.

5. When you are ready to serve, reheat all of the vegetables, except the tomatoes, in the water that they were cooked in. To do so, gently put them into the hot water and allow them to heat through before carefully lifting them out again with a slotted spoon. Alternatively, you may reheat the vegetables in a steamer.

To serve
Divide the warmed vegetables between 4 warm serving plates, making sure that there are a few pieces of each vegetable – including the wedges of tomato – on each plate. Drizzle with the herby sauce and serve immediately with additional sauce on the side.

- 100g (3½oz) carrots, peeled
- 50g (1¾oz) celeriac, peeled
- 100g (3½oz) white button mushrooms, wiped
- ½ tbsp olive oil
- 1 tsp finely chopped tarragon
- 8 squares of pasta dough, preferably from
  an Asian grocer
- 400ml (1¾ US cups) vegetable stock, either
  home-made (page 42) or from a cube
- salt and pepper of your choice

To garnish
- 4 tbsp tomatoes, peeled, cored and deseeded
  (Terms and Techniques, pages 327–8),
  then finely diced
- small handful of chervil sprigs
- 4–6 chives, snipped into small matchsticks
- 16–20 tarragon leaves

GARDEN RAVIOLI IN A VEGETABLE STOCK

135 CALORIES PER PERSON
Cooking and preparation: 30 minutes
Level of difficulty: **
Serves 4

1. Cut the carrots, celeriac, and mushrooms into matchsticks, about 4cm x 2mm (1½ x ⅛in). In a medium-sized covered saucepan, gently sweat the carrots in the olive oil for 3 minutes before adding the celeriac. Sweat the celeriac and carrots together for 3 minutes, then add the mushrooms and sweat for 3 minutes more. Season with salt and pepper. Stir in the finely chopped tarragon and set aside to cool.

2. To make the ravioli, place 4 squares of pasta dough on your work surface. Place some of the cooled vegetables in the centre of each pasta square. Using a pastry brush, lightly brush the edges of each square with water. Lay another pasta square on top of and gently press the edges of the pasta squares together, making sure that there are no openings.

3. Bring a large saucepan of lightly salted water to a simmer and carefully lower the ravioli into the water. Simmer the ravioli gently for 5 minutes, then remove them and refresh in cold water. Drain, cut away any excess dough from the edges of the ravioli and set aside to cool.

To serve
When you are ready to serve, heat the vegetable stock in a medium-sized saucepan. Gently reheat the ravioli in the warm stock and transfer to 4 warm shallow serving bowls. Sprinkle the ravioli with the diced tomatoes and fresh herbs, and ladle some of the warm vegetable stock on top. Serve immediately.

- 150ml (¾ US cup) light whipping cream (30%–35% fat)
- 2 egg whites
- 1 tbsp fructose or the sweetener of your choice (pages 16–20)

Choice of flavourings
- Vanilla: seeds of ¼ vanilla pod (bean)
- Chicory: 2 tsp powdered chicory
- Coffee: 2 tsp instant coffee plus ½ tsp finely ground coffee
- Armagnac: up to 2 tsp Armagnac, bearing in mind that the whipped cream will lose volume slightly with the addition of alcohol

*Fructose: 140 calories
*Aspartame: 130 calories
*Xylitol: 145 calories
*Sugar: 150 calories
*Honey: 150 calories

ULTRA-LIGHT CHANTILLY CREAM

130–150 CALORIES PER PERSON,
depending on the sweetener you use*
Cooking and preparation: 10 minutes
Level of difficulty: **
Serves 4

I prefer this low-fat whipped Chantilly cream to the traditional rich version because it is aerated by beaten egg whites and does not leave a greasy film on the palate. It is based on traditional Chantilly cream but I have greatly reduced the fat content. Because it is impossible to whip cream that has a very low fat content, I have used whole cream – but in an unusually small quantity.

1. Thirty minutes before making the whipped cream, put a large metal mixing bowl and the cream in the refrigerator.

2. Using a balloon whisk or a hand-held beater, whisk the cream until it holds firm, but not stiff, peaks on the whisk. Carefully fold in the flavouring of your choice.

3. In a separate bowl, whisk the egg whites until they are almost firm before whisking in the fructose.

4. Tip all of the egg whites into the whipped cream. Using a wooden spoon or rubber spatula, gently fold the whites into the cream, lifting the cream from the bottom of the bowl and folding it over the top. Continue folding the mixture to together until it is well blended.

5. Use the whipped Chantilly cream immediately to decorate a dessert or keep it chilled for 2–3 hours for later use. There will be no need to rewhip the cream.

- 100g (3½oz) strawberries, hulled and quartered
- 50g (1¾oz) raspberries
- 200ml (⅞ US cup) water
- 300g (11oz) redcurrants, stems removed
- 2 sheets leaf gelatine (soaked) or 1½ tsp powdered gelatine (page 22)
- 1 heaped tbsp fructose or the sweetener of your choice (pages 16–20)

To decorate
- Ultra-Light Chantilly Cream, vanilla-flavoured (page 280)
- 50g (1¾oz) redcurrants, ideally 4 stems
- 4 small sprigs of mint

*Fructose: 225 calories
*Aspartame: 180 calories
*Xylitol: 240 calories
*Sugar: 270 calories
*Honey: 260 calories

REDCURRANT JELLY WITH WHIPPED CREAM

180–270 CALORIES PER PERSON,
depending on the sweetener you use*
Cooking and preparation: 30 minutes, plus 4 hours chilling
Level of difficulty: **
Serves 4

1. Place the prepared strawberries and raspberries into 4 decorative glasses.

2. In a medium-sized saucepan, gently heat the water with the redcurrants. Once the water begins to boil, use a whisk to stir the redcurrants, encouraging them to burst and release their juices. Remove the saucepan from the heat and immediately pass the mixture through a fine sieve, preferably a chinois. You should be left with about 300ml (1¼ US cups) of redcurrant juice.

3. In a medium-sized bowl, dissolve and combine the gelatine of your choice with the warm redcurrant juice, whisking well until the gelatine has completely dissolved. Stir in the fructose and mix well.

4. Cool the mixture quickly by putting it in the refrigerator, checking from time to time until the mixture is lukewarm. Pour the lukewarm jelly mixture over the fruit in the glasses and place them in the refrigerator for 4 hours to set.

To serve
Just before serving, have ready the Ultra-Light Whipped Chantilly Cream. Generously top the jellies with the whipped cream and decorate with the fresh redcurrants and the small sprigs of mint.

- 200ml (⅞ US cup) flavoured base mixture such as fruit juice, custard (page 284) or a milk infusion made from semi-skimmed (2%) milk
- 1 sheet leaf gelatine (soaked) or 1 tsp powdered gelatine (page 22)
- 100ml (⅜ US cup) light whipping cream (30–35% fat), whipped
- 2 egg whites
- 1 tbsp fructose (pages 17–18)

Variations

*Fruit juice, fructose and light whipping cream (30–35% fat): 45 calories

*Custard, fructose and light whipping cream (30–35% fat): 65 calories

* Milk infusion, fructose and light whipping cream (30–35% fat): 42 calories

BAVAROIS

42–65 CALORIES PER PERSON,
depending on the base mixture you use*
Cooking and preparation: 30 minutes
Level of difficulty: **
Serves 8

This basic bavarois mixture has many different applications, depending on the flavouring you use. For example, as well as the suggestions listed here, strawberry or apricot purées can be used. With a little adjustment, the bavarois formula can also be used to produce the verbena-infused semolina mousse (page 283).

1. In a small saucepan, gently heat 60g (2oz) of the flavoured base mixture of your choice, but do not let it boil. Remove from the heat.

2. Dissolve and combine the gelatine of your choice with the warm base mixture, whisking well until the gelatine has completely dissolved. Add the remaining cool base mixture to the warm gelatine mixture, blending well.

3. To set the gelatine, transfer the mixture to the refrigerator. Alternatively, to set it rapidly, place the mixture over iced water for about 20 minutes. The mixture is ready when it is spoonable. If the mixture becomes so stiff that you cannot mix in the cream, you can heat it gently in a bain-marie to loosen it.

4. Whip the cream until it forms soft peaks. Using a spatula, fold about a quarter of the gelatine mixture into the whipped cream, then fold the whipped cream into the gelatine mixture, lifting the mixture up and over the cream until it is well blended.

5. In a medium-sized bowl, beat the egg whites with a balloon whisk until they form soft peaks. Whisk in the fructose. Fold the egg whites into the whipped cream and gelatine mixture, lifting the mixture up and over the egg whites until all is well blended.

Chef's tip

In this recipe, the amount of gelatine used is just enough to hold the mixture together and produce a smooth texture. It is not enough for the bavarois to be turned out from a decorative mould, especially a tall one, and hold its shape firmly. This sort of effect, although dramatic and very popular in the nineteenth century, calls for a firmer, slightly rubbery texture that no longer finds favour with many contemporary eaters. However, if you do want to produce an elaborate turned-out dessert, you should double the amount of gelatine given here.

- 350ml (scant 1½ US cups) semi-skimmed (2%) milk
- 6 tsp fructose or the sweetener of your choice (pages 16–20)
- 3 heaped tsp fine semolina
- 6 sprigs of verbena or mint
- 1 sheet leaf gelatine (soaked) or ¾ tsp powdered gelatine (page 22)
- 50ml (¼ US cup) light whipping cream (30–35% fat)
- 2 egg whites

To decorate
- 4 small sprigs of verbena or mint

*Fructose: 140 calories
*Aspartame: 110 calories
*Xylitol: 150 calories
*Sugar: 165 calories
*Honey: 160 calories

VERBENA-INFUSED SEMOLINA MOUSSE

110–165 CALORIES PER PERSON,
depending on the sweetener you use*
Cooking and preparation: 50 minutes (can be prepared the night before)
Level of difficulty: *
Serves 4

1. In a small saucepan, gently heat 250ml (1⅛ US cups) of the milk with 4 teaspoons of the fructose. Add the semolina slowly while stirring continuously and allowing the mixture to come to the boil. Adjust the heat and simmer the mixture very gently for 7 minutes. Remove the semolina mixture from the heat and leave it to cool.

2. In a small saucepan, gently heat the remaining 100ml (⅜ US cup) of milk with the sprigs of verbena or mint but do not let it boil. Remove from the heat, cover, and let the verbena or mint infuse for 15 minutes. Pass the milk infusion through a fine sieve, preferably a chinois, to remove the leaves.

3. To stiffen the infused milk, dissolve and combine the gelatine of your choice with the warm milk infusion, whisking well until the gelatine has completely dissolved. Set the gelatine mixture over iced water for about 20 minutes, stirring occasionally. When the mixture starts to set, it is ready to be combined with the semolina.

4. Stir the cold semolina mixture into the gelatine mixture. Whip the cream until it forms soft peaks. Using a spatula, fold about a quarter of the gelatine mixture into the whipped cream, then fold the whipped cream into the gelatine mixture, lifting the mixture up and over the cream until it is well blended.

5. To complete the semolina mousse, beat the egg whites with a balloon whisk in a medium-sized bowl, until they form firm peaks. Whisk in the remaining 2 teaspoons of fructose. Fold the egg whites into the semolina mixture, lifting the mixture up and over the egg whites until the ingredients are blended.

6. Spoon the semolina mousse into teacups or the decorative glasses of your choice and chill them in the refrigerator until you are ready to serve.

To serve
Before serving, decorate each mousse with a sprig of verbena or mint.

- 250ml (1⅛ US cups) semi-skimmed (2%) milk
- ½ vanilla pod (bean), cut in half lengthways
- 2 egg yolks
- 1 heaped tbsp fructose or the sweetener of your choice (pages 16–20)

*Fructose: 180 calories
*Aspartame: 140 calories
*Xylitol: 170 calories
*Sugar: 205 calories
*Honey: 200 calories

CUSTARD

140–205 CALORIES PER PERSON,
depending on the sweetener you use*
Cooking and preparation: 30 minutes
Level of difficulty: *
Serves 2; makes 250ml (1⅛ US cups)

Custard takes many forms in the preparation of minceur desserts. Hot or cold, it can be an accompanying sauce for a range of desserts, from fruit tarts to versions of floating islands (see opposite). It also plays an integral role in the composition of certain ice creams, as well as forming the base of slightly stiffened desserts, such as bavarois (page 282). The use of sweeteners as a replacement for regular sugar in the following recipe allows readers to include custard in their repertoire of desserts without unnecessary calories.

1. In a small saucepan, gently heat the milk and the vanilla pod (bean) until the milk starts to boil. Once the first few bubbles rise to the surface, remove the milk from the heat. Cover the saucepan and allow the vanilla pod (bean) to infuse in the warm milk for 15 minutes. Remove the vanilla pod (bean).

2. In a medium-sized metal bowl, beat the egg yolks with a whisk until they are pale and creamy. Gradually pour the warm milk into the beaten egg yolks, whisking to blend well.

3. Return the milk and egg mixture to the saucepan. Heat the mixture very gently on a low heat while stirring with a wooden spoon, using a figure-of-eight movement. Alternatively, cook the custard in a bain-marie. When you feel the mixture starting to 'grab' the spoon, stop stirring and wipe your finger across the spoon: if it leaves a mark, then the custard is ready. If it doesn't, continue to cook the custard, checking for doneness every 10 seconds or so.

4. Remove the custard from the heat and immediately pass it through a fine-meshed sieve – preferably a chinois – to remove any small particles of egg.

5. Stir the fructose into the custard, mixing well. Use immediately if you require it warm. Alternatively, cool it and store in the refrigerator.

Chef's tip
You can also perfume the custard with milk infusions using aromatic herbs such as mint, verbena, thyme, basil, or using lively flavours such as citrus zest. To make the infusion, bring the milk to the boil, remove it from the heat and add the flavouring of your choice. Cover and allow the milk to infuse for about 15 minutes. Filter out the herbs or citrus zest and proceed with the recipe.

- 3 egg whites
- 3 tbsp fructose or the sweetener of
  your choice (pages 16–20)
- 500ml (2⅛ US cups) custard (page 284)

To decorate
- 4 small sprigs of mint

Equipment
- Steamer

*Fructose: 220 calories
*Aspartame: 160 calories
*Xylitol: 235 calories
*Sugar: 290 calories
*Honey: 275 calories

VANILLA FLOATING ISLAND

160–290 CALORIES PER PERSON,
depending on the sweetener you use*
Cooking and preparation: 20 minutes
Level of difficulty: *
Serves 4

1. Cut parchment paper to the size of your steamer tray. Set aside. Preheat the steamer. Use a large mixing bowl and a balloon whisk or hand-held beater to whisk the egg whites until they hold soft peaks. Add the fructose and continue whisking until it is fully incorporated.

2. Use a tablespoon to drop 16 small swirls of egg white onto the parchment-lined tray. Put the tray in the steamer and cook for 1 minute, or until the meringues are slightly puffed up and just set. The meringues can also be cooked in the microwave although they should not be cooked for more than 10 seconds at 800 watts. When the meringues are done, transfer them to a cool plate.

To serve
Have ready 4 shallow-bowled serving plates. Distribute the custard between the plates. Carefully place 3 meringues in the centre each, then place the fourth meringue on top of each trio. Decorate with the sprigs of mint and serve immediately.

Variations
This recipe can easily be modified to create many enticing new flavours. In the recipe for Tropical meringue floating islands (page 309), you replace half of the milk with a blend of exotic fruit juices. Custard also marries extremely well with the flavour of coffee: once the custard is prepared and strained, stir in 2 teaspoons of instant coffee dissolved in the smallest amount of boiled water and a half-teaspoon of finely ground coffee. Simpler still, you can replace the vanilla pod (bean) in the recipe with spices such cinnamon, nutmeg or quatre épices.

ICE CREAMS, SORBETS AND GRANITAS

The supple, creamy texture of ice cream owes a lot to its sugar content: the more sugar it contains, the easier it is to manipulate and make soft and smooth, and easily spooned or scooped. This is usually the case with commercially manufactured ice creams, which contain a great deal of sugar.

In our minceur approach to desserts, the ice cream and sorbet recipes are sweetened with fructose, xylitol, honey or sweeteners other than sugar. Generally speaking, honey affords ice cream the same suppleness as sugar does. In addition, it gives it an exceptionally pleasant taste.

However, using sweeteners to make low-calorie ice creams and sorbets has its restrictions. As we have seen fructose, for example (pages 17–18), has very similar properties to ordinary sugar but because it has almost double the sweetening power, we have to use half as much fructose as sugar in our recipes. This means that the end-result is not supple enough to qualify as an excellent ice cream.

Similarly, aspartame-based sweeteners (pages 18–19) do not have the same texture as sugar, so they cannot provide the desired suppleness either.

For this reason, professional cooks who want to create low-calorie ice creams and sorbets invest in a Pacojet machine. This uses a process known as micro-puréeing that works well with sweeteners. What is more, the Pacojet is able to keep the ice cream or sorbet at an ideal serving temperature and consistency.

You do not, however, need such sophisticated equipment as a Pacojet to make the ice cream and sorbet recipes in this book. No doubt some home cooks will own an ice-cream maker with a sorbetière attachment that will churn preparations to the silkiest of textures. However, recipe instructions are also given for making the preparations very simply in a shallow tray – preferably of metal, which reacts quickly to temperature change.

If you make ice creams and sorbets in this way, you only have to remember to stir them with a fork every half an hour or so to break up ice crystals. You can use them immediately they have been churned or stirred to the right consistency, or you can store them in the freezer and, just before serving, transfer them briefly to the refrigerator or to room temperature, to restore their suppleness. If you are not counting calories, you can also forego the sweeteners and make the recipes using sugar or honey.

The grainy, crystal texture that characterizes granitas does not require the same suppleness as ice cream and sorbet, and so lends itself to a different approach. In fact, a granita can be made very successfully using an aspartame-based sweetener; you do not need to use a special machine. To prepare a granita, start by making a flavoured syrup and freezing it – in much the same way as for a sorbet. Leave it at room temperature just long enough for it to soften slightly and become easy to scrape. Use a fork to scrape across the surface and collect the little ice crystals – the granita. Collect them quickly, before they melt, in a separate tray. Transfer the tray of crystals to the freezer until you are ready to serve.

- 800g (1¾lb) fresh apricots
- 500ml (2⅛ US cups) water
- 3 heaped tbsp fructose or the sweetener of your choice (pages 16–20)
- 4 sprigs of thyme

To decorate
- fresh thyme leaves, stripped from their stems

*Fructose: 140 calories
*Aspartame: 90 calories
*Xylitol: 155 calories
*Sugar: 195 calories
*Honey: 170 calories

APRICOT CARPACCIO WITH THYME GRANITA

90–195 CALORIES PER PERSON,
depending on the sweetener you use*
Preparation time: 30 minutes, plus 12 hours chilling (start 1 day ahead)
Level of difficulty: *
Serves 4

---

1. The day before you want to serve the dessert, prepare the apricots: cut them in half and remove the stones (pits). For the syrup, put the water, fructose and thyme in a saucepan and bring the mixture slowly to a simmer. Cut a round of greaseproof or parchment paper to the same diameter as the saucepan. When the syrup starts to simmer, add the apricots, cover them with the paper – this will ensure that the apricots cook evenly – then cover the saucepan with a lid.

2. Let the apricots simmer over a very gentle heat until tender – usually about 10 minutes, depending on their size and ripeness. Discard the thyme and transfer the apricots and their cooking syrup to a bowl; set aside.

3. To make the granita, strain off half of the apricot cooking syrup into a shallow ice tray. Cover it with clingfilm (plastic wrap) then transfer it carefully to the freezer. Keep the apricots and the remaining syrup, covered, in the refrigerator.

4. The next day, when the syrup has frozen into an ice, remove it from the freezer. Leave it at room temperature just long enough for it to soften slightly and become easy to scrape. Use a fork to scrape across the surface and collect the little ice crystals – the granita. Collect them quickly, before they melt, in a separate tray. Transfer the tray of crystals to the freezer until you are ready to serve.

5. Drain the chilled apricots – setting aside the cooking syrup – and arrange them flat-side down on 4 large flat serving plates. Cover the apricots with clingfilm (plastic wrap) and flatten them with the palm of your hand to create an even layer that resembles a carpaccio.

To serve
When you are ready to serve, remove the clingfilm (plastic wrap). Pour the reserved cooking syrup over the apricots. Add a spoonful of granita to each serving and decorate with a sprinkling of fresh thyme leaves.

- 500ml (2⅛ US cups) fresh or canned pineapple juice
- 150ml (¾ US cup) water
- 2 tbsp amber rum
- 1 lime
- ½ fresh sweet pineapple with skin and 'eyes' removed, net weight of about 200g (7oz)
- 1 large ripe mango

To decorate
- 4 sprigs of mint

Equipment (optional)
- Sorbetière

TROPICAL COMPOTE WITH PINEAPPLE SORBET

120 CALORIES PER PERSON
Preparation time: 40 minutes
Level of difficulty: **
Serves 4

---

1. For the pineapple sorbet, combine 300ml (1¼ US cups) of the pineapple juice, 50ml (¼ US cup or 6 tbsp) of the water and the rum in a large mixing bowl. Remove the zest from the lime using a zester or fine grater. Cut the lime in half and squeeze its juice. Divide the juice into 2 equal portions. Add the lime zest and half of the lime juice to the ingredients in the mixing bowl. Set aside the other half of the lime juice for the compote.

2. Pour the pineapple juice mixture into a sorbetière and churn it to a soft-textured consistency. Alternatively, put the mixture in a shallow freezing tray and stir it thoroughly every half-hour with a fork. The sorbet will be ready when, after several hours, it has a soft, scoopable, consistency. Put the sorbet in an airtight container and freeze until you are ready to serve.

3. For the tropical compote, slice the pineapple lengthways into 4 or 5 long, thin sections. Use a sharp knife to cut away and discard the woody core from each section, then cut the sections into small even-sized pieces.

4. Peel the mango and extract the flesh by cutting the fruit away from either side of the stone (pit). Cut the flesh into 1cm (½in) dice.

5. Combine the pieces of pineapple and mango in a saucepan. Add the remaining 200ml (⅞ US cup) of pineapple juice and the remaining 100ml (⅜ US cup) water, as well as the remaining lime juice. Bring the mixture briefly to the boil. To ensure uniform cooking and to prevent any evaporation, place a circle of greaseproof or parchment paper, cut to the diameter of the saucepan, on top of the mixture. Adjust the heat to maintain a very gentle simmer for 20 minutes, lifting the paper frequently and stirring to ensure the pineapple does not stick to the bottom or sides of the pan. Let the compote cool then transfer it to an airtight container and chill it.

To serve

Have ready 4 chilled serving bowls. Divide the chilled compote between the bowls. Remove the pineapple sorbet from the freezer. Scoop out each portion of sorbet using 2 dessertspoons and pass the sorbet between the spoons to make oval quenelle shapes. Slide a quenelle on top of each portion of compote. Decorate with a sprig of mint and serve immediately.

- 250ml (1⅛ US cups) semi-skimmed (2%) milk
- a generous handful of fresh verbena leaves or mint leaves
- 2 egg yolks
- 8 level tsp fructose or the sweetener of your choice (pages 16–20)
- 1 lime
- 200ml (⅞ US cup) water
- ½ fresh sweet pineapple, skin and 'eyes' removed, to yield about 200g (7oz) net
- flesh from ½ mango, to yield about 150g (5½oz) net
- 1 grapefruit
- 2 oranges
- 80g (scant 3oz) strawberries, hulled
- 80g (scant 3oz) raspberries

To decorate
- 4 small sprigs of verbena or mint

Equipment (optional)
- Ice cream maker

*Fructose: 195 calories
*Aspartame: 180 calories
*Xylitol: 215 calories
*Sugar: 250 calories
*Honey: 235 calories

FRESH FRUIT MEDLEY WITH A FRAGRANT ICE CREAM

180–250 CALORIES PER PERSON,
depending on the sweetener you use*
Preparation time: 50 minutes
Level of difficulty: **
Serves 4

---

1. For the ice cream, bring the milk briefly to the boil in a saucepan, then remove it from the heat. Add the verbena or mint leaves, pushing them down with a wooden spoon to immerse them completely. Cover the saucepan with a lid and leave the milk to infuse for 15 minutes. Strain the milk through a fine sieve set over a bowl and discard the leaves.

2. In a separate bowl, whisk the egg yolks with 6 level teaspoons of the fructose. Combine this mixture gradually with the infused milk, stirring continually to blend. Return the infused milk mixture to a saucepan. Stir with a wooden spoon, making a figure-of-eight movement, over a very low heat, as when making a custard (page 284). When the mixture starts to 'pull' on the spoon and coat it, the flavoured cream is ready. Transfer it to a bowl and leave to cool.

3. Remove the zest from the lime using a zester or fine grater over a small bowl. Set aside. Cut the lime in half, squeeze its juice into the flavoured cream and stir well.

4. Pour the mixture into an ice cream maker and churn it to make a smooth ice cream. Alternatively, put the mixture in a shallow freezing tray and stir it thoroughly with a fork every half-hour. The ice cream will be ready when, after several hours, it has a soft, scoopable, consistency. Put the ice cream in an airtight container and freeze until you are ready to serve.

5. To make the syrup for the fruit salad, combine the 200ml (⅞ US cup) water with the remaining 2 teaspoons of fructose in a saucepan. Bring the mixture to the boil, without stirring, and let it simmer for 1 minute. Pour the syrup into a mixing bowl and leave it to cool for 30 minutes. Add the lime zest to the syrup, then transfer the syrup to the refrigerator until needed.

6. For the fruit medley, slice the prepared half-pineapple lengthways into 4 thin pieces, then cut away the woody core from each piece. Cut the flesh into small, even chunks. Cut the mango flesh into 1cm (½in) dice. Peel the grapefruit and oranges. Use a small sharp knife to trim the peeled grapefruit and oranges free of any remaining pith. Working over a small bowl, cut along each side of the membranes to free the segments. Squeeze the emptied membranes over a bowl to collect their juice. If you like, cut any large segments in half.

7. To complete the fruit medley, combine the chunks of pineapple, the mango dice and the citrus segments and their juice in a large bowl. Stir in the chilled syrup.

To serve
Have ready 4 shallow-bowled serving plates. Distribute the fruit medley between the plates. Arrange the strawberries and raspberries on top.

Scoop out each portion of ice cream using 2 dessertspoons and pass the ice cream between the spoons to make oval quenelle shapes. Slide a quenelle onto each plate. Decorate with a sprig of verbena or mint and serve immediately.

- 4 organic lemons
- 500ml (2⅛ US cups) plus 3 tbsp water
- 6 heaped tbsp plus 1 pinch of fructose or the sweetener of your choice (pages 16–20)
- 200g (7oz) fresh raspberries
- 3 tbsp water

To decorate

- 200g (7oz) fresh raspberries
- 4 small mixed bunches of fresh verbena, mint and rosemary

Equipment (optional)

- Sorbetière

*Fructose: 175 calories
*Aspartame: 70 calories
*Xylitol: 210 calories
*Sugar: 310 calories
*Honey: 250 calories

GARDEN-FRESH LEMON SORBET

70–310 CALORIES PER PERSON,
depending on the sweetener you use*
Preparation time: 40 minutes
Level of difficulty: *
Serves 4

1. To make the syrup for the lemon sorbet, remove the zest from 3 of the lemons using a zester or fine grater over a saucepan. Add 500ml (2⅛ US cups) water and 6 heaped tablespoons of fructose, and bring the mixture to the boil. Remove the saucepan from the heat.

2. Cut all 4 lemons in half and squeeze their juice. Stir the juice into the warm lemon syrup.

3. Transfer the lemon syrup to a sorbetière and churn to a soft-textured consistency. Alternatively, put the mixture in a shallow freezing tray and stir it thoroughly every half-hour with a fork. The sorbet will be ready when, after several hours, it has a soft, scoopable, consistency. Put the sorbet in an airtight container and freeze until you are ready to serve.

4. To make the raspberry coulis, put the raspberries and 3 tablespoons of water in the bowl of a food processor and blend to a purée. Taste, and adjust the acidity of the fruit by adding a pinch of fructose if required. For a smooth coulis, pass the purée through a fine sieve – preferably a chinois – and discard the pips. Pour the coulis into an airtight container and place it in the refrigerator until needed.

To serve

Have ready 4 chilled shallow dessert bowls or glass dishes. Remove the lemon sorbet from the freezer. Scoop out each portion of sorbet using 2 dessertspoons and pass the sorbet between the spoons to make oval quenelle shapes. Put one quenelle into each bowl. Drizzle a little of the chilled raspberry coulis over each helping. Add a few fresh raspberries and decorate with small mixed bunches of fresh verbena, mint and rosemary. Serve straight away.

- 1 litre (4¼ US cups/1 quart) water
- 1 vanilla pod (bean), cut in half lengthways, seeds scraped and set asided
- 1 tbsp Sichuan (Szechuan) pepper
- 8 heaped tbsp fructose or the sweetener of your choice (pages 16–20)
- 4 Williams or Bartlett pears, peeled but not cored and with stems left on
- 250g (9oz) fresh or frozen blackberries
- 50ml (¼ US cup or 6 tbsp) water
- juice from ½ lemon

For the hazelnut spice biscuit (cookie)
- 2 tbsp water
- 1 heaped tbsp icing sugar (confectioner's sugar)
- 1 heaped tsp flour
- 1 heaped tbsp ground hazelnuts
- ¼ tsp ground quatre-épices mix ('four spices': roughly equal parts of white or black pepper, cloves, nutmeg and ginger or cinnamon)

Equipment (optional)
- Sorbetière

*Fructose: 185 calories
*Aspartame: 155 calories
*Xylitol: 200 calories
*Sugar: 230 calories
*Honey: 210 calories

PEAR WITH SICHUAN PEPPER, BLACKBERRY SORBET AND A HAZELNUT SPICE BISCUIT

155–230 CALORIES PER PERSON,
depending on the sweetener you use*
Preparation time: 45 minutes
Level of difficulty: ***
Serves 4

---

1. To make the pepper and vanilla-flavoured syrup, bring the 1 litre (4¼ US cups/ 1 quart) of water, the halved vanilla pod (bean) and its seeds, the Sichuan pepper and 6 of the heaped tablespoons of fructose to the boil in a large saucepan.

2. Immerse the pears in the syrup, placing a coffee-cup saucer or small bread plate upside down on top of the pears. Poach the pears gently for 15 minutes or until the tip of a knife can easily pierce the fruit. Remove from the heat and let the pears cool in the syrup.

3. Drain the pears and stand them upright on a cutting board. Cut each pear widthways, about one-third of the way down from the top, forming a little 'hat' with the pear's stem attached. Set the 'hats' aside briefly. Use an apple corer or paring knife to remove each core, leaving the bottoms intact. Using a melon baller or grapefruit spoon, carefully open up the space left by the core to make a small cavity with a diameter of 2–3cm (¾–1¼in). Place the 'hats' and the bottoms of the pears in the refrigerator until needed.

4. For the blackberry sorbet, put the blackberries, the 50ml (¼ US cup or 6 tbsp) of water, the remaining 2 heaped tablespoons of fructose and the lemon juice in the bowl of a food processor and blend to a purée. Pass the purée through a fine sieve, preferably a chinois, and discard the seeds.

5. Pour the blackberry purée into a sorbetière and churn it to a soft-textured sorbet. Alternatively, put the mixture in a shallow freezing tray and stir it thoroughly every half-hour with a fork. The sorbet will be ready when, after several hours, it has a soft, scoopable, consistency. Put the sorbet in an airtight container and freeze until you are ready to serve.

6. To make the hazelnut spice biscuits (cookies), combine all the ingredients in a mixing bowl. Preheat the oven to 180°C (350°F, gas mark 4). Use a rubber spatula to spread the biscuit dough carefully onto a baking sheet lined with greaseproof or parchment paper. The dough should be about 2mm (less than ⅛in) thick. Bake for 2 minutes.

7. Remove the baking sheet from the oven and use a knife to cut the partially baked dough into two 10 x 5cm (4 x 2in) rectangles. Cut each rectangle in half diagonally to make 4 triangles. Bake the biscuits (cookies) for 6 minutes more or until they are nicely browned.

8. Let the biscuits (cookies) cool on the paper, then transfer them carefully to an airtight container.

To serve

Remove the pear 'hats' and bottoms from the refrigerator and place each pear bottom on a dessert plate. Remove the blackberry sorbet from the freezer and, using a teaspoon, fill each pear cavity with the sorbet. Let some sorbet overflow slightly from each cavity.

Place each pear 'hat' on top of the sorbet and lean a biscuit (cookie) against each pear. Serve immediately.

- 4 Granny Smith apples, unpeeled and washed
- 3 heaped tbsp fructose or the sweetener of your choice (pages 16–20)
- 100ml (⅜ US cup) water

To garnish
- 4 small sprigs of mint

*Fructose: 125 calories
*Aspartame: 75calories
*Xylitol: 145 calories
*Sugar: 180calories
*Honey: 165 calories

GRANNY SMITH SORBET

75–180 CALORIES PER PERSON,
depending on the type of sweetener you use*
Preparation: 15 minutes, plus 4 hours chilling
Level of difficulty: *
Serves 4

1. Cut the apples in half, then into quarters. Remove and discard the cores and the pips, keeping the peel intact as it will lend colour to the finished sorbet. Chop the apple quarters into small to medium dice and spread the dice out on a plate in a single layer. To prevent the apple from discolouring, cover immediately with clingfilm (plastic wrap) and transfer to a freezer for about 4 hours.

2. For the syrup, put the fructose and water in a saucepan and set it over a low heat. When the fructose dissolves, increase the heat and bring the liquid to the boil. Remove this syrup from the heat and leave it to cool.

3. Put the frozen apple pieces in the bowl of a food processor. Add the cooled syrup and blend the ingredients together to make a sorbet mixture.

4. Put the mixture in a shallow freezing tray and stir it thoroughly every half-hour with a fork. The sorbet will be ready when, after several hours, it has a soft, scoopable, consistency. Put the sorbet in an airtight container and freeze until you are ready to serve.

To serve
Scoop the sorbet into 4 ice cream glasses or dessert bowls. If you like, you can pass the sorbet between 2 dessertspoons to make it into oval quenelle shapes. Add a sprig of mint to each helping and serve immediately.

Chef's tip
This light, refreshing, sorbet is an exquisite dessert in its own right. It is also a well-matched companion for the Russet apple mousse (page 304) and, equally, for the Hot apple and lime soufflés (page 324).

- 300g (11oz) fresh raspberries
- 7 tbsp water
- 3 heaped tsp fructose or the sweetener of your choice (pages 16–20)
- ½ sheet of leaf gelatine (soaked) or ½ tsp powdered gelatine (page 22)
- 150g (5½oz) fromage blanc or Greek yogurt (0% fat or low-fat)
- 50ml (¼ US cup or 6 tbsp) light whipping cream (30–35% fat)
- 2 egg whites
- 4 sponge fingers (ladyfingers), cut in half lengthways

To decorate
- 100g (3½oz) fresh raspberries
- 4 small sprigs of mint

*Fructose: 190 calories
*Aspartame: 170 calories
*Xylitol: 195 calories
*Sugar: 215 calories
*Honey: 205 calories

RASPBERRY TIRAMISU

170–215 CALORIES PER PERSON,
depending on the sweetener you use*
Preparation time: 30 minutes
Level of difficulty: *
Serves 4

1. For the raspberry compote, combine the raspberries and 6 tablespoons of the water in a saucepan. Bring the liquid just to the boil, stirring continuously with a wooden spoon. Lower the heat and cook the raspberries for 5 minutes or until they have yielded their juice. Continue stirring the mixture until it thickens to a compote.

2. Add 2 of the heaped teaspoons of fructose to the compote and stir well. Pass the compote through a nylon sieve to separate the juice from the rest of the mixture. Set aside the juice for soaking the sponge fingers (ladyfingers) later. Refrigerate the juice and the strained compote separately.

3. To make the fromage blanc mousse, heat the remaining tablespoon of water in a saucepan. Remove the saucepan from the heat and dissolve and combine the warm water with the gelatine of your choice , whisking well until the gelatine has completely dissolved. Add the fromage blanc and stir well. Transfer the mixture to a mixing bowl.

4. Beat the cream until it forms fairly firm peaks then fold it into the fromage blanc mixture.

5. In a separate mixing bowl, whisk the egg whites to soft peaks. Sprinkle on the remaining heaped teaspoon of fructose and whisk again to incorporate it. Mix about a quarter of the whisked egg whites into the fromage blanc mixture, then combine this with the remaining whites, repeatedly lifting the whites from the bottom of the bowl and folding them over the top of the mixture until all is well mixed.

6. To moisten the sponge fingers (ladyfingers), pour the reserved raspberry juice into a shallow dish and quickly dip the halved sponge fingers (ladyfingers), one by one, into the juice.

To serve
Divide half of the raspberry compote between 4 pretty glasses. Repeat with half of the stiffened fromage blanc mousse, then add the remaining half of the raspberry compote, followed by the soaked sponge fingers (ladyfingers). Finish with a layer of the remaining fromage blanc mousse. Chill the tiramisu in the refrigerator until the fromage blanc mousse is firm.

Just before serving, decorate each glass with whole fresh raspberries and a sprig of mint.

- 900g (2lb) ripe pineapple, with its leaves – a minimum of 8 – still attached
- 3 heaped tsp fructose or the sweetener of your choice (pages 16–20)
- 2 limes
- 4 tbsp dark rum
- ½ tbsp cornflour (cornstarch), mixed with a little cold water
- 200ml (⅞ US cup) fresh pineapple juice
- 2 egg whites
- 1 heaped tsp aspartame or the sweetener of your choice (pages 16–20)
- 4 sponge fingers (lady fingers)
- 160ml (¾ US cup) water

Equipment
- Sorbetière (optional)
- Steamer

*Fructose: 205 calories
*Aspartame: 190 calories
*Xylitol: 215 calories
*Sugar: 225 calories
*Honey: 220 calories

LIME MERINGUE WITH PINEAPPLE

190–225 CALORIES PER PERSON,
depending on the sweetener you use*
Cooking and preparation: 1 hour
Level of difficulty: ***
Serves 4

---

1. Wash and dry the pineapple. Use a serrated knife to top and tail it; discard the top and bottom but set the leaves aside. Leaving the pineapple unpeeled, slice the trunk into four even-sized circles.

2. Remove the fruit from inside each circle without damaging the outer skin – the circles will be used for the presentation. Cut the fruit from one circle into ½cm (¼in) dice and set aside in a small bowl in the refrigerator. Put the fruit from the remaining 3 circles in another bowl and set aside to make the sorbet. Put the 4 pineapple shells on a large freezer-proof plate and transfer to the freezer.

3. For the pineapple sorbet, cut the fruit from the 3 circles into large dice and transfer to a food processor. Add 60ml (¼ US cup or 6 tbsp) of water and one of the heaped teaspoons of fructose. Remove the zest from one of the limes using a zester or fine grater. Cut the lime in half and squeeze out its juice. Add the zest, juice and half of the rum to the food processor and blend to a smooth, loose purée.

4. Transfer the purée to a sorbetière and churn to a soft-textured consistency. Alternatively, put the mixture in a shallow freezing tray and stir it thoroughly every half-hour with a fork. The sorbet will be ready when, after several hours, it has a soft, scoopable, consistency. Put the sorbet in an airtight container and freeze until you are ready to serve.

5. For the pineapple sauce, put the cornflour (cornstarch) blended with water into a bowl and add one-third of the fresh pineapple juice. Pour the remaining two-thirds of the pineapple juice into a saucepan and bring it to the boil. Stir about half of the hot pineapple juice into the cornflour (cornstarch) mixture then return the combined mixture to the saucepan. Simmer for 2 minutes, whisking all the time. Transfer the sauce to a bowl and chill.

6. For the meringues, preheat a steamer and line its tray with greaseproof or parchment paper. Preheat the grill. Remove the zest from the remaining lime and set aside. In a mixing bowl, whisk the egg whites until they form stiff peaks. Gradually whisk in the remaining fructose and the lime zest.

7. Drop 4 large spoonfuls of the meringue mixture onto the steamer tray to make 4 irregular rock-like shapes. Steam for 1 minute. Transfer the steamed meringues to a heatproof plate that fits beneath the grill and grill them – watching them all the time – until the tops of the peaks turn golden brown. Remove from the grlll and set aside in a cool place.

8. Make a cold rum syrup by mixing 100ml (⅜ US cup) of water with the remaining rum and stirring in the aspartame. Set this aside briefly. Trim the pineapple leaves to make an attractive shape, wash them and set them aside in iced water.

To serve
Have ready 4 cold serving plates and the various elements of the dessert.
Put one frozen pineapple shell in the middle of each plate. Trim the sponge fingers (ladyfingers) as needed, to fit inside the shells. Dip the fingers in the rum syrup and put one finger in the centre of each shell. Put about 2 spoons of sorbet over each finger, allowing the sorbet to spread to fill any gaps.

Distribute about three-quarters of the diced pineapple and about half the pineapple sauce inside the pineapple shells. Top each shell with a meringue and decorate with pineapple leaves. Scatter with the remaining diced pineapple and drizzle the remaining sauce around the edge, as desired. Serve straight away.

- freshly squeezed juice from 4 oranges
- 50ml (¼ US cup or 6 tbsp) water
- 1½ sheets of leaf gelatine (soaked) or 1 tsp powdered gelatine (page 22)
- 4 heaped tsp aspartame or the sweetener of your choice (pages 16–20)
- 275g (9½oz) fresh mango, peeled and stone (pit) removed
- 100ml (⅜ US cup) light whipping cream (30–35% fat)

Equipment
- Multi-functional whipper with 2 gas cartridges (pages 36–7)

*Fructose: 170 calories
*Aspartame: 155 calories
*Xylitol: 175 calories
*Sugar: 185 calories
*Honey: 180 calories

MANGO JELLY MOUSSE

155–185 CALORIES PER PERSON,
depending on the sweetener you use*
Preparation time: 30 minutes, plus 2 hours chilling
Level of difficulty: **
Serves 4

1. To make the orange jelly, first divide the freshly squeezed orange juice between two containers: one containing 200ml (⅞ US cup) juice and the other 100ml (⅜ US cup) juice. Heat the water in a saucepan and dissolve and combine the gelatine of your choice with the warm water, whisking well until the gelatine has completely dissolved. Pour the 200ml (⅞ US cup) of orange juice into the saucepan, along with 2 of the heaped teaspoons of aspartame. Stir well. Set aside the 100ml (⅜ US cup) of orange juice for the mousse.

2. Cut 200g (7oz) of the mango into 1cm (½in) dice and divide them between 4 pretty glasses. Pour the orange jelly on top of the mango in each glass, and refrigerate for 2 hours or until the jelly has set.

3. To make the mousse, cut the remaining 75g (2½oz) of mango into large chunks. Put the mango chunks, the remaining 100ml (⅜ US cup) of orange juice, the cream and the remaining 2 heaped teaspoons of aspartame in a mixing bowl. (Should you choose to use sugar, xylitol or fructose, be sure to mix the sweetener with the orange juice before adding it to the mango-and-cream mixture.)

4. Pour the mixture into a food processor and blend well. Pass this mixture through a nylon sieve before pouring it into the multi-functional whipper. Close the whipper and insert 2 gas cartridges. Place the filled whipper in the refrigerator until chilled.

To serve
Remove the chilled glasses and the whipper from the refrigerator. Use the whipper to top the mango jelly in each glass with a generous helping of mousse. Serve immediately.

- 2 very ripe, large bananas
- 3 limes
- 250ml (1⅛ US cups) water
- 2 sheets of leaf gelatine (soaked) or 1½ tsp powdered gelatine (page 22)
- 3 heaped tbsp aspartame or the sweetener of your choice (pages 16–20)
- 150ml (¾ US cup) fresh or tinned pineapple juice
- 100ml (⅜ US cup) light whipping cream (30–35% fat)
- 2 level tsp rum

To decorate
- 4 sprigs of fresh mint

Equipment
- Multi-functional whipper with 2 gas cartridges (pages 36–37)

*Fructose: 185 calories
*Aspartame: 160 calories
*Xylitol: 190 calories
*Sugar: 210 calories
*Honey: 210 calories

BANANA JELLY WITH PIÑA COLADA MOUSSE

160–210 CALORIES PER PERSON,
depending on the sweetener you use*
Preparation time: 30 minutes, plus 3 hours chilling
Level of difficulty: **
Serves 4

1. To make the lime and banana jelly, peel the bananas and cut them into 1cm (½in) dice.

2. Remove the zest from one of the limes using a zester or fine grater. Cut all 3 limes in half and squeeze their juice. Separate the juice into two different bowls: one containing two-thirds of the juice for the jelly and the other containing the remaining one-third of the juice for the piña colada mousse.

3. For the jelly, have ready the 250ml (1⅛ US cups) of cold water. Heat 150ml (¾ US cup) of it until warm but not hot. Blend this with the gelatine of your choice, whisking well until the gelatine has completely dissolved. Stir in the remaining cold water, the two-thirds of the lime juice and the aspartame. Set aside briefly.

4. In a mixing bowl, combine the banana dice with the lime zest. Divide the mixture between 4 pretty glasses. Pour just enough of the jelly on top to cover the banana and set the remaining jelly mixture aside. Transfer the glasses to the refrigerator for 1 or 2 hours or until the jelly has set.

5. Warm the remaining jelly just enough to make it liquid. Remove the glasses from the refrigerator and spoon the melted jelly on top of the jellied banana. Return the glasses to the refrigerator until the top layer of jelly has set. Covering the banana with jelly in this way prevents the fruit from turning brown.

6. For the piña colada mousse, combine the pineapple juice, the cream, the remaining one-third of the lime juice and the rum in a mixing bowl. Stir to blend then put this mousse mixture into the multi-functional whipper. Close the whipper and insert 2 gas cartridges. Shake well and place the filled whipper in the refrigerator until chilled.

To serve
Remove the glasses and the whipper from the refrigerator. Use the whipper to top each banana jelly with a quarter of the piña colada mousse. Decorate each glass with a sprig of mint and serve immediately.

- 1 pineapple weighing about 900g (2lb)
- 4 grapefruits
- 1 tbsp acacia honey

To decorate
- 4 sprigs of fresh lemon thyme

Equipment (optional)
- Electric carving knife

PINEAPPLE CARPACCIO WITH GRAPEFRUIT

110 CALORIES PER PERSON
Preparation time: 20 minutes
Level of difficulty: *
Serves 4

---

1. Use a long sharp knife to remove all the skin from the pineapple. Use a small knife to cut away any remaining 'eyes' from the flesh. To slice the pineapple thinly enough for the carpaccio, either use an electric carving knife or a very sharp chef's knife. If you use an electric carving knife, slice the whole pineapple into large, paper-thin, rounds. If you use a chef's knife, cut the pineapple in half lengthways, then cut out and discard the core. Place each pineapple half flat-side down on a cutting board and slice widthways into thin half-moon shapes.

2. Arrange the pineapple slices in a single layer on 4 serving plates, dividing the portions of pineapple equally. Chill in the refrigerator until required.

3. For the grapefruit and honey juice, cut 3 of the 4 grapefruits in half and squeeze out as much juice as possible, collecting it in a bowl. Blend the honey into the juice and keep it chilled in the refrigerator.

4. Remove the peel and pith from the remaining grapefruit. Cut with a small sharp knife along each side of the membranes to free the grapefruit segments then cut the segments into 1cm (½in) dice. Transfer them to a container and set aside in the refrigerator.

To serve
When you are ready to serve, drizzle the grapefruit and honey juice evenly over the pineapple slices. Distribute the diced grapefruit and a sprig of lemon thyme to each plate and serve immediately.

- 2 eggs, small or medium
- 1 heaped tbsp fructose or the sweetener of your choice (pages 16–20)
- ½ vanilla pod (bean), split
- 1 tbsp Chambord black raspberry liqueur or Kirsch
- 2 heaped tbsp plain flour
- 3 tbsp single (light) cream
- 340ml (1½ US cups) semi-skimmed (2%) milk
- 300g (11oz) fresh raspberries

To serve (optional)
- Raspberry coulis (Garden fresh lemon sorbet page 00)

Equipment
- 4 individual ovenproof flan dishes

*Fructose: 200 calories
*Aspartame: 175 calories
*Xylitol: 215 calories
*Sugar: 240 calories
*Honey: 225 calories

INDIVIDUAL RASPBERRY CLAFOUTIS

175–240 CALORIES PER PERSON,
depending on the type of sweetener you use*
Cooking and preparation: 25 minutes
Level of difficulty: *
Serves 4

---

1. Preheat the oven to 200°C (400°F, gas mark 6). In a large mixing bowl, beat together the eggs and the fructose using a balloon whisk. Scrape the seeds from the split vanilla pod (bean) into the egg mixture and stir in the raspberry liqueur or Kirsch. Whisk in the flour a little at a time and, when it is fully incorporated, gradually add the cream and the milk, continuing to whisk to make a smooth mixture.

2. Distribute the raspberries between 4 individual ovenproof flan dishes. Ladle the egg mixture into the dishes and transfer them carefully to the top shelf of the oven, preferably with a heat source from above.

3. After 14 minutes, test the clafoutis for doneness. To do this, tap the side of the dish: if the mixture stays in place without wobbling, it is done. If it moves and forms a ripple, cook it for a further 2–3 minutes and repeat the procedure. Continue until the clafoutis is cooked through.

To serve
Serve the clafoutis warm. If you like, you can serve it with some raspberry coulis.

- 6 Russet apples (or similar variety), peeled and cut in half
- 3 tbsp water
- 1 sheet of leaf gelatine (soaked) or ¾ tsp powdered gelatine (page 22)
- 2 tbsp Calvados or brandy
- 100ml (⅜ US cup) light whipping cream (30–35% fat)
- 2 egg whites
- 4 heaped tsp aspartame or the sweetener of your choice (pages 16–20)
- little extra water as required

To decorate
- 4 sprigs of mint

Equipment
- Steamer

*Fructose: 210 calories
*Aspartame: 200 calories
*Xylitol: 215 calories
*Sugar: 225 calories
*Honey: 220 calories

RUSSET APPLE MOUSSE

200–225 CALORIES PER PERSON,
depending on the sweetener you use*
Preparation time: 45 minutes, plus 2 hours chilling
Level of difficulty: **
Serves 4

1. To prepare the apples for the mousse and for the diced garnish, place 4 apple halves on one plate and 8 on another. Remove the cores from the 4 apple halves and cut the flesh into 1cm (½in) dice.

2. Preheat a steamer and add the diced apples. Cook the fruit for 5 minutes then transfer it to a bowl. Leave to cool then refrigerate for later use.

3. For the apple mousse, core the remaining 8 apple halves. Cut them into large pieces and place them in a saucepan with the 3 tablespoons of water. Cover the saucepan and cook the apple over a very low heat for 15 minutes or until the apple softens to a compote consistency.

4. Transfer the apple compote to a food processor and blend to a smooth purée. Return 200g (7oz) of the purée to the saucepan and keep it warm. Transfer the remaining purée to a mixing bowl and chill it.

5. Dissolve and combine the gelatine of your choice with the 200g (7oz) of warm apple purée, stirring well until the gelatine has completely dissolved to make the mousse. Add one of the tablespoons of Calvados to the mixture and stir well.

6. Place the saucepan of apple mousse in a bowl of ice or transfer it to the refrigerator but watch it to ensure it remains soft, with a mayonnaise-like texture, so that it is easy to combine with the cream and egg whites.

7. Whip the cream to soft peaks and fold it into the apple mousse. In a separate mixing bowl, whisk the egg whites to soft peaks. Sprinkle on 2 of the heaped teaspoons of aspartame and whisk again.

8. Working quickly, tip all of the egg white into the apple mousse, put a spatula in the centre, then lift the mixture up and over the whites, clockwise, while you turn the bowl in the opposite direction. Continue until all the ingredients are well blended.

steamed diced apples

apple and
calvados compote

apple mousse

9. Divide this lightened apple mousse between 4 pretty china cups and transfer to the refrigerator to chill. Add the remaining tablespoon of Calvados and the remaining aspartame to the bowl of chilled apple purée. Add enough water to thin the mixture to the consistency of a coulis, then chill in the refrigerator.

To serve
Remove the 4 cups of apple mousse from the refrigerator. Combine the reserved diced apple with the apple coulis and spoon this mixture over the mousse in each cup. Garnish each dessert with a sprig of fresh mint and serve.

Chef's tip
To save time, you can use 250g (9oz) of store-bought unsweetened apple sauce instead of making your own apple compote from the 4 apples, as in the recipe.

Variation
You can serve this mousse with a quenelle-shaped scoop of Granny Smith Sorbet (page 296).

- 4 ripe white peaches
- 1 litre (4¼ US cups/1 quart) water
- 9 heaped tbsp fructose or the sweetener of your choice (pages 16–20)
- 1 handful of fresh verbena leaves or mint leaves
- 1½ sheets of leaf gelatine (soaked) or 1 tsp powdered gelatine (page 22)
- 1 lemon
- 40ml (4 tbsp) semi-skimmed (2%) milk
- 100ml (⅜ US cup) light whipping cream (30–35% fat)

To decorate
- 4 sprigs of verbena or mint

Equipment
- Multi-functional whipper with 2 gas cartridges (pages 36–7)

*Fructose: 190 calories
*Aspartame: 155 calories
*Xylitol: 200 calories
*Sugar: 210 calories
*Honey: 205 calories

POACHED PEACHES WITH FRAGRANT JELLY AND LEMON MOUSSE

155–210 CALORIES PER PERSON,
depending on the sweetener you use*
Preparation time: 40 minutes, plus 2 hours chilling
Level of difficulty: **
Serves 4

1. Peel the peaches by nicking their skin and dipping them briefly into very hot water, then into iced water to loosen the skin (Terms and Techniques, pages 327–8). Gently peel away the skin.

2. In a saucepan, bring the water, 8 of the heaped tablespoons of fructose and the verbena leaves or mint leaves to the boil. Adjust the heat to maintain a simmer. Add the peeled peaches to this syrup, submerging them by placing a coffee-cup saucer or small bread plate upside-down on top.

3. Let the peaches simmer for 12 minutes or until the tip of a knife slides easily into the fruit, all the way to the stone (pit); remove from the heat and let the peaches cool in the syrup. When the peaches and syrup have cooled completely, place the saucepan in the refrigerator. Avoid handling the peaches when they are warm because they can easily become squashed.

4. For the jelly, remove the peaches and syrup from the refrigerator. Measure out 250ml (1⅛ US cups) of the syrup and put about half to heat in a separate saucepan without allowing it to boil. Off the heat, dissolve and combine the gelatine of your choice with the warmed peach syrup, whisking well until the gelatine has completely dissolved. Add the remaining cold syrup and stir well; set aside.

5. Use a slotted spoon to transfer the poached peaches to a cutting board and cut each peach in half to remove the stones (pits). Cut each half into large dice and divide the dice between 4 serving bowls. Spoon the jelly over the diced peaches then transfer the bowls to the refrigerator for at least 3 hours, or until the jelly has set.

6. To make the lemon mousse, remove the zest from the lemon using a zester or fine grater and place the zest in a mixing bowl. Cut the lemon in half and squeeze as much juice as possible into a small bowl, strain out the pips, then combine the juice with the zest. Stir in the milk, cream and the remaining heaped tablespoon of fructose.

7. Let the mousse mixture rest for 5 minutes, or until the fructose dissolves, then pss the mixture through a nylon sieve. Pour the mousse into a multi-functional whipper, close the whipper and insert 2 gas cartridges. Place the filled whipper in the refrigerator until chilled.

To serve
Remove the serving bowls of jellied peaches and the whipper from the refrigerator. Fit the whipper with a fluted tip then top each bowl with a generous helping of lemon mousse. Decorate with a sprig of fresh verbena or mint and serve immediately.

Variation
You can use store-bought tinned peaches in syrup instead of fresh peaches, but be warned that they do contain sugar!

- 400g (14oz) fresh rhubarb, or frozen and thawed
- 300g (11oz) strawberries, preferably wild, washed and hulled
- 300ml (1¼ US cups) water
- 3 heaped tbsp fructose or the sweetener of your choice (pages 16–20)
- ½ vanilla pod (bean), cut in half lengthways
- 1 lime

To decorate
- 4 sprigs of mint

*Fructose: 100 calories
*Aspartame: 50 calories
*Xylitol: 110 calories
*Sugar: 155 calories
*Honey: 130 calories

RHUBARB AND STRAWBERRY COMPOTE WITH LIME

50–155 CALORIES PER PERSON,
depending on the sweetener you use*
Preparation time: 45 minutes
Level of difficulty: *
Serves 4

---

1. If you are using fresh rhubarb, trim it and remove the stringy fibres. Frozen rhubarb will already have been peeled. Cut the rhubarb into 1cm (½in) pieces.

2. Depending on the size of the strawberries, cut them either into halves or quarters. Place two-thirds in one bowl (to be used later in the compote) and the remaining one-third in another bowl (to be used as decoration).

3. In a saucepan, heat the water, fructose and the half of vanilla pod (bean). Add the rhubarb pieces to the mixture. To ensure uniform cooking and to prevent any evaporation, place a circle of greaseproof or parchment paper, cut to the diameter of the saucepan, on top of the mixture. Cover the saucepan with a lid and simmer very gently for 10 minutes or until the rhubarb has yielded its juice and thickened to a compote.

4. Add the two-thirds quantity of strawberries to the compote. Stir gently until the strawberries flop, then remove from the heat and set aside. When the compote has cooled, transfer it to an airtight container and chill it in the refrigerator.

5. When the compote is well chilled, remove the zest from the lime using a zester or fine grater and sprinkle the zest over the compote. Cut the lime in half and squeeze its juice into a small bowl. Add the lime juice gradually to the compote according to personal taste and the tartness of the fruit.

To serve
Divide the rhubarb and strawberry compote between 4 shallow-bowled serving dishes. Use the remaining one-third of strawberries for decoration. Top each portion with a small sprig of mint and serve.

- 150ml (¾ US cup) fresh or tinned (canned) pineapple juice
- ½ fresh mango, peeled and stone (pit) removed, the flesh weighing about 150g (5½oz) and cut into large dice
- 10g (¼oz) fresh ginger, peeled and cut into ½cm (¼in) dice
- ¼ fresh pineapple, unpeeled, and weighing about 100g (3½oz)
- 1 lime
- 2 egg whites
- 2 heaped tsp fructose or the sweetener of your choice (pages 16–20)
- 300g (11oz) custard (page 284)

To decorate
- 4 sprigs of mint

Equipment
- Steamer (optional)

*Fructose: 150 calories
*Aspartame: 125 calories
*Xylitol: 150 calories
*Sugar: 175 calories
*Honey: 180 calories

TROPICAL MERINGUE FLOATING ISLANDS

125–180 CALORIES PER PERSON,
depending on the sweetener you use*
Preparation time: 30 minutes
Level of difficulty: **
Serves 4

1. To make the tropical fruit purée, put the pineapple juice, diced mango and diced ginger into the bowl of a food processor and blend as finely as possible. Pass the mixture through a fine sieve, preferably a chinois. Transfer the strained purée to an airtight container and set it aside in the refrigerator until needed.

2. Use a long sharp knife to remove all the skin from the pineapple. Use a small knife to cut away any remaining 'eyes' from the flesh. Slice the pineapple thinly then cut the slices into dice no bigger than 2–3mm (⅛in). Transfer the diced pineapple to an airtight container and place it in the refrigerator until needed.

3. To make the meringue floating islands, preheat a steamer and line its tray with greaseproof or parchment paper. Meanwhile, use a zester or fine grater to grate tiny pieces of zest from the lime onto a saucer; set aside. In a mixing bowl, whisk the egg whites together until they form soft peaks. Gradually incorporate the fructose and the lime zest, whisking until the meringue mixture forms stiff, pointed peaks.

4. Lay the greaseproof or parchment paper flat on a work surface and drop large spoonfuls of the meringue mixture on top to make 4 irregular rock-like shapes.

5. Transfer the paper carefully to the steamer tray. Steam the meringues for 1 minute, then transfer them immediately to the refrigerator. If you do not have a steamer, heat the uncooked meringues in the microwave. Take care not to overcook them – they need less than 10 seconds at an 800-watt setting – or the mixture will turn to marshmallow.

To serve
Remove the diced pineapple from the refrigerator and divide it between 4 shallow-bowled serving dishes. Add a quarter of the custard to each plate. Remove the tropical fruit purée from the refrigerator and pour it over the custard. Finally, remove the meringue floating islands from the refrigerator and place one in the centre of each dish. Decorate each meringue with a small sprig of mint and serve.

- 700g (1lb 8oz) strawberries, washed and hulled juice of ½ lemon
- 150ml (¾ US cup) water for the syrup and infusion
- 4 heaped tsp fructose or the sweetener of your choice (pages 16–20)
- 1 small handful of fresh mint leaves, rinsed and dried
- about 1 litre (4¼ US cups/1 quart) water for the bain-marie
- 2 sheets of leaf gelatine (soaked) or 1¾ tsp powdered gelatine (page 22)

For the pastry bases
- 14g (½oz or 1 tbsp) butter, softened
- 1 heaped tbsp icing sugar (confectioner's sugar)
- 2 heaped tbsp plain flour
- 1 tbsp water

To decorate
- Few strawberries and their leaves or 4 small sprigs of mint

Equipment
- Sorbetière (optional)
- 4 individual moulds or ramekins, about 7cm (2¾ in) in diameter and at least 3cm (1¼in) deep

*Fructose: 170 calories
*Aspartame: 140 calories
*Xylitol: 180 calories
*Sugar: 200 calories
*Honey: 190 calories

UPSIDE-DOWN STRAWBERRY AND MINT TARTS

140–200 CALORIES PER PERSON,
depending on the sweetener you use*
Preparation time: 1 hour, plus 4 hours chilling
Level of difficulty: ***
Serves 4

1. For the sorbet, measure out 250g (9oz) of the strawberries into a bowl. Sprinkle with the lemon juice and mix gently. Bring 50ml (¼ US cup or 6 tbsp) of the water and 2 heaped teaspoons of the fructose briefly to the boil in a saucepan without stirring. Make sure that none of the liquid evaporates. Remove the syrup from the heat and pour it over the strawberries.

2. Stir briefly then turn the mixture into a food processor. Blend to a smooth purée, then transfer the purée to a sorbetière and churn to a soft-textured consistency. If you do not have a sorbetière, you can put the puréed strawberries in a shallow freezing tray and stir the mixture thoroughly every half-hour with a fork. The sorbet will be ready when, after several hours, it has a soft, scoopable, consistency. Put the sorbet in an airtight container and freeze until you are ready to serve.

3. For the strawberry and mint infusion, measure out a further 250g (9oz) of the strawberries and put them in a heatproof bowl. Add the remaining 100ml (⅜ US cup) of water, the remaining 2 heaped teaspoons of fructose and the handful of mint leaves.

4. Make a bain-marie by bringing to the boil about 1 litre (4¼ US cups/1 quart) of water in a saucepan that is large enough to hold the heatproof bowl. Lower the heat to a simmer. Cover the heatproof bowl with clingfilm (plastic wrap) then put it in the bain-marie so that the gently simmering water reaches about halfway up the side of the bowl. Simmer the water for about 20 minutes to infuse the strawberry and mint mixture.

5. Pass the strawberry and mint infusion through a fine sieve – preferably a chinois – to separate the juice from the solids. Measure out 200ml (⅞ US cup) of the warm strawberry-mint juice, then dissolve and combine the gelatine of your choice with the juice, whisking well until the gelatine has been smoothly incorporated. (You can reserve the remaining strawberry-mint juice for another recipe.)

6. For the strawberry tarts, cut the remaining 200g (7oz) strawberries into 1cm (½in) dice and divide between 4 individual moulds or ramekins. Pour the strawberry and mint jelly over the strawberries, filling the moulds to just below the rim, then transfer them to the refrigerator for at least 4 hours, or until the jelly has set.

7. To make the pastry bases, combine the softened butter, icing sugar (confectioner's sugar), flour and water in a mixing bowl. Blend to a smooth dough. Preheat the oven to 180°C (350°F, gas mark 4). Roll out the dough onto a sheet of greaseproof or parchment paper. Use a spatula to flatten the dough into an even layer, about 2mm (less than ⅛in) thick. Use a pastry cutter or a drinking glass to cut 4 circles of dough the same size as the moulds. Transfer the paper to a baking sheet.

8. Bake the pastry bases for about 7 minutes or until golden brown. Remove the bases from the oven, and let them cool. Transfer them to an airtight container until you are ready to serve.

To serve

Have ready the various elements of the dessert and 4 serving plates. Put a pastry base in the middle of each plate. Run the tip of small knife around the rim of each jelly to help free it from its mould. Stand the moulds briefly in hot water, then invert each onto a pastry base and lift the mould away. If the jelly does not slip out easily, repeat the unmoulding procedure.

Scoop out each portion of strawberry sorbet using 2 dessertspoons and pass the sorbet between the spoons to make oval quenelle shapes. Slide a quenelle on top of each upside-down strawberry jelly. Garnish with a few strawberries and their leaves or small sprig of mint and serve immediately.

- 400g (14oz) fresh raspberries
- 100ml (⅜ US cup) light whipping cream (30–35% fat)
- 3 egg whites
- 4 heaped tsp fructose, plus a pinch of fructose or the sweetener of your choice (pages 16–20)
- 3 tbsp water

To decorate
- 200g (7oz) fresh raspberries
- 4 small sprigs of mint

Equipment
- 4 glasses or other pretty containers, capable of being put in the freezer
- Multi-functional whipper with 2 gas cartridges (pages 36–7)

*Fructose: 180 calories
*Aspartame: 155 calories
*Xylitol: 190 calories
*Sugar: 210 calories
*Honey: 200 calories

FROZEN RASPBERRY SOUFFLÉS

155–210 CALORIES PER PERSON,
depending on the sweetener you use*
Preparation time: 20 minutes, plus 4 hours freezing
Level of difficulty: *
Serves 4

1. To make the frozen soufflés, place 4 glasses or other pretty containers in the freezer. Put 200g (7oz) of the strawberries in a mixing bowl. Crush them slightly with a fork, then add the cream and whisk with a hand-held electric whisk to make a coarsely blended purée.

2. Pass the purée through a sieve, preferable a chinois, and discard the pips.
Pour the sieved raspberry cream into the multi-functional whipper, close the whipper and insert 2 gas cartridges.

3. In a separate mixing bowl, whisk the egg whites together until they form soft peaks. Sprinkle on the 4 heaped teaspoons of fructose and whisk again. Empty the raspberry cream from the whipper onto the beaten egg whites. Using a wooden spoon, mix the raspberry cream and the egg whites together, lifting the whites from the bottom of the bowl and folding them over the top of the raspberry cream until the mixture is well blended.

4. Remove the glasses from the freezer and divide the raspberry mixture between them. Return the glasses to the freezer for 4 hours.

5. For the raspberry coulis, purée the remaining 200g (7oz) raspberries with the 3 tablespoons of water, either using an electric blender or a hand-held electric whisk. Pass the purée through a fine sieve, preferably a chinois or one made of nylon, and discard the pips. Taste, and adjust the sweetness of the coulis by adding a pinch of fructose as desired. Transfer the coulis to a covered container and set aside it in the refrigerator until you are ready to serve.

To serve
Remove the glasses of frozen soufflé from the freezer and remove the raspberry coulis from the refrigerator. Stir the decoration of fresh raspberries into the coulis and use this mixture to coat the surface of the frozen soufflés. Decorate each soufflé with a small sprig of mint and serve immediately.

- 400ml (1¾ US cups) semi-skimmed (2%) milk
- 1 heaped tbsp instant coffee powder
- 2 level tsp cornflour (cornstarch)
- 1 egg
- 2 heaped tsp fructose or the sweetener of your choice (pages 16–20)
- 60ml (¼ US cup or 6 tbsp) single (light) cream
- 1 sheet of leaf gelatine (soaked) or 1 tsp powdered gelatine (page 22)
- 2 heaped tsp aspartame or the sweetener of your choice (pages 16–20)

To decorate
- cocoa powder

Equipment
- 4 drinking glasses, capable of being put in a low oven
- Multi-functional whipper with 2 gas cartridges (pages 36–7)

*Fructose: 145 calories
*Aspartame: 125 calories
*Xylitol: 150 calories
*Sugar: 160 calories
*Honey: 155 calories

COFFEE ZEPHYR CREAMS

125–160 CALORIES PER PERSON,
depending on the sweetener you use*
Preparation time: 45 minutes, plus 4 hours chilling
Level of difficulty: **
Serves 4

---

1. To make the coffee cream, heat 200ml (⅞ US cup) of the milk in a saucepan and combine it with the instant coffee powder, stirring well to ensure that the coffee is completely dissolved. Preheat the oven to 95–100°C (200°F, gas mark ½).

2. In a mixing bowl, combine the cornflour (cornstarch) with 50ml (¼ US cup or 6 tbsp) of the remaining milk. Stir the hot milky coffee into the cold milk and cornflour (cornstarch) mixture, then pour the entire mixture back into the saucepan. Bring this to the boil, stirring continuously. Remove from the heat and transfer to a mixing bowl.

3. In a separate mixing bowl, beat the egg with the fructose until pale. Gradually pour this into the hot coffee mixture, stirring continuously. When the mixture is smooth and well blended, pour it into the 4 drinking glasses. Put the glasses on a baking sheet or oven tray and transfer to the oven, ideally, directly below a heat source. Because the oven temperature is low and the glasses are sturdy, there should be no risk of breakage.

4. Bake the coffee creams for 30 minutes or until the cream is barely set - it should wiggle slightly when you tap the glasses. If the creams form ripples on the surface when you tap the glasses, continue to bake them, checking for doneness every 5 minutes or so. Remove the cooked creams from the oven and leave them to cool for 30 minutes before transferring them to the refrigerator to chill for at least 3 hours.

5. To make the milk foam, pour the remaining 150ml (¾ US cup) of milk and the cream into a mixing bowl. Heat one-third of this mixture in a saucepan. Remove the saucepan from the heat. Dissolve and combine the gelatine of your choice with the warm milk mixture, whisking well until the gelatine has completely dissolved. Then add the rest of the milk mixture and the aspartame and stir well.

6. Pour the entire contents of the saucepan into a multi-functional whipper. Close the whipper and insert 2 gas cartridges. Place the filled whipper in the refrigerator until it is chilled.

To serve

Remove the chilled glasses and the whipper from the refrigerator and use the whipper to top each coffee cream with a generous cloud of milk foam. Finish with a light dusting of cocoa powder.

- 1 egg
- 5 heaped tsp aspartame or the sweetener of your choice (pages 16–20)
- 4 heaped tbsp plain flour
- 1 tbsp peanut oil
- 120ml (½ US cup) semi-skimmed (2%) milk, chilled
- 100ml (⅜ US cup) custard (page 284)
- 1 sheet of leaf gelatine (soaked) or ¾ tsp powdered gelatine (page 22)
- 50ml (¼ US cup or 6 tbsp) light whipping cream (30–35% fat)
- 1 egg white
- 2 Bramley, Granny Smith or Golden Delicious apples
- 2 tbsp vanilla extract

To serve
- 200g (7oz) apple sauce, thinned with water to a coulis consistency or 200ml (⅞ US cup) custard (page 284)

Equipment
- Steamer

*Fructose: 245 calories
*Aspartame: 225 calories
*Xylitol: 250 calories
*Sugar: 275 calories
*Honey: 275 calories

ROLLED APPLE CRÊPES WITH VANILLA MOUSSE

225–275 CALORIES PER PERSON,
depending on the sweetener you use*
Preparation time: 45 minutes, plus 3 hours resting
Level of difficulty: ***
Serves 4

---

1. To make the crêpes, mix the whole egg, 4 of the heaped teaspoons of aspartame, the flour and peanut oil in a mixing bowl. When the mixture is smooth, whisk in the cold milk a little at a time to prevent lumps from forming. Place the crêpe batter in the refrigerator for 3 hours to rest.

2. Remove the batter from the refrigerator and pour it into a jug. Heat a dry non-stick crêpe pan over a medium heat (you don't have to grease the pan because there is oil in the batter). The pan is hot enough when a tiny drop of water, flicked from the finger into the pan, sizzles.

3. Pour enough batter into the pan to cover the base. Tilt and roll the pan to spread the batter thinly and evenly over the base, then pour the excess batter back into the jug. With a spatula or blunt knife, cut away the dribble of excess batter from the side of the pan. Continue to cook the crêpe for 20–30 seconds, until the edges start to curl. With thumbs and forefingers, turn the crêpe over smartly.

4. Cook the second side of the crêpe for about 15 seconds, or until pale golden-brown. Slide the crêpe out of the pan. Cook the remaining 3 crêpes in the same way and transfer them to a plate. Cover the crêpes with clingfilm (plastic wrap) and set them aside at room temperature.

5. For the mousse, heat one-third of the custard gently in a saucepan. Remove from the heat, then dissolve and combine the gelatine of your choice with the warm custard, whisking to incorporate the gelatine smoothly. Stir in the remaining custard. Transfer this vanilla-flavoured mixture to a bowl and place over iced water, stirring until the gelatine starts to 'take' and the mixture has the consistency of mayonnaise. (You can also place the bowl in the refrigerator, but then the process will take about 20 minutes.)

6. Once the mixture has reached the correct consistency, remove it from the iced water. Beat the cream until it forms firm peaks and fold it into the mixture. In a separate mixing bowl, whisk the egg white until it forms soft peaks. Sprinkle on the remaining aspartame and whisk again to firmer, but not dry, peaks.

7. Mix this whisked egg white into the vanilla-flavoured mixture, repeatedly lifting the beaten egg white from the bottom of the bowl and folding it over the top of the mixture until all is well blended. Place this vanilla mousse in the refrigerator until needed.

8. For the apples, preheat a steamer. Peel, halve and core the apples, then cut the flesh into (⅜in) dice. Steam the apples for 5 minutes. Transfer them to a container and, when cold, stir in the vanilla extract, turning the fruit to ensure even distribution.

To serve
Lay the 4 crêpes out on a work surface and put one-quarter of the apple mixture in the centre of each. Cover the apple with a generous helping of the vanilla mousse. One by one, roll up each crêpe and place it, seam side down, on a serving plate. Serve with the apple coulis or custard.

A historical titbit
When rolled up, these crêpes are called 'pannequets' in French, which no doubt gave rise to the English word 'pancakes'.

- 450ml (2 US cups) semi-skimmed (2%) milk
- 50ml (¼ US cup or 6 tbsp) single (light) cream
- large handful of fresh verbena leaves or mint leaves, rinsed and dried
- 3 sheets of leaf gelatine (soaked) or 2½ tsp powdered gelatine (page 22)
- 3 heaped tbsp aspartame or the sweetener of your choice, plus a pinch or 2 of extra sweetener
  - for the raspberries (optional)
- 400g (14oz) fresh raspberries

To decorate
- 4 sprigs of verbena or mint

*Fructose: 170 calories
*Aspartame: 140 calories
*Xylitol: 175 calories
*Sugar: 205 calories
*Honey: 185 calorie

HERB-SCENTED PANNA COTTA WITH RASPBERRIES

140–205 CALORIES PER PERSON,
depending on the sweetener you use*
Preparation time: 30 minutes, plus 3 hours setting
Level of difficulty: *
Serves 4

1. Start the preparation of the panna cotta at least 4 hours before you want to serve it. In a saucepan set over a medium heat, bring the milk and cream briefly to the boil. Remove the saucepan from the heat and add the verbena or mint leaves, pushing them down with a wooden spoon to immerse them completely. Cover the saucepan with a lid and leave the mixture to infuse for at least 15 minutes. Strain the infused mixture through a fine sieve set over a mixing bowl and discard the leaves.

2. Ladle about 225ml (1 US cup) of the infused mixture into a saucepan and heat it without allowing the milk to boil; remove from the heat. Dissolve and combine the gelatine of your choice with the warm infused mixture, whisking well until the gelatine has completely dissolved and is smoothly blended. Add this warm mixture to the remaining infused mixture and continue to whisk until the gelatine has been absorbed evenly throughout. Add the aspartame and whisk again.

3. Divide the panna cotta mixture between 4 small dessert bowls or moulds. Put them on a small tray that will fit into the refrigerator and chill for at least 3 hours.

4. To make the raspberry coulis, put half the raspberries into the bowl of a food processor along with 3 tablespoons of cold water, and blend to a purée. Pass the purée through a nylon sieve and discard the pips. Stir just enough sweetener into the coulis to remove any excess sharpness. Cover and set aside in the refrigerator.

To serve
Put the bowls of panna cotta on under-plates. Very gently combine 12–16 of the remaining whole raspberries with the coulis, taking care not to crush the fruit. Divide the coulis mixture between the bowls. Add the remaining whole raspberries to the under-plates, along with sprigs of verbena or mint.

- 500g (1lb 2oz) fresh raspberries
- 3 tbsp water
- a pinch plus 1 heaped tsp of fructose or the sweetener of your choice (pages 16–20)
- 50ml (¼ US cup or 6 tbsp) light whipping cream (30–35% fat)
- 1½ sheets of leaf gelatine (soaked) or 1 tsp powdered gelatine (page 22)
- 2 egg whites
- 4 large choux pastries (bought or home-made)

To decorate
- 4 small sprigs of mint

*Fructose: 165 calories
*Aspartame: 160 calories
*Xylitol: 170 calories
*Sugar: 175 calories
*Honey: 170 calories

RASPBERRY PROFITEROLES

160–175 CALORIES PER PERSON,
depending on the sweetener you use*
Preparation time: 30 minutes, plus 1 hour resting
Level of difficulty: ***
Serves 4

1. To make the raspberry coulis, put 300g (11oz) of the raspberries and 3 tablespoons of water in the bowl of a food processor, and blend to a purée. Taste, and adjust the acidity of the fruit by adding a pinch of fructose if required. For a smooth coulis, pass the purée through a fine sieve – preferably a chinois – and discard the pips.

2. Pour one-third of the coulis into a mixing bowl and set the remainder aside in the refrigerator, to be used for serving.

3. For the raspberry mousse, beat the cream until it forms soft to medium-firm peaks – if the cream is too stiff, it will be difficult to combine with the coulis. Set aside the whipped cream briefly in a cool place.

4. In a saucepan, heat about a quarter of the raspberry coulis from the mixing bowl. Remove the saucepan from the heat, then dissolve and combine the gelatine of your choice with the warm coulis, whisking well until the gelatine has completely dissolved. Whisk in the remaining raspberry coulis from the mixing bowl. Stir a little of the whipped cream into the stiffened coulis, then combine this mixture with the rest of the cream, lifting and folding the ingredients until thoroughly blended.

5. To complete the raspberry mousse, whisk the egg whites to soft peaks in a separate mixing bowl. Sprinkle on the heaped teaspoon of fructose and whisk again to firm, but not dry, peaks. Mix about a quarter of the whisked egg whites into the stiffened raspberry cream mixture. Combine this with the remaining whites, repeatedly lifting the whites from the bottom of the bowl and folding them over the top of the mixture until all is well blended.

6. Split the choux pastries in half. Use a teaspoon or piping (pastry) bag to fill the bottom halves with a generous layer of the raspberry mousse. Replace the tops of the filled profiteroles and chill them in the refrigerator for at least 1 hour.

To serve
Put 1 profiterole on each of 4 serving plates. Coat each one using about half of the chilled raspberry coulis. Use the remaining coulis and the remaining 200g (7oz) of fresh raspberries to decorate the desserts. You can combine these elements if you wish, drizzling the mixture around each profiterole. Add a small sprig of mint to each plate and serve.

Variation
You can also make this recipe with strawberries or blackberries.

- 450ml (2 US cups) water
- 4 tbsp unsweetened cocoa powder
- 3½ heaped tbsp fructose or the sweetener of your choice (pages 16–20)
- 80ml (⅓ US cup) semi-skimmed (2%) milk
- 80ml (⅓ US cup) light whipping cream (30–35% fat)
- 100g (3½oz) sweet chestnut purée or chestnut spread
- 1 tbsp rum
- 2 sheets of filo (phyllo) pastry, thawed if frozen

Equipment
- Sorbetière (optional)
- Multi-functional whipper with 2 gas cartridges (pages 36–7)

*Fructose: 285 calories
*Aspartame: 225 calories
*Xylitol: 300 calories
*Sugar: 350 calories
*Honey: 340 calories

CHESTNUT-CHOCOLATE TIMBALE

225–350 CALORIES PER PERSON,
depending on the sweetener you use*
Preparation time: 45 minutes
Level of difficulty: **
Serves 4

1. To make the syrup for the chocolate sorbet, bring 250ml (1⅛ US cups) of the water, half of the cocoa powder and 2 heaped tablespoons of the fructose to the boil in a saucepan. Reduce the heat to maintain a gentle simmer for 2 minutes. Allow the mixture to cool then pour it into a sorbetière and churn it to a soft-textured consistency. Alternatively, put the mixture in a shallow freezing tray and stir it thoroughly every half-hour with a fork. The sorbet will be ready when, after several hours, it has a soft, scoopable, consistency. Put the sorbet in an airtight container and freeze until you are ready to serve.

2. For the chocolate sauce, bring the remaining water and cocoa powder to the boil in a saucepan, stirring constantly. Reduce the heat and let the mixture simmer gently for 2 minutes. Remove from the heat and stir in the remaining fructose. Set aside the sauce in the refrigerator until needed.

3. For the chestnut mousse, combine the milk, cream, chestnut purée and rum in a mixing bowl. Pour the mixture into a multi-functional whipper. Close the whipper and insert 2 gas cartridges. Shake well and set aside in the refrigerator.

4. For the filo (phyllo) pastry shells, preheat the oven to 180°C (350°F, gas mark 4). To keep the filo (phyllo) moist while you work, cover it with a layer of greaseproof or waxed paper and put a damp tea towel on top. Cut each sheet into 4 identical squares, to give 8 squares in all. Overlap one square on top of the next, giving a quarter-turn between layers to produce a star shape. Repeat with the remaining 6 squares to make 4 stars in all.

5. Gently place each pastry star in a wide teacup or muffin tin. Using a cup that is slightly smaller than the teacup containing the pastry, press the pastry against the sides of the cup to make 4 cone-shaped shells. Bake the pastry shells for 5 minutes or until they are golden brown. Remove them from the oven and allow them to cool.

To serve
Transfer the cooled pastry shells to dessert plates. Remove the chilled whipper from the refrigerator and use to divide half of the chestnut mousse between the 4 pastry shells. Remove the chocolate sorbet from the freezer and place a spoonful of sorbet in the centre of each portion of chestnut mousse. Top each pastry shell with the remaining mousse.

Remove the chocolate sauce from the refrigerator and drizzle it generously over each filled shell. Now you can enjoy this guilt-free delight!

- 4 slices of one-day old white bread
- 1 egg
- 1 egg yolk
- 2 heaped tsp fructose or the sweetener of your choice (pages 16–20)
- 2 vanilla pods (beans), split lengthways to make 4 halves
- 200ml (⅞ US cup) semi-skimmed (2%) milk
- 2 apples, preferably Granny Smith, Russet, Pippin, Pink Lady or other apple variety that holds its shape when cooked
- about 100ml (⅜ US cup) light whipping cream (30–35% fat)
- ½ level tbsp fructose or the sweetener of your choice (pages 16–20)

To decorate
- 4 sprigs of mint

Equipment
- Food ring or cutter, about 10cm (4in) in diameter (optional)
- Steamer
- Multi-functional whipper with 2 gas cartridges (pages 36–7)

*Fructose: 220 calories
*Aspartame: 210 calories
*Xylitol: 230 calories
*Sugar: 245 calories
*Honey: 240 calories

FRENCH TOAST WITH VANILLA-SCENTED APPLE

210–245 CALORIES PER PERSON,
depending on the sweetener you use*
Preparation time: 40 minutes
Level of difficulty: **
Serves 4

---

1. To make the French toast, toast 4 slices of bread and use a food ring, cutter or drinking glass to cut each slice into a circle.

2. Whisk together the egg, egg yolk and the 2 heaped teaspoons of fructose in a bowl. Scrape the seeds from one of the halves of vanilla pod (bean) and stir them into the mixture. In a saucepan, heat 150ml (¾ US cup) of the milk, and stir or whisk it into the egg mixture, blending well. Transfer the custard mixture to a shallow dish.

3. Place the 4 circles of toast in the custard for 2 minutes, or until the toast begins absorbing the custard. Turn the pieces over, then cover the dish with clingfilm (plastic wrap) and place it in the refrigerator until needed.

4. To make the apple topping, preheat a steamer. Peel the apples, cut them in half, core them and cut the flesh into 1cm (½in) dice. Steam the diced apple for 5 minutes or until it softens but retains its shape. Transfer the apple to a covered container and refrigerate it. When the apple is completely cold, remove it from the refrigerator, scrape the seeds from 2 of the remaining halves of vanilla pod (bean) and stir them into the apple. Return the apple to the refrigerator.

5. For the vanilla cream, combine the cream, the remaining 50ml (¼ US cup or 6 tbsp) of milk, the remaining half of a vanilla pod (bean), and ½ level tablespoon of fructose in a mixing bowl. Stir or whisk well, then pass the cream through a fine sieve, preferably a chinois. Pour the strained cream into a multi-functional whipper. Close the whipper and insert 2 gas cartridges. Place the filled whipper in the refrigerator until chilled.

To serve

Preheat the oven to 200°C (400°F, gas mark 6). Drain the slices of French toast, pressing them gently between the palms of your hands to remove any excess custard. Place each slice on a baking sheet lined with greaseproof or parchment paper. Bake in the oven for 5 minutes. Meanwhile, heat through the reserved diced apple in a microwave, allowing about 1½ minutes at 800 watts.

Remove the French toast from the oven and use a spatula to transfer each piece to a dessert plate. Spoon the warm diced apple on top. Place a helping of vanilla cream from the whipper alongside and add a sprig of mint. Serve immediately.

- 20g (¾oz or 1½ tbsp) unsalted butter, softened
- 2 tbsp caster (superfine) sugar
- 3 large apples, such as Pippin, Granny Smith or Braeburn
- 4 tbsp water
- 2 limes
- 4 egg yolks
- 4 egg whites
- 2 heaped tsp fructose or the sweetener of your choice (pages 16–20)

To serve (optional)
- Granny Smith sorbet (page 296)

Equipment
- 4 individual soufflé dishes, about 8cm (3in) in diameter

*Fructose: 220 calories
*Aspartame: 205 calories
*Xylitol: 225 calories
*Sugar: 240 calories
*Honey: 235 calories

HOT APPLE AND LIME SOUFFLÉS

205–240 CALORIES PER PERSON,
depending on the sweetener you use*
Preparation time: 45 minutes
Level of difficulty: * *
Serves 4

1. Prepare the soufflé dishes by brushing them lightly with the softened butter, sprinkling them with the sugar, then tipping out the excess sugar; set aside.

2. For the soufflé mixture, peel the apples, cut them in half, core them and cut into small dice. Put the apple in a saucepan with the 4 tablespoons of water and cover with a lid. Simmer over a low heat, lifting the lid frequently to stir the apples, for 20 minutes or until the apples have formed a compote.

3. Blend the compote to a finer purée, using a stick blender or food processor. Put the purée in a covered container and set aside it in the refrigerator. Once the purée is completely cold, transfer 300g (11oz) of it to a large mixing bowl, reserving the remainder for another recipe.

4. Remove the zest from the limes using a zester or fine grater. Squeeze the juice of the limes. Whisk the egg yolks. Add the zest, juice and beaten egg yolks to the bowl of apple purée and stir well to blend thoroughly. Preheat the oven to 200°C (400°F, gas mark 6), bearing in mind that the oven must be hot before you complete the next step.

5. To complete the soufflé mixture, whisk the egg whites in a large mixing bowl until they form soft peaks. Sprinkle on the fructose and whisk again. Working quickly, tip all of the egg white into the apple and lime mixture, put a spatula in the centre, then lift the mixture up and over the whites, clockwise, while you turn the bowl in the opposite direction. Continue until all the ingredients are well blended.

6. Spoon the soufflé mixture into the prepared soufflé dishes, filling them ½cm (¼in) above their rims. Put the dishes on a warmed baking sheet. Transfer to the oven and bake the soufflés for 8 minutes.

To serve
As soon as the soufflés are cooked and risen, serve them immediately. A quenelle-shaped scoop of Granny Smith sorbet (page 296), served separately in a pretty teacup, makes the perfect accompaniment.

Chef's tip
To save time, you can use about 125g (4½oz) of store-bought unsweetened apple sauce, instead of making your own apple compote, as in the recipe.

TERMS AND TECHNIQUES

Agar: a vegetarian alternative to gelatine, made from sea plants and now widely available in health-food stores. You should be guided by the instructions on the packet but one heaped teaspoon of agar flakes is used with 350ml (scant 1½ US cups) of liquid.

Beat or whisk egg whites: to beat egg whites with a wire balloon whisk or a hand-held electric whisk until the whites expand in volume and create a white foam that forms peaks on the whisk. Egg yolks can also be beaten with a whisk until they become pale and creamy, thus forming a base for many egg-bound sauces and preparations.

Bias, on the: usually refers to a method of cutting meat (or sometimes fish) across the grain at a 45° diagonal angle.

Bind or thicken: to give body to a sauce or stock by blending it with a thickening agent such as cornstarch, flour, egg yolk and, in the case of *Eat Well and Stay Slim: The Essential Cuisine Minceur*, with special puréed liaisons.

Blanch: to partially cook vegetables, herbs or fruit by immersing them in boiling water for several minutes. Vegetables are frequently blanched, then refreshed (see Refresh) in order to reduce their final cooking time. This is also an important step in preparing vegetables and fruit for freezing. Blanching also helps loosen skins from tomatoes, peaches and almonds so that they are easier to peel (see Peel). Citrus zest is also blanched and refreshed to remove its bitterness (see Zest).

Broad beans (fava beans): Once these beans have been shelled from their pods, they must be freed from their individual skins. To do this, plunge the beans into lightly salted simmering water for 3 minutes, then refresh in cold water and drain. Slip the bright green beans free from their wrinkly skins and discard the skins.

Brown or colour: to cook food until its surface acquires a golden or brownish colour. Traditionally, oil or butter is used to brown food but – and especially in *Eat Well and Stay Slim: The Essential Cuisine Minceur* – it can often be coloured without fat if a non-stick frying pan (skillet) is used.

Butterfly: to split food, such as prawns (shrimp) and langoustines, through the middle lengthways, without completely separating the halves. To do this, open up each prawn (shrimp) to resemble butterfly wings: pull the head and legs off, then peel away the shell, leaving the last big segment of shell and the tail firmly intact. With a small sharp knife, score lightly along the back of the prawn (shrimp) in a straight line, stopping just before the segment of shell. If there is a long black intestinal vein, pick it out and discard it. Cut deeper into the flesh to open the prawn (shrimp) to make two wings. These remain joined together at the last segment of shell and tail.

Canelle knife: a corrugating knife or a triangular cutter. Depending on the brand, it may also be called a channel knife. It allows you to cut long channels down the sides of raw vegetables such as carrots and courgettes (zucchini) so that when they are sliced crossways, the slices have a decorative edge.

Ceviche: raw fish marinated in citrus juice, which 'cooks' the fish. Ceviche relies on the use of ultra-fresh fish. Salmon is a popular choice but you can also use sea bass, sea trout, rainbow trout or brill.

Chiffonade: from the French for 'rag', this refers to the technique of cutting long, thin ribbons mainly of herbs and leaf vegetables. It is usually done by stacking the food to be cut, roiling it tightly, then slicing perpendicular to the roll.

Chinois: a very fine-meshed, conical-shaped sieve that directs the liquid being sieved into a bowl. A traditional professional version, known as a chinois-étamine includes a layer of muslin or cheesecloth to trap fine sediment. However, the newer mesh versions do a very similar job.

Compote: the result of cooking fruit and vegetables, covered, using gentle heat, until the flesh breaks down naturally and falls apart.

Confit: applied to certain fruit and vegetables, this is the result of cooking in order to concentrate the flavour. See Tomato Confit (page 81). Lemon Confit is also used in *Eat Well and Stay Slim: The Essential Cuisine Minceur* (pages 214, 242 and 244).

For 10–12 slices, make as follows:

- 1 large unwaxed lemon, washed
- 150g (5½oz) caster (superfine) sugar
- 360ml (1½ US cups) water
- water for preliminary blanching

Cut away the ends of the lemon. Using a mandolin or sharp knife, cut the lemon into thin slices, discarding the pips. To blanch the slices and remove the bitterness from the peel, put them in a saucepan, cover with cold water, bring briefly to a boil, then simmer for 4 minutes. Drain and set aside, discarding the water.

For the syrup, put the sugar in a saucepan and cover with the 360ml (1½ US cups) water. Over a low heat, let the sugar dissolve without stirring it. Increase the heat and bring the syrup to a brisk simmer. Add the blanched slices of lemon. Maintain a simmer for about 25 minutes or until the syrup has reduced by at least a half and the slices look translucent. Strain the confit slices through a nylon sieve set over a small bowl, reserving the syrup for another recipe. Spread the slices out on a plate. Leave them to cool, then put them in an airtight jar and store them in the refrigerator for up to 1 month.

Coulis: a purée of fruit or vegetables that can be used as a sauce in its own right, or combined with other mixtures to make more complex sauces.

Deglaze: to pour a liquid – such as wine, stock or water – into a pan in which food has been sautéed or roasted, in order to incorporate the particles remaining on the bottom of the pan into a sauce.

Degrease: to remove fat from cooking juices by skimming the surface. The juices are usually chilled prior to degreasing, which causes the fat content to rise to the surface and form a solid layer. This can then be scraped away easily with a spoon.

En papillotte: the technique of wrapping food loosely in a paper or foil parcel and sealing the parcel so the food cooks in a steamy atmosphere.

Fines herbes: a mixture of fresh herbs, usually consisting of finely chopped flat-leaf parsley, chervil, tarragon and chives.

Julienne: refers to fine, matchstick-type strips which are most often cut from vegetables, fruit and, notably, the zest of citrus fruit (see Zest). The strips are used for garnish and flavouring. Julienne strips are usually about 2mm (⅛ inch) wide and no more than 4cm (1½in) long. In the case of julienne of citrus, they are made by cutting away the ragged edges from the zest.

Kaffir lime leaves: the fragrant lemon-flavoured leaves of the wild lime tree, kaffir lime leaves can be bought fresh, frozen or dried from Asian grocers and, increasingly, from large supermarkets. You can also order them online. However, if you cannot obtain them, you can substitute lemongrass.

Liaison: an ingredient that acts as a thickening agent to give body to a sauce or stock. Liaisons traditionally include cornstarch, flour, egg yolk. In the case of *Eat Well and Stay Slim: The Essential Cuisine Minceur*, special vegetable and fruit-based purées fulfil the role of a liaison.

Marinate: to immerse raw food for several hours in an aromatic liquid or, sometimes, in dry ingredients such as salt and herbs, in order to flavour or tenderize the food. The mixture for the immersion is known as a marinade. Wet versions include some or all of the following: wine, stock, oil, lemon, herbs, spice and aromatic vegetables.

Mesclun: a mixture of young, tender salad leaves, which ideally includes lamb's lettuce (mâche or corn salad), red oak leaf, chervil, spinach, frisée, sorrel, radicchio, rocket (arugula) and mizuna or mustard greens of some kind.

Peel (tomatoes; also peaches and nectarines): with tomatoes, the peeling process usually goes hand in hand with coring and deseeding. To peel a tomato, first score a cross at its base. Drop it carefully into a pan of boiling water or put it in a bowl and pour over boiling water. Leave it for about 30 seconds or until the skin starts to lift. Remove it from the hot water and plunge into iced water. Peel, halve, core and deseed the tomato.

TERMS AND TECHNIQUES

It is now ready to be sliced, diced or otherwise used according to the requirements of the recipe. The skins of peaches and nectarines are loosened and peeled in the same way.

Pare: to remove the outer skin from a vegetable or piece of fruit using a paring knife or peeling tool.

Pimientos del Piquillo: chargrilled whole sweet red Spanish peppers that are peeled and ready to eat. They are sold in salted water in small jars, and are available in many supermarkets as well as through websites.

Poivrade artichokes: the very small purple variety of artichokes (often from Provence), now available throughout the UK and USA.

Quenelle: originally an egg-shaped poached mixture of creamed meat, fish or chicken. In *Eat Well and Stay Slim: The Essential Cuisine Minceur*, you will often find it also used to refer to oval or egg-shaped purées, sorbets and ice creams. Making the shape involves passing the mixture between two spoons until the desired shape is achieved, then slip a knife underneath each quenelle to release it. In the case of sorbets and ice creams, scoop the portion out of its freezer container using two spoons, and proceed as for other quenelles.

Ras el-hanout:

A Moroccan spice blend, made as follows:

- 1 tsp ground cumin
- 1 tsp ground ginger
- 1 tsp turmeric
- 1 tsp salt
- ¾ tsp sugar
- ¾ tsp fresh ground black pepper
- ½ tsp cinnamon
- ½ tsp ground coriander
- ½ tsp cayenne
- ½ tsp ground allspice
- ½ tsp ground fennel
- ¼ tsp ground cloves

Mix together, and store in an airtight jar.

Reduce: to boil down a liquid to concentrate its flavour and, by the process of evaporation, to thicken it to the consistency of a sauce.

Refresh: to plunge hot food into cold water to stop the cooking process. Vegetables and other items of food are usually refreshed after they have been blanched (see Blanch).

Sauté: from the French 'sauter' meaning 'to jump', the term refers to frying food rapidly over a lively heat, shaking the pan or turning its contents frequently so as to keep the food moving or 'jumping'.

Seize or sear: to cook food, usually meat, briefly over a lively heat in order to colour it and seal in its natural juices.

Sweat: to cook aromatic vegetables or other foodstuffs over low heat, usually in a pan that is covered, for a few minutes, or until they exude their juices without colouring. A small amount of oil or fat may be used in the process.

Turning: this is the action of turning, or rotating, mostly root vegetables as you pare or peel them prior to cooking, in order to create special uniform shapes. It is a way of making carrots, potatoes, turnips and celeriac, for example, look pretty for presentation. Generally speaking you should begin with chunks of vegetable no more than 4cm (1½in) long. For a rugby-ball shape, the sides are then pared away and the top and bottom are cut on a slant. A smaller version of this can be made to look like an olive or a clove of garlic. An easy shape is a barrel, which lends itself well to carrots as well as to cucumber. To make, cut thick pieces of carrot or cucumber in half lengthways, then into quarters to make triangular wedge shapes. Pare the sides until you have a rounded barrel.

Poivrade artichokes can also be turned. The method for doing so is slightly different from that of turning a regular globe artichoke. This is because the poivrade is smaller with a pointed shape – so it has a slightly different inner structure. It is also extremely tender, which means that part of its stem, and relatively more of its heart, can be eaten.

To prevent the artichoke flesh from discolouring as you work, use a stainless-steel knife and have ready a bowl containing lemon juice and water in which to dip the cut surfaces of the vegetable.

To turn and trim the artichoke to its stem and heart, cut its stem to a length of about 3cm (1¼in). Starting at the base end, bend back the tough outer leaves and either snap them off or cut them off at the crease. As you work upwards towards the tip, the leaves will pull away easily without snapping. Continue until you reach the tender, paler leaves. These form a pointed pyramid shape above the base. Cut off the pyramid, leaving the base with its tough dark exterior and its inner heart and choke (the inedible centre).

Using a small sharp knife, trim back the dark green exterior from the stem. Peeling in a spiral – like peeling an apple – pare away the tough green exterior of the base of the artichoke to reveal the heart. Cut away the tough fibres. Peel away the fine petal-like leaves that surround the choke. Remove the choke with a serrated-edge teaspoon or a knife. Peel away any tough outer skin from the artichoke's stem. Place the heart with its section of stem attached in the bowl of acidulated water, ready for use.

Vadouvan: a spice blend that originated in the French Indian region of Pondicherry. The mixture generally has an onion, shallot and garlic base with several Indian spices added, including, but not limited to, fenugreek, curry, cumin, cardamom, mustard seeds, turmeric, nutmeg, clove, and red pepper flakes.

The following is a summary of a recipe found on the website Epicurious.com:
- 900g (2lb) onion
- 450g (1lb) shallot
- 12 garlic cloves
- 60ml (¼ US cup or 6 tbsp) vegetable oil or untoasted sesame oil
- 1 tsp fenugreek
- 1 tbsp fresh curry leaves
- 1 tbsp cumin
- 1 tbsp cardamom
- 1 tsp brown mustard seeds
- ¾ tsp turmeric
- ½ tsp nutmeg
- ¼ tsp cloves
- 1 tbsp salt
- 1 tsp pepper
- ½ tsp hot red pepper flakes

Preheat the oven to 180°C (350°F, gas mark 4). In several batches, pulse the onions, shallots, and garlic in a food processor until they are finely chopped but not completely pulverized. In a large frying pan (skillet), sauté the onions, shallots and garlic in the vegetable oil for 25–30 minutes until they are golden and brown in some parts. Add all of the spices, mix well and transfer to parchment paper-lined baking sheets, spread into a thin layer. Bake in the oven, stirring occasionally, until well browned and barely moist, about 1–1¼ hours.

Zest: refers to the uppermost layer of peel taken from a lemon or other citrus fruit. Although zest is prized for its flavour, scent and oils, its underside has a layer of bitter white pith, which must be removed. Tiny pith-free morsels of zest can be obtained using a zester tool, but larger pieces of peel, for instance to make julienne strips, cannot be zested in this way.

For these you must first peel the citrus into fairly long strips using a potato peeler or a small sharp knife. Then carefully scrape away and discard the peel's white inner pith. To convert the peel into edible zests, blanch and refresh it. To do this, put the strips of peel into a small saucepan; add enough cold water to just cover then bring to the boil over medium heat. Drain the strips, refresh them in cold water and drain again. Some recipes call for this blanching process to be repeated at least twice more. The zests will then be ready for you to use in a variety of ways. To make julienne strips from the zest, cut away the ragged edges, then cut the zest into matchstick strips about 4cm (1½ in) long and 2mm (⅛in) wide.

ALPHABETICAL INDEX TO THE RECIPES

The Essential Cuisine Minceur Recipes
(with an indication of the number of calories per person and the level of difficulty)

INDEX OF RECIPES BY INGREDIENT

ACKNOWLEDGMENTS

Eat Well and Stay Slim: The Essential Cuisine Minceur has its scientific basis in the principles of the White Paper (see page 7), which was developed recently thanks to an initiative by the French Ministry of Health. Once again, I extend my thanks to everyone who contributed to this project.

I also most warmly acknowledge the contribution of the kitchen team at Les Prés d'Eugénie, who worked tirelessly on this stimulating culinary adventure. Most particularly, I would like to thank the following individuals: Jacky Lanusse, Head Chef of the Grande Cuisine Minceur Division; Sébastien Perbost, Head Chef of the Dessert Test Kitchen; and the Chefs, Stéphane Mack and Olivier Brulard.

I am also indebted to Albin Michel and the team led by Nicolas de Cointet who, from the very start, showed great enthusiasm for this new reference book.

I also wish to offer countless thanks to my courageous guardian angels, Adeline and Christine Guérard, who helped on this project while immersed in the constant hive of activity at Les Prés d'Eugénie. And finally, I would also like to give a special mention to the dieticians at the Spa, who conducted the venture with all the expertise, patience and attention to detail that was required.

Michel Guérard

We wish to thank the companies who generously agreed to loan their material for the photographs in this book:
Dibbern (www.dibbern.de),
Mauviel (www.mauviel.com),
Le Creuset (www.lecreuset.fr)
and WMF (www.wmf.fr).